Virginia

HARRISON COUNTY

A Bicentennial Album

THE OFFICIAL PUBLICATION OF THE HARRISON COUNTY BICENTENNIAL COMMITTEE

James M. Pool/Editor
Susan Maxwell/Associate Editor
Lloyd Leggett/Publication Chairman
Edwin Propst/Photography
Edwin Sweeney/Technical Advisor
Gary Martin/Layout Consultant

©1985 Harrison County
Bicentennial Committee
L.C. #85-51415
ISBN #0-9615566-1-7

printed in U.S.A. by:

Walsworth Press, Inc.
Marceline, MO.

regional director:

Don Mills, Inc.
Salem, WV 26426

Publication Committee Members

Jack Sandy Anderson
Alton Bell
Harry Berman
Beulah Cornwell
Dorothy Davis
J. Robert Hornor
Pauline LeRoy
Don Mills
Gale Price
Sharon Saye
George Short
Neva Weeks

FOREWORD

During 1984 Harrison County, West Virginia celebrated its 200th birthday. The Bicentennial celebration was made possible through the work of dozens of persons throughout the area and through the financial support of Consolidated Gas Transmission Corp. and the Humanities Foundation of West Virginia, a state agency of the National Endowment for the Humanities.

This album represents a small portion of the activities which took place during the Bicentennial year and contains a compilation of the stories and events which make the county what it is after 200 years. The cover of the album depicts the Levi Shinn house in Shinnston which stands today as not only the oldest remaining dwelling the county but also as a symbol of the durability of Harrison County and its people through the years.

With respect for the past, with pride in the present and with an unfailing belief in the future The Harrison County Bicentennial Committee is proud to dedicate this album to the people of Harrison County on the 200th Anniversary of the founding of their home.

James M. Pool
Project Director
Harrison County Bicentennial Committee

Jack Sandy Anderson

Alton Bell

Harry Berman

Beulah Cornwell

Dorothy Davis

J. Robert Hornor

Lloyd Leggett

Pauline LeRoy

Gale Price

Sharon Saye

George A. Short

Neva Weeks

THE OFFICIAL SEAL OF HARRISON COUNTY

The Official Seal of Harrison County was adopted by the County Commission on February 23, 1976, and symbolizes the natural beauty and resources of Harrison County. Described briefly, the Seal bears the legend "Harrison County Seal" along with the motto "Freedom and Independence," and the date 1784, the year Harrison County was created. It pictures a deer standing among the hills of Harrison County with the sun rising behind them.

The rising sun symbolizes that Harrison County has begun a time of growth for labor, industry, agriculture, and business. The hills represent the geography and beauty of the County, and also one of the most fundamental rights, land ownership. The words "Freedom and Independence" stand for the strong feelings for freedom our County founders had, and for the fact that Harrison county was one of the first counties of Virginia to initiate the creation of the State of West Virginia. The leaf border symbolizes agriculture, the means our forefathers first used to support themselves.

Bicentennial Committee at work

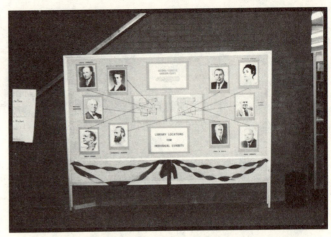

National Figures of Harrison County Exhibit

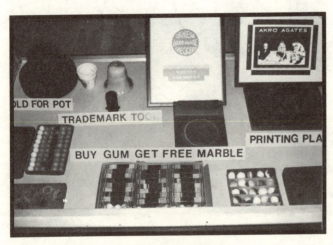

Acro Agate Exhibit

Oil & Gas Industry Exhibit

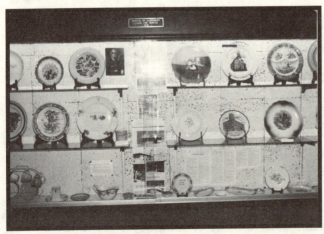

McNichol China Exhibit

Bicentennial Committee at "work"

WEST VIRGINIA HISTORIC COMMISSION, 1964

Origins of Names For Streams, Variety of Community Names

By JAMES M. POOL

The origin of the names of many of the places which we refer to, read about, pass through or in which we even live are derived from a variety of sources. We are surrounded today with a wealth of local history which tells us much of the past of Harrison County simply by examining the origin, meaning and development of the names of our local cities and towns, streams and roads. These names tell us much about not only the area but also the people who settled the area and created many of the names which still exist today.

The sources for these place names are as numerous as the imagination of the persons creating the names. The current events of the time or the prevailing political events of the time led to such names as the districts of Eagle, Union, Grant and Clay, which were named in order for the American Eagle, opposition to succession during the Civil War, Gen. U. S. Grant and the statesman Henry Clay.

Other areas were named for geographical reasons or characteristics such as Coal District, Elk District, Simpson District and Ten Mile District which signified the large amount of coal in one area and the various creeks running through other individual areas.

In all there was an unending source of names for both the early and latter-day pioneers to choose from in this area. Some of these sources and examples of the names taken from them include: pioneer heroes (Harrison County, Hacker's Creek, and Clark District, named for Benjamin Harrison, John Hacker and George Rogers Clark); early occupations or industries (Lumberport, Peddler's Run, Sugar Camp Run); local persons (Davisson's Run, Reynoldsville and Wilsonburg) and the pioneer's mental world reflecting his feelings and aspirations (Quiet Dell, Good Hope, and Industrial).

In many cases an interesting story exists behind the local name which has been memorialized by the use of the name for a certain location. In Harrison County there are several of these for us to examine:

Adamston: A small hamlet formerly on the outskirts of Clarksburg, incorporated in 1903 and named for Josias Adams, former owner of the farm where the village began.

Anmoore: Incorporated town in Harrison County located in Simpson District first called Steelton, changed in 1905 to Grasselli and changed in about 1915 to the present name which

5

is from Ann Moore's Run which was named for a local woman, Ann Moore.

Bingamon & Big Bingamon Creek: Named for the famed Indian fighter Samuel Bingamon who fought with a band of Indians on the Jeremiah Hess farm (formerly located on a hill behind the Wyatt School) and reportedly killed all of them earning the naming of the area and the stream.

Bridgeport: Area originally known as Powers Fort as early as 1771 when it was a small outpost built by John Powers. The present name arose because the first bridge in Harrison County outside of Clarksburg was built across Simpson Creek in 1803 and the town was legally established on lands of Joseph Johnson in 1812.

Brown: Area of Tenmile Creek in Sardis District formerly known as Brown's Mill was originally named for John Brown, a grist mill operator and one of the first settlers of the area.

Clarksburg: City on the West Fork River established by legal enactment in 1785. Some authorities attribute the name to Capt. William Clark of the Lewis & Clark expedition while others say it was named for an early pioneer who was an expert trapper, hunter and fisherman. The weight of authority states that the name is derived from the early pioneer hero Gen. George Rogers Clark.

Dawmont: This village was originally called Dawson but was changed due to another Virginia town with the same name. The present name consists of syllables from Dawson Coleman, at one time a part owner of the Dawson Coal Company, and for Rosemont, the name of the company's coal mine.

Enterprise: Settled by the Charles McIntire family in 1773 the name first attached in 1875 as a result of James Harrison, the first postmaster, who recalled a story from the Civil War of a traveler who came through the area and upon observing several men and their horses getting work done at the blacksmith shop was prompted to exclaim "My, what an enterprising place this is."

Gypsy: This name supposedly arose because bands of gypsies often camped in the area but better authority attributes the name to Caroline "Gypsy" Watson Fleming or her daughter, Caroline Fleming Ward (born 1868), who shared her mother's nickname, the wife and daughter, respectively, of Gov. A. B. Fleming of Fairmont who owned coal lands nearby.

Industrial: A station on the Baltimore & Ohio railroad located within the corporate limits of Salem in Tenmile District, the town owes its being to the West Virginia Indusrial Home for Youth which is located in the area.

Kincheloe & Kincheloe Creek: Both the creek and the village were named for the first explorer of the area and its first permanent settlers, the Daniel Kincheloe family.

Lost Creek: Several trees in the Lost Creek valley were found by the first explorers to bear the letters "T. G." cut into their bark. The explorers believed that the man who carved the initials had been lost or in the alternative according to the philosophy then prevailing it was not the man who was lost but the region through which he wondered, hence the name of the stream and the area located in Grant District.

Lumberport: Originally known as Ten Mile, this area was established by the legislature's enactment in 1838 and once had a boatyard located there where up to 1800 logs were floated down Tenmile Creek, dressed by hand and floated on rafts up the Monongahela to Pittsburgh.

McWhorter: Henry McWhorter came to the neighborhood of Jane Lew in Lewis County from Pennsylvania in the 1780s and founded a community in Grant District about two miles from Jane Lew known as McWhorter. Between 1846-1848 the name was changed to McWhorter's Mill and it merged with Jane Lew. In later years another village grew up around

certain mines of the Jane Lew Coal and Coke Co. and took the name of the original settlers of the area.

Miles End: In 1809 John George Jackson constructed a grist mill on Elk Creek at the mouth of Murphy's Run near the village of Industrial about a mile from Clarksburg. For many years this extinct town was known as "Factory" and in 1814 the legislature established the town naming it Miles End. The bed of the mill can still be traced but the last building was torn down in July 1907.

Mount Clare: Originally knows as Turtle Town and referred to as Byron by the B&O railroad people, this town also took the name Brown's Creek from its location in Grant District. In 1872 when the B&O planned its route through the town the name was changed to Mount Clare from the section of downtown Baltimore where the railroad shops were located.

Nutter Fort: Located on Elk Creek at Nutter Run near Clarksburg the area was named for Thomas Nutter, who built and maintained an Indian fort at that location which served as a refuge for the early settlers during the Indian wars.

Pine Bluff: This village was originlly known as Shinn's Mill in honor of Jeremiah Shinn, landowner and miller, until approximately 1920 when it received its present name from the pine trees that grew above the bluff over the entrance to a coal mine located there.

Pinnickinnick Hill: The literal translation of the name of this high hill overlooking Clarksburg is "what is mixed" and is derived from the Algonquin tribal dialect meaning a mixture prepared by the Indians of tobacco, summac leaves and the inner bark of a species of dogwood, used for smoking by the Indians and the early settlers of this area.

Rinehart: This village on Little Tenmile Creek in Sardis District was named for Hollis Rinehart, a contractor who built nearby the Hartzell Tunnel of the Baltimore and Ohio Short Line Railroad. The tunnel, seven eights of a mile in length, was begun in about 1900 and required two years for building.

Romines Mills: Located on Gnatty Creek in Elk District the town is named for Captain John D. Romine who was born in 1825 and resided on a farm of about 75 acres near Rockford, approximately four miles away.

Salem: Originally 40 families led by Samuel Fitz Randolph came to this area in the Tenmile District from Salem, N.J. in 1788. Their settlement was first called New Salem and was chartered by the legislature in 1794 but the name was later shortened to Salem.

Sardis: This area near Katy's Lick in the district of the same name like areas such as Canaan, Goshen and Bethel derives its names from the scriptures and most likely is named for the ancient Biblical city of Sardis in Asia Minor.

Shinnston: Levi Shinn and other sturdy, independent Quakers from New Jersey established the town which bears his name on the West Fork River at Shinn's Run in Clay District in 1818. The area was settled as early as 1773 but the establishment of the town came years later.

Stonewood: The Elk Creek Development Company in 1910 laid out lots nearby and named the new community east of Clarksburg, Stonewall Park. Residents of the adjoining community had named their town Norwood. After World War II the two towns decided to incorporate as one and a contest was held to name the new combined town. Sixth-grader Charles Childers of Norwood School won the suggestion of Stonewood combining part of the two names and the town was incorporated Dec. 17, 1947.

Viropa: This village in Clay District was founded by coal operators in approximatley 1902 and the name represents the states of the principal owners of the coal, namely Virginia, Ohio and Pennsylvania. Three companies successfully mined coal here during the years: The Fairmont, the Watson, and the

Consolidation Coal companies.

West Milford: In 1817 Jesse Lowther conveyed two acres along the West Fork River to Samuel Clemens and Jacob Romine on which they erected a mill, a short distance above a much-used crossing place or ford of the river and around which a village gradually clustered. The town was incorporated as Millford on Jan. 15, 1821, but the name was afterwards changed to West Milford owing to the fact that there was already another town by the name of Millford in Virginia.

Wolf Summit: Located on Limestone Creek in Tenmile District this area received its name from Perry Wolf, the head of the first family to settle in the area and from the fact that its location on the Baltimore & Ohio railroad was at the top of a grade in the roadbed at the highest point on the road between Grafton and Parkersburg and is a characteristic use of railroad terminology in the nineteenth century.

Wyatt: This little village located on the banks of Big Bingamon Creek in Eagle District was settled in 1865 by Eli Sharp. He raised geese for a living and the town was originally known as Goosetown. In later years, however, Dr. Z. W. Wyatt brought the village through an epidemic of diptheria and the grateful citizens renamed the town in his honor in 1873.

Zeising: This area, also known as Spelter, was originally named for Richard Zeising, manager of the chemical plant which was built there in 1910.

————

Various bodies of water throughout the century have evolved with a history of colorful names which reflect not only the humor of the early settlers but also the simplicity of their times and their thinking. The followng examples indicate that perhaps, in substance, a name is no more than what it is designated to identify.

Buffalo Creek: This name originated from the abundance of buffalo near this area in the early days of the county's settlement.

Cherry Camp Run: A group of hunters spent the night camping under the wild cherry trees in this area and gave the stream its name.

Chub Run: This small stream was named for a type of fish caught in the area and fried as an alternative to wild game.

Gnatty Creek: This was a very slow flowing body of water and the pools formed in many areas fostered an abundance of gnats or flying insects.

Hacker's Creek: Withers in his "Chronicles of Border Warfare" writes that the Indian name for the creek meant "muddy water." This tributary of the West Fork River is named for the pioneer John Hacker who settled here in 1770.

Hooppole Run: Along this stream hickory poles used in making barrel hoops were cut and used in that industry.

Indian Run: Capt. Thomas Harbert and Capt. Samuel Bingamon were pursuing a group of Indians when they found an Indian entangled in the branches of a fallen tree. After killing him they buried him by the stream nearby and gave the stream its present name.

Mudlick Run: A deer lick was located nearby and the run was kept muddy by the vast number of deer visiting the lick.

Pigtail Run: The course and direction of this stream which circled around like a pig's tail led to its present-day name.

Rock Camp Run: A group of hunters made camp one evening under a large, outcropping rock and gave the stream its name.

Rooting Creek: During the warm summer months the level of water in this creek would drop exposing the tree roots in the streambed.

Sugar Camp Run: There was a number of maple sugar trees which led to the establishment of a sugar camp here by early settlers.

Tenmile Creek: The mouth of this body of water is supposedly located ten miles from Clarksburg.

Turtletree Fork Run: A number of turtles were found in this stream and some of the larger ones were captured and hanged from a tree by the local tavern.

Two Lick Run: There were two deer licks located here in the early days where hunters waited for deer to appear.

West Fork River: The tradition is that this river was called "Muddy River" by the Indians. The significance of the name is purely directional and pioneer explorers reported it as being the west fork of the Monongahela River as the river was originally called.

The gallery of local place names is an integral part of local history but may, in many cases, be of little value when the meaning behind the name which has existed for years becomes obscured or forgotten. No matter now frequently the local name may be used, historically speaking, it is nothing more than a sound unless one knows or cares about the person or incident behind the name which led to the first use of the name itself. From this knowledge, or desire to know the roots of our local history, grows the local pride which make a community or a county or a country great.

John Simpson - First European Settler To Settle In The Harrison County Area

BY LLOYD LEGGETT

After the Treaty of Paris in 1763, ending the French and Indian War, France surrendered its claim to the Ohio Valley to England. This included the present day Harrison County. In the same year, King George III issued a proclamation forbidding any of the colonists from settling there.

The stated reason was for the protection of the colonists. But the practical reason was that King George III did not want the expense of policing the Ohio Valley from Indian attacks. The colonists were faced with a choice; obey the proclamation or defy it to reap the vast richness of the Ohio Valley. The spirit that brought settlers from their European homes to an untamed continent would not be halted on the Atlantic Coast. The Ohio Valley would be settled, legal or not. The colonists openly defied the King's proclamation.

The type of person it took to settle such an untamed land was much heartier than an average European Colonist. One such settler, cut from this strong stock, was John Simpson. He is credited with being the first European Colonist in the Harrison County area. A trapper and an explorer, John Simpson was also attracted by a need for solitude and a dislike of civilization. He opened up Harrison County for settlement.

John Simpson originally trapped in western Pennsylvania, but the French and Indian War, coupled with William Penn's purchase of land from the Indians in western Pennsylvania, brought more settlers to the area than he was comfortable with. He would have to move on. In 1761, four colonial British soldiers from Fort Pitt, now Pittsburgh, deserted to do some trapping and exploring on their own. They were William Childers, Joseh Tinsey, John Pringle and Samuel Pringle. They headed north along the Monongahela as far north as the present Geneva, Pa. After staying more than a year, they moved on to Looney Creek, then the most western settlement, where they were spotted and apprehended as deserters. John and Samuel Pringle, however, escaped and hid until early 1764.

During this year, they were employed by John Simpson in trapping. They were determined to move further west. Convincing Simpson with a promise of woods free from other hunters, they moved west. The Pringles wanted to leave because they feared arrest for deserting.

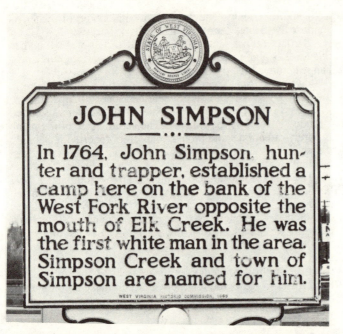

JOHN SIMPSON

In 1764, John Simpson, hunter and trapper, established a camp here on the bank of the West Fork River opposite the mouth of Elk Creek. He was the first white man in the area. Simpson Creek and town of Simpson are named for him.

WEST VIRGINIA HISTORIC COMMISSION, 1969

They crossed the Cheat River at the Horse Shoe, now in Tucker County, on their way to the present Harrison County. But Simpson, a loner, quarreled with one of the Pringles and they split up. The Pringles continued on to the Buckhannon River, and up to the mouth of a small branch called Turkey Run. They set up camp in a hollow sycamore tree, close to the present town of Buckhannon. Simpson crossed the river near

the mouth of Pleasant Creek. He then came upon another water course and called it Simpson Creek, which still bears his name.

He continued west and came upon waters of what he called Elk Creek, named for the vast number of elk he saw in the area. On the opposite side of the West Fork River, not far from what is known as the Stealey Farm, he made camp and began trapping in Harrison County. He used this camp as his headquarters for his trapping, not wishing to stay in one place very long.

After remaining about a year, Simpson returned east to the South Branch Valley. He carried all the furs he could to trade for the much needed ammunition and supplies. After a year of solitude, he once again spoke with other human beings.

At the time of his arrival at what is now Clarksburg, there was not a single acre in northwestern Virginia under cultivation. He was the first European Colonist to stand upon the banks of the West Fork River. One can only imagine the loneliness felt by being alone for over a year. But Simpson craved his solitude and disliked returning to civilization even for short periods of time.

Being a trapper in the early years of pre-Harrison County demanded a cold-hearted spirit and the story is told that John Simpson got into an argument with one of the Cottrils over a peck of salt. Cottril was found dead near Simpson's cabin with his gun cocked. He was probably killed by Simpson. As there were no courts in this area at that time, justice was not served.

In 1781, the commissioners appointed to settle the claims of unpatented lands at its session granted a certificate of ownership to John Simpson for 400 acres of land near the West Fork River. It included the Stealey Farm. Simpson never perfected the title to his land, but sold it to Nicholas Carpenter who perfected it. In 1786 Carpenter built a home which stood on the land for over 100 years.

With civilization creeping up on him, Simpson moved further west into obscurity. West was the only direction for such a man with the constant advance of civilization always a step behind him. The Harrison County which he helped open would later chase him off. He desired only solitude and good game land for trapping. One can only speculate on where he went — perhaps to Ohio — but his presence is still felt in Harrion County with Simpson Creek and Simpson District.

Scope of Harrison County in 1784 Recalled as Bicentennial Begins

BY DOROTHY DAVIS

Throughout 1984 people living along the drains of the West Fork River will be celebrating the bicentennial of Harrison County that in 1784 stretched from the Maryland border to the Ohio River and from Monongalia County to the southern boundary of present Braxton County.

To understand how people in Northwestern Virginia looked on their world in 1784, when Harrison County was formed, one must see the life and death struggle in which the settlers lived.

Twenty years before the 1780s British law forbade any subject to go beyond the headspring of the streams which flowed into the Atlantic Ocean. So with only an occasional hunter and trapper wandering the woods beyond the Alleghenies, the Indians felt the white man had as much right as they to the bounties of nature and did not molest men like the Pringles who were AWOL from the British forces at Fort Pitt, and spent three years living in a tree trunk near the Buckhannon River.

In 1786 the British by treaty bought from the Indians all land east of the Ohio River through to the Tennessee River and

although the British did not change the law forbidding settlement of the area, citizens along the seaboard took the last purchase as a sign that they could now move into the new land, build cabins, plant crops, and live permanently.

By the early 1770s the pressure of many settlements had made Indians hostile especially towards Virginians who through encounters had earned from the Indians the label "Long Knives". Virginia governor, Lord Dunmore, wanted the forks of the Ohio at Fort Pitt included within the boundaries of Virginia. He did nothing to quiet the frontier. Then came the American Revolution.. The upshot was Indian wars from 1774-1783 and threat of Indian attacks until 1795, when the Treaty of Greenville ended Indian incursions forever.

In 1773-74, with Indian war imminent, the general at Fort Pitt and the governor of Virginia ordered settlers who lived west of the Allegheny mountains to move east to protected areas. Instead, the newcomers stayed and built a string of forts along the Monongahela and the West Fork rivers with the last strong hold West's Fort in the 1984 town of Jane Lew. The Monongehela-West Fork line was the frontier for the longest period of time of any frontier in the history of the United States for it existed as frontier for 14 years from 1774 until the founding of Marietta, Ohio, in 1788.

The British during the American Revolution fueled the Indian war with both arms and propaganda causing settlers to "fort up" during good weather and live warily in their cabins during months when with the leaves off trees and snow on the ground, Indians could be seen or tracked.

The chief interest of all men was saving their own lives and the lives of other settlers on the frontier, a feeling so strong that in June 1788 when representatives west of the mountains went to the convention in Virginia to vote on ratification of the U. S. Constitution, 15 of the 16 from present West Virginia

PRINGLE TREE

This hollow sycamore is the third generation tree that provided a home for the first settlers in this area of West Virginia. John and Samuel Pringle, after fleeing from Fort Pitt, lived here 1764-1767.

WEST VIRGINIA DEPARTMENT OF CULTURE AND HISTORY, 1983

county by the name of "Harrison" to be formed at the house of George Jackson at Bush's Fort (Buckhannon) on July 20, 1784.

The name chosen for the new county was that of the man who was governor of Virginia from November 1781 to November 1784 and who would be named governor again in 1791. Choosing the name of an active politician started a pattern which the assembly followed in naming most of the counties in present West Virginia between 1787 and 1860.

Throwing in a great chunk of wilderness along with the few settled areas in forming a new county had been the policy of the Virginia Assembly for 50 years before they placed under the jurisdiction of the court of the new Harrison County so much land that eighteen of the 1984 West Virginia counties lay wholly or partly in Harrison County in 1784. The legislature intended for portions of the new county to break off as settlers pushed into wilderness. The first to break away was the Tgyart's Valley settlement at Beverly in 1787 to form Randolph County because with Clarksburg chosen as county seat by the first Harrison County Court, people felt anyone living near Beverly could not readily reach the courthouse.

In the act creating Harrison County the legislature had ordered the justices at the first meeting to name a city near the center of the county for county buildings. They chose Clarksburg probably because the Tygart's Valley River is too rocky to travel and at Clarksburg Elk Creek, a large stream, flows into the West Fork River thus making many sites for mills and sufficient streams for travel when primitive roads were muddy.

voted to ratify the Constitution for one reason: they thought a strong federal government might end the Indian menace. And it did, for it was General Anthony Wayne's successful foray that caused the Treaty of Greenville in 1795.

The subject other than Indians that caught the ear of anyone living on the drains of the West Fork and the Tygart's Valley rivers two hundred years ago was valid deeds to property. In the 1770s settlers had made blazes on trees to mark boundaries of the land they hoped some day to own legally; and after the Virginia General Assembly in 1779 passed land laws which allowed citizens to register, beginning in 1781, 400 acres given free by right of settlement, people needed to enter deeds and plats in the record books of a county government.

With no land ownership, little need existed for a courthouse before 1781, something lucky for anyone living along thw West Fork River because until 1779 citizens had to travel to Staunton, Virginia, to reach their courthouse. In 1779 the legislature hooked the West Fork River area onto Monongalia County whose courthouse in Morgantown was some 60 miles away. This helped a little for at times, when the river was filled with water, men could go by boat to Morgantown and could walk home over paths through the woods.

The American Revolution ended in 1783 and British incitement of Indians ended. Men living in the Tygart's River Valley settlement, the Buckhannon settlement, and the West Fork settlement drew up a petition in which they asked for a new county for their three settlements which they said lay parallel to each other and from 64 to 87 miles from the county seat.

The settlers stated, "It is not in our power from our local situation and late distresses from our common enemy to have the enjoyment of the laws of our county that our fellow citizens have as our court of justice is now affixed by law and all public offices are in the farthest part of the county from us." More than 250 men signed the petition handed to the Virginia General Assembly May 21, 1784.

In a few days the assembly passed an act authorizing a new

Harrison County Bicentennial Celebration 'Kickoff' Today

The yearlong bicentennial celebration of the formation of Harrison County will kickoff today at the Waldomore, according to project publicity coordinator Charles Miesner.

Following the presentation of the Official Bicentennial Calendar of events for 1984 at 4:30 p.m. at the Waldomore to the area media, a gathering of committee members of the Bicentennial project is scheduled from 5-6 p.m.

Former Harrison County House of Delegates member and state Republican Committee Chairman John F. McCuskey is serving as chairman of the Bicentennial project.

The yearlong celebration, coordinated by historian-in-residence and project director James Pool, will be observed with three methods, Miesner said.

First there will be public activities, including a festive "Harrison County Week" in the spring, highlighted with a parade, an autumn pageant, historical tours and bicentennial programs during the annual Italian Heritage Festival

Also there will be exhibitions, workshops, films and shows commemorating 200 years of the rich and diversified heritage of Harrison County.

Finally, the story of the great and small portions of the history of Harrison County will unfold with the ongoing publication of articles on the people, events, and folklore of that history, Meisner noted.

The celebration is the result of many hours of effort by many people.

The Bicentennial project is to be presented by the county bicentennial committee, with financial assistance from the Humanities Foundation of West Virginia, a state program of the National Endowment for the Humanities.

The Harrison County's 200th Birthday Activities Updated

HARRISON COUNTY Commission met with Historian-in-Residence Jim Pool and Bicentennial Committee member Merle Moore for an update on activities for the coming county celebration. The Harrison County Bicentennial Committee is chaired by John McCuskey and charged with planning for the County's 200th birthday. The committee received a grant from the West Virginia Humanities Foundation which was matched with a local grant from Consolidated Gas Corp. to help with the planned events. Pictured left to right are: Tom Keeley, commissioner; Ruby Keister, commission president; Pool, Miss Moore, and Frank Lopez, commissioner.

Two Lick Cave - A Refuge for Indians

By JAMES POOL

When Columbus discovered America the territory within the boundaries of what is now West Virginia was inhabited by a tribe of Indians known generally as the Eries, but more particularly called the Cat Indians, after the panther which was the totem or symbol which they worshiped. This Indian Nation inhabited the country from the Cumberland River to the Great Lakes and controlled the area of what is today West Virginia, Ohio and western Pennsylvania.

To the east of the Cat Indians dwelled another tribe known as the Adder Indians or more generally as the Iroquois which existed peacefully with the Cat Indians for many generations. During the period from about 1655-1671, however, the Cat Indians went to war with the Iroquois following a quarrel at a meeting to renew an existing treaty in which an Iroquois chief was killed. The war proved very costly to the Cat Nation for by 1671 it had been wiped out and all of West Virginia was controlled by the Iroquois.

The Cat Indians, however, were a superior race of people in many less warlike aspects of their civilization. During the period of their existence in this area they put vast tracts of land under cultivation, having felled the trees, cleared the land and planted crops. Numerous prior generations of the tribe had fashioned distinct ideas of justice, good government, social virtues and honesty which were similar to those depicted in James Fenimore Cooper's famous Leatherstocking Tales, such as the "Last of the Mohicans."

Evidence of the cultural development of these early inhabitants of Harrison County may be found in a small sandstone cave on Cambell's Run across the Two Lick Bridge near Good Hope. As early as September of 1889 the Department of Ethnology in Washington, D.C. sent a representative, W. H. Holmes, to examine this cave or rock shelter because the walls were said to be covered with petroglyphs or rock carvings. Now, the field of ethnology is basically a science which deals with the division of mankind into races and their origin, distribution, relations and characteristics but it is for certain that Holmes appreciated neither Indians in general nor the cave which he had been sent to examine. Henry Haymond in his "History of Harrison County" recounts in detail the report which Holmes compiled which consists of a quasi-graphic description of what he observed carved on the walls of the cave followed by the

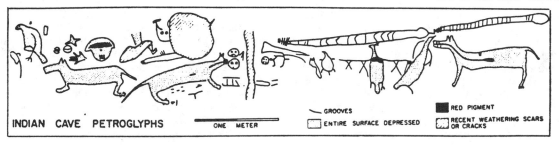

INDIAN CAVE PETROGLYPHS — ONE METER — GROOVES — ENTIRE SURFACE DEPRESSED — RED PIGMENT — RECENT WEATHERING SCARS OR CRACKS

totally ill-founded conclusion that "Although many of our aboriginal races are known to have devoted much time and care to the delineation of personal and clan totems it seems to me that no other than the deep and lasting motives connected directly with religion would be equal to the production of such elaborate and otherwise useless works."

Fortunately, more enlightened scholars have taken the opportunity to examine the cave and the wealth of historical information which these supposedly "useless works" provide with regard to the cultural development of the early inhabitants of Harrison County. One of these was the late Professor William B. Price of Salem College who is credited with providing interpretation of the carvings which may be observed on the walls of the cave even today.

The MacDonald cave in the Two Lick area of Harrison County is about 20 feet in diameter and is nearly circular in shape. Rising to a height of nearly six feet in the center the petroglyphs or Indian carvings on stone contained in the cave are found for the most part upon the back wall in the recesses of the cave and are a mural-like series of engravings about 20 feet long and about four feet high. In all about 28 different figures are to be found on the wall of the cave.

Contrary to the earlier Holmes interpretation, the Two Lick carvings are not the products of superstition designed to appease various unknown gods supposedly worshiped by the Cat Indians. Instead, they represent a mural of intelligent thought and commentary upon social values which these early inhabitants of Harrison County recorded upon the walls of this well-sheltered cave for later generations much the same as other cultures have recorded their history and beliefs in various books and monuments.

The petroglyphs begin at the extreme left of the entrance of the cave where Professor Price notes that a wild turkey has been depicted to show not only the value which the early inhabitants placed upon this bird as a source of food but also to show their respect for the bird as one of the wisest in the forest and one of the hardest to stalk due to its keen senses. For these reasons it is given a place near the entrance in order that it may keep watch and protect the cave from intruders.

Professor Price further notes that the carved face of the Great Spirit watches over all occupants of the cave. Since the Cat Indians believed that all life came from the sun, they felt that the Great Spirit, like the sun was dangerous to meet face to face and therefore a red mask is painted over the upper portion of the face across the eyes. The paint used was most likely made by mixing red hematite iron ore with a substance that would make it adhere firmly to the stone. Some writers claim this substance was probably human blood and Ripley's "Believe It or Not" relates a similar usage in a bridge which was built hundreds of years ago in Asia for which the King ordered enough slaves killed to furnish blood to be mixed with the mortar to increase its strength. A few years ago this particular bridge was still standing in perfect condition as is the paint on the carvings in the Two Lick Cave which is still red after hundreds of years. As one continues into the cave the figures of two panthers about half size are carved below the face of the Great Spirit in the cave. The panther was the totem or symbol of the Cat Indians and they believed that the seat of all life was in the heart. The red line leading from the mouth of each of these animals to its heart signifies that words come to the mouth from the heart and the mouth then gives expression to the feelings of a person outside the body of that person.

The figure of the bobcat is also found near those of the larger beasts. As the face of the Great Spirit represents Life so the skull represents Death. This figure is carved near the head of one of the panthers along with an arrow pointing in a northerly direction. A pair of eyes are also located beneath the first skull while a second skull may be found in a group of carvings consisting of a skull, two turtles, a fish and a rattlesnake. Another rattlesnake is carved further along the wall.

There are indications that additional carvings existed both above and below those described here and shown in the sketch of the petroglyphs, but these other engravings are too indistinct today as a result of disintegration within the general cave area and the wearing process upon the rock contained in the cave.

The cave itself is located in such a place that one can walk nearly right next to it and not realize that it is there. This fact reportedly led raiding Indians in early Harrison County who knew of the cave's existence to use it as a place of refuge for many years until as late as 1792.

Alexander Scott Withers wrote in his classic work entitled "Chronicles of Border Warfare" that in May of that year Indians attacked John Waggoner and his family in a field on Hacker's Creek, near Good Hope. Unarmed and separated from his family the elder Waggoner managed to escape and ran for aid to the fort returning with a rescue party in a short time. In the meantime however, the Indians had made off with Mrs. Waggoner and the six children of the family. In an effort to slow the pursuit of the rescue party following them the Indians killed and mutilated the mother and three of the children and left the bodies upon the trail.

The Indian raiding party was never captured or even located for they managed somehow to escape successfully while passing through the Two Lick area where the rescue party pursuing them lost their trail. The three remaining children seized by the Indians, two daughters and an eight-year-old son named Peter, lived with the Indians for varying periods of time — the eldest daughter escaping after a brief confinement and the second daughter being returned at the close of the war in 1795.

The son, however, voluntarily remained with the Indians for more than 20 years. He married and began to rear a family before being located by relatives and upon their urgings eventually left his Indian family and unwillingly returned to his original family in Harrison County. The attempts of Peter Waggoner's Indian wife to find him again among the white man's civilization is an Evangeline-like love story for another time, but Peter Waggoner's story is perhaps even more interesting and ironic.

Upon his return Peter related to more than one person how the Indians had taken him and his two sisters and avoided the rescue party chasing them by hiding. The rescuers had approached very near the place where the Indians and their captives were concealed but, as Peter vividly recalled no one saw nor heard them in their hiding place in the sandstone cave near Two Lick with the strange pictures on the walls.

He Never Knew His Indian Wife Had Tried To Find Him

BY JAMES GAY JONES

A common presentation of the relations between the Indians and the early American settlers has been that of constant enmity and hostility. Moreover, the Indians were usually portrayed as totally uncivilized, were generally referred to as "savages," and were considered to be incapable of experiencing the normal human feelings of love and compassion for others. In their desperate struggle to preserve and defend their homeland from the encroaching settlers, the Indians were often involved in acts of a heinous nature; yet, from their viewpoint, the settlers were no less guilty of similar acts in their attacks upon them. Despite the fact that both sides

were equally guilty, frontier folklore has preserved the image of the pioneer as a folk hero and that of the Indian as a "beast of the forest."

There were some people, however, who observed the Indian from a different viewpoint. Throughout the years of settlement of Harrison County it was not uncommon to find Indians living, by their own choice, among the settlers. Also, there was intermarriage between members of the two races. Probably the two best known examples of this were that of John Rolfe, a gentleman of Jamestown, and Pocahontas, daughter of Chief Powhatan; and that of Boling Baker, a frontier British soldier, and Arcoma, daughter of Chief Cornstalk. Lesser known were the countless others of lower social status who married and lived normal lives in their communities.

Most marriages of an interracial nature came about because the white persons involved had previously spent some time as captives of the Indians. Although there was some stigma attached to some such marriages at the time, that seems no longer to be true as many of their descendants who live in this Southern Appalachian area at the present time point with considerable pride to their Indian ancestry.

One aspect of Indian social life which compared quite favorably with that of the settlers were the strong bonds of parental and filial love that existed in their home life. Indian women who lost a husband or sons in battle experienced the same immeasurable grief that anyone can know. Sometimes, to fill the aching void in the lives of persons who had suffered such a loss, braves would be sent out to capture frontier white children for adoption into those homes. Once a person was adopted, he was granted a status fully equal to what would have been given to the one he replaced in the family.

In May 1792, Tecumseh, chief of the Scioto Shawnees, with two warriors, came into the western plateau area of the Allegheny Highland for the avowed purpose of capturing some children for adoption. On Hacker's Creek they captured the wife and five children of John Waggoner and immediately started back toward their homes west of the Ohio River. Fearing they might be captured, the Indians urged the captives to travel as fast as they could for some time without any rest. When Mrs. Waggoner and her two youngest children became so exhausted they could barely move, their captors killed and scalped them. The three remaining children, Peter and his sisters Mary and Elizabeth, were able to conceal their

weariness so well that their captors looked upon them with admiration and continued westward with them.

On their arrival in the Shawnee village on the Scioto, Peter was at once adopted by a woman who had lost a son shortly before this time. In spite of his deep sorrow over the tragedy that had struck his family, Peter soon adjusted to his new surroundings. In fact, he came to like the Indian mode of living so well that after the signing of the Treaty of Greenville in 1795 when the Shawnees released his two sisters, he preferred to remain with the Indians.

When Peter reached manhood, he married a Shawnee maiden whose parents lived on Paint Creek, a tributary of the Scioto River. It was there that the young couple made their home and, in time, became the parents of two children. Peter was happy there and was very much attached to his family.

In 1815, after the War of 1812 had ended there was a great westward movement of the American people across the Ohio to take up new homesteads. Among those migrating was Peter Booher of Hacker's Creek, who had been a neighbor of John Waggoner for several years. On his arrival in the Paint Creek section of the Scioto River Valley, he came upon a band of friendly Indians. Among them was a man whose resemblance to John Waggoner was so marked that Booher at once was convinced that this man was John's long lost son. Soon after this, Booher was able to get word back to John of the finding of his son, Peter.

Nearly 22 years had passed since John Waggoner had lost his wife and children. Although his two surviving daughters had been released from captivity, his life had still been exceedingly lonely since that day when tragedy struck his home. Now that his only living son had been located, he felt a strange surge of happiness as he set out to visit the Indian settlement on Paint Creek.

A few days later, John was overcome with joy when he stood before his son and threw his arms around him. His joy, however, soon turned to dismay when Peter refused to leave his family and return to his father's home. John now saw his son as practically a total stranger. It was a distinct shock to him to realize the extent of the indoctrination of Peter into Indian culture. His long black hair, the large earrings, and his slow speech in broken English were completely alien to the appearance John had expected.

When John again asked his son to return home with him, Peter, with firmness in his voice, replied: "This is my wife, these my children, this my home."

John then asked him to go back with him to the old family homestead for a short visit. He suggested that Peter could give his wife and friends his word of honor he would return to them by a certain date. After thinking this over for a time, Peter agreed. Although he gave his wife a firm promise he would return to her, she became disconsolate. With tears welling up in her eyes, she said to him: "If you go, me no see you more."

Soon after John and his son arrived back at the homestead on Hacker's Creek, people from throughout the community came to see the former neighbor boy who had grown up to become an Indian brave. The curiosity of the people made Peter restless and he anxiously looked forward to the time when he would return to his family. John was disappointed to see his son's growing restlessness. He had hoped that Peter would change his mind about returning to the Indian way of life after spending some time at the place of his youth. When he saw that Peter had not changed his mind and had begun to make preparations for his return, some of the neighbors were called in to help keep him under guard so he could not leave.

When Peter realized what was being done to him, he became desperate. One day while his father was sitting at the loom, Peter grabbed a bow and arrow and shot at him. Since Peter was a skilled bowman, he must not have intended to fatally injure his father because the arrow glanced off the top of his head, making only a superficial scalp wound: yet, the blow was strong enough to knock him to the floor.

After this, Peter was more closely guarded until the time of his return had passed. From that time on, he made no further effort to go back to his family because he had failed to keep his promise and thereby had disgraced himself in the eyes of his wife's people. Moreover, he knew it would be unsafe to go back now.

In adjusting to his new situation, Peter had his long hair cut shorter, his earrings were removed and his Indian apparel replaced with that of the style of the border settler. However, there was one characteristic that had so firmly become a part of his nature that he was never able to change. Throughout the remainder of his long life, he was a man of few words and remained proud of his Indian training and culture.

Some time after Peter had decided not to return to the Scioto country, a fairly young Indian woman came into the settlements along Jesse's Run and Hacker's Creek. She looked weary and forlorn and, to some, appeared to be partially demented. Occasionally, when stopping at a house for a drink of water or some food, she inquired of the whereabouts of Peter Waggoner. Even though the people felt sorry for her, they suspected she was Peter's Indian wife who, in a final desperate effort, had come looking for him and refused to tell her where Peter lived. They thought it best that they should not see each other again. Therefore, they directed her to go to places where she would not find him.

At one home where the Indian woman was given overnight lodging, she sang and danced almost all night long as an invocation for guidance to find her husband. When she was later found dead near the mouth of Hacker's Creek, she was quietly buried there and Peter Waggoner never knew that his Indian wife had wasted her life away looking for him.

Levi Shinn - The Founder of Shinnston

BY LENA GOLDEN
JACK SANDY ANDERSON

Among Harrison County's early settlers was Levi Shinn (1748-1807) who came to the West Fork Valley with his brother Jonathan in the fall of 1772. He was born and grew to manhood near Burlington, New Jersey.

Burlington was where his great grandparents, John and Jane Shinn, had settled upon their arrival from England in or about 1678.

Levi Shinn's grandfather, James Shinn, in 1697, married Abigail Lippincott, thereby allying himself with a prominent and influential family that was actively involved in the affairs of colonial New Jersey. In 1740 Levi Shinn's father, Clement Shinn, married Elizabeth, daughter of Robert Webb, and to them were born seven children. Four of these children — Clement, Levi, Jonathan and David — became Harrison County pioneers, although David eventually settled in Hampshire County and there ended his days.

In 1772 Levi married Elizabeth (1755-1813), daughter of James and Mary Capon Smith and half-sister of Aaron Smith, a noted Simpson Creek pioneer. A family tradition has it that soon after his marriage he set out to explore what was then the wilderness of western Virginia for the purpose of choosing land upon which he could establish a home. In the West Fork Valley in 1773 he found this land, and on this tract he built a two-story log home that is now one of West Virginia's few

remaining from the Revolutionary War era.

Details about the original Shinn settlement are rather vague, but the best available evidence indicates that Shinn established a permanent home there sometime between 1775 and 1778. It is known that he and Elizabeth lived for a while on Apple Pie Ridge, a region not far from Winchester, Virginia, and it is generally assumed they came from there to present Shinnston. At any rate, by 1778 the log house had been built, and the Shinns were busy at work clearing their land and struggling for survival in a rich but often hostile wilderness.

A man above the ordinary, Shinn soon became a leader in his part of the county. Records and tradition alike reveal him to have been an educated, frugal, and honest individual who in later life was able to amass what was then a considerable fortune. His neighbors frequently sought his counsel, and he was always ready to help those in need.

Although reared in a strict Quaker household, Shinn soon discovered that Quaker tenets had to be abandoned if he were to survive on the frontier where death from Indian attack was ever a possibility. Bearing arms was a necessity, and in the 1770s and 1780s he helped protect the frontier by assisting in the building of fortifications and by responding to alarms that warned of immediate danger. Some of his descendants believed that he served in the militia during the years of Indian warfare, but thus far no authentic record has been found to prove this.

In or before 1785, the exact date is not known, Shinn built a gristmill a short distance from the mouth of Shinn's Run. This mill proved to be of importance since it formed the nucleus around which grew the village that gradually developed into today's city of Shinnston. Milling was necessary in early times and seems to have run in the family for the immigrant ancestor, John Shinn, was a miller in colonial New Jersey and at least three of Levi Shinn's sons at one time or another were engaged in milling.

His extensive lands mostly obtained by grant, included some of the choicest acreage in northern Harrison County and provided a goodly inheritance for his children. However, in 1793, he sold the valuable tract upon which the main section of the town and of East Shinnston today stand. His brothers Clement and Jonathan were the purchasers, and it was the latter's heirs who caused the land to be laid off into lots and sold, thereby laying the foundation for a town. Levi Shinn had obtained this tract of over six hundred acres in 1784 as part of a preemption warrant he had for one thousand acres. His original tract containing his farm and home was acquired in 1773 and consisted of about four hundred acres. Another large tract he owned was to the west on the waters of Bingamon Creek, and it was upon this tract that the village of Pine Bluff developed.

Tradition tells us that Levi Shinn was an unusually strong individual and spent hours working on his farm and in his mill. He was well known for his honesty and for his generosity to people in need. Both he and his wife were hospitable by nature, and their home was always open to relatives and friends. For the most part, Shinn chose to live quietly and unassumingly and was not active in the political life of the county. Shinn and his wife, Elizabeth, had nine children who grew up in the Harrison County area. He was a member of the Simpson Creek Baptist Church. In 1807 with his family around him he died and was buried in the family cemetery in Shinnston.

In time, Shinn's oldest child, Clement (1773-1840), gained possession of the original log house. An industrious person, he managed with care his inheritance, added to it, and died a well-to-do man. Most of his wealth came from milling and raising livestock.

Following Clement's death and some complicated legal transactions, his heirs sold the log house to David Morris,

whose descendants owned it until the mid 1900s. By the 1840s when this sale occurred, the pioneer era in the West Fork Valley was over, the log houses had become decidedly old-fashioned. Frame dwellings of planed lumber, often large and elaborate, and red brick "mansions," as they were called in ante-bellum days, were fast replacing them. A quirk of fate is the fact that through the marriage of David Morris's great-granddaughter, Mabel Fleming, to one of Levi Shinn's great-great-grandsons, Claude S. Randall, the log house once more passed into possession of a descendant of its builder. In 1959 Estelle Randall and her brother, George, children and legal heirs of Calude S. and Mabel Fleming Randall, sold the Levi Shinn House to Richardson Lumber and and Construction Company. In 1972 the company deeded the house as a gift to the Shinnston Historical Association, which now owns it and employs it as a headquarters and museum. The Levi Shinn House, which is one of West Virginia's oldest houses, was entered on the National Register of Historic Places in 1973.

The Fate of the Children Overshadowed The Joy of the Couple's Eventual Reunion

There is often a great deal of difference between the recording of the historical event and the event itself. Such is the case with the heroic ordeal of Phebe Cunningham who was captured and held by Indians after being attacked in the Bingamon Creek area of Harrison County nearly 200 years ago. The following story was related by Mrs. Leah Beall, the granddaughter of Phebe Cunningham, to her grandchildren as it was related to her by her grandmother following her return from captivity among the Indians. The story is interspersed with references to the versions of the same events as recorded by the various historians in the course of compiling their accounts of the same incident.

Grandma and the children were eating dinner when the shadow of the Indian's tomahawk fell on the threshold. Grandpa and grandma were born in the same year, 1761, and were married when nineteen years old by a lay minister, Calder Haymond, at Prickett's Fort, I think in 1780. Henry, their first child, was four, their next Lydia, was three, their third, Walter, was two, and the baby, Thomas, was six months, when all, except Thomas, were killed by Indians on Aug. 31, 1785. At first, grandpa and grandma settled on Tenmile Creek, but later moved to land on Bingamon Creek, where Thomas' brother Edward, and his family then lived. Edward's wife's maiden name was Sarah Price.

The day the Indians came, grandma, then 24-years-old, a tiny woman, and always very charming, had washed a beautiful red and white coverlet and put it on the fence to dry. The Indians came up out of the woods and crouched behind the fence and the coverlet. Signs told they had been there for two or three hours watching.

One of the Indians—a tall, very fat one, painted for war all red and yellow and black crossed the yard and entered cabin at noon time. On the table were bear meat, new potatoes cooked whole, with fresh-picked peas, apple sauce, a fresh-baked vinegar pie and sweet milk. The Indian paused beside the table and fingered a potato from the pot, and saying "Do ween dah," which in the Wyndotte tongue is "potato," popped it into his mouth. He then ate the pie and drank the pitcher empty of sweet milk. Afterwards he went to the window that opened next to Edward's house, which was 60 feet away, and joined to grandpa's house by a gallery. It was then that Edward, looking from his kitchen window, saw him, and told Sarah to hand him his rifle. A moment later the Indian fired at Edward, and Edward fired back, without harm being done by their shots. The Indian then asked grandma how many men were in Edward's house. She replied by showing him her fingers and thumbs.

He frowned worriedly, "Augh sagh?" he said.

Later, when a captive, grandma learned that "augh sagh," was Wyndotte for "ten."

The Indian ate another potato, then went and pulled the ticks off the beds and heaped the ones with straw together and set them afire, and ripped open the ones with feathers and shook the feathers onto the flames which caused a very thick smoke.

(It has been said that he took an ax and started chopping a hole in the wall before he set the house afire, but grandma said this was not true.)

When the house was filled with smoke, and much of the smoke was going out the door, he jerked grandma from her chair and shoved her across the room. At that moment another Indian ran from the woods into the yard, and Edward shot him, and he fell and crawled off under the fence, looking back at Edward's house and dragging his leg. The Indian in the house watched until his companion was out of sight, then he drew his tomahawk and sank its blade into two-year-old Walter's head, and quickly took the little brown-haired fellow's scalp.

Grandma said as this happened there was not a sound in the house except those made by the Indian's hatchet and knife and the crackle of the fire. Later as the Indian led her from the house with a baby in her arms and Henry and Lydia hanging onto her skirts, Edward called her name, and told her not to lose hope, but to expect a rescue. She, the children, and the Indian, were then hidden from Edward by the smoke pouring from the doorway but she heard Edward's voice, and for a little while, her spirit was uplifted by it.

After grandma and the children were taken from their burning home into the woods where the wounded Indian and two of his companions were, Henry and Lydia, were murdered and grandma and little Tommy were taken off...

(Wither's "Border Warfare," beginning on page 369 — writes of this phase of the attack and capture as follows: "Despairing of accomplishing further havoc, and fearful of detection and pursuit, the Indians collected together and prepared to retreat. Mrs. Cunningham's eldest son was first tomahawked and scalped; the fatal hatchet sunk into the head of her little daughter. Then they took the child's body by the arms and legs, and slinging it repeatedly against a tree, ended her suffering with its life. Mrs. Cunningham stood motionless with grief and in momentary expectation of having the same dealt to her and her innocent infant. But no! She was doomed to captivity, and with her helpless babe in her arms was led off from this scene of horror and woe.

"The wounded Indian was carried on a rough litter, and they all departed, crossing the ridge to Bingamon Creek, near which they found a cave that afforded them shelter and concealment.")

L. V. McWhorter, historian of the West Fork River Valley, stated that "The cave in which Mrs. Cunningham was concealed is on Little Indian Run, a branch of Big Bingamon Creek, and in Harrison County, West Virginia."

Mrs. Beall again: Grandma said she and the baby were taken over the hill to a large overhanging rock, where the Indians had heaped brush and logs, and made a den. In this den they were held for four days, until the wounded Indian died, and twice during this while the men searching for them came so near that grandma heard their voices and understood what they said. On the fifth day, they were taken from the den and

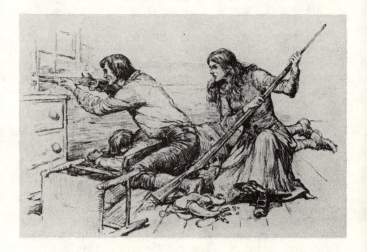

the long journey to the far west of the Ohio River began. On the ninth day, little Tommy was chopped to death by the Indian who killed Walter, and his body left in the open for the wolves.

Grandma was taken to the territory which later became Madison County, Ohio to a Wyandotte town there, where the chief was a kindly Indian called "Darby." (Big Darby Creek is about 20 miles west of present Columbus.) She was not treated badly after she became acquainted with the Indians and their white captives, some of whom became her friends. Among the white captives she met there, she remembered William Wells, Henry and Christopher Miller, brothers; Jonathon Adler; Mrs. Elizabeth Martin; Mrs. Sally Fleming and her little daughters. The first person she saw there whom she had known before her capture was Benjamin Springer. She remembered him for his being often at Prickett's and Coon's forts, and once visiting her home with Col. Martin. He was a cousin of Nathaniel and Nathan Springer of Monongalia County.

Mr. Springer attempted to ransom her, before he left for his home in Kentucky; but the Indians would not bargain with him for her, and he was very sad about it, and promised to get word to grandpa, and let him know where she was and that she was alive and safe. This he did, but the news reached grandpa after grandma was released and on her way home.

Mrs. Beall's narrative ends with her grandmother an Indian captive. M. K. Lowther, in her History of Ritchie County, pages 69 and 70, completes the Phebe Cunningham story, as follows:

When the home of her captors was reached, she received no barbarous treatment, but she was filled with fear and apprehension of some impending doom. Everything about her seemed to bode evil. She was delivered into the hands of the father of the wounded and missing Indian, and was compelled to wear soiled clothing, which was regarded as a bad omen for a captive. And thus for three years here captivity continued.

A conference, preparatory to a treaty between the whites and the Indians, was pending, when, one evening, she noticed and unusual commotion in the village and learned that the presence of the great Simon Girty occasioned it.

She determined to ask him to intercede for her release, and on the following day, seeing him passing by on horseback, she went to him and lay hold of his stirrup and implored his interference on her behalf, which at first, was only met with derision; but though the heart of this chieftian had been long a stranger to tenderness and sympathy, her entreaties finally succeeded in touching his better nature and he made intercession for her, secured her release, made provisions for her ransom, and had her conveyed to the commissioners who negotiated the treaty.

During the autumn of 1788, she was taken to a great Indian conference, at the foot of the Maumee rapids, and while here, Captain Girty brought the case before the British agent (Alexander) McKee, who furnished the trinkets for the ransom, and she was set free; and from here she went to Kentucky with two gentlemen, who came to this conference in quest of their captive children.

After much difficulty and no little delay, she (Phebe) reached her old home — the home of Edward Cunningham in Harrison County — and found that her husband, on hearing of her release, had gone in quest of him. Depressed by this disappointment of not meeting him, and by the thought of the danger and peril that attended his every footstep, she could not enter into the spirit of rejoicing that her homecomeing had occasioned; but in a few days, her husband, learning that she was homeward bound, returned, and was joy unspeakable, clasped to his bosom the long lost wife.

Though the rememberance of the tragic fate of their children shadowed the joy of their reunion, yet time alleviated their sorrow, and other and more fortunate children came to bless their home.

Major William Haymond - Trail Blazer

By DOROTHY DAVIS

William Haymond, first surveyor of Harrison County, once returned home to find his house cinders and his wife distraught. He calmly said, "We still have a kitchen," the kitchen then being a unit separate from the house.

A man would need to be impassive in crisis to have survived that which Haymond had already met at the time the fire occurred when he lived with his wife and young family near Rockville, Maryland. Already Haymond had traveled in 1755 at the age of 15 with Gen. Edward Braddock on the ill-fated attempt to take Fort Duquesne, had gone with Gen. John Forbes when the British won the Forks of the Ohio and established Fort Pitt in 1758; and had returned to the Ohio country in 1759, after enlisting in the Virginia regiment commanded by George Washington to help garrison the land along the Monongahela and the Allegheny rivers.

In 1773 Haymond sold his farm in Maryland and moved with his wife, four children and several slaves to land along the Monongahela River in Augusta County, Va. His son later

wrote that the family lived for a time at two different sites before they arrived at Kearns' Fort at Morgantown, where the son said he and his family planted corn in the ground where Morgantown now stands.

The 1770s were a propitious time for bright, ambitious frontiersmen, for institutions were being formed. The Virginia Assembly authorized Monongalia County cut from Augusta County in 1776. William Haymond held many positions in the new county: justice of peace, deputy surveyor, coroner, sheriff. An army man, Haymond commanded Prickett's Fort in 1777; he won his majority and performed as an officer of the Virginia militia throughout the American Revolution.

After the Virginia Assembly passed land laws in 1779, Haymond sat at spots all over Northwestern Virginia as a commissioner to register tomahawk rights to acreage during which time he entered in his name 800 acres on Hacker's Creek in present Harrison County.

After settlers along the West Fork and the Tygart's Valley rivers had petitioned for a new county, William Haymond donned a bear coat, climbed a horse, and rode to Williamsburg to take the test he must pass to certify him as a surveyor of the county in the making. Like most pioneers, he was adept at many things. His son said that he thought his father had trained in earlier years as a wagoner, that his father could make with his hands anything he wished from iron or wood, and that his father had always been good at mathematics.

At Morgantown during a smallpox epidemic William Haymond had lost two children and six slaves to the disease; so it was a slimmed-down family the son remembered helping move, at age 13, in October 1784 to Clarksburg in the new county of Harrison. Their faithful horses Slider and Prince, plus two borrowed horses, pulled the family possessions on the five-day trip from Morgantown to Clarksburg, where the son said he felt "quite lost" because he knew no one. They stayed for a time at a house across from James P. Bartlett's tavern before William Haymond "bought 60 acres of land for

60 pounds, about three quarters of a mile above town, where we moved with Slider and Prince and built a house for an office.''

William Haymond left the moving to his sons for he was very busy. September 21, 1784, he presented to the Harrison County Court his commission as surveyor and was sworn in. His work would take him over a vast territory from the Maryland border to the Ohio River and the waters of the Kanawha River. The Virginia Assembly named Haymond a trustee of Clarksburg when it incorporated the town in October 1785; the Harrison County Court appointed him to help draw up specifications for a courthouse in 1787; the trustees of Randolph Academy appointed Haymond, John McCally, and Daniel Davisson Sept. 16, 1788, to superintend the raising of a building for the school; the governor appointed Haymond a justice of peace.

February 16, 1788, William Haymond qualified before the county court as commissioner of the road to be cut from the State Road near Kingwood to the mouth of the Little Kanawha River. His son wrote in the 1840s of the difficulty the commissioners in 1788 met in laying out the road west from Clarksburg: ''The commissioners commenced viewing from Clarksburg to the Ohio River, but would get lost in coming back. They then started with a compass to Clarksburg, and ran a due west course and struck the Ohio River six or eight miles below Marietta. They then marked the road back to Clarksburg keeping the west line for a guide. The road was then cut out.'' A traveler who passed over the road in the 1790s reported it to be little more than a path through the woods. Haymond found his wife sick when he returned from a trip to view the new road. She died in December 1788. Haymond married Mary Powers, a widow, Dec. 29, 1789.

When voters came to the courthouse Jan. 7, 1789, to vote for an elector to choose the first president of the U. S., 18 of them refused to vote for the man who was the candidate because they did not know him. The results were Robert Rutherford 112 votes and William Haymond 18 votes even though Haymond did not want the office and was not present at the time the votes were cast.

In 1791 Haymond bought 200 acres on Zack's Run, where he built a cabin for a home. The son remembered killing several turkeys on the road the October day the Haymonds moved their possessions to Zack's Run. (The cabin stood on land on the southeastern edge of Floral Hills Memorial Gardens until the 1970s, when the logs were found too poor to transport. The stones used in the Chimney were carried to Fort New Salem on the Salem College Campus).

Haymond described a meteor he viewed when he was on a surveying expedition and encamped in the woods west of Clarksburg about 1800, a meteor whose explosions and brilliant light created terror among the pioneers: ''Agreeable to my own observations, and taking in view the observations of several others, who saw the light rise up previous to its spreading, the origin of the phenomenon must have been between the west and northwest from me, at the distance of about five or six and 20 miles, at or near the Buckeye Bottom (west of Salem).''

A veteran juryman having served as a member of juries in county courts and as a grand juror in General Court in Morgantown in September 1789, William Haymond was a member of the Grand Jury of the first circuit court held in Clarksburg in 1809 and he was foreman of jurors during the meeting of the Grand Jury of the first U. S. Court held west of the Allegheny Mountains in Clarksburg on March 22, 1819.

Major William Haymond died Nov. 21, 1821, after serving as principal surveyor of Harrison County for 31 years. His son Thomas was sworn in as surveyor in January 1822 and served 31 years, or until 1853; Cyrus, a brother of Thomas, served as surveyor of the county for 17 years or until 1871;

and Sidney, a son of Cyrus, then was county surveyor for four years. One family supplied principal surveyors of the county for 89 years.

At the end of the 19th century when the extraction of fossil fuels made exact property lines mandatory, less difficulty with land measurement existed in Harrison County than in most other West Virginia counties because the Haymonds had been very accurate in their work. Sons had served apprenticeships under fathers for years before becoming principal surveyors.

Surveying instruments used by the Haymonds can be viewed in the collection of the museum of the Harrison County Historical Society housed in the Stealey-Goff-Vance House, 123 West Pike Street in Clarksburg.

Harrison County 200 Years And 2 Days Old Today

By DOROTHY DAVIS

In 1984 Harrison County is celebrating the Bicentennial of an act of the Virginia Assembly which ordered an area of land west of the mountains from the Maryland border to the Ohio River to be organized into a county named Harrison. The land area of the new county was so extensive that the Virginia Assembly between 1787 and 1860 authorized eighteen new counties to be formed wholly or partly from land originally included in the boundaries of Harrison County.

Throwing under the jurisdiction of one county court a land area so huge as to be ungovernable followed a policy of the Virginia Assembly started in 1734 when Orange County was created to include all Virginia lands west of the Blue Ridge Mountains to the ''uttermost limits'' which embraced all of what today is West Virginia, Kentucky, Ohio, Indiana, Michigan, Wisconsin, and a large part of Virginia. Orange County was reduced in size in November 1738, when the Virginia Assembly assigned present West Virginia, except the Eastern Panhandle, to Augusta County with a county seat in Staunton, Va. From 1747 to 1776 the land area of present Harrison County lay within boundaries of various speculative land companies, all of which failed; but which, when active, fed the flames of contention between Pennsylvania and Virginia as to which state was entitled to the land at the forks of the Ohio at Fort Pitt. After Lord Dunmore arrived in Williamsburg, Va., Dec. 12, 1771, to be the governor of the Virginia Commonwealth, he quickly caught the speculative fever of delving into western lands and in the summer of 1773 traveled to Fort Pitt to see for himself the state of affairs of settlers there as a result of the claims of both Virginia and Pennsylvania to lands at the head of the Ohio River.

HARRISON COUNTY WEST VIRGINIA

1784

200 YEARS

1984

Lord Dunmore said that he found "upwards of ten thousand settlers" at Fort Pitt without magistrates or militia. The settlers begged the governor to give them the protection of the laws of Virginia. On Sept. 7, 1773, Lord Dunmore was back in Williamsburg, where on Oct. 11, 1773, he and his council established the District of West Augusta which included the forks of the Ohio at Fort Pitt and what in 1984 is Harrison County.

The justices of the district would naturally be chosen to represent farflung portions of the district, few of which would be more distant from Fort Pitt than the West Fork River. So the governor named William Lowther one of the first justices no doubt because "during the starving year of 1773 his exertions to mitigate the suffering" of settlers on the Buckhannon River, Hacker's Creek, and the West Fork River were so successful that he was the most respected citizen in the southern part of the district.

Lord Dunmore and his council would have made the northwestern lands of Virginia a county instead of a district had a state statute not prevented the governor from forming a county. But with the District of West Augusta an ongoing entity, the Virginia Assembly officially established the district the same day it outlawed the district when the legislative body authorized in October 1776 the formation of Ohio, Monongalia, and Yohogania counties from the land that it had just delineated to make up the District of West Augusta.

Boundaries set by the assembly for the District of West Augusta and for Monongalia County in 1776 left settlers along the tributaries of the West Fork River and along the tributaries of the Tygart's Valley River in the county of Augusta with its county seat in Staunton. A trip down the rivers to Morgantown, the county seat of Monongalia County, or even a trip on horseback or on foot by path and road to Morgantown was possible; the journey over the mountains to Staunton was next to impossible. The complaints of settlers along the tributaries of the Monongahela River were so loud that in May 1779, two and one-half years after the formation of Monongalia County, the Virginia Assembly added the lands in present Harrison County to Monongalia County.

The plea most often used by citizens in Virginia who petitioned for a new county to be formed was inaccessibility of the county seat. And the plea was valid in an age when to cast a vote a person must travel to the county courthouse; when the justices sitting at the county courthouse established all roads, issued all licenses, established all law and order, and tried legal cases; and when the militia in which all male citizens served mustered at the county seat.

The first three years of the five years they lived under the jurisdiction of Monongalia County, the people along the drains of the West Fork River and its tributaries ran often to Richard's, West's, or Nutter's forts for protection; and in June 1781 most of the men from the West Fork River and the Tygart's Valley River met at Nutter's Fort near the mouth of Elk Creek to travel under William Lowther and George Jackson to Pittsburg to join George Rogers Clark for a projected mission to take Detroit from the British.

By 1783, when the Indians were quiet enough for settlers to leave forts for their lands and those who had fled Bush's Fort for Nutter's Fort in 1782 were again in their cabins along the Buckhannon River, citizens bagan to think about voting and the difficulty of a trip to Morgantown. Already administrators of the land laws passed by the Virginia Assembly in 1779 had recognized the hardship of a long trip to the county seat when they assigned commissioners in 1781-82 to sit at the house of Samuel Lewellen in Clarksburg to register land claimed by the settlers. The Virginia General Assembly agreed that citizens could not cope with a county seat one hundred miles from their settlement when it authorized in October 1783 that a poll of voters in April of each year would be taken by the sheriff "at the house of George Jackson, at the place called Boush's (Bush's) Fort, on the Buckhannon River," the Monday after the poll at the courthouse in Morgantown.

One can imagine how the sheriff of a county felt about mounting a horse a few days after he had conducted a poll of voters in the countyseat to ride one hundred miles over paths in the woods to the home of a citizen to conduct a second election. He surely would favor a division of the county started a few months later as attested to by John Evans, Monongalia County Clerk: "I do hereby certify that a division of this County has been Advertised on two different Monthly Court days."

Evans' certification accompanied a petition signed by more than two hundred fifty men and submitted to the Virginia General Assembly on May 21, 1784:

"To the Hon. the Speaker and Delegates of the House of General Assembly of the Commonwelth (sic) of Virginia — The Petition of the inhabitants of Tigers Vally (sic), Buckhannan (sic) and Westfork Settlements Humbly Sheweth — That your Petitioners were formerly a part of Augusta County, and for sometime past hath been added to Monongalia County, find many and grate (sic) dificultys (sic) in being joined to the same since the return of peace with our late Indian enemy. Which your Petitioners begs (sic) leave to lay before your

Honourable House — We being three Distinct Settlements nearly parallel (sic) in situation and partly opposite to each other and nearly adjoining the Green-Brier Line, have it not in our power from our local situation and late distresses from our Common Enemy to have the Injoyment of the Lawes of our County that our fellow Citizens have, as our Court of Justice is now affixed by Law and all publick Offices are in the further part of the County from us —

"Our distance as computed from the waters of said Settlements are Viz. from Tigers Vally, Eighty Seven Miles, Buckhannan nearly the same, and Westfork Sixty Four — Which distance together with the badness of the way, not only makes it disagreable (sic) but almost impossible in the Winter and wet Seasons of the Year to Travill (sic).

"Flattering ourselves that if your Hon. House would be Graciously pleased to lay us off in a Distinct County, that in a short time we should get our Damages sustained by the Enemy repaired, and have it in our power to become Usefull members of the Community, Well knowing it our duty to Exert ourselves to preserve our national Credit —

"Our Request being Granted, will lay us under the Gratest Thankfullness And We in Duty Bound shall Pray."

On the outside of the folded petition is the statement: "that the petition of divers Inhabitants of the County of Monongalia praying that all that part of the said County including the Settlements of Tygers Valley, Buckhannan & Westfork may be laid off into a distinct County is reasonable." The Council of the State of Virginia sent to the governor a list of twelve names it "advised" the governor to name as justices and the name of the man it "advised" to be named sheriff, as stipulated in the act passed by the assembly early in June 1784:

"Be it enacted by the General Assembly, That from and after the twentieth day of July next, the county of Monongalia shall be divided into two distinct counties, by a line to begin on the Maryland line, at the fork ford on the land of John Goff, thence down the said creek to Tyger's valley fork of the Monongalia (sic) river, thence up the same to the mouth of Biggerman's creek, thence up the said creek to the line of Ohio County; and that part of the said county lying south of the said line, shall be called and known by the name of Harrison, and all the residue of the said county shall retain the name on Monongalia..."

The name assigned the new county was that of Benjamin Harrison, the governor of Virginia, who served as the chief executive of the state from November 1781 to November 1784 and was again chosen by the legislature for the post in 1791 but died before the second term of office began. The choice of a Virginia politician active at the time of the passage of the act for the new county for the county's name started a pattern which would continue for the next seventy years in naming new counties west of the mountains in Virginia.

Naturally the governor, as advised by the State Council, tried to appoint as justices men from every section of land included within the borders of the county. The governor could ignore representation from lands west of the West Fork River for a line manned by forts from the forks of the Ohio up the Monongahela and West Fork rivers to West's Fort at present Jane Lew in the upper reaches of the West Fork River was the frontier and would remain the frontier until the founding of Marietta, Ohio in 1788.

From the upper Tygart's Valley River area the governor named for justice Benjamin Wilson who lived four miles from Beverly; from the horseshoe bend of the Cheat River near the present town of Parsons the governor named as justice Salathiel Goff; from the lower Tygart's River Valley, Jacob Westfall and Henry Delay; from the Monongahela River area, Patrick Hamilton; from the lower West Fork River, Thomas Cheney; from the West Fork River near Clarksburg, Nicholas

Carpenter and John P. Duvall; the upper West Fork River, William Lowther; from Simpson's Creek, John Powers, James Anderson and William Robinson.

Having been named a justice by the governor did not mean that the appointee helped run the new county. A search of the records of the court show that Patrick Hamilton who lived almost eighty miles from Buckhannon, did not attend one meeting of the court in two years after he qualified in July 1784 as justice. The names of those recommended by the justices at the first meeting of the court to be sent to the governor in the future "to fill the office of the peace for said county" were men who lived near enough to the county seat to join justices already appointed in carrying out the work of the court: George Jackson, John McCally, John Sleeth, John Wilson, Cornelius Westfall, John Goodwin, Edward Jackson, Benjamin Robinson, John Prunty and Robert Maxwell.

The court followed the provisions of the act passed the month before by the assembly. Benjamin Wilson administered the oath of allegiance to the Commonwealth to John P. Duvall who then administered the oath to the other justices. William Lowther produced a commission from the governor dated June 14, 1784, naming Lowther sheriff and was sworn in by Duvall with George Jackson and Benjamin Wilson as the sheriff's securities.

The court named Benjamin Wilson clerk for the new county, They recommended that the governor appoint William Haymond as principal surveyor; James Anderson and Nicholas Carpenter, coroners; John P. Duvall, county lieutenant; Benjamin Wilson, colonel; Henry Delay, lieutenant colonel; and Willliam Robinson, major. They ordered many roads to be laid out. They appointed seven constables.

The waterways influenced the choice of a site to hold court and erect public buildings. The Tygart's Valley River is too rocky either to be navigated or to be developed. The West Fork River is less rocky and land where Elk Creek flows into the river, land awarded by right of settlement to Daniel Davisson and Andrew Davisson, had already been picked as most propitious for a county seat before the court held its first meeting. On the land was a settlement called Clarksburg. The court voted to erect public buildings on land donated by Daniel Davisson and Joseph Hastings.

The work of George Jackson, the most ambitious politically of the founders of the county and a man described as "very much disposed to have his own way in anything he was connected with" can be seen in the choice of the place for a county seat when during the first meeting, the court gave Jackson permission to build a mill on Elk Creek in or adjoining Clarksburg. Jackson was in the process of moving his family to Clarksburg in July 1784.

The house in which this first court was held stood near the present town of Buckhannon in the neck of the loop of the river, about one mile east of the Upshur County Courthouse, and is said to have been built by John, the father of George Jackson. It has long since been torn down and no part of it is now standing. It was surely a primitive log structure probably less comfortable than the ordinary later operated by George Jackson in his residence in Clarksburg.

The second meeting of the Harrison County Court was held in the house of Hezekiah Davisson in Clarksburg, the town where the court has met each month from August 1784 to July 1984.

The land included in Harrison County in 1784 would not stay intact long for within two years residents of the Beverly settlement in the Tygart's Valley thought the court in Clarksburg too far away to serve their needs. In 1787 the Virginia General Assembly passed an act forming Randolph County. By 1798 the Harrison land along the Ohio River had filled with enough people for the assembly to create Wood

County. The counties formed entirely or partly from land originally in Harrison County are:

Barbour, 1843; Braxton, 1836; Calhoun, 1856; Doddridge, 1845; Gilmer, 1845; Jackson, 1831; Lewis, 1816; Marion, 1842; Pleasants, 1851; Pocahontas, 1821; Randolph, 1787; Ritchie, 1843; Taylor, 1844; Tucker, 1856; Upshur, 1851; Webster, 1860; Wirt, 1848 and Wood, 1798.

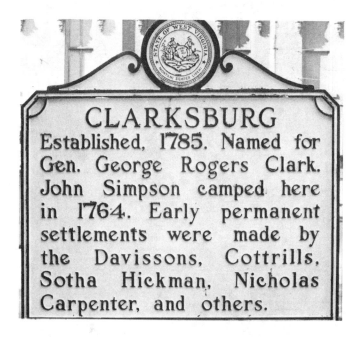

CLARKSBURG Established, 1785. Named for Gen. George Rogers Clark. John Simpson camped here in 1764. Early permanent settlements were made by the Davissons, Cottrills, Sotha Hickman, Nicholas Carpenter, and others.

Sotha Hickman - One of The Origional Settlers in the Harrison County Region

BY GALE PRICE

Sotha Hickman was one of Harrison County's earliest settlers, first coming to the region in 1771 and settling in the area in 1772. Hickman was born on the Sugar Land Bottom on the Potomac River near the present town of Rockville, Md., in 1749.

Explorers from Maryland discovered the southern tributaries to the Monongahela River in the late 1760s, and Hickman and his companions may have been following their lead when they ventured into the Elk Creek area.

On the last day of December 1791, he and some companions were camped on Ann Moore's Run while hunting and looking for suitable land for settlement. They ventured onto the bottom where Brushy Fork empties into Elk Creek (visible from Rt. 20 south, just north of Quiet Dell). There they found buffalo, turkeys, and a bear. Impressed with either the abundant game or the area's geography, several members of the party laid claim to land in the area.

Sotha Hickman claimed land farther north along the Elk Creek, at the site of the present Elk View Cemetery. He settled there with his family in the spring of 1772. His claim was about a mile north of Thomas Nutter's Fort, while Levi Douglass laid claim to the 400 acres immediately beside Brushy Fork.

Hickman laid claim to another thousand acres of land in 1773. This land, which he did not occupy for some years, lay somewhere between Brushy Fork and Zack's Run, and probably included the present community of Quiet Dell. He settled on that thousand acres of land sometime after 1779 (when he was at least temporarily run off his Elk View land by raiding Indians). He was living on his Quiet Dell property at

the time of his death in 1831.

It appears that Sotha Hickman fit the popular image of the boastful frontiersman. He bragged that his son, Arthur, was the first white child born in Harrison County, and claimed that he was the first working farmer in the county: "I raised the first crop of corn that was raised in this county an' I owned the first rooster that ever crowed in this county."

He lived a colorful life, being taken prisoner by Indians (along with trapping companion Levi Douglass) in the 1770s, fighting Indians for 14 months under Col. William Lowther, and nearly being seized by Indians while fishing on Elk Creek, in addition to being run from his home by an Indian raiding party.

Accounts exist of Hickman and Douglass being taken into Ohio by Indians following their capture during their trapping expedition. Hickman and Douglass escaped during some celebration by their captors and fled back home, travelling four days without food before they managed to kill a bear. According to the accounts, they ate themselves sick on bear meat and recovered their health only after drinking the mineral oil they found floating on the surface of the Hughes River.

Another account tells how Sotha Hickman held onto the night's catch after his fishing party was surprised by Indians along Elk Creek.

Hickman retained a hatred for the area's indigenous inhabitants throughout his life. One of his favorite expressions was "Dod blast their yaller hides." Like many frontiersmen,

he appeared to have the notion that the land was there for the taking and land not settled and farmed was land not owned. No doubt the Indians' efforts to chase him from their hunting grounds appeared to Hickman as the malice of savages.

After the Indian wars, Sotha Hickman apparently settled into a quieter life. He lived out his days on his Quiet Dell farm, continuing to devote his autumns and winters to hunting and trapping. One biographer attests to his companionable disposition.

Hickman outlived his fellow settlers, not dying until about his eighty-third year. He died at his home in the Quiet Dell area and is buried in Haymond Cemetery on Zach's Run. His marker reads: Sotha Hickman, Va. Mil. Rev. War 1748-1831.

Keeping Settlers In Forts Was Militia's Problem

BY DOROTHY DAVIS

At the first meeting of the Harrison County Court on July 28, 1784, at the home of George Jackson near Buckhannon, Benjamin Wilson administered the oath of allegiance to the Commonwealth of Virginia to John P. Duvall who had been named by the governor a justice of the peace of the new county. Then Duvall swore in the eleven other men appointed to be Justices: James Anderson, Nicholas Carpenter, Thomas Cheney, Henry Delay, Salathiel Goff, Patrick Hamilton, William Lowther, John Powers, William Robinson, Jacob Westfall, and Benjamin Wilson.

William Lowther, whom the governor had appointed, took the oath as sheriff and the justices recommended William Haymond for surveyor; James Anderson and Nicholas Carpenter, coroners; John Duvall, Benjamin Wilson, Henry Delay, William Robinson, officers of the militia.

John Pearce Duvall, named by the governor as lieutenant for the county, held the position with perhaps more responsibilities than any other county officer in 1784. His job was to protect the settlers from attack by Indians.

Duvall wrote Governor Patrick Henry in September 1785 that he had 250 men and 214 guns for the defense of Harrison County. The men Duvall counted were members of the Virginia militia, which by law all men must enter at age 16. Some militia were "spies" assigned to roam the woods to look for signs of Indians; others, stood guard at stockades and forts to which settlers ran in times of trouble. Men not on active duty met for militia drill once each month.

Keeping people in forts was one problem of the militia. Indians struck in summer for they could be tracked through the snow and seen when leaves were off the trees in winter. Who wanted to be cooped up when the weather was nice? Withers writing in 1831 explained the attitude of the settlers as to "forting up"; "That persons should be going out from the forts when the Indians were so generally watching around them, expose themselves to captivity or death may at first appear strange and astonishing. But when the mind reflects on the tedious and irksome confinement, which they were compelled to undergo; the absence of the comforts and frequently of the necessaries of life, coupled with an overweening attachment to the enjoyment of forest scenes and forest pastimes, it will perhaps be a matter of greater astonishment that they did not more frequently forgo the security of a fortress... they could not brook the restraint under which they were placed."

In 1784 the line from Fort Pitt up the Monongahela River and the West Fork River was still the frontier and had been the frontier for ten years. It would continue to be the frontier until 1788, when Marietta was settled by the Ohio Company.

The popular route used by both Indians and settlers to and from the Ohio River to present North Central West Virginia was a trail which followed the Little Kanawha River. Even though several Virginia Militiamen were stationed at Neale's Station at the mouth of the Little Kanawha River in an attempt to plug entry into the upper reaches of the West Fork River,

Indian incursions were frequent as shown by the Hacker's Creek settlement being broken up completely in 1779 and Bush's Fort near Buckhannon being burned in 1782. And attacks continued. In 1792 Indians killed four members of the Waggoner family on Hacker's Creek and carried off three others of the family to Detroit.

The string of forts starting south of Pittsburgh followed the rivers south to Jane Lew, where West's Fort ended the structures built in 1774 at the start of the Indian wars. The strongest one in the southern end of the fortifications was Nutter's Fort on Elk Creek in the present city of Nutter Fort. Withers in 1831 said it gave protection to settlers from the source of the West Fork to the mouth of the Tygart's Valley River. It was here that the Buckhannon settlers came just before the destruction of Bush's Fort and where many of the Hacker's Creek Settlers came in their time of trouble.

The smaller forts gave protection from small incursions. In addition to Bush's and West's, Richards' Fort, sometimes called "Lowther's" or "West Fort," stood near West Milford. The Harrison County Court erected in the 1930s a marker by the road just north of West Milford at the site where Richard's Fort probably stood.

A small fort built by John Powers stood on Simpson Creek a mile or so north of Bridgeport. In this fort William Powers kept a diary as he grew up. Alexander Withers used William Powers data for much of the material found in "Chronicles of Border Warfare."

Fort Coon was a small fort on the west bank of Coon's Run three miles from the West Fork River; Fort Jackson stood on Tenmile Creek in Sardis District to protect farmers in the neighborhood. Fort Harbert was a blockhouse on Jones Run; McInture Blockhouse stood in Enterprise. Daniel Davisson built a blockhouse-type dwelling near the corner of Chestnut and Pike streets in Clarksburg; and settlers in Salem erected a blockhouse after they arrived on Salem Fork of Tenmile Creek in 1790.

Duvall sometime in the 1780s moved to an island he owned in the Ohio River near Parkersburg. He continued to be county lieutenant but the work of protecting settlers near the county seat fell to William Lowther of the militia. After Duvall emigrated to Kentucky in 1792, Col. William Lowther was named lieutenant of the militia in Harrison County.

Col. Benjamin Wilson - Soldier, Settler, Named the County Court Clerk in 1784

DOROTHY DAVIS

Benjamin Wilson, who administered the first of the oaths of office to a justice at the meeting of the Harrison County Court July 20, 1784, and later at the same meeting was named clerk of the county, was born in Shenandoah County, Va., Nov. 30, 1747, and moved as a boy to Hardy County in present West Virginia.

Virginia Gov. Lord Dunmore chose Wilson, a 27-year-old lieutenant, to be a member of the governor's staff for the foray west that culminated in 1774 in Dunmore's War. Wilson was with Dunmore at Camp Charlotte when Cornstalk came to negotiate a peace treaty. Wilson late in life wrote that he had heard the finest orators in Virginia, Patrick Henry and Richard Henry Lee, "but never have I heard one whose powers of delivery surpass those of Cornstalk on that occasion."

On the way home from Ohio Wilson saw for the first time the Tygart's River Valley and was so impressed with its beauty that he bought out the tomahawk rights of two settlers to land four miles from Beverly and soon moved his wife and children to the valley.

During the Indian Wars which started in 1774, violence increased when the British at Detroit incited the Indians to strick the frontiers of the former British colonies, and continued until 1795. Benjamin Wilson "performed his duties and offices with such skill and good judgement as to become a tower of strength to frontier settlers and (to prevent) the whole settlement from being abandoned." He was made colonel during the American Revolution; he built in 1774 Wilson's Fort on his land.

Anytime an Indian raid occurred in the Tygart's River Valley runners went for Col. Wilson who "with his wonted promptitude and energy" went in pursuit of the marauders, often to the waters of the Little Kanawha River and most often returned to Wilson's Fort only after the volunteers who accompanied Wilson outvoted him and others who wanted to pursue the Indians farther.

In 1782 when John Evans was Monongalia County Lieutenant and Benjamin Wilson was commander of militia, Wilson wrote the War Office in Richmond that he already had 22 families in his fort and should like to stand his ground for if he should break, the whole valley would follow his example; that the militia was distributed among the several forts but must be fed by the people; that provisions ordered sent from Rockingham County had not arrived. Wilson wrote the governor in December 1782 that he had 68 effective men in Tygart's Valley; 18 at Horseshoe; 80 at West Fork; and 25 at Dunkard Bottom.

Benjamin Wilson would be undaunted by the journey from Beverly to Clarksburg after the Harrison County Court at its first meeting near Buckhannon chose Clarksburg as the place to erect county buildings. He probably would have continued to live on his land near Beverly and to travel back and forth each week to perform his work as county clerk had not

Randolph County been formed from Harrison County in 1787. We know Wilson lived near Beverly in July 1787 for John Haymond, son of Major William Haymond, traveled from Clarksburg with his wedding attendants to marry Benjamin Wilson's daughter Mary at Beverly July 3, 1787. The wedding party from Clarksburg camped out all night under a cliff of rocks a short distance from Philippi on the Tygart's Valley River.

After his land fell into the new county, Wilson continued to stay in the Tygart's River Valley long enough to represent Randolph County in Richmond at the convention that ratified the U.S. Constitution in 1788. He moved to the Clarksburg area sometime between 1788 and 1791, the year he bought 400 acres on Simpson's Creek from William Lowther. He needed to be near his work for he was taking on more and more responsibilities as shown by his acceptance of appointment as trustee of Randolph Academy in 1788.

For securing help from the state or the federal government to protect settlers from Indians in the last years of Indian wars Benjamin Wilson had more clout than other citizens. The two outstanding military figures — George Jackson and William Lowther — both were 10 years younger than Wilson and looked to Wilson to appeal for military assistance as shown in a letter from Benjamin Wilson to Gov. Beverly Randolph, a letter that William Lowther carried to Richmond in September 1789: "Our people are dispirited as they have soon felt the direful effects of an efficient treaty with the Indians in which they had put some confidence. They would soon be otherwise for which purpose I earnestly request that the bearer, Major William Lowther, may be called before your Board and examined as touching the late incursions in the county and a copy of their testimony sent to Congress that they may be acquainted with the sufferings of their people and ill effects of

COLONEL BENJAMIN WILSON
NOV. 30, 1747 — DEC. 2, 1827
COLONEL VIRGINIA MILITIA IN INDIAN AND
REVOLUTIONARY WARS; BUILT WILSON FORT NEAR BEVERLY.
MEMBER OF VIRGINIA ASSEMBLY 1783-86. SECURED
CREATION OF HARRISON COUNTY, 1784, AND BECAME ITS
FIRST CLERK FOR 30 YEARS; MEMBER VIRGINIA CONVENTION
1788 RATIFYING U.S. CONSTITUTION. PIONEER SETTLER
AND INDUSTRIALIST OF THIS VALLEY.
TO HIS MEMORY, IN 1942, BY HIS GREAT-GRANDCHILDREN
GERTRUDE BROWN WILSON AND ROBERT R. WILSON

the partial treaties."

Part of the trouble in Harrison County during the last years of Indian wars lay in the fact that the county lieutenant, John Pearce Duvall, lived on an island in the Ohio River at the mouth of the Muskingum River. Banjamin Wilson, on hearing that the Indians who had killed Nicholas Carpenter and Carpenter's son near the Ohio River were headed for the West Fork River, directed captains on the frontier in October 1791 to send out 10 scouts for a few days until the arrival of Col. Duvall at Clarksburg. Duvall wrote Gov. Henry Lee in December 1791 requesting that Benjamin Wilson be appointed to muster the men for the counties of Harrison and Randolph. Duvall had migration to Kentucky in his head and according to a letter written by Wilson to the governor May 6, 1792, "The County Lieutenant is about or has removed out of this county and has put a number of imperfect papers in my hands so that I cannot render a full satisfaction to your Excellency's requisition." The governor responded by naming William Lowther county lieutenant as soon as he read Wilson's letter. Wilson continued to be concerned with Indian depredations for he wrote Gov. Henry Lee in March 1793: "I arrived safe home with the charge of money from the Treasury."

Wilson's work in Clarksburg was business enough without taking on responsibilities of the militia. In 1789 the court appointed him, along with George Jackson and William Haymond, to view the courthouse building and make certain the contractor Thomas Bartlett conformed with the specifications and in 1796 the court named the same three citizens to draw up plans and oversee the building of a new stone jail.

In addition Wilson carried on extensive business ventures among them the operation of a flour and sawmill and woolen mill on Simpson Creek near his home. He farmed extensive acreage of land in the county.

After his first wife Ann Ruddell died, Wilson married Phoebe Davisson of Harrison County. Wilson was the father by his first wife of 12 children and by his second wife, 17 children, the last of whom was born July 20, 1820, when Col. Wilson was 73-years-old.

Col. Wilson was described by an historian as a "man of affairs, of a genial kindly disposition, good conversational powers, of sound judgement and good sense, of stalwart person and dignified bearing, a vigorous intellect and a daring and courageous frontiersman. His character and integrity were without a blemish, and he was of commanding presence and possessed of that elegance of manner pertaining to a gentleman of the old school.

Records extant in 1984 in the Harrison County Courthouse show that Benjamin Wilson was meticulous and thorough as county clerk. His good sense and logic shine through in a few words he wrote into the record of the county in 1796.

John Evans and Wilson had spent long hours drawing up an agreement as to the percentage of wolf tax and public building tax collected by Monongalia County in 1784 that should be paid Harrison County. In August 1796 two commissioners from Monongalia County appeared before the Harrison County Court to allege wrongs in the settlement made by Evans and Wilson. The Harrison County Court asked the visiting commissioners to establish the wrongs, but the two refused to do so. The Harrison County Court decided not to reopen the tax-division controversy for as Wilson put it: "there appears to be no wrongs to right."

Benjamin Wilson resigned as clerk of Harrison County in October 1814 when he had completed 30 years' service as clerk. He was succeeded by his son John who served until 1831 making 47 years that one family oversaw the business of the county.

Wilson died at his residence on Dec. 2, 1827, two days after his 80th birthday. Surviving him were 24 children, 73 grandchildren, 32 great grandchildren, and one great great grandchild making a total of 130 descendants.

First Court House Begun in 1786
Preceded by Pillory and Stocks

BY DOROTHY DAVIS

At the first meeting of the Harrison County Court held at the house of George Jackson at Bush's Fort near Buckhannon July 20, 1784, the 12 justices appointed a month earlier to run the new county decided to erect county buildings on land offered the court by Daniel Davisson and Joseph Hastings.

At the time, with Indian attack still so prevalent that one of the first justices — Nicholas Carpenter — would lose his life when Indians struck his party in camp just across the river from Marietta, Ohio, seven years later in 1791, settlers in Clarksburg had built cabins adjoining side by side and extending from Elk Creek westward on both sides of present West Main Street up the hill to form a kind of fort. It was all they needed for protection from small parties of the foe for if scouts should bring news of great numbers of Indians headed for the West Fork River area, the settlers could go quickly to Nutter's Fort which was a stronghold two miles to the east along Elk Creek.

Perhaps the penchant of mountaineers for erecting public buildings atop hills was the reason; or maybe for some other reason, the court chose to put the courthouse at the western end of the village on the northeast corner of present West Main and Second streets and the jail with pillory and stocks across the street where the Presbyterian Church stands in 1984.

The court, after accepting the gift of land, was in no hurry to build a courthouse since court could be held in homes for a time. The mandatory structures were those necessary to

restrain the criminal.

In March 1785 the justices gave Daniel Davisson a contract to build stocks, whipping post, and pillory before the April meeting of the court; and gave John Prunty the contract to build a jail which was reported as finished on November 15, 1785.

The contract for a courthouse was let to Thomas Bartlett in March 1786. In drawing up plans the court gave detailed instructions for the erection of nine pillars built two feet below the surface and eight feet above as foundation for the 36 by 26-foot frame structure covered with a roof of black or red shingles. Specifications called for a raised platform for the justices, a sheriff's box, a jury box five feet high with stairs, and stairs to go up to the jury room which was the loft of the building. Bartlett finished the courthouse in 1789.

The court used the whipping post in January 1788 after a female prisoner who was charged with taking goods from Joseph Wilkinson was ordered to "the publick whipping post and there to receive ten lashes on her bare back, well laid on"; and the court used the post again eight months later when it ordered a prisoner to have 39 lashes and then be delivered to "David Hughes, constable, who shall convey him to Isaac Anderson, said Anderson to convey him to the next constable who is to convey him instantly out of the county, or the said Anderson to convey him out of the county himself."

County buildings did not satisfy citizens long. In 1796 the court ordered the sheriff to contract for a new stone jail. By 1803 citizens clamored for a new courthouse but fought so violently over the site that the erection of the structure was delayed.

From the start of the county two bright ambitious men, George Jackson and Benjamin Wilson had often been at loggerheads. Their contention carried over to their sons, both as intelligent or even more intelligent and ambitious than their fathers. In the first decade of the 19th century Benjamin Wilson Jr. wanted the new courthouse built on Wilson land near the southwest corner of present West Main and Third streets, land on which the western portion of the Harrison County Courthouse stands in 1984. John George Jackson, eager to develop his land east of Elk Creek, offered to give a stone house which he would remodel into a courthouse plus two lots if the court would move to East Main Street.

The court quarreled. Jackson petitioned the Virginia Assembly that decided January 18, 1811, that the court could build on land to be donated by Benjamin Wilson Jr.

The two-story brick building with large coal grates in each end of the first floor, which consisted of a single courtroom with a stairway to the jury room on the second floor, cost $3,700 plus $250 for a bell for the cupola, a bell purchased in Pittsburgh. The court bought one dozen Windsor chairs for the building and moved in the structure in 1813. In 1816 the court built two small offices east and west of the courthouse for the county clerk.

The whipping post which stood back of the second courthouse near the jail was a large trunk of a tree planted firmly in the ground with two large iron rings, one on each side, through which the culprit's arms were sent so as to embrace the post and allow his arms to be tied on the opposite side.

In 1853 the circuit court issued a mandamus directing the county court to build a new courthouse. James P. Bartlett agreed to erect on the site of the second courthouse a two-story building for $8,000. In 1856 the court first met in the new building. Citizens entered a hallway with stairs on each side to the jury room above. Doors from the hallway led to the office of the county clerk and to a large courtroom used by both the county and the circuit courts.

The third courthouse must have been the meeting place for every organization and every social event in the town for a visitor to Clarksburg in 1861 described it as "a most extraordinary specimen of architecture, which is used for every purpose besides its legitimate one; for fairs, balls, parties, political indignation and other meetings.''

January 10, 1887, the county court let a contract for $46,-650 for the fourth county courthouse, this one to be built on the site of the second and third buildings. During the years of construction court met in the Bartlett Hotel that stood on the corner of West Main and South Third steets on the lot that had been bought by the court in 1885.

Finished in 1888, the red brick fourth courthouse pleased no one during the more than 40 years it was used. Citizens complained that the arrangement was inconvenient; that the building had insufficient floor space. The structure is remembered by many Harrison Countians for it was not razed until 1931.

Luckily the county court had laid a levy for the fifth courthouse in 1928 and had the money in hand when the financial crash came in 1929. Most of the $650,000 had been spent and the structure was nearing completion when the Great Depression was felt in the county circa 1931. The courthouse was dedicated in November 1932.

The third jail was constructed of stone in 1816 at a cost of $1,000 on the back of the lot of the second courthouse on Main and Third streets. The two-story jail, with the sheriff's residence attached, faced Mechanic Street (Washington Avenue). A fourth jail was built 1869-1870 of red brick on the site of the third jail. On December 21, 1904, the court awarded contracts for $75,566.60 to build a sheriff's residence facing on Third Street and a stone jail to be constructed in the rear of the residence. In 1977 the jail and sheriff's residence were razed and replaced with a Correctional Center which contains a jail, meeting hall, the county health department, and sheriff's offices.

Harrison County Bar Honors Guests

HONORED AT THE Harrison County Bar Association's dinner meeting held Monday evening at Bridgeport Country Club were Stewart McReynolds, seated left, and Howard Calpan, to his right. They were recognized for their ''individual outstanding commitment and dedication to the highest professional standards in the practice of law.'' The Clarksburg law firm of McReynolds and Caplan is the oldest one in the county and is a direct successor to Davis and Davis established in 1895. Standing from left are Carmine Cann, president; H. G. Underwood, vice president; John McCusky, Bicentennial Committee Chairman, and James W. Martin, member of the Bar's Social Committee. State Supreme Court Justice Richard Neeley was the speaker. Music was furnished by the Dave Satterfield Quartet from West Virginia University.

John Powers - Scout and Frontiersman

BY NEVA WEEKS

The first settlers to take up land in the Simpson Creek area were James Anderson, Andrew Davisson, John Wilkinson, Joseph Davisson and John Powers. Here John Powers obtained 400 acres of land on Simpson's Creek, Harrison County, below the present town of Bridgeport, adjoining the land of James Anderson, and it is where he built Powers Fort.

William Powers, son of John, was born in Frederick County, Virginia, Nov. 9, 1765 and came with his father to Simpson's Creek. At the age of 15 he became an Indian Scout when, in March 1781, he enlisted in Monongalia County, Virginia, for nine months in Capt. Joseph Gregory's Company of Indian spies. He reenlisted in March 1782. He was stationed at Powers Fort on Simpson Creek and acted as a scout n territory that afterward became Ohio, Tyler, Wood, Lewis, Harrison and Randolph counties. Powers was made ensign of a company of scouts in March 1783 and was assigned as an Indian spy in Monongalia County.

The following incident was told by Major William Powers to Benjamin F. Shuttleworth of Clarksburg:

''An Englishman during the early settlement of North West Virginia was traveling on horseback from Clarksburg to Marietta, lost his way in the woods, and after night came on saw a light in the distance and, upon approaching, found it to be from an Indian camp. A state of war existing at the time, he was apprehensive of his safety, but was protected by the leader of the party, who gave him food and a blanket to sleep on, and the next morning guided him to the Marietta trail and gave directions to enable him to reach his journey's end in safety.

''Many years afterwards a showman had engaged a party of North American Indians and taken them to England to exhibit them in their native costumes, to the people of that country.

''One evening while the party was entertaining a large audience in a London Theatre with their dances, war songs and other customs of their people, a gentleman present raised a great outcry, attracting the attention of the house. Upon investigating it was discovered that he had recognized in one of the Indians performing on the stage, the very one who years before in the Virginia forest had rescued him from his perilous condition and acted towards him the part of the good Samaritan.'

On April 4, 1783 he marched from Powers' Fort to the mouth of Bingamon Creek where he ''stationed part of his men on the site of an old Indian town,'' the remaining ones he stationed ''at the mouth of Jones Run.'' These men made regular scouting tours while Powers traveled from station to station in the capacity of commander. Powers was one of the scouts who searched for the Indians that raided the home of Thomas Cunningham on Bingamon Creek in 1785; he was with Col. William Lowther during the attack on Hughes River in 1781 when the Leading Creek captives were rescued and with Lowther on the Little Kanawha River in 1787.

William Powers was well educated for his day and knew every man able to bear arms on the frontier. He was five feet six inches tall, well built, spare and erect. He had dark hair and a light complexion. While he continued his scouting for Indians, his father was busy helping to shape up the community around him. He found many things to do and being a man of integrity and perseverance engaged in many. His first appointment to office was in 1784 as a justice of the peace.

By this time the county court decided that a jail was needed. On March 18, 1785 it was ordered built. It was a log structure and Powers and Nicholas Carpenter were to be in charge. John Powers reported that it was completed in November of that year.

JOHN POWERS' FORT

On Simpson Creek is site of fort built by John Powers, 1771. Nearby is grave of Col. Benjamin Wilson, soldier and settler. Here lived Joseph Johnson, only Virginia governor from west of Alleghenies; first elected by popular vote.

WEST VIRGINIA DEPARTMENT OF CULTURE AND HISTORY. 1981

The General Assembly in October 1786 appointed a commission consisting of William Haymond, Nicholas Carpenter, Thomas Webb, John Powers and Daniel Davisson to lay out and open a wagon road from some point on the state road to the mouth of the Little Kanawha River, now Parkersburg. The road was first made from Clarksburg in an eastward direction to a place on Cheat River, where it joined the state road. A traveler in going east from Clarksburg in 1790 spoke of a wagon road near Cheat River. But the work going westward seemed to be delayed for sometime and taken up again after a traveler reported nothing could be found but a blazed trail through the woods between Parkersbug and Clarksburg.

On April 23, 1788 George Jackson, Benjamin Wilson, Nicholas Carpenter and John Powers took the oath as trustees of Randolph Academy. About this time they were looking for a teacher and had received a letter from Rev. George Towers, lately from England, and a well-qualified teacher, signifying his willingness to accept the appointment as teacher at the Academy at a salary of $250 per year.

Meanwhile William Powers had settled near West's Fort in the Jane Lew area, with his wife, the former Hannah Stout. While he resided away from the center of activities in Harrison County, he was familiar with the early settlement, and stated that at a meeting of the settlers one of the Shinns suggested that the town of Clarksburg be named after General George Rogers Clark, which was assented to and the community of a few log cabins clustered together was named Clarksburg.

Although John Powers lived out his life span near Bridgeport, no record has been found where he is buried. His son William died June 6, 1856, and was buried in the Broad Run Cemetery in Lewis County.

It Was Nearly Dark As The Two Children Approached The Massacre Site

By JACK SANDY ANDERSON

Over a hundred years ago a ten-year-old boy, Fred Sandy, and his little sister, Flo, were walking home from Enterprise. They had spent the afternoon visiting their aunt and uncle, and the hours had sped by. They had paid no attention to time until they noticed the sun slipping below the western horizon. It was now late evening, and they were hurrying to get home before dark. The path on which they were walking wound along the crest of the ridge separating Enterprise from the Bingamon country, where they lived, and passed within a few feet of the McIntire massacre site.

Here in the long-ago John McIntire and his wife had been killed by Indians.

According to some people, this was a haunted place; and for years there had been stories told of scary things seen and heard in its vicinity.

Fred and Flo knew these stories, for like most country children of their day they enjoyed ghost stories and always listened to them with rapt attention. Moreover, they had heard the story of the McIntire massacre time and time again from their Granny Jane, whose mother had been the only McIntire daughter; and they had once been allowed to hold in their hands the old cap worn by Mrs. McIntire on that fateful day when she and her husband had been brutally murdered. Granny Jane inherited the cap, along with other relics, from her mother and kept it locked in the top drawer of the big cherry bureau in the spare bedroom of her house.

It was nearly dark as the two children approached the massacre site. Going through their minds were the stories they had heard, and they were feeling a little scared and wishing they had not stayed so long in Enterprise.

Suddenly, in front of them appeared a shimmering mist. They stopped and stood still, frightened but yet fascinated by this strange, unworldly sight. As they watched, the mist grew thin; and in it they saw a long-haired woman struggling with a painted Indian. On her face was a look of terror, and her hands were uplifted to defend herself from the tomahawk the savage held above his head. For a moment longer they watched. Then, Fred grabbed Flo by the hand, and they ran from the path and into the woods below it.

Not until they reached the bottom of the hill did they stop. When they had caught their breath, Fred asked his sister, "Do you know what we saw?"

"Yes," she answered. "We saw the McIntire woman getting killed by an Indian."

"You're right. But we mustn't tell anyone, not even Mama. This will be our secret, Flo, and no one else's."

And for many years it was. Only after Flo had long been dead, and he was an old and feeble man did Fred tell their secret to one of his favorite grandchildren. Later, the grandchild, who thought it an interesting story, told others in the family.

The McIntire massacre occurred in May, 1791, and was one of the last Indian depredations in the West Fork Valley. John McIntire and his wife Rachel were among Harrison County's early settlers and established their home at the head of what later came to be called Nutter Run, a tributary of Bingamon Creek. At or near present Enterprise lived several of John's brothers and also his only sister, Sarah, and her husband, Uriah Ashcraft. John's father, Charles McIntire, had acquired land at Enterprise before the Revolution and during that war had served both in the army and in the navy, where he attained the rank of ensign. Tradition has it that John was the oldest child in the Charles McIntire family and that he, too, served in the Revolution.

Trading labor was a common frontier practice, and John and Rachel were returning home from Enterprise where they had been working for his brothers, who had previously worked for them. Not long after crossing the ridge and going down the Bingamon side, they encountered an Indian war party. Escape was impossible. Death came swiftly and violently to the unfortunate couple.

A little later the Indians continued toward Enterprise and passed by Uriah Ashcraft's cabin which was located not far from the top of the ridge on the Enterprise side and near the path leading to the Bingamon country. Alerted by the sound of his dog barking, Ashcraft went to the door of his cabin to investigate and saw the Indians. He had seen John and Rachel go by minutes before and now feared for their lives as well as for his own. He tried to shoot at the Indians, but his rifle would not fire. He then yelled as loudly as he could to attract the attention of the McIntire brothers who lived some distance away. They heard him and came running up the hill. Apparently the Indians decided it was not wise to fight several white men with rifles and quickly disappeared into the woods.

Ashcraft and the McIntire brothers followed the Bingamon path to ascertain the fate of John and Rachel. Soon they found John's body. He had been tomahawked, scalped and stripped. They could find no trace of Rachel and assumed that she had been taken captive by the Indians.

Word was sent to Clarksburg for help in pursuing the Indians and a pursuit party was organized and set out to overtake the Indians. There were eleven men in the party, among whom were William Haymond Jr., John Haymond, George Jackson, John Harbert, Benjamin Robinson and Christopher Carpenter. The Indians were overtaken on Middle Island Creek. They fired at their pursuers, narrowly missing Jackson and John Haymond. Some of the men in the party then shot at the Indians, who were running up a hill to escape. One of the Indians was wounded so badly that he left a trail of blood but nonetheless was able to get away. It was decided not to continue the pursuit, and the men collected the belongings which the Indians had left behind. Among the belongings was the scalp of Rachel McIntire. When the men returned to the West Fork Valley, an intensive search was launched in the area where the McIntires had been attacked. Rachel's body was then found.

It was later learned from Joseph "Indian Joe" Cunningham, who in 1791 was a prisoner in an Indian town in Ohio, that four Indians were in the party responsible for the McIntire massacre. Only one of them, he said, returned to the town. The other three died from being shot by members of the pursuit party.

Long handed down in the Bingamon country is a tradition that the Indians who killed John and Rachel came by their cabin as they traveled toward Enterprise. There was so much noise coming from it that they thought a large number of people were inside and quickly went on. The noise was being made by the McIntire children playing with a pet bear cub. Had it not been for this, they no doubt would have suffered the same fate as their parents.

The McIntire children were one daughter, Elizabeth, and four sons — Charles, Joseph, Isaac and Zadoc. The last named, who did not die until 1885, was the youngest and served heroically in the War of 1812.

The cap worn by Rachel McIntire on the day of the massacre is still in existence. It was found near her body and was given to Elizabeth, who in 1797 married Christopher Nutter. She passed it on to her daughter, Jane, wife of Blackley Martin, who not long before her death in 1888 presented it to her daughter, Mattisonia, wife of Abraham Hess. The cap has remained in the Hess family ever since, and for several years was owned by Mattisonia's grandson, the late H. Clare Hess, who displayed it in a glass case in his Mannington home.

Daniel Davisson - The Label 'Proprieter of Clarksburg' Was by Past Historians

By DOROTHY DAVIS

The label "proprietor of Clarksburg" given to Daniel Davisson by past historians is apt. Davisson owned all the land Elk Creek encircles in the Water Street area of Clarksburg to the mouth of the creek by right of settlement in 1773 and by law after he registered his 400 acres when, land commissioners sat in Clarksburg in 1781.

Daniel Davisson arrived on Elk Creek at the age of 25 with his young wife Prudence Izzard Davisson, whom he married in Philadelphia. They were surrounded by kin, for Daniel's father and mother, Obadiah and Elizabeth Davisson, and Daniel's brothers Isaac, Josiah, Obadiah, Nathanial, Hezekiah and his sister Elizabeth had all emigrated west to the West Fork River from Millstone Run near Princeton, N.J. And there were more kin: an uncle Andrew Davisson and his family had emigrated too.

Daniel's brother Hezekiah claimed the land west of Daniel's in the Adamston-Limestone Creek area. The father and most of the brothers of Daniel staked out claims south of Clarksburg in the general area of the present-day Nathan Goff Armory and Davisson's Run. Andrew Davisson's 400-acre claim began with the Monticello Avenue area in Clarksburg and extended east, land he soon sold to move to Anmoore. His family staked out claims for acreage on Simpson Creek.

Daniel Davisson and his wife, Prudence built in 1773 a log cabin which stood in the present Chestnut Street area of Clarksburg near Elk Creek. The bowl of land they claimed settlers thought propitious for a village probably because it lay fairly flat and had accessible everywhere a good-sized creek that gave settlers a road in any kind of weather and entry to the West Fork River a few hundred yards away. After Indian wars began in 1774, anyone living on Daniel Davisson's land had the protection of Nutter's Fort just two miles to the southeast and one of the sturdiest forts in the upper reaches of the Monongahela River.

By 1778 Davisson had let a number of settlers build cabins on either side of present West Main Street hill from the creek west to the sites in 1984 of the First United Presbyterian Church and the Union National Bank Plaza. One cabin joined the next to form a wall that made the tiny village a fortification.

The Harrison County Court decided at its first meeting near Buckhannon in July 1784 to place the county buildings on Davisson's land, and George Jackson asked at the same meeting permission to build a dam and grist mill on Elk Creek a hundred yards south of the eastern edge of the village. The court held its second meeting at the house of Hezekiah Davisson in Clarksburg. Daniel Davisson gave the court land at the western end of the village to place a courthouse and made plans to build himself a residence across from the courthouse on the northwest corner of present Second and West Main Streets. Already the court had licensed Daniel Davisson, George Jackson and Evan Thomas to keep an ordinary, or inn, and had set the rates they could charge for spirits.

It was 1787 before the court ordered a couthouse built and one writer said it was 1790 before Daniel Davisson finished a house near the courthouse for his family and ordinary guests. If so, his wife Prudence got little done on court days but run from their Chestnut grove residence to wherever the court met since the records of courts in the the 1780s are filled with statements like: "Daniel Davisson with wife Prudence acknowledged the deed for Lot No. 10... Daniel Davisson with wife Prudence acknowledged deed to Thomas Barkley; Daniel Davisson with wife Prudence, two lots to Isaac Washburn." The first U.S. Census taken in Harrison County four years before 1790 lists for Daniel Davisson seven white souls, two dwellings, and four other buildings.

Daniel Davisson was everywhere in the 1780s. He viewed the road "to Levi Shinn's" and filled an order of the court "to build stocks, whipping post, and pillory" in 1785; he collected from the court a shilling for candles he furnished justices in 1786; he accepted a place on the committee to superintend the erection of a building for Randolph Academy in 1788 and proved to the court he had worked 20 days in 1788 and 30 days in 1789 as a commissioner helping to cut out the road from the State Road near Kingwood to the mouth of the Little Kanawha River; he presented the court a commission of captain in the Virginia militia in 1789; and a year later conveyed land to the regular Baptist Church named Hopewell which was built just below the site of the present Daniel Davisson Cemetery on the south side of West Main Street near the Chestnut Street intersection.

The court's acceptance in 1790 of Hezekiah Davisson in

place of Daniel "to keep the road in repair from ford of Elk in Clarksburg to Limestone Creek and from the courthouse to mouth of the Elk" is a signal that Daniel Davisson would focus his attention on his ordinary-store-residence across from the courthouse. The Davisson establishment during the decade was so much an adjunct of the courthouse that by 1795 the court authorized Daniel Davisson to keep the courthouse key and "to sweep the courthouse clean for a year at 15 shillings" and by the end of the decade allowed Davisson "$12.50 for his room to hold court in for 1 year." Daniel examined those who applied for surveyor in the county. Of course, the Davisson ordinary was the gathering place for the men and the site for gossiping and planning practical jokes as shown in a suit in the court in 1791.

George Jackson owned the town's mill, had sat in the legislature of the state since the formation of Harrison County, and had designs on a seat in the U.S. House of Representatives where he, in the future, would be the first man west of the Allegheny Mountains in Northwestern Virginia to sit in that body. Jackson has been described as a man who liked to have his own way. In 1790, angered by tales passed around in the Davisson ordinary, Jackson brought to court a suit against Isaac Peterson and Daniel Davisson for slander. the Court handled the suit lightly, and the jury found a verdict in Jackson's favor and set the damages at seven shillings.

Jackson lost for the first time a bid for election, a seat in the 1791 Virginia Assembly, and was so enraged he wrote the governor of the state. Jackson told the governor that the Harrison County sheriff "had caused to be carried to the jury concealed in a teakettle a quantity of ardent spirits with which to make merry over his case… Ill-disposed persons at the last election had used this circumstance to his (Jackson's) injury, by saying the County of Harrison was represented by a gentleman whose character was valued at seven shillings. Having found this out only within the past ten or twelve days, he has thought it proper to report the facts to the Executive and ask for redress in the premises, etc."

So on Aug. 15, 1791, the Harrison County Court heard a suit brought by Jackson against the 12 jurors each one of whom was fined two shillings "for drinking one quart of apple brandy while in retirement." Jackson was appeased.

In 1799 the governor of Virginia issued a commission as major in the 11th Regiment of the Virginia Militia to Daniel Davisson and in the same year the governor received the names of Daniel Davisson, William Powers, Benjamin Webb, Richard Bond, John Righter, and Hedgeman Triplett as likely men to be named justices in Harrison County. Voters in Harrison County sent Daniel Davisson as a delegate to the Virginia Assembly in 1801 and again in 1802.

The last entry for the tavern license for Daniel Davisson was recorded in 1804. He had kept through the years a residence on the northwest corner of present Chestnut and West Main streets as a farmhouse. It is not known in which housing unit Prudence Davisson died in 1806.

By 1817 Daniel Davisson was the oldest of the justices in term of service, a record that made him that year the one the governor named to be High Sheriff of Harrison County. Daniel Davisson died in 1818 at the age of 71 and was buried in the Daniel Davisson Cemetery across the road from his farmhouse.

They Followed the Buffalo Trails

By DOROTHY DAVIS

In his late years someone asked Humphrey Faris, who served as a member of the House of Delegates in the Virginia Assembly 1819-1820, how he traveled from Bridgeport in Harrison County to Richmond to attend sessions of the legislature. "We followed buffalo trails," he replied.

And so did every other Harrison Countian who used the roads until heavy equipment developed during World War II made possible the building of interstate highways. Every main highway in the state until the 1960s followed what was first a buffalo trail, then an Indian trail, and finally a road built by citizens.

The first settlers in Harrison County were not so isolated from the outside world as most people think. Even though the new county was a stretch of wilderness that extended from the Maryland border to the Ohio River, one to four days of walking in the last decades of the eighteenth century could take an early settler to the settlements along the South Branch of the Potomac River.

Late each fall the early settlers near a village like Clarksburg brought their furs and ginseng to town to be packed by professionals who would organize a train of a number of horses to carry products to market in Winchester, Va., where the load was exchanged for gunpowder, salt, calico, tools, and cooking pots. The horses were tethered together one after another with a lead horse in front. At night

the men operating the train made camp along the paths they traveled through the woods. Other than Winchester, the towns from which travelers "brought the news" were Staunton, which had been the county seat from 1779; Morgantown, which had been the county seat from 1779-1784; Richmond, where legislators went each December; and later Marietta, after the Ohio Company from Boston settled in 1788 where the Muskingum River flows into the Ohio River.

People circa 1795, when the Indian threat ended forever, must have thought the modern age had arrived for they could freely jump on a horse or walk anywhere they wanted. John Reynolds arrived in Clarksburg in 1798 in the first large or four-horse wagon brought into the county. John George Jackson wrote James Madison, Jackson's future brother-in-law from Clarksburg on Sept. 25, 1800, telling Madison that Jackson had been in Morgantown where he talked with an intimate friend of Albert Gallatin who said that Pennsylvania would give "the immaculate Jefferson" a majority of its votes in the coming presidential election and that Jackson's father, George Jackson, would call upon Madison at Montpelier on the elder Jackson's way to Washington to serve in the U.S. House of Representatives.

The post rider who carried the mail was a medium of communication in the early years of the county. In 1808 George Jackson, who by then had moved from Clarksburg to Zanesville, Ohio, and was a member of the Ohio Assembly that met in Chillicothe, wrote an angry letter to his son in Clarksburg because he heard from "the post" when the rider passed through Chillicothe, that the son in Clarksburg had suffered a concussion but was better because the post had seen the son on the street in Clarksburg when the post rider passed through the town a few days earlier. No one but the post had told the father of the son's illness.

Luther Haymond, who wrote in his diary that he had been no farther from his home in Clarksburg than Monongalia County, during his eighteenth summer in 1828 mounted his horse Christopher Columbus and went to Baltimore via the Preston County glades, Harper's Ferry and Frederick. He enjoyed so much riding behind the steam engine which ran on a track for miles in Baltimore and viewing Fort Henry that the next summer Haymond traveled again on his horse Christopher Columbus to Baltimore. His 20th summer he rode his horse to Richmond and reported that after leaving Staunton to return home, the first night he was in the Greenbrier country; the second night, in Beverly; and the next night in Clarksburg.

By this time Haymond was an inveterate wanderer. In 1831 he traveled to visit an uncle in Indiana and bragged to his diary that he made the 300-mile return trip to Clarksburg in just eight days, of course on his faithful horse Christopher Columbus.

In 1832 the Virginia Assembly authorized the building of the Northwestern Turnpike from Romney to Parkersburg, a road that opened in 1838 when the stagecoach began regularly scheduled runs from Parkersburg to Winchester. Inns were built along the way to house travelers including the drovers who drove from inn to inn, which provided corrals for the animals on the way to market, the cattle and hogs from Harrison County to Baltimore.

Old stagers and drovers sat in front of the courthouse in the 1850s telling tales of foreboding as to what would happen when the tracks then abuilding brought trains to the county. Cattle, the drovers said, would lose so much weight from sheer fright while being transported to Baltimore that livestock producers would lose money. Far better it would be to let the drovers take the cattle to market over the Nothwestern Turnpike. To quiet the fears, the railroad company after the Baltimore and Ohio opened in 1857 equipped the cattle cars with leather straps which held each animal firmly in place and the railroad company allowed the owners of stock to ride free of charge with their animals to Baltimore.

1860 is the date, roughly speaking, when Harrison County homes shifted from cooking at the open hearth to preparing food on the woodburning stove for the railroad built through the country in the mid 1850s carried as freight the cookstoves that had been too heavy to carry over the mountains in wagons.

Railroads so eclipsed the highways that roads everywhere fell into so poor condition that they were mudholes in winter and dusty trails in summer. If a person wanted to travel from Bridgeport to Clarksburg or Salem to Clarksburg, he rode the train. And by 1900 travel from Shinnston to Clarksburg and from Weston to Clarksburg was by train or after 1906 by trolley if one lived in Shinnston and 1913 by trolley if one lived in Weston.

Then came the automobile which signaled the demise of the train. No longer did little boys dream of becoming locomotive engineers or railway conductors. Instead they looked forward to driving the family touring car to Winchester after the Northwestern Turnpike was paved in 1928. For a few years the thing to do was to take a picnic lunch, drive to Winchester and then down the Shenandoah Valley to visit a limestone cave and return to Harrison County the same day after stopping several times on the moutains to pour water into the radiator of the car and to patch tires that had been punctured along the way.

Samuel Fitz Randolph - Land Buyer For Settlers of The New Salem Community

BY GALE PRICE

Samuel Fitz Randolph, the founder of Salem, was born in Piscataway, New Jersey in October 1738. He came from a

family of Seventh Day Baptists, decendants of some of America's very early settlers.

His ancestors came to Plymouth County (now Massachusetts) from Nottinghamshire, England sometime around 1630. His grandparents settled in Piscataway. They, like his parents and himself, were members of the Seventh Day Baptist

Church in Piscataway. His wife, Margaret Fitz Randolph, was also a member of the Piscataway congregation.

Samuel Fitz Randolph served in the Revolutionary War, as an ensign in the Second Regiment of Sussex County, New Jersey. The war spurred Randolph's interest in lands to the west, and he and his wife purchased land in Fayette County, Pennslyvania in the late 1780s. They went west with the other church people and were among the founders of the Woodbridge Seventh Day Baptist Church in 1789.

At about the same time, Samuel Fitz Randolph made a sight-unseen purchase of a tract of land lying on the waters of Ten Mile Creek in what was then Northwestern Virginia.

In 1790, a group of Baptists from the Shrewsbury Church in New Jersey moved to Virginia and attempted to establish a settlement at White Day Creek, not far from Samuel Fitz Randolph's Pennslyvania holdings. They found their land unsatisfactory. Samuel Fitz Randolph persuaded them to journey south and inspect his Virginia lands. They found the waters of Ten Mile much more favorable for habitation and moved south to settle there.

Samuel Fitz Randolph and his wife remained in Woodbridge until 1792, and only then moved south to join the Shrewsbury settlers in Harrison County, Virginia.

The new settlers purchased their own holdings in the New Salem area, but Samuel Fitz Randolph tract proved the center of the settlement. He had a portion of the land laid out in streets and lots in the form of a town. In 1794, the General Assembly of the Commonwealth of Virginia officially recognized the status of the town of New Salem. It is likely that Samuel Fitz Randolph named New Salem after Salem, New Jersey. but that supposition is not a matter of official record.

Randolph's own house near the northern end of one of New Salem's cross streets, was a matter of a few hundred feet from the town's church and cemetery.

Samuel and Margaret Fitz Randolph spent the rest of their lives as Salem residents and members of the New Salem Seventh Day Baptist Church. They had nine children: Mary, Sarah, Elizabeth, Jesse, David, Rhulanah, Johnathan, Margaret and Nancy. Samuel Fitz Randolph died February 25, 1825, Margaret Fitz Randolph died February 29, 1832. Decendants of their sizable family continue to be among the prominent families of Salem and of West Virginia.

One of their decendants, Corliss Fitz Randolph, wrote "A History of Seventh Day Baptists in West Virginia," a major source of information of the founding of Salem. Fourteen years later in 1919, another grandson wrote the 13-page "Reminisences of Salem in Pioneer Days." Issac Fitz Randolph's little book contained information of another sort: " My father and two other neighbors...made it a practice for a number of years to kill each fall sixty bears, 20 to a family. My father never wore a shoe until he was 12 years old. He would slide on the ice barefooted."

While some of us may doubt that Samuel Fitz Randolph sent his sons out barefoot in mid-winter, just as we may doubt that the Randolph family personally destroyed West Virginia's entire bear population, we can probably agree that Samuel Fitz Randolph led a rigorous and adventurous life. He live to the age of 86, sired a thriving family, and founded a community.

Samuel Fitz Randolph was buried in the Salem cemetery, his marker simply reads "In Memory of Samuel Fitz Randolph...." His wife, Margaret Fitz Randolph, is buried along side him.

"Harrison County: Birthplace Of Eighteen West Virginia Counties"

By SHARON SAYE

In 1784 when Harrison County was formed it was the largest county west of the Alleghenies. It stretched from the Maryland line west to the Ohio River, north of Fairmont and south beyond the present counties of Calhoun and Braxton. But, by the very nature of its size, it was reduced to ever more managable portions in the next 75 years. Until 1850 there were no restrictions on the creation of counties and so 18 were formed from the original area that was Harrison County in 1784.

Taxes were collected, votes cast, legal disputes settled, marriage licenses obtained, deeds, wills and marriages recorded, county officials chosen, mills, bridges and roads decided upon, all at the county seat. The monthly court sessions took on a festive atmosphere as citizens gathered to take care of legal matters and trading; they were also infamous for the drinking and fighting that occurred. Attending court sessions was thus vital to the citizens, but in the case of those who lived in the far-flung reaches of Harrison County the journey to Clarksburg could be long and arduous. Even with the current highway system a trip from Parkersburg or Glenville can be tedious, but two hundred years ago with few roads and genuine horsepower, citizens were quick to opt for the formation of their own county court.

In 1816 citizens as close as Lewis County found it difficult to travel to the Harrison County seat and also felt that the county court ignored their interests in favor of Clarksburg's. Almost every county was formed because of the distances involved in traveling to the nearest county court as well as the desire for more local control over their own government. An Act of the Virginia Assembly was required for the formation of a new county; this often took some political maneuvering. Tucker County sent a lobbyist to Richmond; Lewis County turned out the vote to put a politician favorable to their wishes in the Assembly. Counties were then named for well-known Virginians or famous Americans.

Once the act was passed the county court met at the location designated to establish the county government. Until the Constitution of 1850, the governor of Virginia appointed the justices of the peace for life. These justices recommended nominations to the governor for the positions of sheriff, surveyor, and militia officers. They appointed their own clerk, assessors and constables. None of these officials were elected by local residents until the Constitution of 1850 mandated justices, sheriffs and other county officials be elected for short terms.

In 1838 the Virginia Assembly passed an act permitting a new county to be formed if its citizens petitioned the Assembly, posted a notice, and voted favorably on the creation of the new county. In 1850 further retrictions regarding size and population were placed on the formation of counties.

One of the most important considerations of the new county court was the location of the county seat. In most counties the matter was easily resolved, but in a few counties the conflict lasted for years. An act of the House of Burgesses had to resolve the situation in Wood County; the Supreme Court made the final decision in Randolph; in Calhoun the controversy lasted 13 years, and an armed raid by Parsons' residents settled the problem in Tucker County.

In all, 18 counties were formed from all or parts of Harrison County. In 1786, Randolph was created, then Wood in 1798, Lewis in 1816, Pocohontas from parts of Randolph in 1821, Jackson in 1831, Braxton in 1836, Marion in 1842, Barbour and Ritchie in 1843, Taylor in 1844, Gilmer and Doddridge in 1845, Wirt in 1848, Upshur and Pleasants in 1851, Tucker and Calhoun in 1856 and Webster in 1860.

Two years after its creation Harrison County lost a substantial amount of territory with the establishment of Randolph County. It was named for Edmund Jennings Randolph, governor of Virginia during the year of its founding.

Col. Benjamin Wilson, the renowned Indian scout, built a fort near what is now the town of Beverly and was vital in the creation of the new county. The first county court was held at his home on May 28, 1787 where he and his fellow justices organized the county's government. They elected a president of the court, made nominations to the governor for sheriff, surveyor, coroner, and offices of the militia. They admitted lawyers to practice in the county, issued marriage licenses, authorized tax rates and heard judicial cases. They also made plans for the county seat; James Westfall, one of the justices, offered land on which to locate the future county court. Originally named Edmondton the town's name was changed to Beverly, supposedly in honor of Gov. Randolph's mother. It remained the county seat until the growth in population of Elkins in 1890 created a movement to change the county court. This set off a ten-year squabble between the two communities that was finally resolved in 1899 when the Supreme Court decided in favor of Elkins.

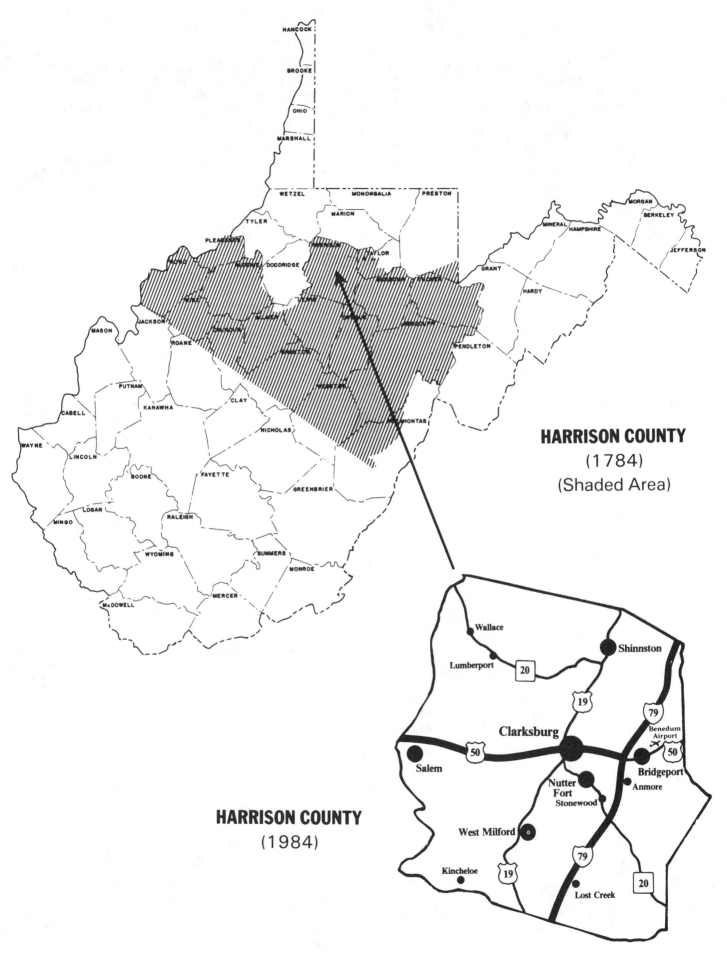

HARRISON COUNTY
(1784)
(Shaded Area)

HARRISON COUNTY
(1984)

In 1790 the population of Randolph County was 951 persons and it was the largest county in the state. All of Tucker, parts of Barbour, Upshur, Pocohontas and Webster were formed from land designated as Randolph County in 1786. Despite territorial losses Randolph is still the largest county in the state.

In 1799 a second county was formed by the House of Burgesses and was named in honor of James Wood, governor of Virginia from 1796-1977. Wood County then covered an area of approximately 1,400 square miles. Its population in 1800 was 1,217 persons and its total tax revenues were $1,257. The first court met Aug. 12, 1799 at the home of Hugh Phelps near Neal's Station. Controversy immediately developed over the location of the county seat. Three communities vied for the honor: Neal's Station, Vienna and Williamstown. Dr. Joseph Spencer who established the town of Vienna lobbied for its selection. The results were two county courts, one at Neal's Station, the other at Vienna and each claiming jurisdiction. The House of Burgesses finally required both county boards to meet and iron out their problems. John Stokley's offer of two acres for a court house and square in Stokleyville which is now a part of Parkersburg, was accepted and a hewn log courthouse was built. Jackson, Wirt and Pleasants counties were later formed from portions of Wood.

Lewis County was named for Col. Charles Lewis who was killed at the Battle of Point Pleasant in 1774. Because of the dense forest and lack of roads people were isolated; the nearest post office until 1798 was Winchester, Va. With the concentration of settlers on the Upper West Fork, Buckhannon, and Little Kanawha Rivers, residents desired to form a new county. They also felt neglected by the county seat which focused its attention on the development of Clarksburg. Residents were determined to elect members to the Virginia Assembly from Harrison County who would be favorable to their petition. They selected Col. John McWhorter. Opposition developed from the northern regions of Harrison County to the formation of Lewis County. The battle waged over whether or not Col. McWhorter would be elected.

Since all voting was done at the county seat at Clarksburg, McWhorter had to persuade constituents from the southern part of the county to travel to Clarksburg to vote for him. The results were something of a gala event. Frontier settlers arrived carrying game they hunted on the way. Roasting their venison they slept in the open since the northern contingent had reserved all available rooms. Col. McWhorter was duly elected and he introduced the bill establishing Lewis County that passed on Dec. 18, 1816.

When first formed the county was 1,754 square miles, but shrank to its present size with the formation of Ritchie, Gilmer and Upshur counties. The county seat was established in 1818 on a farm of Henry Flesher and was named Preston in honor of the governor of Virginia. When Preston County was formed the town's name was changed to Flesherville, but finally it was named Weston in 1820.

Pocohontas County was named for the famous Indian Princess and was formed from parts of Bath, Randolph and Pendleton in 1821. It had been the hunting ground of the Shawnee and was first settled in 1749 by Jacob Marlin and Stephen Sewell. Surveyor Andrew Lewis discovered them in 1751 although Sewell had removed himself to live in a hollow sycamore tree after a quarrel over "relagian." Sewell moved on to Greenbrier County where he was killed by Indians. The first county seat was at Huntersville which was founded at the cabin of John Bradshaw who raided supplies for pelts from the local hunters. In 1891 the voters decided to change the county seat to Marlinton.

Jackson County was founded in 1831 from parts of Wood, Mason and Kanawha, and was named in honor of Andrew Jackson, the seventh president of the United States. John Warth's home at Willow Grove was the temporary county seat until Jacob and Ann Starcher donated eight acres for the county court on land once settled by William John and Lewis Rogers in 1768. Starcher petitioned for a charter which was rapidly approved on Dec. 5, 1832. The town was named in honor of Harry Ripley who according to Legend drowned crossing Mill Creek while on a preaching circuit. The total revenue of the county court that first year was $887.25.

Citizens tired of the long trips to Charleston, Summersville or Weston to attend the county court prepared a petition for the establishment of a new county from parts of Lewis, Kanawha and Nicholas; the petition was passed in 1836 and Braxton County was created.

It was named in honor of Carter Braxton, one of the signers of the Declaration of Independence. Braxton had a population of 2,371 persons of whom 400 were eligible voters in 1836. The first county court was held at the home of John D. Sutton on April 11, 1836 where Sutton, originaly named Newville, was selected as the county seat.

There was cosiderable opposition from Monongalia and Harrison counties concerning the formation of Marion County, but William S. Morgan, a delegate at the Virginia Assembly, and William Willey, state senator, successfully defeated the opposition and the act was passed on Jan. 14, 1842. It was named for Gen. Francis Marion, "The Swamp Fox" of Revolutionary War fame. Middletown was designated the county seat; it was founded by settlers on the west bank of the Monongahela River because it was near a meeting house named Middletown for the obvious reason that it was midway between Clarksburg and Morgantown. Because another town in Frederick County, Virginia, was also named Middletown, the community was re-named Fairmont in 1843.

Barbour County was created on March 3, 1843 from parts of Harrison, Lewis and Randolph counties and named in honor of Philip Pendleton Barbour, a noted statesman who served as secretary of war under John Quincy Adams. The first county court was held at the home of William F. Wilson with all the justices present; plans for the court house were drawn up and a committee appointed to oversee the building. The county court was to be on a farm owned by William F. Wilson that had originally been settled in 1780 by William Anglin. The town was also named in honor of Philip Barbour; the county court ordered it to be called Phillippa, but various misspellings later, the county seat of Barbour County is Philippi.

The existence of Ritchie County can be credited to the construction of the Northwestern Turnpike from Winchester to Parkersburg during the 1830s which sparked population growth sufficient to warrant the creation of a new county. It was formed in 1843 from parts of Wood, Harrison and Lewis and named for Thomas Ritchie, a distinguished Virginia journalist. The county seat is Harrisville which was founded in 1822 on land owned by Thomas Harris.

Edward J. Armstrong, a delegate from Harrison County, was primarily responsible for the creation of Taylor County. In 1843 he took a petition signed by every landlord in the proposed county area to the Virginia Assembly. The act passed on Jan. 19, 1844 and the first county court was held at Williamsport in April of the same year. Taylor was named for Sen. John Taylor of Virginia and included parts of Harrison, Barbour and Marion counties. Williamsport was named county seat since it was the largest town and was re-named Pruntytown since John Prunty owned all the land upon which the town was situated. The county seat was moved to Grafton in 1878.

Gilmer County was created in 1845 from Lewis and Kanawha counties and named for Thomas Walker Gilmer, a congressman and governor of Virginia. The first county court met at the home of Salathiel G. Stalnaker on March 24, 1845.

A major controversy developed over the location of the county seat. The earliest county courts met in DeKalb, but voters preferred the town of Glenville. This change did not meet with the approval of all the justices. The county clerk adamantly refused to bring the records to the new location. Thus on June 25, 1845 the county court met in both sites. The Glenville supporters could not carry on official business without the records so they decided to return to DeKalb stealthily. Entering the court room at the end of the day they used their majority votes to carry a motion to adjourn to the house of Thomas Marshall in Glenville the following morning. The matter of the location of the county seat was thereafter resolved.

Philip Doddridge was a United States congressman and state legislator, and a distinguished lawyer from Brooke County. When a new county was formed in 1845 from parts of Harrison, Tyler, Ritchie and Lewis counties it became Doddridge County in honor of this respected citizen. The first county court was held at the home of Nathan Davis in the town of West Union which became the county seat.

Wirt County was formed by the Virginia legislature in January 1848 from Wood and Jackson; it was named for William Wirt, a Virginia politician. The county seat is Elizabeth, named for Elizabeth Woodyard Beauchamp, the wife of David, son of one of the first settlers in the area, William Beauchamp.

Opposition from Lewis County delayed the existence of Upshur County by three years, but finally, in March 1851 the act establishing the county from parts of Lewis, Randolph and Barbour counties was passed. It was named in honor of Abel P. Upshur, a Virginia statesman who died tragically while secretary of state under John Tyler when the Naval vessel, Princeton, exploded on the Potomac in 1844. The first county court was held at the home of Andrew Poundstone in Buckhannon which was selected as the county seat.

Pleasants County has a mystic element in its history. Residents of the area began discussion in 1842 about forming a new county, but it was not until 1851 that the act was passed. The new county included territory from Wood, Tyler and Ritchie and was named for James Pleasants Jr., a United States senator and governor of Virginia. Area revenue was not sufficient to support even a small government; so, pledges were sought as early as 1848 for $4,500 to erect public buildings in the new county seat. It took four years to raise the funds.

The mystic element derives from the establishment of the county seat of St. Marys. Legend has it the Alexander Creel had a vision of the Virgin Mary while asleep in his cabin on a steamboat bound for Wheeling. The vision pointed out a location on the Virginia side of the Ohio River and told him it would be a happy and prosperous city. Creel purchased the land and named the town St. Marys because of his experience.

Citizens in the northern part of Randolph County found it inconvenient to travel to Beverly, the county seat, and petitioned the Virginia Assembly for the formation of their own county. Apathy from the local delegation greeted their petition; so, William Ewin, a prominent St. George attorney was sent to Richmond to lobby for its passage. Judge John Brannon from Lewis County supported the petition and helped ensure its passage.

Tucker County was established on March 7, 1856 and named for Henry St. George Tucker, a prominent politician and attorney. The first county seat at Westernford was re-named St. George in honor of his son. It continued as the county seat until 1893 when citizens voted for Parsons as the new location. This resulted in virtual warfare between the two communities when citizens of Parsons carried out an armed raid on the St. George court house removing all the county records and equipment including the court house bell.

Tucker County is the location of the Fairfax Stone placed in 1746 to mark the western boundary of the estate of Lord Thomas Fairfax. The Fairfax Stone has been instrumental in establishing the state's present boundaries and is considered to be one of the state's most important historic markers.

Calhoun County was created on March 5, 1856 from Gilmer County. It was named in honor of John C. Calhoun, the famous American statesman from South Carolina. The act also suggested three sites for the county seat at Bigbend, Arnoldsburg and Grantsville; thus creating a 13-year controversy as the county seat moved from one location to another before it was finally established in Grantsville in 1869. A local attorney grew so disgusted with the situation that he re-located to a neighboring county with a fixed county seat.

Webster County was the last county to be created before the separation from Virginia. Residents of the area found it difficult to travel the 50 odd miles to the county seats of Randolph or Braxton counties and attempted as early as 1848 to establish an independent county, Their initial efforts failed as did their petition to the Virginia Assembly in 1852, but finally, a new effort in 1859 met with success and Webster County was created on Jan. 10, 1860 from parts of Nicholas, Braxton and Randolph counties. It was named for Daniel Webster, the famous New England orator.

The county seat was originally called Fork Lick, then Addison, after one of the early settlers, but it is now known as Webster Springs. The first elections were held in May 1860, but the outbreak of the Civil War disrupted the organization of the new county. During the war no county courts were held or taxes collected. In fact, since neither the North nor South established a government in the county, the area became known as "The Independent State of Webster." At the end of the war, the Webster County government was officially formed.

The great boom in counties ended with the formation of Webster in 1860 leaving Harrison County in almost its present form. An addition was made to Taylor in 1863, and a boundary line was changed between Barbour and Harrison in 1871 leaving the county with its present form.

Early Life in Salem

By DOROTHY DAVIS

Until 40 families of Seventh Day Baptists settled on the headwaters of Tenmile Creek in 1790 and built a blockhouse near the forks of Patterson and Tenmile creeks to protect themselves against the Indians, the only structure in the area was a hunting lodge erected by Nicholas Carpenter and used by him occasionally when he hunted and trapped for wild game. Samuel Fitz Randolph had purchased the tomahawk rights to the land, sight unseen, from the widow of Joseph Swearingen and had encouraged the congregation of the Shrewsburg (N.J.) Seventh Day Baptist Church to settle the land. In 1792 Fitz Randolph joined the group that had already built log cabins around the blockhouse. An act of the Virginia Legislature on December 19, 1794, read: "Be it enacted by the General Assembly: That the lots and streets as already laid off on the lands of Samuel Fitz Randolph in the County of Harrison, shall be and hereby are established a town by the name of New Salem, and John Patterson, John Davis, Samuel Lippincott, James Davis, Zebulon Maxon, Benjamin Thorp, Thomas Clayton, William Davis, Jacob Davis, George Jackson and John Haymond, Gentlemen, constitute and are appointed trustees thereof." When the danger of attack by the Indians disappeared, the settlers — many of them — bought farmlands in Harrison, Doddridge, and Ritchie counties and established homes on their lands until, in the 1850s, "there were scarcely more than a dozen houses in the village."

One of the contractors hired to build the Northwestern Turnpike in the 1830s, a Mr. Fenten, opened the first store in the town, a business taken over later by Peter and Isaac Randolph. Across the street from this store, which was located near the original blockhouse, stood the old log tavern kept for decades by Peter Randolph in the sructure built and first occupied by Peter's grandfather, Samuel Fitz Randolph, the founder of the colony.

The town, named "New Salem" by the settlers, was called "Salem" by the railroad company that built its road through the town (1854-56) and was referred to as "Salem" by most of its citizens. For decades mail directed to the village traveled often to a little hamlet in Greenbrier County or to Salem near

crossing; Daniel and Preston Randolph operated a store, "The Randolph Company." The inns were the Furbee House and the Mountain State Hotel. The Mountain State Hotel was a large rectangular structure with imposing, double-decked circular verandas appended to the front and located on the site of the First Baptist Church.

Structures in the town until around 1898 started a few hundred feet east of the site of the blockhouse erected in 1790 and extended to the Salem College building. Back Alley (Valley Street) had residences and Robert Gordon's mill; High Street was filled with livery stables and a woolen mill, all of which burned in July 1900, when a fire that started in the woolen mill burned the buildings on the north side of downtown High Street.

The land west of the college was farm land owned by R. T. Lowndes.

Roanoke in Virginia; in 1885 the Post Office Department agreed with the little town in the southern part of the state which had petitioned to drop the letter S and become "Alem"; the Post Office Department in 1885 officially dropped the "New" from New Salem in Harrison County.

There were about 25 dwelling houses in Salem in 1885. Henry Towles ran a shoe shop (in which the Methodist Church was organized in 1851); Robert Gordon had moved from Sycamore Dale and opened a gristmill; Henry Hawker operated the post office, a hardware-tinware business, and the carriage repository later bought out by W. E. Leonard, who in the late 1880s was the town blacksmith; Jesse Randolph owned a planing mill; Albert Gains ran a store at the railroad

In 1897 posters distributed in Harrison County announced that a committee, designated by the state legislature to spend $10,000 to establish an Industrial Home for Girls, had decided to locate the institution in Harrison County and was investigating sites for the buildings. A committee was formed to work to secure the state institution, and to formulate a plan whereby residents could purchase 38 acres on a hill of the Lowndes farm to deed to the state in order to influence the legislature-appointed committee to choose the Salem community for the projected "Home." After the committee had considered all the sites offered by Harrison County communities, it named the Salem one the most ideal. Now Salem citizens were in a predicament: Lowndes would sell no less than 190 acres, the entire farm; and the period from 1893-97 had been known as a "hard time" period when like other villages, Salem with a population of less than 1,000 had a hard time maintaining itself. The townsmen, determined to have the institution, formed a company and sold stock among themselves at $25 a share to raise the $1,730 down payment on the land and businessmen personally endorsed notes for the rest of the sum owed.

Luckily the story had a happy ending for after deeding 46 acres of the land to the state, the company divided the rest of the 190 acre plot into lots and at three sales, two in 1897 and one in 1898, sold off all the land it owned. When the company dissolved on Dec. 3, 1900, it divided a profit of $3,000 over and above expenses among its stockholders. The company had inadvertently added to the community what would soon be the entire Third Ward of the town.

Salem had its heyday at the turn of the century when the oil boom doubled the population. "During the first years of the oil developments, Salem had its siege of outlawry as is always the case when a fluctuating population makes up the temporary population of a community; saloons, speakeasies, houses of ill-repute, gambling dens held high sway in the little city," a 1919 newspaper account stated.

Concerned citizens waged continuous war on the evils of the town. During the winter of 1901 a temperance group organized to buy the town's newspaper and printing shop; ironically enough, just two hours after this deal had been arranged on Dec. 14, the plant was discovered to be on fire with the outcome that the whole business section of the town was entirely destroyed. While the fire raged it is said that looting of business houses went rampant and that for two days whiskey, pillage and reckless riot ruled the once quiet streets of the city. Men costumed in women's clothing taken from the stores that afterwards burned paraded the streets hilariously filled with whiskey and the excitement of the conflagration.

The fire spread from the printing shop on Water Street to burn every business house in the block northwest of Main and Water streets; jumped Water Street to burn Dr. Edwin A. Wilson's house and front-yard office on the northeast corner of Water and Main streets and every other building on both sides of Main Street to Irwin Street; and moved on south as far as the railway station. In the weeks following the fire, if a citizen saw any of his property in another's possession, he pointed out that the item was rightfully his; invariably the rightful owner was handed the article he claimed.

The Salem holocaust — the greatest in the number of buildings burned in the history of the county benefitted the town in that new Main Street buildings, most of them brick structures, rose in place of the ramshackle wooden buildings thrown up haphazardly in the nineteenth century. An opera house, built on the west side of Water Street a hundred feet from where the street intersects High Street, replaced the Main Street theater which had burned. For 20 years road companies presented plays in the opera house; then a bakery occupied the building until it was destroyed by fire on Feb. 12, 1930. The 1901 fire seemed to burn out the excesses of the boom days. After the town was rebuilt citizens voted into force a new city charter giving the mayor a tight legal rein.

In 1938 when J. D. Muldoon —a Salem College professor —was mayor, the city administration started a movement to build a city building. The citizens voted $12,000 in 1939 to erect a building for city offices. At the time the offices of the city and the fire department were housed in rented quarters on the corner of Main and Irwin streets. The Salem Volunteer Fire Department owned a lot on the corner of High and Valley streets which was donated to the city. City officials bought a stone quarry and used federally-financed Works Progress Administration labor to cut stone and lay up the outside walls

of the city structure. Federal funds amounting to $30,952 were allotted toward constructing the building; 20 WPA workers were employed. The WPA ran out of money when the masonry reached the upstairs windows; so the fire department and the city finished the work. The new building dedicated Sept. 16, 1940, housed the fire fighting equipment, city offices, a jail, an apartment, and a large auditorium controlled by the fire department until January 1965, when the city council was given responsibility for it. A large vacant space back of the city building became the site of a carnival sponsored by the fire department each August as a means of raising money to purchase equipment.

After World War II the consensus of the citizens was that time had arrived to work for a solution to Salem's greatest problem — water, either too much or too little. One effort toward more effective city administration started when the council appointed a committee in 1947 to draw up the city-manager plan of government which was voted in by residents Sept. 23, 1947. The city manager administration went into effect July 1, 1948, with instead of a six-person council as under the mayor plan, a council of three, with each council member representing one of the three wards in the city. The council continued to choose a mayor from its members. In June 1963 citizens voted to return to the strong-mayor plan of government with six council members, the same plan first voted in 1906.

During the 1930s and the 1940s a saying common among Salem citizens ran: "If it rains one hour, the fire siren will ring to summon help for flood victims." An army engineer called in to survey the town's woe frankly said, "You have made your own problems." It is true that Main Street and several business places are built over the bed of Jacob's Run just before the stream flows into Tenmile Creek. A hard rain caused the stream to overflow into the streets; a deluge sent water over parking meters and once, in 1944, halfway up the post office steps. Citizens knew that after the WPA had cleared the creek of refuse in 1936 no floods had occurred for three or four years; in 1951 citizens — in a campaign led by the Business and Professional Woman's Club — raised $10,-000 to finance the widening and deepening of the creek beds. This community effort helped to attract the federal government to the site as an area for a pilot project in stopping the erosion of lands in the headwaters of streams.

The Upper Tenmile Watershed project was a plan to stabilize and to control the amount of water running down channels of Salem Fork of Tenmile at a given time and a plan to treat every surface acre of the 5,325 acres (100 farms) included in the project to soak up water like a sponge and thus slow down the rate of water runoff. Seven floodwater retarding structures, each dam high enough to trap at least a three-inch storm, were built during the project; in addition, four miles of stream channels were improved by widening, deepening and reshaping the stream beds. Congress appropriated $328,000 to build the eight dams. Farmers planted one-half million seedling trees, built farm ponds, improved grazing practices and woodlands. Toward the total cost of the project, the federal government paid $366,000; the City of Salem, $250,000; the Upper Tenmile Watershed Association, $87,000. Salem has not suffered a flood since the project was completed in 1958. The Upper Tenmile Watershed project, started in 1957 and, dedicated on completion at a ceremony at the Glenn L. Post farm on Sept. 11, 1958, won the honor of being the first of the several watershed projects authorized by Congress to be finished within the time specified. The U.S. Geological Survey and the Unted States Weather Bureau each week since 1958 have measured sedimentation and run-off water in order to learn whether control of streams at their source is an effective procedure.

The City of Salem voted a $250,000 bond issue in 1954 (to be repaid in 1988) to purchase land and build a dam for a lake that is both a part of the Upper Tenmile Watershed project and a reservoir of water to supply the homes and businesses of the town. Before 1954 wells pumped water from the ground for the city system and since the supply was inadequate, a high percentage of the time when residents turned a faucet, air instead of water flowed from the pipe. Citizens were so incensed by water shortage that in 1940 the council leased the system to A. Page Lockard and went out of the water-supply business. This action made the system more efficient, but took away so much revenue from the city coffers that the council again took over the system in 1942. In May 1968 the Economic Development Administration granted $479,000 to be matched by a $479,000 loan from the Farmers Home Loan Administration for a reservoir, a water treatment plant, a 3,000-gallon storage tank, and 11 miles of new water lines to update the Salem water system.

The two-mile-long Main Street has changed very little in appearance since the business district was rebuilt after the 1901 fire. In 1924 Methodists built the town's largest church on the same plot of ground where the congregation had worshipped in a clapboard structure for almost 30 years (an earlier stucture on the opposite hill had burned in 1902). Baptists bought the land on which the Mountain State Hotel had stood in 1912, razed the inn, and built a stone church dedicated June 13, 1913. The schoolhouse was torn down in 1903, when a new brick structure was built on the hill above the site of the former school on Main Street. Two grade schools, Van Horn on West Main and Harden on East Main were built by the Salem Independent School Disrict in 1922. The Furbee House on the corner of West Main and Irwin streets was razed in 1941 so that the Randolph Brothers could build a paint and wall paper store on the site. The Post Office Department bought the Jesse Randolph property, destroyed the old house, and constructed, at a cost of $75,000, Salem's first government-owned post office building in 1940. Salem College tore down the Joel Randolph home in 1961 to build a college cafeteria on the site. The United States Government built a $328,000 National Guard Armory (Underwood Armory) in 1960 on land donated by Salem College on Rt. 50 just west of the city limits.

Through the years Salem has grown in population, and the college has expanded, bringing in students from other states. Due to the new highways which have brought Clarksburg and other cities closer, many of the privately-owned shops and stores are no more. As time goes on Salem is becoming more and more what its founders may have desired — a peaceful educational and recreational center.

Col. William Lowther - Noted Defender, Protector of Northwestern Virginia

BY DOROTHY DAVIS

The Buckhannon Hacker's Creek settlers had the jump on most other settlements on the waters of the West Fork and the lower Tygart's Valley rivers by four years because the Pringles led men in 1768 from the South Branch to the tree where the two Pringles had lived from 1763 to 1767.

John and Samuel Pringle had stayed on the Buckhannon River for four years because they were AWOL from Fort Pitt and afraid of arrest should they return to their home on the South Branch of the Potomac River. They had lived in a tree on land which the British forbade their subjects to enter. But in 1768 when the British bought by treaty from the Indiams all land east of the Ohio River, people interpreted the purchase to mean they could settle in what had been forbidden territory.

Because the Pringles had already explored a route through the wilderness, they could start out immediately in 1768 whereas it took most others a few years to push off. It was 1773 before the trickle of settlers to the waters of the West Fork River became a flood. Several permanent settlers were on Simpson Creek earlier -James Anderson, 1771; Jonathan Stout and John Powers, 1772. Nicholas Carpenter and William Robinson were on the West Fork River in 1772 and Thomas Nutter was on Elk Creek in 1772. But it was 1773 when the Davissons and Sotha Hickman settled in what would be later Clarksburg; when Levi Shinn settled in Shinnston; when Thomas Harbert settled Lumberport and Charles McIntyre was in Enterprise. So many people were on the waters of the West Fork River without crops to harvest that a crisis arose so great that 1773 became known as "the starving year."

The Hacker's Creek people, among whom were the Jackson, Hugheses, Cutrights, Ratliffs, Hackers and Sleeths, had had time by 1773 to harvest crops and to learn good sites for hunting game. One of their members had the organizing

ability needed to meet the crisis of too many people for the food available to feed them. William Lowther had married, probably in Moorefield, Sudna the daughter of Thomas Hughes, who had followed the Pringles on an exploratory trip in 1768 and had settled on Hacker's Creek with his family in 1769. Lowther and his wife and oldest children had followed in 1772, when Lowther was 30 years old and a seasoned frontiersman for his rifle, which is extant in 1984, has carved on the stock "Fort Seibert 1768" plus a notch which may indicate having an encounter with an indian.

A contemporary wrote of William Lowther: "Colonel William Lowther was called the defender and protector of Northwestern Virginia. He defended in time of war; protected in time of famine; and if it had not been for his energy and sympathy for his fellow beings in the year 1773, the inhabitants of the infant settlement might have perished with hunger. He roamed amidst danger and alarm, killed venison, elk, buffalo, and bear and thus supplied all their wants." Even in normal times grain was so short in spring that a son of William Lowther wrote that once before the new crop matured his grandfather (Robert Lowther) visited bringing a knapsack of biscuit. The child tasted it, then threw it down and called for "jerk", which was strips of dried venison and the food to which the child was accustomed.

The skill he exhibited in 1773 may be the reason that when the Governor Dunmore-inspired District of West Augusta was formed in 1775 as part of the effort to include the Pittsburgh area within the borders of Virginia, William Lowther was named a justice of the district. When the governor of Virginia

looked at the list of proposed justices for the new county of Harrison in 1784, he appointed for sheriff of the new county the one man who had had experience as a justice - William Lowther.

But it was as "defender and protector of Northwestern Virginia" that people from the West Fork River to the Ohio River looked to William Lowther from 1774 to 1775. The 13 notches with the words "Kanawaha Fork Fall 1774" carved into his rifle show that Lowther was in the Battle of Point Pleasant in Dunmore's War. A man who was a ranger and a spy in Northwest Virginia during the American Revolution, when the British at Detroit agitated the Indian Wars that swept the frontier, wrote that Col. Benjamin Wilson and Col. William Lowther assumed the authority for the organization and disposition of troops in the country, paid off soldiers, recommended the appointment of officers, etc. Lowther in the first years of the war was a captain. He left Nutter's Fort on June 21, 1781, with a company of men from the Tygart's Valley and West Fork rivers area, to join Gen. George Rogers Clark in Pittsburgh for a trip down the Ohio to Louisville from whence they were to march to Detroit to rout the British. So few men reported to Pittsburgh and Wheeling that the campaign was scrapped, but not before Clark had made Lowther a major. Lowther left Clark at the mouth of the Little Kanawha River on Aug. 11, 1781, and walked up the Little Kanawha River to his home.

William Lowther received a commission as colonel in the Virginia militia in 1793 "when had the whole command of Northwester Virginia... He was charged to take care of the different stations on the Ohio River. He visited each station on the river, supplied them with ammunition and provisions, gave direction for defense, had rangers appointed to observe the movement of the enemy, and what could be done by any mortal being in person he performed with unabaiting zeal."

Lowther was ubiquitous during the Indian wars. In almost every account of Indian massacre cited by Withers, Lowther either gave chase after an attack or "rode up" about the same time as the Indians struck. One man who served under Lowther wrote that the preachers on the frontier were "very fearful and frequently quoted this passage of scripture 'the wicked flee where no man persueth but the Righteous are as bold as a Lyon' and they would ask Col. Lowther how the passage could be true for the Preachers were fearful but Col. Lowther was bold as a Lyon."

A letter written by Col. William Lowther from Morgantown, June 7, 1792, reveals his military responsibilities: I have under my command in Harrison County by order from the executive and ensign, two sergeants, two corporals, and forty privates. I was authorized to appoint two scouts by the executive, which I have complied with. I have two scouts at the mouth of the Little Kanawha, the other two on the frontier of the West Fork Settlement. The rangers, I thought proper to submit the distribution to a council of officers of Harrison, who advised me to station them in three detachments, which I have done along the West Fork Settlements, about forty miles, with a small deviation to wit: to the Little Kanawha, being an exposed part of the county, and a small station near the mouth, I sent a sergeant and 11 men with the two spies or scouts. In Randolph County, I have under my command a lieutenant, two sergeants, two corporals, and 25 privates, the distribution of which I also left to a council of the Randolph County officers which they have done as followeth: the lieutenant and fifteen privates including the sergeant and corporal in the upper end of the (Tygart's) valley and a sergeant and eleven men at the Buckhannon settlement."

Unlike most energetic men on the frontier, William Lowther had little interest in political or financial aggrandizement for himself. Other than a trip to Richmond to serve as a delegate to the U.S. Constitutional Convention in Virginia, no record exists of his having left his duties in Northwestern Virginia. He amassed little acreage except that on which he lived: "His purse was not his own; his neighbors shared it with him.

Lowther was five feet eleven inches in height and weighed

about 180 pounds. He was always cheerful or as a contemporary put it: "he was cheery and undismaid amidst the most trying circumstances in life." Lowther had a high forehead, prominent nose, firm mouth, greyish blue eyes with arching brow. He was strong, sinewy, erect, proud, determined "yet loving and tender as a child." That he was loved is shown by the number of his friends who named their children for him, among them George Jackson whose youngest son was named "William Lowther."

The treaty of Greenville in 1795, which ended the Indian Wars, ended Lowthers work as Lieutenant of Harrison County but retirement to his farm did not last long. In 1797 when Wood County was formed out of Harrison by act of the Virginia Assembly, Col. William Lowther was named by the governor as the first sheriff of the new county.

The farm to which William Lowther moved from the mouth of Hacker's Creek sometime before 1781 is south of West Milford overlooking the West Fork River. Other than a period circa 1784 when his duties as sheriff required him to live in a house in the 100-block of West Main Street in Clarksburg, Lowther lived all his years in his cabin on the farm where he died Oct. 28, 1814 at the age of 72. The well which supplied his home with water is extant in 1984. His grave marker can be viewed in 1984 in the Lowther Cemetery reached by walking a few hundred yards south of the spot where his home once stood on the road leading from West Milford to Mt. Clare. The Col. William Lowther Chapter of the Daughters of the American Revolution, located in Salem, maintains the Lowther Cemetery.

He Rode The Catfish Until It Died Of Exhaustion Near Pittsburg

BY JACK SANDY ANDERSON

Flowing through northern Harrison County is meandering Bingamon Creek, a stream that once formed a part of the boundary between Monongalia and Harrison County when the latter was created in 1784. The countryside through which it flows had a rugged beauty marked by steep wooded hills, narrow valleys, and, here and there bottomland ideally suited for farming. By 1800 several settlers had established homes on its waters and were successfully wrestling a living from what a few years before had been a dangerous wilderness.

The people that we call Indians were the Bingamon country's original human inhabitants. When they first came is a question which no one can answer, but artifcts have been found dating back thousands of years. By the time the white man arrived, the Indians no longer maintained permanent living sites here, but nontheless still claimed the area and resented the advent of the pale-skinned newcomers who were destroying their ancient forest land. For a long time the Bingamon settlers lived with the contstant threat of Indian attack, and some of them — such as the Cunningham brothers, Thomas and Edward — were involved in the fierce border warfare about which so much has been written.

Bingamon Creek has had its name for over two centuries. It was named for a legendary but yet real frontiersman, Samuel Bingaman (or Bingamon), who must have been an extraordinary individual. Facts about him are few, but they are sufficient to prove his existence and to indicate beyond doubt that he possessed unusual strength, courage and daring.

From Kercheval's "A History of the Valley of Virginia" first printed in 1833, it is learned that in the 1750s Indians attacked Bingaman's home. An excerpt from this book is as follows:

"....seven Indians surrounded the cabin of Samuel Binga-

man, not far distant from the present village of Petersburg, in the county of Hardy. It was just before daybreak, that being the time when the Indians generally made their surprises. Mr. Bingaman's family consisted of himself and wife, his father and mother, and a hired man. The first four were asleep in the room below, and the hired man in the loft above. A shot was fired into the cabin, the ball passing through the fleshy part of young Mrs. Bingaman's left breast. The family sprung up to their feet, Bingaman seizing his rifle, and the Indians at the same moment rushing in at the door. Bingaman told his wife and father and mother to get out of the way, under the bed, and called to the man in the loft to come down. He, however, never moved. It was still dark, and the Indians were prevented from firing, by a fear of injuring one of their number. Bingaman, unrestrained by any fears of this kind. laid about him with desperation. At the first blow his rifle broke at the

breech, shivering the stock to pieces; but with the barrel he continued his blows until he had cleared the room. Daylignt now apearing he discovered that he had killed five, and that the remaining two were retreating across the field. He stepped out, and seizing a rifle which had been left by the party, fired at one of the fugitives, wounded and tomahawked him. Tradition relates that the other fled to the Indian camp, and told his comrades that they had a fight with a man who was a devil — that he had kiled six of them, and if they went again, would kill them all. When Bingaman, after the battle, discovered that his wife was wounded, he became frantic with rage at the cowardice of the hired man, and would have dispatched him but for the entreaties of Mrs Bingaman to spare his life. She recovered from her wound in a short time."

According to the same book, Bingaman was a member of a pursuit party that chased a number of Indians who in the fall of 1756 attacked and killed several settlers in the vicinity of Fort George (Petersburg). The Indians were overtaken at Dunkard Bottom on the Cheat River. Bingaman was ordered by the captain to stay behind and guard the horses. This, however, he considered demeaning, and refused to obey. He followed behind his comrades, leaving the horses unguarded. One of the pursuit party, an overzealous young man, fired prematurely at the Indians. Immediately, they began to flee. Bingaman decided to go after the largest of them, an Indian giant-like in size. Throwing his rifle aside, he sped after the fleeing man. When the caught up with him, he split his skull with one mighty blow of his hatchet. Several other Indians were also killed, and the pursuers lost not a single man.

The captain, who a few days earlier had argued with Bingaman, started to reprimand him. "I ordered you to stay and guard the horses," he harshly said. But before he could speak further, Bingaman replied in a tone of voice just as harsh: "You are a rascal, sir; you intended to disgrace me; and one more insolent word and you shall share the fate of that Indian." He pointed to the giant Indian warrior he had just killed. The reprimand did not continue.

It is not exactly clear just what the connection was between Bingaman and the stream that bears his name (really, two streams, since there is also a Little Bingamon Creek). When I was a child forty or so years ago, I heard some old-timers say that the creek was named Bingamon because in the long-ago Samuel Bingaman had rescued two white girls from Indians camping on its waters at or near what is today the village of Wyatt. Others said that before the Revolution Samuel Bingaman hunted and trapped in the area and often camped along the creek. Which is the correct version? I do not know. Perhaps both are true.

No doubt Bingaman participated in other remarkable incidents that did not get recorded in history books. As years passed by the stories about him became distorted and exaggerated and ultimately took on a mythological flavor. Story-telling in pioneer days (and even in my childhood) was an important and favorite pastime, and embroidering a good take to make it better was far more unusual.

Some of the stories about him that have survived the years would have us believe he was at least fifteen feet tall and so strong that he could easily bend a rifle barrel into the letter S, his initial. He could, so it was told, move his cabin by simply running his head through the roof and walking away with it. Bears were no match at all for him, as he would jump on a bear's back and then proceed to beat the unlucky animal to death with his bare fists. He could kill Indians, when he chose, by tying their legs together in knots an leaving them to the mercy of hungry wolves. Once he straddled a tremendous catfish in the Monongahela River and rode it until finaly it died of exhaustion near Pittsburgh.

A story I have always liked is the one about his encounter with the dreadful Ogua, a two-headed dragon-like monster believed in by some Indians and also by some frontiersmen. An early letter written by a young man at Fort Harman (Marietta, Ohio) to his parents in Connecticut refers to this creature: "There is an animal in this country which excites the admiration of all who have had an opportunity to view it; being amphibious, it resides in the water during the daytime, but at night repairs to the land in quest of its prey; which are deer. They lie in the deer paths undiscovered, behind an old stump, until the deer, unaware of its enemy, passes over him; this creature immediately seizes him, and entangling him in its tail, which is fifteen feet in length, and notwithstanding all the deer's exertions to free himself, draws him to the water, where he drowns an then devours him... They live in a large muddy bank, where we can find no bottom; it has two heads, in shape resembling a turtle...."

Bingaman supposedly had his encounter with an Ogua on the Cheat River. The monster was resting after having eaten two hogs when Bingaman came upon it (apparently this Ogua liked hogs as well as deer). He grabbed it and cut off one of its heads, causing it to lose its ability to see in straight line. The Ogua began flopping around in a circle that got smaller as it tired. At last the circle was so small that the mythical moster swallowed itself and thus disappeared.

Many decades have come and gone since Samuel Bingaman first gazed upon the creek the bears his name. The pioneer era in whic he so bravely lived ended generations ago, and the men and women who knew him have long been dust. Yet his memory lingers on in the Bingamon country, where even today when thunder booms and echoes among the hills, old-timers will say: "Don't be afraid. That's just old Sam Bingaman cuttin' up and actin' a fool."

Shinnston - Established in 1778

BY JACK SANDY ANDERSON

Shinnston was settled by members of the Shinn family who by 1778 had established a permanent settlement. A log house built in 1778 by Levi Shinn (1748-1807) still stands at the southern edge of the town and is today believed to be Harrison County's oldest house. A grist mill built by Levi Shinn near the mouth of Shinn's Run in or before 1785 formed the nucleus around which a village developed. In 1818 Shinnston was chartered as a town by the Virginia General Assembly, and a post office was established soon thereafter. In 1852 it was incorporated and in 1877 reincorporated. It is presently operating under a charter obtained in 1915.

The oldest house now standing in the main part of town is the "Old Stone Mansion" on Charles Street. It was built about 1821 by Aaron Shinn and his wife (Mary Pigott), who according to tradition carried the stones from the river in leather aprons. There are several other houses over a century old. Some of the more interesting ones are the Dr. Jacob H. Fortney House on the West Side, built soon after 1848; the David Edgar Foreman House on Main Street, built before 1864; the David Mahlon Shinn House at the top of Clement Street, built in 1869; the Dr. Emory Strickler House at the top of Main Street, built in 1853 by the McCord family; the Solomon S. Fleming House on Main Street, built prior to the Civil War; and the Benjamin Franklin Lowe House on Bridge Street, now the Lowe Public Library, originally a small cottage built in the 1870s and later enlarged to resemble the Abraham Lincoln House in Springfield, Ill.

The first church was organized by Methodists in 1786 in the home of Jonathan Shinn (1752-1817). Today there are three Methodist churches; First United Methodist at the corner of Rebecca and Pike Streets, built in 1976-77 to replace an earlier church that occupied the same site; Christ United Methodist Church on Main Street, built in 1898; and Otterbein United Methodist on Clark Street, West Side, built in 1923. Baptists organized a church in 1885 and in 1891 erected a church building on Rebecca Street that was replaced by the present yellow brick church which was dedicated in 1916. North Shinnston Baptist Church on Drain Hill was built in 1924. In 1905 Disciples of Christ (Christian Church) organized in Shinnston and in 1906 built a church, still standing, at the corner of Charles and Pike streets. St. Ann's Catholic Church on Pike Street was constructed in 1952-53 and replaced a wooden church that had served the parish for nearly 30 years. Church of Christ members dedicated a church on Pleasant Avenue in 1971; and the Church of the Lord Jesus Christ on Hood Avenue, West Side, was dedicated in 1973.

The early schools in Shinnston were subscription schools, and the first one was taught in 1813 by Rev. Asa Shinn. The first free school was held in a two-story building at the corner of Pike and Walnut streets in 1865 and was taught by William B. Wilkinson. Built in 1860 for a town hall and academy, this building served as a public school (Clay District School No. 4) until 1895 when a brick school building was erected on upper Mahlon Street. Clay District High School, later Shinnston High School, became a reality in 1907 and held classes in the 1895 building. In 1916 classes were held in a new brick high school building on the hill overlooking the town. This building is now Shinnston Middle School. Shinnston High School

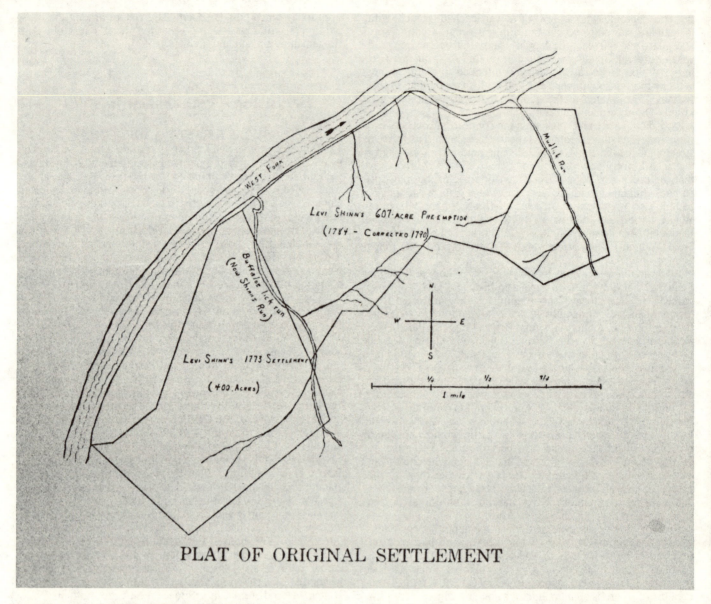

Levi Shinn's 607-Acre Preemption
(1784 - Corrected 1790)

West Fork

Muddy Run

Buffalo Lick Run
(Now Shinns Run)

Levi Shinn's 1773 Settlement
(400 Acres)

N
W — E
S

¼   ½   ¾
1 mile

PLAT OF ORIGINAL SETTLEMENT

ceased to exist in 1978; and today high school students attend Lincoln High school, located along U.S. Rt. 19 a short distance south of the corporation limits. The 1895 building, which has been greatly enlarged and modified through the years is the present elementary school.

Shinnston grew slowly but steadily throughout the 19th century. Its stores, shops, mills, and taverns were widely patronized; and it became the shopping center for the surrounding countryside. During the nineteenth century there were numerous tradesmen and businessmen who contributed toward the community's development. The first tannery was built by George Kirkpatrick and was later operated by John B. Lowe, Rezin K. Shinn, and William P. Hall. William and Frederick A. Stoey had a tannery which was located a little distance up Shinn's Run. There were two wagon shops — one on Main Street owned by Benjamin Tyson Harmer Sr., also a funeral director and casket maker; and one on Walnut Street owned by Jacob Helmes. Some of the early storekeepers were Elder Levi Shinn, who had the first store in 1810; Robert McGee, William P. Hall, Jacob Martin, Dr. Jacob H. Fortney, John Marshall Knox, Solomon S. Fleming, William E. Swiger, Benjamin Asa Reeder, Allison Robinson, Jesse V. Martin, and Van Davis. Apothecary shops were owned by Dr. Peter Davis and Granville D. Hall and Van B. Hall. Albert Shore, Jacob Crim, and James P. Stout had blacksmith shops. Shoe shops were owned by Samuel O. Shinn, B. F. Saint, and Alex Ogden. Justis Jarrett and Eugenius Clark, both of whom were skilled cabinetmakers, had ferries as did also Dr. Jacob H. Fortney. Edward Ebert was the town's hatter. William Knox had a saddler's shop near the pottery he and his relatives, the Haughts, had opened in the 1870s on Main Street. This pottery was in operation until the 1890s; its operators were Knox and Haught; William Haught and Sons, John L. Haught and Co.; Knotts, Dillinger, and Huhn; Wilkinson and Fleming; and last, A. Conrad. The early doctors were Jesse Flowers, Jacob H. Fortney, John H. Ogden, James Denham, Peter Davis, Emory Strickler, Zachariah W. Wyatt, and Charles Oliver Henry.

Mills were vital in the early days, and Shinnston had several that served the community and neighboring areas. The first mills utilized water power, while the later ones utilized steam. Some of the men engaged in milling were Levi Shinn, Clement Shinn, Seth Shinn, Howard T. Shinn, Jeremiah Shinn, Solomon S. Fleming, Daniel Riblett, George J. Riblett, Jesse V. Martin, William Sullivan, Henry Sullivan, John H. Griffith, John M. Fortney, Charles L. Steel, John Nay, James Jackson, Bart Clark, Benjamin F. Lowe, Joseph B. Harrison, George W. Harrison, Taylor Harrison, and Jason M. Kester.

One of the early town's most noted places was the Red Lion Tavern, immortalized in Granville Davisson Hall's *Daughter of the Elm* as the ''Blue Boar.'' Some of its owners and/or proprietors were William E. Lyon (who probably built it in the 1840s), William S. Sandy, Benjamin R. Patton, David Morris, Jacob Long, Granville D. Nay, James Stealey, James Wamsley, Judd Dent, Rawley M. Fortney, Benjamin Asa Reeder, and John W. Carder. Another well-known tavern was the Busy Bee, kept by David Mahlon Shinn. Supposedly the first tavern in Shinnston was one kept by William Black; in it in 1835 was held a memorable Fourth of July celebration.

It was in the 19th century, during the years just before the Civil War, that a notorious outlaw band flourished in the area. Nearby Big Elm Farm, on which stood the gigantic elm tree that gave the farm its name, was the band's headquarters. Granville Davisson Hall (1837-1934), who grew to manhood in Shinnston, wrote a fictionalized account of this band in a novel he entitled *Daughter of the Elm*. First published in 1899, it proved so popular that several editions have been printed through the years.

When the Civil War erupted in 1861, the majority of the town's inhabitants favored the North; and many of the men served bravely in the Union Army. In late April, 1863, Confederate soldiers under William E. Jones raided Shinnston in what has long been known as ''Jones's Raid'' and engaged Union forces in a brief skirmish near the Maulsby (covered) Bridge at present Gypsy. Livestock, particularly horses, and food supplies were appropriated by the invaders who otherwise did no great harm to the town and its people. Shinnston was touched by the deplorable guerrilla warfare that raged in the West Fork Valley during the Civil War years, and tragic incidents occurred that engendered bitter feelings which lasted for generations. Solomon S. Fleming, who was elected mayor when the town was incorporated in 1852, was one of Harrison County's leading Union supporters and took part in the activities that led to the formation of West Virgnia as the 35th state in 1863.

In the last quarter of the 19th century there were several milestones in the town's history. The first bridge to span the West Fork at Shinnston was constructed in 1876 and was such a novelty that people came from miles around to gaze upon it. The great flood of 1888 swept away this two-span bridge, but it was soon replaced by another bridge that still stands, though no longer is in use. (In 1930 the so-called new bridge, located downstream from the old one, was opened to traffic.) In 1886 the first telephones were installed. This was the same year that witnessed the installation of the first street lights. These lights burned oil and were in use until 1899 when natural gas lights replaced them. In 1914 electric street lights became a reality. The railroad reached the town in 1890 and was heralded with much enthusiasm. In 1906 the streetcar came to the town; and people were able to travel to Fairmont and Clarksburg quickly, comfortably, and cheaply. It ceased operation in 1947. Charles Ashby Short built the first theater, Short's Opera House, at the corner of Pike and Station streets in or about 1889; it was destroyed by fire in 1906. In 1897 appeared the first issue of ''The Shinnston News,'' a weekly newspaper that still exists and that is as popular today as it was then. In 1899 the first bank, the Farmers Bank, was established. The present Bank of Shinnston dates from 1932.

During the fading years of the last century and the first years of this century Shinnston grew rapidly and became a town in fact as well as in name. This sudden growth was chiefly due to the development of natural resources — coal, oil, and gas —in the area. Coal mining came to be an industry of paramount importance in the local economy as numerous mines of varying sizes sprang into existence. For a time Shinnston resembled a boom town as the tranquility of a rural village gave way to the hustle-and-bustle of an energetic industrial town. Automobiles, at first little more than curiosities, steadily increased in number as the new century advanced and by the 1920s had replaced the horse and buggy.

Throughout this century the town has successfully overcome a number of serious problems and survived the stresses caused by two world wars and Korean and Vietnamese conflicts. Its elected representatives have been instrumental in maintaining and promoting the town's welfare despite frustrating difficulties that at times seemed insurmountable.

During the years of World War II there occurred a terrible freak of nature known as the Shinnston Tornado. On the evening of Friday, June 23, 1944, this monstrous tornado roared across the West Fork at Lucas Mill and struck the residential areas of Solon, Pleasant Hill, and South Shinnston. John L. Finlayson's book *Shinnston Tornado* published in 1946, is a definitive account of this tragic phenomenon that claimed many lives and caused great devastation.

Today Shinnston has a population of approximately 2,800 persons and remains the shopping center for the surrounding countryside. The coal industry is still important in the local economy, even though some of the once well-known mines no longer exist. Although it takes pride in being progressive and up-to-date, Shinnston remembers and appreciates its past. No matter what problems the coming years may bring, Shinnston will be able to overcome them and look forward to a prosperous and happy future.

Jesse Lowther - Established The Town by The Name of Milford in Year 1821
BY PAULINE G. LeROY

Jesse the fourth of Col. William Lowther's five sons, was born July 21, 1773.

Some old records say that his birth occured a scant six weeks after his family came to theis area, but most authorities now place their arrival in 1772. He was the first white child born in the ''Lowther Settlement'' located about one and a half miles north of present-day West Milford.

William Lowther had married Sudna, the daughter of Thomas Hughes, while their families were living in the Moorefield area. Thomas and the rest of his family moved west shortly thereafter, settling on Hacker,s Creek in what is now Lewis County in 1768. The Lowthers, with their three oldest children, Robert, Thomas and William, followed four years later.

Evidently the Lowther family did not stay any length of time on Hacker's Creek. William was closely identified with the area around Nutter Fort in the earlier days of its existance and the residence always identified with him was a large homestead on West Fork River about seven miles below Clarksburg.

His cabin is described as measuring 16 by 20 feet with joist of flattened timbers, three and a half by seven and a half inches.The fireplace was nearly five and a half feet high. Although the cabin was considered to be commodious according to its location and date of construction, the addition of a fifth child , Elias, 1776, must have made days when weather allowed outside activities even more precious despite the hardships and dangers which were ever present.

When he was well-along in years, Jesse related to a neighbor two incidents from his childhood that recalled the hard lifestyle of the frontier.

''When my father with several other families settled on the West Fork River,'' said Jesse, ''grain was so scarce that it was impossible to buy corn for bread. They were compelled to rely on game for food until a crop could be raised. It was agreed that my father and Jesse Hughes, the best hunters in the party, should furnish provisions while the others cultivated and cleared the land. These two hunters not only supplied plenty of game and fish for their own people, but they gave assistance to others in need on Hacker's Creek. Before the crop matured, my grandfather (Robert, "the Quaker" Lowther) visited us, bringing a knapsack of biscuit. I was then a small boy and my mother gave me one. I tasted it, threw it down and called for 'jerk' (strips of dried venison). Mother cried at the thought of living in the wilderness so long that her children had forgotten the use of bread."

At another time when the inhabitants were driven to the fort by Indians, provisions became extremely scarce. Just as starvation seemed imminent, a large turkey lit on grapevines growing near the stockade and Co. Lowther shot it. With the garrison rifles protecting her, Jesse's mother ran out of the fort and brought in the turkey. " God has sent this to preserve our lives," she said.

Jesse's brother, William told his descendants about the Lowther childrens daily lives — clearing land and plowing and hoeing corn from daylight until dark with an hour alloted at noon. During that hour, however, according to William, he not only ate but was expected to spend any free time weaving,

ATTENTION ! ! !

The Clarksburg Rifle Blues,

UNDER the command of Capt. E. Marsh, will attend a company muster in Clarksburg on the

4th day of July,

armed and equipped as the law directs, and well supplied with ammunition to celebrate the day. It is expected that particular attention will be paid to the above.

By order.

AMOS KEYS, O S.

N. B. The usual course will be pursued.
June 18. 1825.

Attention ! ! !

THE men attached to the company commanded by Capt. Alexander L. Paxton, will attend a company muster at Milford, on the 4th day of July next at 10 o'clock, armed and equip, ed, with a sufficiency of ammunition to celebrate the day.

By order.

JESSE G. LOWTHER, O. S.

June 18 1825.

Many nights were spent in burning brush and logs in order to make use of every available moment.

By the srping of 1778, with the American Revolution in full swing, the British considered loosing the Indians against the colonists a legitimate method of warfare.

Gen. Lachlin McIntosh, the commander of Fort Pitt, built Fort McIntosh on the Ohio River to protect that part of the frontier, impending the Indians' invasions in that area, but directing them into the settlements of the Monongahela Valley and its upper tributaries.

The settlers in these areas, aware of the storm that would break upon the frontier in the spring, had spent the previous winter repairing old forts and block houses and building new ones.

During the first week in May a double tragedy struck the Lowther-Hughes family.

A war party of about 20 Indians came into Hacker's Creek and Upper West Fork areas and the residents in these locations moved to West's and Richard's forts, respectively.

During the day women and children stayed in the forts under the protection of a few men while the rest continued to do their normal farm chores, working in groups for safety's sake.

Several men were working in a field on Hacker's Creek, clearing land, plowing and fencing, when they were taken unaware by the Indians. Jesse's grandfather, Thomas Hughes, his uncle, Jonathan Lowther, were killed.

Two of the men ran to Richard's Fort to give the alarm; however, the murder of Isaac Washburn had already put the inhabitants of that area on guard.

The Indians left shortly thereafter, unpursued.

In 1791, at athe age of 18, Jesse married Mary Regan, a daughter of Jacob Regan, a Revolutionary War veteran of Dutch descent. They lived in the "Lowther Settlement" until 1797 when they, with Jesse's brothers and their families, moved to Ohio.

Jesse and Mary established a home on Neil's Island, about four miles below Parkersburg.

After Wood County was formed from Harrison in 1798, William Lowther served as its sheriff, Jesse as a justice of the peace, and Elias as an officer in the militia.

Repeated bouts of "chills and fever" drove them back toward their former home within 10 years. Part of them, including Jesse and his family, returned to the West Fork, while others,Elias among them, elected to relocate on the Hughes Riverin Ritchie County.

In 1807 George Bush conveyed a 130-acre tract of land to Jesse. About eight years later, assisted by Samuel Hoff, Jesse laid out on this site what would become the town of West Milford.

Samuel Clemens and Jacob Romine brought two acres of this land in 1817. They built an eight-foot dam across the West Fork that backed up the river for several miles and a gristmill and sawmill. This was the first sawmill in the district. It had a perpendicular saw run by an under shot water wheel and so much power that a community began to grow around it.

An Act was passed on Jan. 15, 1821, by the Virginia Assembly that provided "That ten acres of land on the West Fork River, the property of Jesse Lowther in the County of Harrison, as the same is already laid off into lots and convenient streets, shall be established a town by the name of Millford, and that Robert Lowther, Jacob Coplin, and Robert Maxwell, Gentlemen, be and they are thereby appointed trustees thereof."

"Mill-ford" seemed an appropriate name for the new town since it designated the shallow water below the dam where settlers crossed the river.

A post office was opened in January 1827. Jesse served as the town's second postmaster, from Jan. 21, 1829 until postal

...ided to discontinue that office in June 1833.

...t Creek post office served both communities for a ... the petitions of West Milford citizens secured the ...ent of their office. At this point Washington postal ...iscovered that there was another "Millford" in ...ginia, so "West" was added to the Harrison ...tion's name and, in the process, it also lost an "l." ..., the Lowthers raised two small grandsons, who ...ildren of their son Robert, a physician who had ...Mississippi. Both Robert and his wife died within a ... of time and the children were brought to live with ... parents.

Jesse died in October 1854, and is buried near West Milford. Following his death, Mary went to Pullman in Ritchie County, to live with their daughter, Mary Ann Hall.

The Lowthers' other children were; William, who settled at Oxford in Ritchie County; Sallie Lowther Morris of Gilmer County; Margaret Lowther Mitchell and Sudan Lowther Maxwell, who stayed in the West Milford area; Jesse Jr., a doctor who died in Arkansas; Elizabeth Lowther Lester, of Lewis County; Uriah, who died as a child; Druzilla Lowther Morgan and Millie Lowther Wyer, both of whom lived in Ohio, and Ellis, who died in Wirt County.

The Legend of Peter Crowe...

He Seemingly Came from Nowhere And Settled in The Bingamon Area

BY JACK SANDY ANDERSON

Who was Peter Crowe, the strange man who seemingly arrived from nowhere well over a hundred years ago and settled in the wooded Bingamon Country where he soon became the subject of many eerie tales? I first became aware of him in 1946. I was then a student at Wyatt and one noon hour went into Gilmer Cunningham's store where I bought a small booklet entitled, "Hidden Powers."

This was, I discovered, an account of Crowe written by Lawrence H. Martin, a descendant of the family into whose midst Crowe appeared one winter night in the long-ago.

Through the years I have read it many times and always find it fascinating. Hundreds of students have greatly enjoyed it, for nearly every year I read it to my classes. They like to speculate about him and what sort of man he truly was and how the weird stories about him developed. The Peter Crowe legend is a part of Harrison County's heritage, and I hope it will survive the years and be enjoyed by future generations.

It has been my privilege and good fortune to have known a few men and women, now all passed away, who were living links to our area's pioneer era. One of them was Maggie Glover Davis. Born in 1869 and gifted with unusual powers of observation and an exceptional memory, she spent her long lifetime in the Bingamon country and knew more about the early inhabitants than anyone else whom I ever interviewed. Not long before her death, she told me of the time she met Peter Crowe.

She was a little barefooted girl of about four or five playing outside in the yard when she spied on an old man slowly walking up the hill toward the house. When he finally got to the house, he asked her to bring him a drink of water and to tell her father (George Washington Glover) that he wished to see him. As soon as he had gone, Maggie asked her father who the old man was, and her father replied: "Why, that's old Pete Crowe!"

Maggie remembered him as being of rather striking appearance. He wore a linen duster to protect his dark clothes, had long hair, and was stooped with age. He looked one straight in the eye, and spoke in a penetrating voice that was clear but soft. She was not sure just where he lived, but assumed it was not too far distant, perhaps somewhere between Big Run and Little Bingamon. She thought he died not long after she met him. If so, his death would have occured around 1874.

According to tradition, Peter Crowe came to the Joseph Martin homestead near Wyatt on a winter night during a blizzard. Yet no snow was on his clothes nor were they even damp. When he left the following morning, he made no footprints in the fresh snow. Upon his return, also at night, no one was aware of his presence until, as if by magic, he was seated in a chair near the fireplace and began speaking. It was noted by the Martins that his lips did not seem to move and that he spoke in two different voices — one near and calm, the other distant and agitated.

The Martins had several children who at once became Crowe's devoted friends. He had a wonderful way with the young and could entertain them by the hour with riddles, tales, tricks, and making clever things such as corncob castles and stick-and-bark wigwams. Adults, too were charmed by him: for when he chose, he could relate stories that held them spellbound. But there were times when he was withdrawn and terribly still, as if, perhaps, he were communicating with beings ordinary eyes could not see.

He stayed for sometime with the Martins before acquiring land a few miles away on which he built a simple log cabin. He paid for the land and paid the Martins for his board with gold

coins that shone like they had been but recently minted. As the years went by, Crowe's reputation as a person with supernatural powers grew steadily. He had few real friends, other than the Martins, for most of his Bingamon neighbors were a little afraid of him. Yet they respected his abilities and did not hesitate to call on him when in need.

His knowledge of remedies based on familiarity with the area's medicinal plants, saved more than one ailing neighbor, and he became known far and near for his ability to stop bleeding. It was said that many would have bled to death had it not been for him.

If Peter Crowe were indeed a witch, he did not practice the black arts. What powers he commanded were used for good, not evil. His presence, so his neighbors believed, caused butter to come quickly, chimneys to draw better, yarn to reel without trouble, and knots and tangles in the manes and tails of their horses to disappear. They observed, too, that dogs no matter how vicious, never barked or growled at him. Unbroken colts and wild horses turned uncannily gentle when he was about, and he could mount and ride them with perfect ease. Some said that at night he would ride them through the sky.

Probably the most spectacular demonstration of his remarkable powers took place when he rescued a small child from the angry flood of Bingamon Creek. It was summer, and a cloudburst struck the upper Bingamon country. Within a short while the normally small and quiet stream had turned into a raging torrent that threatened all who lived along its banks. A small crowd of people, including Crowe had gathered to watch a house across the creek being swept away. Suddenly an anguished cry was heard above the sound of the roaring water. There on a large rock just below where the house had stood was a child. Crowe disappeared from the crowd, and soon reappeared on the rock with the child in his arms. In a matter of seconds he seemed to glide across the frightful stream with his precious burden. Those present felt they had witnessed a miracle and were so filled with awe that for a time they could not speak.

Tradition has it that Crowe spent his last years alone and seldom ventured forth from his cabin. To the surprise of some of his contemporaries, he was unable to ward off the ravages of time. The years took their toll of him, as they do of every mortal, and he grew bent and feeble. Eventually —inevitably — like all that have been given the great gift of life, he bowed his head and passed from this earthly scene. Even to this day, so it is said, the grass on his grave remains always green.

Col. Benjamin Robinson - Frontiersman, Soldier, Legislator, Settled Lumberport

BY MRS. CREEL CORNWELL SR.

Benjamin Robinson was born July 7, 1758 in Virginia, a son of William Robinson, a pioneer settler on Robinson's Run, for whom the Harrison County stream was named. While a resident of Carolina County, Virginia, he raised a company of Minute Men in the Revolutionary War.

He was promoted to the rank of colonel in 1776 and was in the battles of Brandywine and Germantown.

He applied for a pension Dec. 24, 1832, from Harrison County. It was granted.

Col. Robinson was the Harrison County member of the Virginia House of Delegates from 1797 to 1798.

During 1803 and 1804, Robinson was a trustee of the Randolph Academy which was chartered in 1787 in Clarksburg.

His first wife was Magdaline Webb. She was the daughter of William Webb and Mary Margaret Webb. His second wife was Mary Assom Wilkinson.

———

Col. Robinson founded the settlement that grew into Lumberport on part of 400 acres of land he owned in 1775. Settlers in the Lumberport area formed a frontier community on Jones Run shortly after the Revolutionary War. In addition to Robinson, individuals who established homes in the settlement were Thomas Cunningham, John Hull, Captain Thomas Harbert, John Wood, Samuel Harbert, Nathan Reece, Peter Cornelius, John Cornelius and Elizabeth Cornelius.

Robinson became known as a man of great force of character who took part in the Indian conflicts. On July 2, 1784, at the home of George Jackson on the Buckhannon River, he was appointed a Justice of the Peace.

At the April 1785 term of the Harrison County Court Robinson, William Robinson, Enoch James and Daniel Davisson were appointed viewers to mark a road from Skillings Ford on the West Fork River, past Levi Shinn's mill site, to Clarksburg, keeping as close to the river as the situation would permit.

At the April 1788 term of court Robinson qualified as a captain of militia and J. Bartlett and John Thomas as ensigns.

In 1789 Robinson was an elector.

At the June 1790 term of Court, Thomas Cheney presented a commission as sheriff, but made oath that he could not procure security. The court recommended John McCalley, William Hammond and Robinson as proper persons to fill the office. On July 21, 1794 Robinson gave bond and qualified as sheriff.

The following story was retold by Henry Hammond in his History of Harrison County:

"In the year 1791, the Indians killed James or John McIntire and wife a mile or two above the mouth of Bingamon Creek. Five or six of us when we heard the news, started and went to Ben Robinson's. We followed the Indian's trail down the creek about a mile below the three forks the Indians had just come through. Here was a fresh trail. They were Christopher Carpenter, John Hammond, John Harbert, Jackson, Robinson and myself. We stripped ourselves and lightly as we could, tied handkerchiefs around our heads and proceeded to travel as fast as we could. The Indians appeared to travel very carelessly. It was May. The weeds were young and tender. We could follow a man very easily. We went about seven or eight miles, passed where the Indians had stopped to eat. Arriving on a bank, Jackson turned around and said, 'Where do you think they have gone?'

"With that he jumped down the bank and we proceeded down on the beach, a short distance, when one of the Indians fired. I think we were about 40 yards from them, we on the beach, they on the bank on the same side of the creek. We started on the run and had run ten or 15 yards when the other three fired. Then we were in about 30 yards of them. At the first gun, Jackson wheeled around and said 'Where did that gun come from?' John Harbert and brother John discovered them first running up the hill. They fired. Ben Robinson and myself ran and jumped on the bank where the Indians left their knapsacks. I fired a third shot, the Indians were 60 yards off. They had run up a very steep hill. Robinson shot at the same Indians that I did. I heard him or one of them talk after I shot. Jackson and Carpenter shot last. We then ran a little to the right from where the Indians had run up the hill. I was the first on top with the company I was with (the other men had joined us and two or three went around the hill in another place).

"We then turned down to where the Indians had got on the top of the hill. There we found a blanket, belt, knife, scabbard and blood. The Indian had bled considerable. He went about a quarter of a mile and cut a stick which we supposed was to stop the blood. We followed him about a mile when we then

LUMBERPORT

Near blockhouse built by Thomas Harbert and others about 1775. This was the home of Col. Benjamin Robinson who was a soldier in the Revolution. He led a company at Brandywine and Germantown and also saw Indian service.

thought it dangerous to follow, thinking he had his gun with him and would hide and kill one of us. To my mortification we returned. We could have trailed him anywhere. On our return we found his shot pouch. Had we found it first, I think we would have overtaken him. About 10 yards after his gun was found.

"We returned to the Indians' place of attack where we found all their knapsacks, one shot pouch (having previously found one), four hatchets and all their plunder (including the woman's scalp). Here on examination we found that Brother John had been shot through the handkerchief just above his ear and Jackson through the shirt sleeve near his waist.

"We thought at the time we had wounded two Indians. We sold our plunder for about $20 among which were some curious affairs."

In April 1790 as Samuel Hall was engaged in ploughing a field for Robinson he was discovered by a small party of Indians and shot, tomahawked and scalped. The murder was

discovered by Mrs. Robinson. Surprised that Hull did not come to the house as usual, to feed the horses and get his own dinner, she went to the field to see what detained him. She found the horses some distance from where they had been working. Presently she saw Hull lying where he had been shot. The field in which this occurred was for many years known as the "Hull Field."

On June 21, 1802 the county court granted Col. Robinson permission to build a dam across, and near the mouth of Tenmile Creek and to erect a saw and grist mill, he was known as a man of great determination who had lived in the area since 1775 as a successful frontiersman. When the mill was completed the first industry began in the village.

Beginning in the early 1800s and continuing for several years, large quantities of timber were rafted from Lumberport to market in Pittsburgh. The town derived its name from this practice.

County Bicentennial Committee Opens Covered Bridge Exhibit

THE HARRISON COUNTY Bicentennial Committee announces the opening this week of the Covered Bridges of Harrison County exhibit. The month-long display is located on the first floor of the Clarksburg-Harrison Public Library and may be seen from 9 a.m. to 8 p.m. Monday through Friday and from 9 a.m. to 5 p.m. on Saturday. The Covered Bridges of Harrison County exhibit highlights the existing covered bridges of the area with photos by George Ashby Short. Short is a professional photographer who spent part of his life working in the west with the late, renowned Ansel Adams. He also has a personal stake in such an exhibit since his father, Charles A. Short, was a covered bridge repairman from Shinnston and worked on many of the area bridges. The small exhibit is one of many which are slated during Harrison County's 200th birthday. Funding for Harrison County Bicentennial projects is provided by the Humanities Foundation of West Virginia, a state program of the National Endowment for the Humanities, and by the Consolidated Gas Transmission Corporation.

Strange Happenings, A Tale of A Ghost That Was Reported Seen At Haywood

BY JACK SANDY ANDERSON

In my opinion, no historian, past or present, has done as much as Fairmont's Glenn D. Lough to reveal the true early history of the West Fork Valley. His many fine articles in the Fairmont newspapers, his own historical newspaper, "Awhile Ago Times," and his monumetal book "Now and Long Ago," all bear impressive testimony to his success in discovering how thrilling and important this history really is. It is due to him that we now know of the tragic death of Jacob Fisher at present Haywood in 1758.

This was a year when our valley was still a dangerous wilderness with Indians to be wary of. The French and Indian War was raging; and the French, whom the Indians favored over the English, were encouraging Indian attacks against the frontier settlements.

In the Shenandoah Valley four Frenchmen and about 50 Indians raided the Mill Creek settlement where they murdered several settlers, destroyed a number of houses, and captured 48 persons, among them a 12 or 13-year-old boy named Jacob Fisher. Traveling westward, they, in six days reached Haywood, then the site of an ancient hunting camp called by

the Indians "The Beaver's Head" because the West Fork here, as it curves from the east to the west and back to the east, makes the outline of what they thought resembled that animal's head.

They decided to camp for a time, and on the second day held a council at which they agreed to amuse themselves by burning one of their unfortunate captives. Jacob was chosen and was ordered to gather the firewood. Sensing what was about to happen, he cried and had to be beaten before he obeyed. The wood was ignited, and Jacob was forced to run the firey ring until the rope wound tight around the tree. He then had to reverse his direction until he again came into the fire. This was a slow, horrible, agonizing way to die; and poor Jacob lasted from near noon until darkness had fallen.

More than two centuries have passed since this terrible thing happened. Yet we may assume that Jacob is still not at rest, for his ghost has allegedly been seen several times down through the years. In this day of sophistication when skepticism and cynicism are all too common, it is indeed a brave person who openly expresses his belief in ghosts. The realm of the supernatural, while entertaining to read about, does not truly exist. Or does it?

What was it that John Williamson and his sister Evaline saw at Haywood in July of 1870? In the dark of evening they saw a fire burning brightly around a large tree; but when they came near, it disappeared and no trace of anything burning could be found. And who was the boy that George Shinn saw on a cold winter day in 1874 when he was in the woods near Gypsy Hill? And twenty-six years later who was the boy who Benny Griffin saw crying by the river at Gypsy Grove? I wonder — so do many others.

And in 1908 who was the disappearing boy that Emmett Baker, then a lad of ten, saw emerge from the woods with the Baker family cow? In a letter to Mr. Lough, which was printed in one of Lough's articles in the Fairmont Sunday newspaper, Mr. Baker related his unusual experience as follows:

"One evening I played too long and let the cow get lost. I was still searching for her after dark, and was terrified because ghosts were very prevalent in those days, and I was then a firm believer. While searching the site of the Fisher boy tragedy, I approached a woods nearby and the cow came walking out, driven by a boy who vanished as I drew near.

"Sure, I knew it's foolish to tell about a ghost in these enlightened Flying Saucer times, but I was sure that I had seen a ghost, and I high-tailed it for home to fetch my Dad. 'There's no such thing as ghosts. It's all in your head,' he said. And so on until we were back to the cow. Now we're back to the cow again, still standing near the same spot. As we approached, I heard someone crying. Dad said, 'No need to cry, there's nothing there.'

"I said, 'It's not me, Dad. It's over there by that tree. Let's go see.' And Dad said, 'It's way past milking time. Let's hurry on home with the cow.' Dad pretended to think that it was monkey business by someone. I'm sure no one in Haywood ever heard the Fisher boy's story, or knew that we were in that vicinity."

Strange happenings are far from rare in this valley of ours. Ever since the first settlers felled the virgin forest and built their homes, tales defying explanation have been told and handed down from one generation to another.

Well do I remember a number of them that were told to me by some of my family on snowy winter evenings when the wind blew mournfully through the nearby woods. Who am I to say that these tales are only figments of the imagination? Life holds countless mysteries, many of which mortal man shall never solve.

Rev. George Towers - Teacher, Brought Change to The Northwestern Counties

By PAULINE G. LeROY

"I thank God there are no free schools nor printing and I hope we shall not have, these hundred years, for learning has brought disobendience and heresy and sects into the world, and printing has divulged them and libels against the best Government. God keep us from both."

This, in 1671, was the reply of Sir William Berkeley, governor of Virginia, to an inquiry made by an English official concerning the provisons made for public instruction in that colony.

This attitude was not prevalent among the first trans-Allegheny pioneers, who very soon displayed concern for the education of their children and suppported the establishment of "old field" schools.

Unfortunately, early life on the frontier was so hard and demanding on the efforts and time of every member of a family that children could be spared for, at best, only a few weeks of school during the mid-winter. Indifferent skill in reading, spelling, writing and mathematics was the usual result.

"The neighborhood of Clarksburg," wrote historian Henry Haymond, "was peopled by an excellent class of pioneers and at a very early period took high rank as an educational center, and its influence was widely felt."

In evidence of the truth of this statement, Harrison County was barely three years old when the Randolph Academy was chartered by an act of the General Assembly which also provided that on the second Monday in May, 1788, a meeting would be held in Morgantown to "fix upon some healthy and convenient place within one of the counties of Ohio, Monongalia, Harrison and Randolph for the purpose of erecting therein the necessary buildings for the said Academy." Clarksburg was selected as a site which met the requirements.

The law at this time required one-sixth of the county surveyors' fees to go to the support of William and Mary College at Williamsburg, but this act stipulated that the surveyors for the four counties mentioned would turn in that amount for the support of Randolph Academy instead — an indication that this was to be an institution of no little importance.

The Academy's charter stated that the school was to be free from church control.

William Haymond, John McCally and Daniel Davisson comprised a committee appointed to oversee the building of the Academy; however, it wasn't until early 1793 that John Haymond, serving the Academy's trustees as a clerk, recorded the following:

"Resolved that the Randolph Academy be built of wood and... agreeable to the original plan, except the cupalo (sic) and be let this afternoon to the lowest bidder, under the immediate direction of the Board, and to be completely finished on or before the first day of November next in a workmanlike manner.

"Resolved also that the purchaser give bond with approved security.

"Resolved also that the undertaker (low bidder) be paid his money by three installments, to-wit: one third when the frame is raised, the second third at finishing said house and the other third in six months after the said house is finished."

David Hewes was the low bidder, agreeing to undertake the project for a sum of 179 pounds and to be finished on or before Nov. 1.

The following June, Haymond laid before the board a letter from Rev. George Towers expressing his willingness to accept an appointment as a teacher at the Academy at a rate of $250 a year, to be paid in quarterly installments.

Having a building and a teacher, the trustees next advertised for students with this notice:

"The Trustees of the Randolph Academy notify the public that they have erected in the town of Clarksburg, Harrison County, Virginia, a commodious building, in order to carry into effect the laudable design of the Institution, and according have employed as a tutor in the said Academy the Rev'd George Towers, lately from England, a gentleman of undoubted character and abilities, who has engaged to teach the Latin and Greek Languages, the English Gramatically, Arithmetic and Geography. The price of tuition will be, for the Latin and Greek, $16, for Geography, $6, for Reading, Writing and Arithmetic, $5 per annum, to be paid quarterly. Genteel boarding can be had in the town or neighborhood on reasonable terms."

On April 19, 1796, George Towers went into the Harrison County court to take the oath of general government. The following April, the court authorized Towers "to celebrate the rites of matrimony."

Evidently parental acceptance of the Academy was positive, for when Isaac Van Meter of Hampshire County came through Clarksburg in 1801 on his way to the Ohio, he recorded, with some surprise, that there was "an Academy on an elevated piece of ground near the town" where "we were informed.... nearly fifty children are generally taught...."

Eighteen-year-old John Scripps, an unbound apprentice, spent five years in Clarksburg, starting in 1803. Writing about his experiences later he pointed out that "being naturally addicted to study and literary pursuits... drew me to the attention of the better class.

"Rev G. Towers, a Presbyterian clergyman and Professor of the Academy and his wife were the only religionists in the town. They gave me access to their large and select library. He was sociable and instructive and at his special request I visited him two or three evenings every week. Both he and his wife smoked as an incentive to study and he kept a pipe constantly for my use. Everybody then used tobacco and amid its frgrant fumes I derived much instruction.

"Mr. Towers preached regularly twice a month in the Academy, but he had no church members."

Towers was certainly qualified and a popular member of the community but his school had problems that were not of his making.

During Randolph's first years, its governing board, which Towers served for a time as clerk, spent most of its time worrying about the morals of the Academy's students and financial problems.

In November 1804, the board agreed to institute suits against surveyors for the fees stipulated for the school's maintenance. The following month, its members decided instead to send copies of a letter outlining their position to the principal surveyors in Brooke, Ohio, Wood, Monongalia, Randolph and Harrison counties by the board's treasurer,

Major Benjamin Robinson.

Evidently this wasn't effective, for the minutes of February 18, 1806, revealed the school's grave financial condition. "Ordered," they state, "that the Rev'd George Towers be allowed the Sum of twenty dollars — it being for interest on money due him from this board and that the Clerk of this board do give the Said Towers an order on the treasurer for the Same... The Sd. 20 dollars being the full amount of interest due him from the Board up to this date."

About 1812 Towers joined several other prominent residents of Clarksburg in the formation of a company for the purpose of conducting a banking business. Under the name of the "President, Directors and Company of the Saline Bank of Virginia" they issued notes, received deposits and discounted paper, but failed initially to apply for a legal charter as required by state law.

A charter was applied for, but for some reason, was never obtained.

The United States brought suit against the institution in the U.S. District Court with the decision being made in the defendants' favor. When an appeal was taken to the Supreme Court, its members affirmed the original decision and dismissed the bill.

The troubled bank finally ceased operation about 1828. some 12 years after Towers' death.

Randolph Academy, still struggling financially, was finally sold in 1841 and razed to make way for the Methodist-affiliated Northwestern Virginia Academy which, after 1865, came under the jurisdiction of the district school system.

The third building on the same site, which opened for classes in 1895, is still known as Towers School, as a tribute to the first teacher of the Randolph Academy. The street on which it is located, Hewes Avenue, commemorates David Hewes, the builder of the original school.

Schools Were Abandoned Log Cabins

By DOROTHY DAVIS

Citizens of Northwestern Virginia who met in Morgantown in 1787 to decide where to build Randolph Academy that the Virginia Assembly had chartered for west of the mountains chose Clarksburg for the site.

The hope of the assembly on issuing the charter was that the academy could be to the Virginia lands north of the Little Kanawha River what William and Mary College had been to Tidewater Virginia. This was not to be for roads were so poor that few other than Clarksburg youths could attend the school and trustees of the institution had no funds with which to work. Trustees did not have the "36- by 20-foot wood and frame building" northeast of the junction of Hewes Avenue and Second Street in Clarksburg ready for occupancy until the fall of 1795.

What lifted Randolph Academy above the usual subscription school was the instructor. Somehow the trustees engaged in 1795 George Towers, an Oxford man and a Presbyterian minister, who had just emigrated from England, "to teach the Latin and Greek languages, the English Gramatically, Arithmetic and Geography."

Once in recent years when a historian asked a county resident why Harrison County had supplied far more outstanding men to the state and the nation than any other county in the state, the answer came quickly: "George Towers." He followed academic standards during the 19 years he taught at the school that gave the youths a thorough classical education and set a tone that continued after his death in 1814 and after

the Methodist Church took over the institution in 1840. The Methodist Church built a new building named Northwestern Academy, a building converted into a federal prison and hospital in 1861 when Clarksburg was a supply depot for Union troops.

Many men active in the new state movement in the early 1860s had been attached to the Clarksburg school. Francis H. Pierpont taught Randolph Academy in 1838. Gordon Battelle was principal of Northwestern Academy 1843-51; Alexander Martin, 1851-54. Battelle and Martin were largely responsible for the public school laws written into the first constitution of the State of West Virginia, laws that required counties to divide into districts with boards of education that must provide free of charge schooling for children within the borders of the district.

The subscription schools the free schools replaced had been largely family affairs described well by Luther Haymond, born in 1809 and as a child a pupil in the subscription school: "The schools were generally old abandoned log cabins with furniture of slabs with holes bored in each end and pins driven in them for legs… It was the custom for the teacher or master, as he was called, to go around in a neighborhood and procure subscriptions for as many scholars as the head of the family could furnish and pay for. The tuition was about two or two and a half dollars per scholar, which was sometimes paid in linsey, linen or grain."

For several decades after the formation of West Virginia, district boards had sufficient revenue only for one-room schools with instruction similar to that in the old subscription school. Since the law provided for the establishment of "independent districts" to be carved out for citizens who wished to tax themselves heavily for schools, three independent districts existed in Harrison County in the 19th century.

Clarksburg Independent District, which had established in 1867 the second school for blacks to be opened in West Virginia, started Clarksburg High School in 1888 and for many years boards of education in districts without high schools paid the tuition for pupils who wished to attend school beyond the eighth grade to travel to Clarksburg to school. Pupils dropped out of the Clarksburg school to attend a local high school as boards of education established high schools in their districts. Salem had a high school in 1903; Shinnston, 1906; Bridgeport, 1910; Lumberport, 1912; Lost Creek, 1915; West Milford (Unidis), 1915; Sardis, 1916; Bristol, 1918; Coal District (Victory), 1920; Clark District (Roosevelt-Wilson), 1921.

A parochial grade school opened by the Catholic Church in 1866 in a building near the old B&O Depot on East Pike Street began with a system that grew into St. Joseph's Academy for girls in 1872 which in 1876 moved into Centennial Hall on the corner of Maple and East Pike Streets, where both boys and girls were schooled. Xavierian Brothers arrived in 1914 to teach in Clarksburg after opening St. Mary's High School for boys. In 1927 girls from St. Joseph's transferred to a coeducational St. Mary's and after Notre Dame High School opened in 1955, St. Mary's became a grade school.

In 1876 Broaddus Female College moved from Winchester to the Bartlett Hotel beside the Harrison County Courthouse. The head of the school bought ten acres in Haymond Grove (Chestnut Grove) for the school, built Willis Hall and then sold the property to the Baptist Convention. Payne Hall, built in 1905 for offices, classrooms, dining rooms and 22 dormitory apartments for Broaddus College, stands in 1984 on Broaddus Avenue in Clarksburg. The school moved to Philippi in 1908.

The Seventh Day Baptist Church opened Salem Academy

in Salem in 1888. Even though the school received a charter for ''Salem College'' in 1890, it continued to operate, in conjunction with the college, an academy where high school subjects were taught until 1926. In 1958 the College established a branch in Clarksburg.

Mr. Elliott of Wheeling was the first president of a business college established in Clarksburg in 1881. In 1911 the name of the school was changed to West Virginia Business College.

THE CIRCUIT RIDERS

by JAMES POOL

In the early days of settlement on the Appalachian frontier, the sparseness of the population prevented the establishment of churches in much of the area for a considerable period of time. Even though some of the people were said to be ''natural-born hell-raisers,'' most of the people there were honest and God-fearing. Many of them had spent the early days of their youth in eastern communities under the stabilizing influence of religious teachings; therefore it was with misgivings they missed this in their isolated wilderness homes, especially in the performance of marriage ceremonies and burial rites. The coming of the circuit riders partially solved some of their problems; however, other needs remained unfulfilled until an increase in the population made it feasible to have a full-time minister to dwell among them.

The circuit rider was most often an ordained minister of an established church which sent him into this wilderness to renew contacts with the isolated settlers. In preparation for his mission here, his training came largely from other dedicated ministers, who, in their time, had served on other frontiers east of the Appalachian Highland. A number of these minsters had gained considerable renown, even while the colonies were still within the British Empire, for their bold, and sometimes dissenting, remarks. It was said that they ''feared God and nothing else.''

The circuit rider, usually by horseback, traveled into this mountainous region where roads were almost unknown and trails were few and, at times, impassable. Because of the difficulties of travel and the extent of territory to cover, he would be unable to visit some localities more than once in a period of two or three years. Consequently, funeral services and marriage ceremonies would have to be postponed until the circuit rider appeared. With the frontiersmen being thoroughly practical, they went ahead and buried their dead; also, they granted permission to those who planned to be married to live together as husband and wife until the coming of the circuit rider who would formally unite them in the bonds of wedlock. By the time the minister arrived in some communities, couples awaiting the performance of the marriage rites often had a child or two to participate in or witness the ceremony.

One of the more interesting circuit riders in the early days of Harrison County was the Rev. John A. Williams who spent much of his life in the itinerant service of the Methodist Episcopal Church.

Rev. Williams attended school at the Northwestern Academy in Clarksburg, which stood on the site of the Towers School of the 20th century. Upon completion of his studies Rev. Williams was licensed to preach and moved his wife Eleanor and fourteen children to the Sycamore Creek area of the county. There he commenced to preach the gospel at many points throughout central West Virginia while riding circuit in Lewis, Upshur, Randolph, Webster, Tyler and Doddridge counties, as well as in his home county of Harrison.

Haymond Maxwell Sr. in his monograph covering 50 years of history of the Sycamore Creek Valley of Harrison

County entitled ''The Story of Sycamore'' recounts an early tale handed down from generation to generation in which the Rev. Williams, if not the leading actor was at least the central figure — somewhat in the manner that the lamb is the pivotal point or activity in the sacrificial feast.

It seems, as the story goes that ''the parson having been directed by the Presiding Elder to conduct a series of religious services in a mountainous interior section, many miles from Sycamore, proceeded by arduous horseback journey to the designated community. Having reached there late in the afternoon of the second day's hard riding, he stopped at the mountain cabin and sought food and shelter for himself and his horse.

The queen of the home — the mountain housewife — hospitably, if not graciously, told the lone traveller that he was welcome to share their humble and frugal board. She said that her husband was out on his trap line and would return in the evening, but that the hour of his arrival was uncertain as he was frequently much delayed by the unexpected emergencies arising in his trapping activities.

In the little half-open barn, the hardy traveler stabled and fed his tired and hungry horse. Then, having gone to the house, the minister was bid ''have a chair and sit down.'' He did so, and the conversation proceeded.

After a while, he asked his hostess if there were any infidels in the community. She promptly replied that she did not know whether there were or not; that he (the minister) might look in the shed alongside the barn and see if there were any hides of that kind among her husband's assortment. The preacher replied ''Madam, I fear you are in the dark.''

"Yes, she said, "I know I am. For sometime I've been trying to get Bill to cut another hole in the wall."

Supper was presently over and darkness was upon the face of the land, but Bill had not returned. The sole room of the cabin was large and, among other furnishings, accommodated two beds. The hour for retirement having arrived, the guest was assigned to the bed in the "back corner." The other and bigger bed the woman proceeded to occupy. This sort of arrangement in the accomodation of guests was common on log cabin days.

Perhaps an hour after the hostess and her guest had retired to their separate couches, the lord and master of that particular mountain castle came stalking into the room. He was a giant, with viscious looking beard, high-top boots, coonskin cap, and fists like two mauls. The parson, wide awake, lay still. The giant threw fagots on the fire and looked directy toward the guest bed. Then, seating himself before the newly-revived fire, he crossed his legs, drew his long hunting knife from its scabbard and proceeded to strop it on his boot. All the while he kept casting what seemed to be threatening glances toward the stranger in bed. The parson thought his time had come. His suspicion was crystallized into conviction when the mountain man arose and with gleaming knife held high, started in the direction of the visitor's bed. The preacher's heart almost stopped. He was about to spring to the floor and, empty handed and against all odds, fight for his life, when he realized that the husky hunter was not directing his activities toward either the guest bed or its occupant. The giant was not bellicose; he was merely hungry. Straightway he proceeded to cut some generous slices from a quarter of venison hanging nearby the peacher's bed.

Great was the relief of the clergyman. His sense of security became complete when, a little later, the big bearded man, after having eaten heartily of bread and meat in front of the burning logs, knelt in prayer before joining his dutiful wife in peaceful slumber.

The parson slept well, but doubtless dreamed of Goliath.

Col. George Jackson - Indian Fighter, Pioneer, Adventurer and Mill Builder

BY GALE PRICE

From 1784 to 1929 a mill sat at the foot of Main Street hill in Clarksburg, near the present intersection of Main Street and Water Street. That mill was built by one of Harrison county's most dynamic early settlers, Col. George Jackson.

George Jackson was born in Cecil County, Maryland, Feb. 9, 1749. His father, John Jackson, moved west while George Jackson was small, going first to Moorefield, and then to a site on the Buckhannon River in 1769. In 1773, George Jackson entered a land claim of his own for 400 acres on the second Big Run.

Jackson was named captain of the band of Indian fighters organized at Buckhannon in 1779. Captain Jackson was prominent in defense of the area throughout the Revolutionary War. Accounts of his bravery and his commitment to duty abound. He commanded the scouts who maintained the line of blockhouses from Buckhannon to the Ohio River and was frequently out with scouting parties until the end of hostilities.

Harrison County was formed through the influence of Jackson and his fellow Buckhannon settlers. They argued that their Buckhannon River settlement was too far from Morgantown, the Monongalia County seat, to allow them access to their government. In October 1783, the Virginia General Assemblly authorized a poll of voters by the county sheriff for those settlers unable to journey to Morgantown to vote. The poll, not surprisingly, was to be taken at George Jackson's house.

The next year, Jackson got the rest of his wish. The Virginia Assembly assigned boundaries to Harrison County, and directed that the county court hold its first meeting at George Jackson's house on the Buckhannon River. That first court named Jackson Justice of the Peace, named Co. William Lowther sheriff, and gave Jackson permission to erect a mill on the Elk Creek at Clarksburg.

Jackson erected his mill in 1784, and moved to his new place of business in Clarksburg. His mill was the second in the county, the first being erected in 1776 a short distance upstream on Elk Creek at the entrance to the "narrows." George Jackson's mill was the first built with the express permission of the county court.

According to information in the "History of Harrison County" by Dorothy Davis, "The mill itself was a small log affair with millstones or buhrs, of native sandstone and cogwheels of wood. The mill which stood about one hundred feet south of the Main Street Bridge in Clarksburg, was rebuilt and equipped with machinery after wagons could be brought to the county. Jackson sold the business in 1815 to Dr. William Williams who opereted the mill until Sept. 24, 1829 when he sold it to Dr. Michael Gittings, who owned it for 24 years and probably changed from water power to steam power. The new owner, John S. Carlile, was the proprieter for only two years before the long-lived concern passed to Samuel R. Steel. In 1876, R. T. Lowndes and John Chorpening bought the mill after Steel went bankrupt; the Lowndes-Chorpening interests continued operating the money-making business until 1919. Finally, in 1923, the building fell to the last owner of the property, the Clarksburg Automobile Co., which tore down the structure in 1929."

Jackson increased his power and prestige with his move to Clarksburg. The county court moved to Clarksburg with Jackson, although it did meet at the house of Hezekiah Davisson, not Jackson's, until the court house was built in 1787.

Jackson established, again with the permission of the county court, a ferry across Elk Creek. In 1795, Jackson along with fellow commissioners William Robinson and William Haymond, were authorized to contract with someone to build a bridge across Elk Creek on Main Street. He clearly did not allow his interest in his ferry to stand in the way of progress.

Although he had no formal training in the law, Jackson was accepted before the Harrison County Bar in 1784. There is evidence that he may have practiced before that date, and that he may have represented clients before the Monongalia County Court.

He also continued his activities as an Indian fighter, and was qualified in open court as Lieutenant Colonel of Militia in 1787. There are accounts of his leading expeditions against the Indians as late as 1791.

George Jackson did not confine his interests to the Harrison County area, but was active in state and national politics as well. He served in the Virginia Convention to ratify the Constitution of the United States, where he voted in favor of the Constitution. He served six terms as a representative to the Virginia Assembly, and served three terms in the United States House of Representatives.

Col. George Jackson's self-taught manner and his frontier style evidently caused a bit of amusement in Philadelphia. Some members of Congress found one of his rough-phrased speeches amusing, and Jackson was provoked into saying he would go home and send his son John to Congress, and the members would not laugh then.

Jackson made good his threat a few years later. When he retired from Congress, his son John George Jackson ran for

and won his father's seat. John George Jackson had the formal education in the law his father lacked, and shared the dynamic bearing of his father. John George Jackson proved an influential member of Congress, as well as a highly successful businessman and public figure.

About 1806, Col. George Jackson left the Harrison County area. He moved West to the Zanesville, Ohio area, where he erected a mill and again began other enterprises. He represented his county in the Ohio Legislature and continued his vigorously active life. He died at his home in Zanesville in 1831.

George Jackson was a pioneer, an adventurer, and a builder. He was one of those people who look at a piece of land and see how they can transform it. With his vision, George Jackson helped create Harrison County. By raising his son, John George Jackson, with the same kind of vision, George Jackson helped mold Clarksburg's future. Though the mill George Jackson built in Clarksburg is long gone, the county he helped establish has reached its bicentennial and its county seat remains in the city he helped build.

A Phantom Deer Appeared

BY JAMES GAY JONES

Many of the early settlers who had little or no opportunity to acquire a formal education were, nevertheless, fully capable of adjusting to the rigorous environment in which they lived. They usually adapted quickly to new situations and sometimes faced situations they could not understand.

As a result, a lack of knowledge of some aspects of what they experienced would be filled in by their imagination and their training in the superstitions of the border. Consequently, there arose a substantial amount of folklore built around unusual happenings which, while often chilling in the initial

experience, continued to be highly entertaining in the retelling in less exciting times.

In the area of the upper Monongahela River Valley when it was still largely a wilderness, there appeared to a number of persons an unusually large phantom deer. What made it more

intriguing was that a phantom dog often made its appearance in the vicinity about the same time the deer was seen. Whenever those people who had observed the phenomena got together, they discussed and compared their experiences. In doing this, they hoped to dispel from their minds any lingering doubts they may have that what they had seen might have existed only in their imagination. In such discussions it was generally agreed that the similarities of their observations were sufficient evidence to prove the existence of the phantoms.

When John Holden set out early one morning to hunt deer, he purposely left his dog at home. Sometime later as he quietly moved through the woods, he saw a dog, which he thought was his own, come trotting past him and sniffing the ground as if trailing something. He whistled and spoke softly to it but it acted as if it did not know he was there. It ran back and forth a number of times and circled about him a time or two, but he was unable to gain its attention. What made it more uncanny was the fact that despite the dryness of the leaves through which it ran, the dog made no noise as it trotted about. Finally it made a wide circle and disappeared behind some buckberry bushes.

A half hour or so later, John was surprised to see a large deer standing alone in a wide clearing about 20 yards away. Since he was concealed by some bushes and with the wind coming in his direction, he was sure the buck was unaware of his being there. For a time John just stood there, awe-struck with the beauty of the scene. Then slowly he raised his momentarily to see his dog trot past again; on looking back to where the buck had stood, he saw that it was gone.

The open space which surrounded the spot where the deer had been standing was so extensive that it was practically impossible for it to have run to the adjacent woods without his having seen it go. He believed the only explanation for its sudden escape, no matter how illogical it might appear to some, was that it simply vanished in its tracks. Being somewhat unnerved by this experience, he had no further interest in hunting for the remainder of that day. On his return home, he noticed that his dog was leashed to a tree in the backyard where he had left it when he went out hunting earlier that day.

William Schoolcraft, who lived on the headwaters of the West Fork River, a tributary of the Monongahela, was a noted hunter and, for a time, was a school teacher in his comunity. Since he was better educated that the average person of his time and locality, some thought it quite uncharacteristic of him when he reported having had a strange experience with the phantom deer. Widely known for being a person of integrity and discreetness, the story he told was accepted as gospel truth.

Schoolcraft related that while out hunting one day, he saw a large buck standing on a narrow ridge some distance away. The ground was covered with snow at the time which seemed to give the deer a bolder and more striking appearance. Since there was a deep gulch between them, he did not try to get closer to the deer for fear of alarming it and scaring it away. Even though the distance to the point where the deer stood was considerable, Schoolcraft believed it well within range of his rifle; since he was a deadshot, he decided to fire at it from where he was standing.

After taking careful aim, he fired but the deer did not move. He quickly reloaded his gun and fired again but still there was no reaction from the deer. Now feeling considerable vexation, he again reloaded, took deliberate aim, and on the firing of his rifle for the third time, the deer disappeard.

Schoolcraft reloaded his rifle, then made his way across the gulch and up the hill toward the point where the deer had been standing. When he arrived at the place, a strange sensation came over him when he could find no tracks or any evidence that a deer had been there; the snow lay deep and unmarked by any living thing.

Still trying to view the incident in a logical way, he decided he could be mistaken about the location, when went back to where he had been when he shot the deer. He positioned himself in his former tracks and looked again toward the ridge. To his amazement he could clearly see his own trail in the snow which led directly to the place where the phantom deer had stood. Now completely baffled , he could only shake his head in disbelief. So it was considerable relief when he later heard that others, likewise, had seen the phantom deer.

Downtown Lumberport Once Site of Boatyard, Lumber-Grist Mill

By LLOYD LEGGETT

Settlers in the Lumberport area formed a frontier community on Jones Run shortly after the Revolutionary War years. Individuals who established homes in the settlement were Thomas Cunningham, John Hull, Captain Thomas Harbert, John Wood, Major Benjamin Robinson, Samuel Harbert, Nathan Reece and Peter Cornelius, John Cornelius and Elizabeth Cornelius.

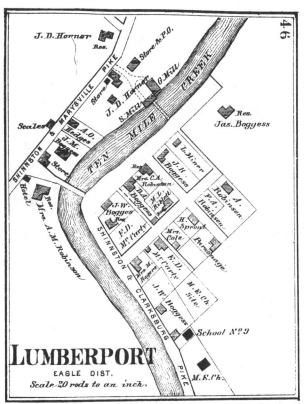

Major Robinson was granted permission by the county court on June 21, 1802, to build a dam across the Tenmile Creek and to erect a saw and grist mill on land owned by him. He originally had settled in the area around 1775.

"Ten Mile Creek" was the name of the first post office established on March 1, 1836. Below Major Robinson's mill, James Y. Hornor owned and operated a boat yard, where he loaded the vessels he built with lumber from the mill and when the water rose sufficiently high, floated the boats with their cargoes to Pittsburgh. "Ten Mile Creek" was in effect a Port for the lumber business. On March 31, 1838, the citizens of "Ten Mile creek" petitioned the Virginia Legislature for a charter including a "Plat of town of Lumberport containing eight and one-half acres. The above is a correct plat of the

town of Lumberport laid out pursuant to an act of Assembly of Virginia (signed) Thomas Robinson, James S. Griffin, J. Martin.'' The Virginia General Assembly on April 3, 1839, enacted ''that not exceeding ten acres of land, the property of James Y. Hornor and David Robinson (a son of Major Ben), lying on ten Mile Creek near Robinson's Mill in the county of Harrison, so soon as the same shall be laid off into lots with convenient streets and alleys, shall be and the same is hereby established a town by the name of 'Lumberport.' On December 19, 1838, the Post Office Department changed the name of the village office from ''Ten Mile Creek'' to ''Lumberport.''

William Ferguson established the first store in Lumberport sometime around 1833. Ferdinand Y. Hornor operated a store in the town in 1863, His business was raided by Jones's men during the civil war.

The Circuit Court of Harrison County, West Virginia, incorporated the town of Lumberport on Sept. 18, 1901. Officers elected at the first election were J. W. Wadsworth, mayor; J. E. Boggess, recorder; George D. Griffin, Lee Boggess, J. B. Payne, E. D. McCarty and L. M. Harter, councilmen. The town began to grow.

A. B. Sharp, who taught more than fifty years in Lumberport schools described the Lumberport he first saw in 1907:

''When we arrived in Lumberport, we came by train and found a small town, large enough to support a 4-room school located where the grade school stands in 1965.

''In 1907 Mr. Lee Boggess and family lived in the house now occupied by the Lumberport-Shinnston Gas Company. Mr. Boggess operated a general store on the corner of Bridge and Main Streets, which the Pure Oil Station now occupies. Mr. Walter Riblett was the clerk in the store. Mr. Boggess was also operating a livery barn near the Ten Mile Creek bridge. The large house that is still standing. Mr. James Stark lived in what is known as the Dr. Bates property. This home had been built by the late James D. Hornor. The Nancy Griffin family, consisting of Mrs. Nancy, Miss Narcissaa and Ellis E. Griffin and his wife, Eva, lived in the old brick home on the corner of Main and Chestnut streets, a residence now owned by Mrs. Florence Hill and a house said to be one of the oldest homes in Lumberport. Mr. Enoch McCarty ran the McCarty Hotel.

''A new Opera House had been built (1903) a short time before our arrival on the site where the post office building (dedicated May 20, 1961) now stand. The front of this structure was occupied by the Bank of Lumberport whose cashier was Mr. Vance L. Hornor. A small room by the side of the bank was used by Mr. Alden Sprout for a barber shop. One the top floor of the opera house was a lodge room. The rear of the building contained a large show house with a balcony. In 1907 regular shows were presented here by traveling troupes. The seats were not fastened to the floor so that the room could be used for dinners and other public gatherings. The school used the opera house to present their plays and programs.

''The old grist mill, which stood on the bank of Ten Mile

Creek and back of the present show house, belonged to the Hornor Hardware Company and was being operated by Gordon Cambric. The mill ground both corn and wheat, the wheat being ground by the roller process. It was in this mill that the late Michael Benedum, while being employed met with a serious accident which might have cost him his life but for the quick thinking of Mr. Cambric who shut off the machinery in which Mr. Benedum's arm was caught.

"In 1907 Grant McCarty operated a carriage shop in a building that stood back of the present Robinson Motor Co. building. The lower room was used for a blacksmith shop by Mr. Luther Harbert, the smith. The Odd Fellows Hall stood where the drugstore is now located. The first floor of the building was used for a drugstore operated by Dr. Roberts. John W. Wadsworth had a watch repairing business in a small building near where the three-story Martin building stand."

The current form of government stands as the typical strong council/mayor form. The mayor is elected for a 2-year term. A recorder is also elected to serve a 2-year term. The current mayor is Ronald G. Wright. The five council persons are Randy Barker, Frank Hall, Hoseph Hall, William McQuaid II and Charles "Bill" Reynolds. The recorder is Rick Scott.

The strength of Lumberport is not found in a booming industy, business center, or a higher educational institution. Lumberport's strength is in the fact that it is a nice town in which to live. It is far enough away from urban centers to offer its citizens solitude and a nice quiet place to live and rear chidren. And yet it is close enough to urban centers to offer cultural and social contacts needed for a well-balanced life. A citizen of Lumberport can have a good neighborhood that is peaceful and low in crime, while enjoying the benefits of the surrounding communities. Lumberport stands as a unique community among those communities which make up Harrison County in 1984.

Alexander Scott Withers - Writer

By NEVA WEEKS

In 1831, an interesting volume appeared from the press of Joseph Israel of Clarksburg in northwestern Virginia. The text on the border wars of the western section of the state was prepared by Alexander Scott Withers. It was well-received at the time of publication, when works on that subject were few, and was avidly read by descendants of the people so graphically described in the work.

Historians received it with high praise. Mann Butler, the historian of Kentucky, declared that it was "a work to which the public was deeply indebted," composed with "so much care and interest." The late Samuel G. Drake, the historian of the Red Man, said it was "a work written with candor and judgement." Having been issued in a remote corner of the state and being designed primarily for local circulation, almost every copy was read by a country fireside until scarcely legible. The author took great pains to be authentic, and his chronicles are considered by western historians to form the best collection of frontier life and Indian warfare that is printed. There are still a few original calf skin-bound copies to be found in the hands of collectors.

In 1829, in Covington, Va., Hugh Paul Taylor, published in the nearest village paper, "The Fincastle Mirror," a series of articles over the signature of "Son of Cornstalk." The series covered a period of 40 years from 1740 to the close of the Revolutionary War. Taylor had scarcely put these articles into print, when he died at an early age. These articles formed at least the chief authority for several of the earlier chapters of Withers' book.

Soon after Taylor's publication, Judge Edwin S. Duncan of Peel Tree, then Harrison County, residing in the heart of the region rife with stories of Indian wars and hair-breadth escapes, made a collection of materials, probably including Taylor's publication, but his professional and judicial services were so great that he turned over to Withers his historic gatherings.

Other writers in the field of western history, particularly Noah Zane of Wheeling and John Hacker of the Hacker's Creek settlement, freely furnished their notes and statements for the work. William Powers, along with Hacker, provided much of the source material for the book and Powers purchased Hacker's interests in the notes and statements following the latter's death. Joseph Israel subsequently bought the manuscript and employed Withers to prepare it for publication.

Withers had a wealth of materials regarding the first settlements, Indian wars of the region now comprising West Virginia, information concerning Dunmore's War, and material concerning several military campaigns from the western borders of Virginia and Pennsylvania into the Ohio region during the Revolutionary War.

Withers for his good services in the field of western history, well deserves to have his name and memory perpetuated as a public benefactor. Descending, on his father's side, from English ancestry, he was the fourth of nine children in the family of Enoch K. and Jannet Chinn Withers, who resided at a homestead called Green Meadows near Warrenton, Va. It was here he was born Oct. 12, 1792 — the third centennial anniversary of the discovery of America by Columbus. His mother was the daughter of Thomas Chinn and Jannet Scott, born in Scotland and a first cousin of Sir Walter Scott.

Spending his early years in home and private schools, he became a lover of books. He read Virgil at the age of ten; and in due time entered Washington College and later studied law at William and Mary College where he received his degree, and was admitted to the bar in Warrenton. He practiced there for three years. His father died in 1813 and he abandoned his law practice (which he did not like) and for a period of time managed his mother's plantation.

In August 1815 he married Melinda Fisher, a most estimable lady a few years his junior, and by 1827 he had a growing family, consisting of two sons and three daughters. He looked to the great West for his future home and field of labor and moved to western Virginia. He first located in Bridgeport where he devoted much time in collecting materials and writing his "Chronicles of Border Warfare."

In June 1941 Mrs. John J. Lang of Bridgeport wrote: "Hidden away from the public eye, at the end of a country lane just three miles south of Bridgeport on Rt. 23, is the farm once owned by Alexander Scott Withers, and where he wrote the book "Chronicles of Border Warfare." He bought this farm in 1826 and resided here from five to seven years, writing almost continually during these years.

"My grandfather, Parker Pepper, knew him well. I have heard my mother recall how he asked him one day 'Why don't you cut the bushes and weeds near your door?'

" 'When I finish this book, I shall pay someone else to cut them,' Withers replied."

CHRONICLES

OF

BORDER WARFARE,

OR

A HISTORY

OF THE

SETTLEMENT BY THE WHITES,

OF NORTH-WESTERN VIRGINIA:

AND

OF THE INDIAN WARS AND MASSACRES,

IN THAT SECTION OF THE STATE,

WITH

REFLECTIONS, ANECDOTES, &c.

BY ALEXANDER S. WITHERS.

CLARKSBURG, VA.

PUBLISHED BY JOSEPH ISRAEL,

1831

The publisher, Joseph Israel, took deep interest in the work, as his advertisement of it suggests. He must have realized ample recompense for the work, as he had subscribers for the full edition issued; yet for some cause, he failed pecuniarily, and Withers received nothing for his diligence and labor in producing it, save two or three copies of his work. He used to say, that had he published the volume himself, he would have made it much more complete, and better in every way; for he was hampered, limited, and hurried —often correcting proof of the early, while writing the later chapters.

After this worthy but unremunerative labor, Withers turned his attention to Missouri for a suitable home for his old age. He was disappointed in his visit to that new state as the richer portions of the country, where he would have located, were more or less unhealthy. So he returned to West Virginia, and settled near Weston in Lewis County, a fine healthful region of hills and valleys. Here he engaged in agricultural pursuits and served several years as a magistrate.

The death of his wife in September 1853 broke sadly into his domestic enjoyments. His family was now scattered and his home was made with his eldest daughter, Mrs. Jannet S. Tavenner, and her husband, Thomas Tavenner, who in 1861 moved to a home near Parkersburg. Here Withers lived a retired, studious life, until his death occurred on Jan. 23, 1865. He is buried in the Hill Cemetery in Weston.

Withers had no talent for the acquisition of wealth, but he met with marked success in acquiring knowledge. He was an admirer of ancient literature, and in his last days read the Greek classics in the original. A rare scholar, a lover of books, his tastes were eminently domestic. He was, from his nature, much secluded from the busy work about him. Nearly six feet tall, rather portly and dignified, he was kind and obliging to all. He was a true Virginia gentleman of the old school, and a pioneer in his own right in the history of Harrison County and the frontier life in Trans-Allegheny Virginia.

Voting in Virginia - In The Late 1700s

By DOROTHY DAVIS

To vote in Virginia in the late 1700s a man must travel to the county seat, enter the courthouse, and after a clerk had announced his name, speak the name of the person for whom he wished to vote. A second clerk then registered the vote in a poll book.

The voter had no problems remembering the names of the candidates, for other than a vote for a presidential elector once every four years, the only offices for which a citizen cast a ballot were for a memer of the U.S. House of Representatives and for state legislators. The Virginia governor appointed the sheriff and the justices who in turn appointed other county officers. The Virginia Assembly elected the two U.S. senators.

Citizens in the Tygart's Valley complained so loudly about the inconvenience of a trip to the county seat in Morgantown to vote that in 1783, a few months before the legislature passed an act to form Harrison County out of Monongalia County, it authorized the sheriff of Monongalia County to travel to the house of George Jackson on the Buckhannon River to hold a special election for people on land drained by the Tygart's Valley River. One reason people on the West Fork River did not complain was that their stream, less rocky that the Tygart's Valley, could be navigated in the election months of November and April by canoe.

The choice of Clarksburg in 1784 for a county seat did not solve the voting problems of Tygart's Valley River settlers. Three years later they asked and were given the new county of Randolph because they said it was inconvenient to reach the

Harrison County courthouse. And the same complaint from people on the Ohio River caused Wood County to be cut out of Harrison in 1798.

Voters at the Harrison County courthouse who announced their vote for an elector at the first presidential election in 1789 showed their displeasure of voting for the sole candidate, Robert Rutherford, whom they did not know. While 112 dutifully voted for Federalist Rutherford, 18 announced the name of William Haymond who was the principal surveyor of Harrison County and a man the voters knew even though "Haymond did not offer himself as a candidate and neither was he present at the time he was voted for."

Not being present showed that Haymond had no wish to be chosen for candidates were expected to be present at the election held in their home county and to speak to the crowd in the courthouse square. Sometimes a window sash was removed from the courthouse so that the speaker would have a place to stand. Sometimes a candidate would have a barrel of whiskey rolled into the square, the head knocked out and tin

cups hung around on the barrel, and all his supporters invited to partake. Revelry followed as well as fist fights, quarrels and general hilarity.

The presidential election of 1840 created more uproar and excitement in the county than any election before or since. The so-called "Log Cabin and Hard Cider" campaign took place between the Whig candidate William Henry Harrison and the Democratic candidate President Martin Van Buren. The sedate and aristocratic Whigs knew that in order to win the election they must avoid being labeled the old Federalist Party and that they must stir up enough excitement to disguise the fact that they were really "a discordant combination of the odds and ends of all parties." A banner "We Stoop to Conquer" carried in a Whig parade in Baltimore on May 4, 1840, epitomized the spirit of the Whig campaign planned from the start to capture the imagination of the common man much as Andrew Jackson had stirred the masses in 1828 and 1832. The Whigs resolved to "prostrate our opponents with the ... weapons, with which they beat us."

After an anti-Whig newspaper had derided Harrison with "Give him a barrel of hard cider and a pension of two thousand a year, and, our word for it, he will sit the remainder of his days in a log cabin," the Whigs turned the statement into slogan and symbols for the campaign: "Log cabin and hard cider." The campaign was the most remarkable ever known and did immensely solidify the people into party ranks. Prior to the time parties had been largely among the politicians and governing class. Now the voters ranged themselves on one side or the other and entered the struggle with intense feeling. The Whigs took advantage of the situation very skillfully and out demagogued the Democrats. They became the champion of the "poor man" against such "aristocrats" as Martin Van Buren, who (the Whigs insisted) actually had gold spoons upon his table. Those around him carried gold headed canes and devoured the people of substance The much belabored, frilled and ruffled shirt which the Whigs had been accused of wearing was not worn by Van Buren and his satellites. On the other hand Gen. William H. Harrison ... was a pioneer, who after his brilliant services to the country was content to live in a log cabin and drink hard cider instead of the costly wines served at Van Buren's tables....

The log cabin with the raccoon skin on the door became the party emblem, hard cider the party beverage. A log cabin of buckeye logs, where this timber abounded, was raised in every Whig settlement. Songs celebrating Harrison's victories at Tippecanoe and the Thames took precedence of oratory. "Tippecanoe and Tyler too" became the campaign slogan. The country went wild with enthusiasm, and the popular demonstrations exceeded anything known up to the time of the Civil War. Farmers named their horses "Tip and Ty." A couple in Cincinnati baptized their twins Harrison and Tyler; another Whig couple named their triplets William, Henry, and Harrison; the Thomas A. Horner family who lived on Duck Creek in Harrison County, would name the son born to them in 1841 William Henry Harrison. Every time western hens laid eggs they reputedly cackled 'Tip-tip! Tip, tip! Tyler!' A U.S. senator in 1840 described the ethusiasm thus: "Since the world began there was never before in the West such a glorious excitement and uproar among the people."

Late in the summer of 1840 William McGranaghan started publication of "The Harrison Whig" in Clarksburg with the words: "He (Harrison) is one of Virginia's own sons, and a true representative of the Virginia blood. As Virginians — as citizens of Harrison County, a name for which we are indebted to his illustrious father, one of themost efficient patriots of the Revolution, we are proud to do him honor — proud to be ranked among those who consider him entitled to the highest honor in the gift of free people."

Believing that "The steam must be kept up," the triumvirate running the Whig campaign nationally — Thurlow Weed, Horace Greely, and Wiliam H. Seward, encouraged politicians in the centers of Whig culture to stage series of activities. In Wheeling Whigs raised in August a liberty pole 321 feet high "the tallest and best Harrison pole in the Union," and sent out word that a "Great Democratic Whig Convention of the three great states, Pennsylvania, Ohio and Virginia," would be held in Wheeling on September 3, 1840.

A group of "forty or fifty" men from Clarksburg, decided to join the fun in Wheeling. The men traveled on horseback reaching Middlebourne the first night on the road and Moundsville the second night. The next morning they arrived in Wheeling: "their horses were turned out on pasture and the company assigned quarters. Wheeling ready for more than 30,000 visitors stocked "a public table with 360 hams, (meat from) 26 sheep, 20 calves, 1,500 pounds of beef, 8,000 pounds of bread, 1,000 pounds of cheese, and 4,500 pies."

It was a wonder how a place the size of Wheeling could contain such a mass of people, but they did it with the most extraordinary liberality and kindness, without money or price. Parlors, halls, porches, stables were used to sleep in and when they were filled those not so fortunate as to get shelter slept on the lawns.

Parades, speeches, music were the order of the day and a great time was had.

The party did not return in a body, but broke up into groups and returned by different routes. All reached home safely.

Harrison was elected and the Whigs all over the country went wild with joy as they were not accustomed to electing presidents.

Clarksburg illuminated and to make things lively, someone set a deserted house on fire, which stood on the hill back of Hornor Avenue, which added more fire and light to the jollification. It was a great time, and the old town was painted red in honor of the occasion.

Tour Offers Guide Down The Path of 'Yesterday'

By MYRA LITHERLAND

Just outside your own front door, a pleasant sojourn into Harrison County's past awaits.

It's a little like the exciting trip Dorothy took over the rainbow into the Land of Oz. Once there, she saw common, everyday things and places - sights familiar to her, scenes she took for granted - in a way she never had before.

The Harrison County excursion holds no sinister tornado to fling one over the rainbow into a strange and magical place - it only offers a threshold to cross, your own automobile or a sturdy pair of walking shoes, and a guide to some fascinating historical landmarks in the area.

The scenario may be nowhere as exotic as the Land of Oz, but it can be fully as entertaining.

Actually, a compilation of five separate excursions, the Harrison County Bicentennial Tour, created as a part of the countys' current 200th anniversary celebration, is the product of months of research and study by two county residents, Barbara Brennan Highland and George Ashby Short.

Mrs. Highland, with much invaluable assistance lent by such people as Emily Harrison Windoes of Clarksburg, began work on the project late in the summer of 1983, delving into volumes of early Harrison County data. Short joined her several months later to compile the necessary maps of the area.

Recently in beautiful old Waldomore's second-floor geneological rooms, steeped in its gentle aura of yesterday, Mrs. Highland and Short paused at one of the room's long library tables to discuss their monumental project, and how and why they became involved in it.

"I grew up on East Main Street", Mrs. Highland explained, "in the house that my great-grandparents built.

My grandmother was born in 1850, and lived to be 92," she continued, adding that the tales of early county history she heard recounted "at her grandmother's knee" kindled her first fires of area historical appreciation.

That appreciation grew as she did, so that for her the compilation of the needed information was literally a labor of love.

Mrs. Highland said she began by delving reams of material, both at West Virginia University and the Clarksburg-/Harrison Public Library. She also conducted extensive interviews with area senior citizens, to glean from them recollections of an earlier way of life.

The result was a volume of material so extensive it was almost too weighty to handle, and she was forced to begin a process of elimination.

"I found that I couldn't include things in the tour that aren't here anymore," Mrs. Highland said. "For instance, the first sawmill in Shinnston - How can you tell people that on that site a sawmill once stood, but it's not there now? I couldn't do that - I had to concentrate on existing buildings and landmarks.

"Also, a theme for the tour was necessary, and I started out with 'Transportation in Harrison County,' in keeping with the theme of the Bicentennial celebration, but I had to abandon it. I couldn't do it in the time frame I had."

The multi-talented George Short, relatively silent up to that point, spoke up.

He explained that he hadn't attempted to record every road in the county on his maps, but had concentrated upon "the main roads, where the points of interest were."

He echoed Mrs. Highland's feelings that only existing points of interest should be included on the maps. "I decided it had to show Harrison County as it is, not how it was," he said.

Short, a native of Shinnston, is an accomplished artist and photographer. He returned to this area in 1979 after living in Ohio, then retiring to California, where he studied art as a means of enhancing his photographic talents.

Upon his return to West Virginia, he found, upon studying accounts of early Shinnston history, virtually nothing recorded about life during the first quarter of the century in that area. "That was the time I was growing up there," he said. "I found no mention of families and places I knew existed.

There was a big gap in the historical data."

Short decided to remedy the situation and put his recollections into print, writing on "The Cultural and Industrial Development of Shinnston."

As a result, he was asked to speak before members of the Shinnston Historical Society.

"I ended up being president of the group!" Short said, adding that he went on to address the Harrison County Historical Society in Clarksburg, and ultimately was named president of that group, also.

In fact, he was head of both groups concurrently for a three-year period.

Other involvement included membership in the Sons of the Revolution and the Harrison County Bicentennial Steering Committee. Through that, he became involved with the tour cartography.

The end result of the pair's "teamwork" was the Harrison County Bicentennial tour. With its five separate excursions outlined, it includes both walking and driving trips.

The walking tour encompasses the downtown Clarksburg area, but as the pair explained, many streets were omitted from the map for the sake of convenience.

"If we had included them all, it would just have gotten too confusing," Mrs. Highland explained. "We just concentrated on the streets where the historic sites are located; and there are some areas we had to leave out, where there are some really fine, old homes. If we'd included everything, the route would have zig-zagged back and forth and been nothing but a maze."

She added that only the exterior of many of the historic old buildings listed on the city tour may be viewed - they're private residences and not open to the public. "We have to respect the privacy of the people who live there," Mrs.

Highland stressed, but added that most public places are accessible.

The Harrison County Bicentennial Tours include:

Number 1, Sites 1-13 - Southeastern Harrison County, a beautiful 42-mile rural driving tour encompassing the West Milford - Lost Creek areas. It covers such areas as the Civil War earthworks atop Lowndes Hill; the circa 1840 authentically-restored log cabin home of Mr. and Mrs. A. M. Quilly Ward of Peel Tree, and Haymond Cemetery, where Major William Haymond Sr., sergeant under Col. George Washington in the French and Indian War and officer in the Revolutionary War, is buried.

Number 2, Sites 14-23 - Northeastern Harrison County, the Bridgeport area, entered on Route 50, from the West. It includes the William Johnson house, on the corner of Main and Virginia, circa 1840, built by William Johnson, the brother of Governor Joseph Johnson; the Benedum Civic Center, the restored home of oil wildcatter and philanthropist Michael Late Benedum, now housing the city's public library as well as a community swimming pool located on the grounds, and the W. T. Law covered bridge, built over Simpson Creek in 1881. The bridge recently suffered storm damage, but restoration plans are currently underway.

Number 3, Sites 24-50 - Northern Harrison County, the Shinnston-Lumberport area, one of the more extensive tours in the group, highlights such historic landmarks as the Maulsby Bridge in Gypsy. Only the piers remain of Harrison County's longest and most celebrated covered bridge, the site of the Jones-Imboden raid during the Civil War, in 1863; the Levi Shinn house, one of the state's oldest dwellings. Built in 1778 by Jonathan and Clement Shinn who settled Shinnston, the log house is open to the public occasionally, and the Nancy Griffin house in Lumberport, built by Henry Clay Hedges, one of the oldest in town. It is said that the original part of the house was a log building, possible built as a fort.

Number 4, Sites 51-55 - Western Harrison County, the Salem area, a drive of about 35 miles, which includes the site of the Salem Blockhouse, pinpointed by a marker. Under the side porch of the cottage directly across the road from the marker is the well that supplied water to the first community of Salem in the 1790s, and Fort New Salem, built in the late 1960s for use by students in the Heritage Arts Division of Salem College's Art Department. It consists of log structures donated by landowners in surrounding counties, arranged in the style of a settlement of the 1770s. Heritage arts demonstrations are conducted on the grounds of the fort, which is open to the public weekends from late April through October.

Number 5, Sites 1-38 - The City of Clarksburg walking tour, which includes a pleasant stroll past such areas as the Stuck Log Cabin on Chestnut Street, believed to be the only log house in the city; Christ Episcopal Church, with its lovely stained-glass windows, built in 1853 on land donated by Burton Despard, and the Stealey-Goff Vance House, built in 1807 by Jacob Stealey, a tanner. After several periods of private ownership through the years, today the house is the headquarters of the Harrison County Historical Society, in addition to serving as a museum.

This list of Harrison County historical points of interest barely skims the surface - a plethora of others is detailed in the self-guided tour brochure. Although there are many areas to be visited, each tour's directions are clear, concise and simple to follow, and because each can be taken at one's convenience and leisure, they're sure to be pleasurable, as well as educational.

Harrison County's no "Fairy-Tale Land," but an excursion through the area, with the direction of Mrs. Highland and George Short's comprehensive guide, is certain to be as enjoyable as any odyssey through "Oz."

The illustrated guides, which include all five tours, are available at both the Clarksburg/Harrison Public Library and at the Clarksburg Chamber of Commerce office.

I Wasn't Scared, But Didn't Care to Stay And Hunt for That Dog

BY WILLIAM B. PRICE

The clock was just striking four in the morning when I was awakened by my wife calling my name, "Hars! Hars Turner! Wake up!"

Now when I sleep, I sleep — and am in no hurry to get up at four o'clock, but I did open my eyes.

I asked, "What in the world is the matter Matilda?" I thought it strange that she was already up and dressed.

"Pa," she said. "I've been most uneasy all this night, and I've had the most horrible dream three times already."

I told her to lie down a minute and tell me her dream, because she always said a dream would not come true if told before breakfast.

"Yes, Pa," she said, "I must tell it all and then I'll get breakfast while you feed the horses and cows."

This is the dream as she told it on that early morning in the spring of 1869:

"Pa, I heard screaming in Bart's house; then a figure left the house and ran through the fog to the barn. Suddenly a light appeared at the door, and a figure carrying a lantern entered the barn; another figure dashed out of another door and ran back to the house. There were more screams and something that sounded like blows on flesh, then all was still. An' Pa, I dreamed that same dream three times. It was so clear and real I just had to get up, and then I thought I'd better wake you."

I got up, reassured her it was only a dream, started a fire in the fireplace, lit a lantern, and went to the barn to feed the horses and cows while she got breakfast.

After breakfast, we lit a lantern and went to the barn to milk. It had been foggy when I went to the barn earlier, but now the fog seemed to roll up from the creek like a great gray blanket, so thick that the lantern scarcely lighted the path ahead of us.

We had almost finished milking when there came a "Hello," from the big road. Going to the cowshed door, I answered, "Hello!"

"Mr. Turner! Mr. Turner! There's trouble down at Bart's place. Will you come down to the road?" I recognized the voice of one of the Stephens boys.

Well, I went to the road and the boy told me that one of Bart's girls had come to their house about three o'clock and told them that her dad had hit the two little kids in the trundle bed with a poker, that her mother had run screaming to the barn, and that her dad had lighted a lantern and followed her. She had run out the back door to the Stephens' house. She was afraid her father had killed the two little children and wanted the neighbors to try to do something. The boy asked me if it would be all right for the neighbors to come to my place to decide what to do. I told him that would be fine.

Pretty soon more than a dozen men were at our place ready to help if they were needed. Wat Dye, who was a natural leader, was asked to make the plans for approaching the house.

It was decided that Wat and I ride down the road to Bart's place and call him from the big road and engage him in conversation while the other men moved closer to the house from the woods.

When we reached Bart's house, Wat called several times before the door was cautiously opened and Bart's face appeared. Wat said, "Bart, 'I'm having a logrolling Saturday and would like for you to come down and help. I have a barrel of cider that hasn't been opened and we'll have plenty to drink as well as plenty to eat.''

"I can't come as I won't be home," said Bart.

"We'll need you badly, Bart, and would like for you to bring your mule and a pair of grab hooks. Gonna be a lot of logs to roll if I get that patch ready for corn.''

As we talked, the door opened wider and Bart stepped out on the porch. By this time we could see the men coming to the back of the house, and we tried to keep Bart talking loudly so he wouldn't hear them.

Said Wat, "Bart, do you have a log chain and a cant hook you could bring along Saturday?''

Bart began to get louder and yelled, "I tell ya, I hain't going to be at home.''

About that time the door behind the man opened and Bart was seized by two of the Rowe boys. A pair of check lines were wrapped around him, and he was tied to a tree in the yard where he raved and struggled to free himself.

Inside the house, the little children were found in a trundle bed where they had died from the blows of a heavy poker.

The mother had been strangled and lay on the floor of the kitchen, partly covered by an overturned table. The buckwheat batter she had mixed the evening before had risen and had run over the crock onto the hearth of the kitchen fireplace.

Several slices of pork shoulder were already in the skillet for frying the morning meal. The salt gourd by the side of the fireplace lay on the floor with the salt scattered on the hearth. On the floor was a tablecloth from the overturned table, three broken plates and two shiny bowls from which the two small children usually ate.

The hand of a good woman was in evidence in the neat old-fashioned kitchen, but now that hand lay cold and still in death partly covered by a piece of a broken blue bowl. On the mantle a kerosene lantern still burned. By its side were two little cornshuck dolls with shoe-button eyes. Also, on the mantle, a big square clock ticked away the minutes.

We sent word to my wife and some of the other women to come and look after the dead woman and the children.

Hank Danks rode to the post office and brought the justice of the peace who lived there. Wat Dye and the justice soon had a paper written up and Bart was taken to Clarksburg to be placed in the county jail.

During the wake, a dense fog rolled up from the bottom, and a ghostly figiure in white appeared, bearing a light and moving from the barn toward the house. Then it disappeared, and a sound like a moaning child followed by a scream of terror — all faint and sounding far away — were heard by those watching by the side of the three homemade coffins.

After the funeral, the house was closed and the surviving child was sent to live with an aunt down the creek from Bart's place. Bart was later adjudged insane and sent to Weston State Hospital some 25 miles down the river. A sale was held to dispose of Bart's property, and the money was placed in trust for the little girl.

The house was closed up and I went down there to get the dog. It was a foggy night, and, when I saw a light on the road, I supposed it was a neighbor and went on. I was surprised when the light seemed to move toward the house. Of course I wasn't scared, but somehow I didn't care to stay around and hunt for that dog. I went home! After that the light was seen most often early in the morning when a fog rolled up the hill from the valley.

One night Si Funk was coming past Bart's place, walking real fast. He wanted to run but had often heard that a person running from a ghost would run himself to death. On this particular night he had just passed the farm gate which led to the barn when he heard a noise behind him. When he glanced back, something ghostly and white loomed in the road moving toward him. He forgot all about the admonition not to run and started down the road. All the while he could hear footsteps following behind. As he wondered what to do, he remembered that he had heard that a ghost would not cross a stream of water. Recent rains had filled the nearby creek to the top of its banks. Si made for the creek. As he struck the water, he bailed out the whole creek in a single splash and then landed on the other side. Sure enough, the ghost was gone. The next day a neighbor found tracks in the muddy road where a man had been running; also the footprints of an animal with cloven hooves.

Si Funk himself told the story of his narrow escape the next time he came to the post office, Wat Dye just heehawed and " 'lowed as how the devil waz jus' pertectin' his property.'' He didn't tell poor Si that a pet steer of his would follow anyone —especially if the person were running.

During the summer there was no fog, and no lantern or light was seen. Then, as a young man who had been courting his girl was returning to his home in the early morning hours, he heard that awful scream from the kitchen and he saw the light at the cabin and the running figure moving toward the barn. He wasn't a cowardly fellow, but, somehow, he didn't stop to inquire as to what was going on.

Once when old Nancy Forney — returning home from a baby case — saw the moving lantern, she ran after the figure and asked "What in the name of the Father and the Son and the Holy Ghost do you want?" The figure stopped and held the light high above his head, and there was heard a mournful scream as if some soul were in torment. The wind sighed through the big white pine by the cabin, a screech owl called from a nearby thicket. Then, the light went out and all was still.

Bart continued to live at the hospital, and when fog enveloped the great stone building he often raved and then seemed to be in another place. He seemed to feel that someone was after him, trying to take him away. Sometimes he called his wife's name and then called for her to protect him from some danger.

Upon checking with the folks of the neighborhood in which Bart had lived, it was learned that the lantern and the figure were seen at his home place at exactly the same time he had the raving spells and the blackouts in the hospital. Groans were sometimes heard coming from the bedroom where the little ones were found in the trundle bed or from the kitchen where Mrs. Bart's body was found cold in death.

It is said that a shanty man who came to the neighborhood decided to live at the place while engaged in building one of the covered bridges for which that locality was noted. He was a bridge builder by trade, and by no means a tramp in any sense of the word. He knew nothing of the ghastly murders that had been committed there, and, of course, nothing about the running figure or the light. He had been there for perhaps a week when, suddenly, early one morning, he heard a scream and several thuds as if something were striking flesh. This was followed by the moaning of childish voices, and a flash of light that seemed to follow a fleeing figure to the barn and then back to the house from which came a scream and more thudding blows in the kitchen.

The man thought it had all been a dream and said nothing about it. Later, when the bridge was almost finished, he heard the tale about the murders and the reappearance of the light and the running figure. He then told of his own experience remembering that it had been during a night of heavy fog.

It is said that a teamster, by the name of Barns, who did not believe any of the tales he had heard was obliged to leave a loaded wagon in front of the old barn at Bart's place. When he returned the next morning about four o'clock and saw a light near his wagon, he thought nothing of it, as it was still quite dark and very foggy. He was riding one of his horses and leading the other. Since the horses were harnessed, the trace chains made a jangling noise as they passed over rough spots in the road.

As he neared the wagon, Barnes saw the silhouette of a large man holding the light high above his head. "Hello," Barnes shouted.

Then, suddenly the light went out and the fog lifted, leaving neither man nor lantern.

Bye and bye a new owner moved into Bart's old house. He placed a gas light in the yard which lighted the whole area between the house and the barn. Then Bart died and the mysterious moving-light was seen no more.

'Chained Down To Hell's Brazen Floor... To Rain Cinders Of Black Damnation To Fry Out The Fat Of Your Pride And Grease The Dungeons Of Hell With'

By DOROTHY DAVIS

Energetic missionaries of the Baptist and Methodist churches with a belief in democratic church organization, fiery evangelism, and a lay clergy moved through the frontier soon after the first settlers arrived.

James Sutton, a Baptist minister traveling from Redstone (Uniontown), gathered in 1774 a group of settlers on Simpson Creek in present Harrison County into the first Baptist church to be formed in Northwestern Virginia. Methodist Bishop Asbury preached in Clarksburg in July 1788.

The difficulties met by the traveling clergy are caught by Bishop Asbury's description: "We journeyed on through devious lonely wilds, where no food might be found, except what grew in the woods or was carried with us. We met with two women who were going to see their friends and attend the

A dedicated circuit preacher. No matter what the odds against him were, he always kept going. If his horse died, he walked. His dedication lasted throughout his lifetime.

quarterly meeting in Clarksburg. Near midnight we stopped at A_____'s, who hissed his dogs on us; but the women were determined to get to the quarterly meeting, so we went in. Our supper was tea. Brother Theobus and Cook took to the woods; old _____ gave up his bed to the women. I lay along the floor on the few deer skins with the fleas. That night our poor horses got no corn; the next morning they had to swim across the Monongahela. After a twenty-mile ride we came to Clarksburg; and man and beast were so outdone that it took us ten hours to accomplish it. I lodged with Col. Jackson."

Bishop Asbury presided over the quarterly meeting in a building owned by Daniel Davisson. A Hopewell Baptist church which stood on West Main Street in Clarksburg disappeared soon after 1802. Ira Chase, a clergyman sent by the Baptist Convention to report on the state of religion in Clarksburg, wrote in 1818: "Nothing but the graveyard appeared where the Hopewell meeting house once stood... There was no church of any denomination and there were but few, very few, professors of religion, and some of these were not very correct in their morals. On Lord's Day I preached in the Court House to a very small assembly and again in the evening."

Despite Rev. Chase's dreary report, the frontier church was far from dead. The Hopewell Baptist Church is said to have joined with members of the Seventh Day Baptist Church who had dropped out from the group bound for Salem in 1790 and had stopped near Hepzibah. They had formed a society which would organize the Hepzibah Baptist Church in 1822. So many small Baptist churches formed all over the county at such sites as Coon's Run, Center Branch, Brushy Fork, Jones Run that by 1838 nine churches in Harrison County were dismissed by their mother association to form a new Broad Run Association.

Methodist circuit riders had organized in the 1780s Methodist societies in the homes of Jonathan Shinn in the present town of Shinnston; Benjamin Webb's near Bridgeport; and Isaac Washburn's at Good Hope.

The fiery evangelism of the Great Awakening, which began along the Eastern Seaboard in the 1720s and reached Eastern Virginia in the middle of the Eighteenth century, appeared in the western mountains in the 1780s and lingered through the Nineteenth century in the form of camp meetings and revival, or protracted, meetings.

Camp meetings occurred in the fall during harvest. Entire families traveled as far as 20 or 30 miles with supplies to camp for the week that the religious meeting continued in the open air. A Clarksburg newspaper advertised on July 24, 1824, "a Camp meeting at Sickamore Creek, Harrison County, on the road leading from Clarksburg to Weston, on the old ground, west side of the river, to commence on the 16th day of September next, and to continue for five or six days, at which time and place we invite the serious of every order to meet on the ground, and join with us to implore the mercy of God and to promote our own salvation."

Lorenzo Dow, the great traveling preacher preached in Clarksburg in the '30s. He preached his sermon in the grove near the Monticello Spring but the preacher who could draw the largest crowds at camp metings and revivals in general was the Rev. Samuel Clawson. He preached the doctrine of eternal damnation and pictured the future punishment of the wicked in such vivid terms that even the rough element of Clarksburg grew decent for a time at least after his visit.

John C. Johnson wrote this description of the church revivals held in Bridgeport in the late 1800s: "Many great revivals, called protracted meetings, were held in (the Brick Church)... and the firey eloquence of Rev. Samuel Clawson and others aroused the greatest enthusiasm. The church was always crowded, and people came for miles to attend the meetings. Order was not always as good as it should be, and men sometimes came to meetings with a bottle of firewater in their pockets. Rev. Clawson once rebuked some bad behavior in the following language: 'Thank God, the day is not far distant when you will be chained down to Hell's brazen floor, and the devil, with his three-pronged harpoon, will pierce your reeking heart and rain down on you cinders of black damnation to fry out the fat of your pride to grease the dungeons of Hell with.' "

Mr. Clawson never remained long in one place. His parting remark was usually that he had "another half acre of hell to grub out" in the community to which he was going.

The camp meetings supplied the double purpose of religious instruction and social enjoyment. They lasted from one to two weeks during which the families shut up their homes and lived in tents and shacks on the camp ground. Great quantities of food were prepared and taken to the grounds and further cooking was carried on at huge camp fires. Three services were held each day and between times the people enjoyed a social intercourse not possible during the labors of the rest of the year.

The longest-lived camp meeting in Harrison County occurred each year at Gypsy from the 1840s until the second decade of the 20th century. By the 1870s meetings at the campground in the grove of ancient chestnut trees on the farm of Aaron Vincent were an institution. People met for reigious services in a large square. On the west side was the preacher's stand, a raised platform with a roof and open on all sides. The seats on both sides of a center aisle were two-inch-thick planks placed on small logs that in turn rested on stone supports. Lighting for the evening services was furnished by torches made of tin buckets with bails and lids; on the side of the containers were one or two spouts equipped with candle wicking. Filled with kerosene, the buckets were hung on the tree trunks and lighted.

Surrounding the site for meetings were family-owned "tents," rough buildings planked up and down Yankee style and a story and a half in height. Harvey W. Harmer, a former Clarksburg attorney, recalled in 1944: "In 1878 the camp meetings began on Aug. 21 and closed on Aug. 28. My father had a tent on the ground and we always moved out there for the camp meetings taking two wagon loads of furniture and a cow."

The preachers' tent to which tentholders contributed furnishings was occupied by 10 or more ministers. A boarding (food service) tent and a huckster tent helped to frame the place of worship. Assisted by his brother, Frank Woolard sold candy, cigars, peanuts and watermelons which were hauled by wagon from Clarksburg.

After the building of the Monongahela River Railroad in 1888, the camp meeting in its closing years had its largest attendance. H. G. Bowles superintendent of the railroad, on one occasion brought as speaker famed Georgia evangelist, Rev. Sam Jones, and ran 15 special trains that carried 15,000 people, some of them from as far away as Parkersburg, to the campground.

Bridge at Millford...
A Vital Link On The West Milford And New Salem Turnpike
MRS. CREEL CORNWELL SR.

Nestled among beautiful rolling hills and stately woodlands, the picturesque community of West Milford has an interesting, historical background.

In 1807 George Bush conveyed a 130-acre tract of land to Jesse Lowther, fourth of Col. William Lowther's five sons, born July 21, 1773, and the first white child born in the Lowther Settlement located about one and a half miles north of present-day West Milford. Richards Fort near Sycamore protected the settlers — William Runion, Conrad and Isaac Richards, Charles and Isaac Washburn, Richard Kincheloe, John Neeley, James Kain, John Yerkey, William Carder, George Post, Jacob McConkey, William Lowther and Lowther's sons Robert, Thomas, William, Jesse and Elias — in case the Indians should attack.

In 1772 Col. Lowther and his brothers-in-law Jesse and Elias Hughes, starting from the present site of Clarksburg (to which they had recently moved from the South Branch) followed the West Fork of the Monongahela to its headwaters near the present site of Weston and crossing the divide followed Sand Fork to the Little Kanawha and proceeded to name the tributary streams, including the Hughes River.

Early in 1773 Lowther built below the site of West Milford a cabin which was still standing in 1908. There he lived until his death in 1814. Jesse Hughes settled on Hacker's Creek.

Although a neighbor of Hughes, Col. Lowther (1742-1814) was quite a different type of frontiersman. He was a man of character, poise, and bearing. As a consequence, he was a leader among his neighbors. During the entire Revolutionary War and for some years after, Lowther was one of the most active defenders of the Hacker's Creek settlement. In fact, he was to that region what Capt. Samuel Brady was to the extreme Northwest of Virginia. Lowther was the first justice of the peace for the district of West Augusta and the first sheriff of both Harrison and Wood counties. His family intermarried with families of the Buckhannon Valley.

West Milford was laid out about 1815 by Jesse Lowther assisted by Samuel Hoff.

In 1817, Jesse Lowther sold two acres of the 130 acres he had secured from George Bush in 1807 to Samuel Clemens and Jacob Romine so that the two men could build a dam across the West Fork River and a gristmill and sawmill. This was the first sawmill in the district. It had a perpendicular saw run by an undershot water wheel and so much power that a community began to grow around it. The eight-foot dam Clemens and Romine built backed the river up for a distance of seven miles.

Farmers brought logs from their farms and had logs sawed into boards to build homes and other buildings on their farms. "In 1819 Jesse Lowther who owned land on the west side of the river laid out ten acres of land into blocks, streets, and alleys for the town of West Milford — the same streets that we

use today,'' said Mrs. Bertha Lynch in a special interview in 1983 with Charles Taylor of West Milford. The sidewalks were built of flat stones laid side by side. Two of these sidewalks are still in use — the one in front of Melissa Windon's and the Dussart's homes on School Street and the one now covered with grass grown over in front of the Patterson home.

On January 15, 1821, the Virginia Assembly enacted, "that ten acres of land on the West Fork River, the property of Jesse lowther in the County of Harrison, as the same is already laid off into lots and convenient streets, shall be established a town by the name of Millford, and that Robert Lowther, Jacob Coplen, and Robert Maxwell, Gentlemen, be and they are hereby appointed trustees thereof.'' The shallow waters below the mill dam, where the settlers crossed the river, made Millford a fitting name for the new town. Post office officials decided in June 1833 to discontinue the office they had opened Jan. 26, 1827 (Jesse Lowther served as the town's second postmaster from Jan 21, 1829 until the postal officials discontinued it). The Lost Creek post office was designated to serve both communities.

The Lost Creek post office served the area for a decade, until the petitions of West Milford citizens secured the reestablishment of their office. At this point Washington postal authorities discovered that there was another Millford in eastern Virginia, so the prefix West was added to the Harrison County location's name, and in the process, it also lost an l. The post office opened June 19, 1844.

The name West Milford was given to the town because the mill was on the west side of the ford in the West Fork River.

West Milford has been noted for its many citizens, men of culture, usefulness, and influence — but probably none of them excelled Bennett D. Rider. He was a mechanic, machinist, teacher, merchant, photographer, postmaster, miller and gentleman. He remained in business in West Milford until his death on Oct. 11, 1890. His mill was in continuous operation for 95 years and in all had 20 different owners. Clemens and Rider owned it for 63 of the 95 years.

In the early days of the town between 1821 and the War Between the States, every man seemed to have a trade and a place of business. Each made a good living for his family. None was rich, but each had a very comfortable living. The citizens ran a tannery, saddle, cabinetmaking, furniture, blacksmith, barrel, wagon and an undertaker's coffin shops, five general stores, and dressmaking shops in homes.

The first store was owned by Joseph Clemens and Jefferson West.

"I can remember going to five different stores as a child. The stores were general stores, hardware, some clothes such as working clothes, hose, shoes, dress goods, nails, and groceries (almost all one needed),'' said Mrs. Lynch.

In the brick house which still stands on Mill Street lived E. J. Rider who was a photographer and took several early pictures of the town. Some of these pictures are in the "History of Harrison County'' by Dorothy Davis.

In 1852, the West Milford and New Salem Turnpike sold shares to people living along a projected 30-foot highway that would run from the Weston Road above Lost Creek via Duck Creek and Sycamore to the Northwestern Turnpike at Wolf Summit. The company, rather than build a bridge over the West Fork River, ran the road through the ford at West Milford. It was not until 1872 that a bridge company was organized with a Duck Creek resident, John Smith, as president and two West Milford residents, Clark Helmick and Bennett Rider, as members.

The Harrison County Court agreed to subscribe to $2,000 in shares in the bridge company and on Aug. 11, 1875, after the company had indebted itself $725, voted to pay the total cost. The wooden bridge opened soon after 1875, and the main street leading from the town was called Pike Street.

One of the more interesting former residents of West Milford was one of the physicians who lived in and served the area in earlier years. Dr. L. A. Davidson was not a graduate of a medical school. Apparently he "read medicine'' under the tutelage of a local physician prior to commencing his medical practice about 1886 in West Milford. The doctor developed a liquid medicine called "Suzanna'' which was manufactured by the Ray-Vise Medicine Company of West Milford. The trademark for Suzanna was registered on April 19, 1892. A bottle is stored among the memorabilia of the Harrison County Medical Society.

In May 1907, Dr. Davidson was appointed by Gov. Dawson to serve as a delegate representing West Virginia at the national meeting of the American Anti-Tuberculosis League in Atlantic City. Here the doctor intended to proprose that an anti-tuberculosis hospital be built by the league at West Milford. A site for the institution had been selected on a plateau just east of West Milford. Apparently the proposal was rejected for no further information was revealed.

In 1883, West Milford had three general stores, one saw mill, a flour mill, one furniture store, two saddle and harness shops, three blacksmith shops, two wagon and carriage shops, a hotel, two shoe shops, three doctors, a lawyer and four ministers. Jacob Fox ran the hotel, a two-story log structure on Back (Mill) Street during the War Between the States and for several decades following the conflict. Oldsters still remember Polly Davis's boarding house in the residence of Dr. Davidson who bequeathed the property that stood opposite the Methodist Church on Pike (Main) Street to her. The food served there was so inviting that for 10 years or so after automobiles became popular many Clarksburgers drove to West Milford to eat Sunday dinner at the inn. Herman Ladwig operated a casket shop on his farm to the south of town from the 1850s until shortly before his death in 1904; A. A. Ladwig was the town blacksmith until 1930.

On Jan. 22, 1885, the Circuit Court of Harrison County entered an order incorporating West Milford under the laws of the state: "A certificate under oath of Rufus Holden, James A. Clark, and Richard W. Stonestreet was this day filed showing that a majority of all qualified voters residing in the described boundaries, containing 160 acres, have been given in due form of law in favor of the incorporation of the town of West Milford in the County of Harrison, bound as herein set forth.'' No records exist as to the first officers elected by the citizens of West Milford.

After the flood of 1888, which destroyed the bridge and forced travelers to ford the river, the townspeople reasoned that the logical move was to do away with city government. The consensus held that the court might not rebuild the bridge for years and that at times of high water the section of the corporation which lay to the east and across the river would be inaccessible. (The court surprised the populace by building a one-way bridge — the first bridge had been a wider structure — in 1889). This iron bridge was used until the new bridge was built in 1980. In spite of the replacement of the bridge, the citizens reincorporated that part of the town on the west bank of the river, eliminating from the corporation "the other side of the river.'' But West Milford gave up its charter in 1910 because the cost of the streets and bridge was so high the citizens decided to let the county court shoulder the responsibility. The town was reincorporated in 1920. Since that time citizens have elected a mayor and five councilmen every two years.

Education has always been a priority in the town. Four school buildings have been used. Sometime before the Civil War a one-room school building was erected on the ground now owned by Orance Titus. The pupils had to pay tuition as the public school system was not established in Harrison County until 1863. Pupils from 6 to 12 years of age attended the one-room school. During summer terms held at West Milford, young men and women from Clarksburg, Shinnston, Salem and other places attended the select school where college courses were taught. Many men who later became doctors, lawyers, bankers, and businessmen attended the select schools.

In 1865 the two-room school was built on the ground where Unidis High School formerly stood.

The third school in 1918 did away with the two rooms and a four-room building was built. That school was still in use when the high school was built. The high school was started in 1911 with one teacher and 17 students. Fifteen persons graduated and two quit. This was a two-year-course high school and was called a third class high school. G. W. Hawkins was the teacher. In 1915, the West Milford High School became a first class one. The school was named from a contraction of the first three letters of the two words "Union District."

In the fall of 1965, Unidis and Lost Creek high schools consolidated and became South Harrison High School, located midway between the towns of Lost Creek and West Milford. This structure was built for 500 students. In February 1984 a new six-room annex was dedicated to house the seventh grade and a similar structure is being built for additional students. It is projected to be completed by September of 1985.

Today, West Milford is a quiet, country town with a population of about 600 persons. According to Bertha Lynch, "Our town is quiet and the people are very friendly. We help each other."

In many ways this sums up the history of West Milford and its people. From the earliest settlers under the guidance of Col. Lowther to its residents today, the people of West Milford help not only each other but their neighbors and all who are fortunate enough to pass through the area.

From a Ball of Fire
to a Headless Man

BY JOHN RANDOLPH

Some 15 years ago when I first started collecting stories in the Marshville Community, I found a variety of tales telling about strange lights appearing and disappearing.

It seems that the damp hollows and damp evenings, created a most conductive situation for these happenings. Nevertheless in that time, and yes, even today, if you are walking along at late dusk or after you might encounter the "will-of-the-wisp" or as the British call it "the friar's lantern."

Roy Hurst told about walking with a group up Grass Run in the early spring after a church gathering and saw a ball of fire roll along the ground for "ever so far" and disappear in the creek bank.

Aunt Mary McKown told of a relative whose son had left home to seek his fortune. The father and son were very close. The son promised that if anything happened to him he would send his father a sign. Some time later as the father came from the barn with the evening's milking, a ball of fire appeared on a fence post and jumped from post to post all the way to the house. Some time later word came that the boy had been killed just at the time his father had seen the fire balls.

Another account tells of a young lad lost in the woods. He was guided home after dark by tiny lights glowing in the path ahead of him.

Ruth Ann Musick in her collection of folk tales entitled "The Telltale Lilac Bush" related the story of the old peddler and the ball of fire.

No one noticed when the old peddler rode toward the residence of his bachelor friend. This was his third month in town, and the neighbors were used to seeing him go one day and return a week later.

This evening he was tired, nervous, and wanted a shave so he asked his friend to shave him. The bachelor agreed, and began preparing for the task. He lathered the peddler's face, stropped the razor, and began shaving him. The bachelor was hard-pressed for cash, and knowing the peddler carried a rather large sum of money, he decided to take advantage of circumstances, and cut his throat then and there. Then he cut the body into several parts and, taking them into the garden, buried them in the hotbed. He turned the horse loose, headed it out of town, and hoped it would wander far off.

The bachelor searched the peddler's clothing and rifled the baggage, taking the money and some of the jewelry. The remainder he burned or buried. Before burying the body, he removed a ring from the peddler's finger.

Afraid that stray dogs might smell the buried body and dig it up, he went out a couple nights later, dug up the body, put the pieces in a sack, and went to the river late at night. Coming to a whirlpool, he put rocks in the sack, tied it, and tossed it into the pool. In his haste he forgot to dig up the head of the body.

About five months later, a circuit judge, in town to hold court, rode down the road by the river. When he came within 200 yards of the whirlpool, he saw a ball of fire above the road.

The judge could not imagine what caused such a thing, so he stopped the horse when he came to the spot where the ball of fire was. To his amazement, the ball of fire changed form and became a headless man. This headless man got into the judge's buggy and told him the whole story of his death, and the circumstances connected with it. He wanted the judge to indict the bachelor on a charge of murder.

The judge, however, afraid people would think him insane for bringing a case before the court without a corpse for evidence, let the matter drop. He did, however, make inquiries. The only information to come forth was that the bachelor was seen wearing the peddler's ring and had acquired about $2,000 several months before but no one knew what had happened to the peddler.

John George Jackson...

He Was Vexed That He Had A Wish Beyond Clarksburg

BY DOROTHY DAVIS

John George Jackson saw almost as much change in his lifetime as does a 20th-century man for Jackson was born in September 1777 in Bush's Fort near Buckhannon and, living thirty years after all Indians had disappeared, saw the National Road open up the West and the birth of steam power. Jackson, the third generation of Jacksons to know Bush's Fort, was given the name of his grandfather John and his father George who had traveled in November 1776 to the South Branch of the Potomac River to marry Elizabeth Brake.

When the Virginia Assembly formed Harrison County in 1784, John George was a seven-year-old lad living in the George Jackson ordinary near the Jackson gristmill which stood on the west side of Elk Creek about a hundred yards south of the present bridge at the foot of East-West Main Street Hill.

As a boy John George transferred goods to military stations all over Northwestern Virginia after the governor had awarded his father in 1791 the contract to muster and provision rangers in the area. He attended school taught by Rev. George Towers at Randolph Academy in Clarksburg. Jackson accompanied his father on business trips to Richmond, where the lad bought books on surveying, and visited his father in Philadelphia after George Jackson went in 1795 to the city to represent the Third District of Virginia in the U. S. Congress.

Rufus Putnam in 1797 named the 20-year-old John George deputy surveyor of Ohio lands in present Muskingum and Licking counties. Young Jackson made two experienced Bush's Fort hunters, Elias Hughes and John Ratliff, members of his party and struck out from Marietta in July 1797. He finished the job in November.

Perhaps young Jackson met the Payne girls when he visited his father in Philadelphia. However it was, John G. Jackson courted Mary Payne, a sister of Dolly Madison, and married her at the Madison residence at Montpelier, Va., in October 1800.

John G. Jackson built a home for his bride on the northeast corner of present Maple Avenue and East Main Street in Clarksburg and began the practice of law in his office in the west wing of his home. He won a seat in the Virginia Assembly and when his father in 1802 announced he would retire from the U. S. Congress, the younger Jackson traveled a candidate's route in the First Congressional District of Virginia from Randolph to Brooke to Wood counties and won a seat in the U. S. Congress in 1803.

Then followed years of traveling via the Preston County glades to Harewood near Charlestown, where lived Mary Payne Jackson's sister Lucy Washington, to Washington for sessions of Congress and then home again to Clarksburg at the end of sessions; and years of both joy and sorrow for Mary Jackson's mother, in Clarksburg to care for her ailing daughter, died in October 1807 just four months before her daughter Mary would join her in death. Both Mary Coles

Payne and Mary Payne Jackson are buried in the Jackson Cemetery on Philippi Street in Clarksburg.

John J. Jackson's career in congress ran from 1803 to 1817 except for one session when he did not announce candidacy because he was recuperating from an almost fatal wound inflicted by a fellow congressman in a duel fought in Bladensburg, Md., on December 4, 1809. He traveled to Clarksburg in a wheeled vehicle in the spring of 1810 accompanied by Jonathan Jackson, who would marry in 1818 and in 1824 would have a son Thomas Jonathan (Stonewall) Jackson. Jonathan Jackson lived in his cousin John G.'s house in Clarksburg and handled the John G. Jackson law practice, when the congressman was in Washington, for more than ten years.

At the time of the duel the congressman was corresponding with Mary Meigs of Marietta, Ohio, whose father had been governor of Ohio, U. S. Senator from Ohio, and in 1814 would be appointed postmaster general of the United States. Jackson married Mary Meigs in Marietta July 19, 1810. They returned to Clarksburg to live in the East Main Street residence. Jackson thought his political career was at an end. He wanted to establish industry. He instructed workmen who planted hundreds of acres in crops including fields of flax and of teasel, the seed for which Jackson had brought from the East; he ran an advertisement in the "Clarksburg Byestander" in October 1810: "I will give cash for sheep as I wish to buy 500 or any less delivered at Clarksburg."

The sheep, the teasel, the flax would supply materials for Jackson's mills at the industrial site he was building one mile from his house at Mile's End on Elk Creek in present Anmoore. The flax gave warp for cloth in the fulling mill and seed for his oil mill. The heads of the teasel would be split and fastened in cylindrical frames that would revolve against cloth in the fulling mill to raise the nap.

Still Jackson could not get politics out of his system. He wrote James Madison: "I am vexed that I have a wish beyond Clarksburg, but dame nature is to blame, not I. She infused the fire...". April 1811 Jackson was "taken up" and elected to the Virginia Assembly and while he served in the body the next January, the Virginia Senate elected him brigadier general in the Twentieth Brigade of the Virginia militia.

When the governor in 1812 ordered General Jackson to supply and detach for federal service one rifle company of fifty men and Jackson's stream of letters to President Madison did not speed up federalization of Virginia militia, Jackson took a complement of mounted riflemen and rode to General Harrison's headquarters in Franklinton (Columbus) to volunteer for service. Harrison declined the offer and Jackson returned to Marietta.

Jackson was back in the U. S. Congress in 1813 and back in the building on the corder of F and 15th streets in Washington that he had bought in 1810. Dolly Madison would send word for Jackson to come to the President's House as soon as she would hear her brother-in-law was in town.

Jackson could never persuade Mary Meigs Jackson to live in Washington even though her mother and father lived in the nation's capital. His wife's preference for Clarksburg plus the fact that James Madison was leaving the presidency and returning to Montpelier were probably the reasons Jackson did not seek office in 1817.

Jackson had established a saltworks on the West Fork River in the general area where stands in 1984 the Nathan Goff National Guard Armory. While Jackson was in Washington 1813-1817 his Uncle Edward Jackson ran the industry. Now J. G. would take over that business plus the industries at Mile's End which the owner labeled "The Factory": a furnace for producing iron, a forge, a rolling mill, a nail factory, a woolen factory, a tannery, a fulling mill. In addition Jackson owned three grist mills, three saw mills and a toll bridge plus numerous houses and buildings near the establishments.

He needed waterpower and transportation for the merchandise he turned out. He needed money. So he launched The Monongahela Navigation to build, with the help of the Virginia Board of Public Works, dams to retain enough water to assure a flow in the West Fork River twelve months in the year. He helped launch the Saline Bank on West Main Street in Clarksburg. Both ventures failed, the navigation company when a spring freshet in 1823 took out several dams and the bank when it refused payment in October 1819 when an agent of the U. S. Government requested it to redeem its notes.

The governor of Virginia appointed Jackson in March 1818 to be one of the twenty-one commissioners to lay plans for a proposed state university. Jackson signed the report of the commissioners at the close of the meeting at Rockfish Gap on August 4, 1818, and returned home to lobby the Harrison County legislators to vote to locate the university in Charlottesville.

President Monroe in March 1819 appointed John George Jackson judge of the U. S. Court in the first federal district to be established west of the mountains in Virginia. Of course, Jackson established the court in Clarksburg and thus lay the foundation for the town's distinguished bar.

John George Jackson died at the age of forty-eight at his residence on East Main Street in Clarksburg March 28, 1825. He is buried in the Jackson Cemetery on Philippi Street.

Milling, The Most Important Industry In The Developement of West Milford

By MRS. CREEL CORNWELL SR.

The mill was one of the most important buildings in the development of early Harrison County. Cities such as Clarksburg, Shinnston and Lumberport, to name only a few, developed as a result of the existence of a mill. Each mill was unique in many ways but perhaps one of the best known was the West Milford mill which during its history was destined to have many different owners, and to play a very important part in the business and welfare of the people of Harrison County.

Samuel Clemans and Jacob Romine decided to enter into a partnership to build and operate a grist mill on the West Fork River, about nine miles south of Clarksburg. The site selected by them was on the farm of Jesse Lowther.

On June 16, 1817, Jesse Lowther conveyed to them two acres on the West Fork River and on Aug. 22, 1817, Romine filed his petition in the county court for a permit to build a dam across the West Fork River, to put an abutment on the lands of Thomas Estlack, for the purpose of driving a grist mill and other machinery. Estlack approved the petition, waived notice, and gave his [1]consent.

The court then made an order that a writ of ad quad damnum be directed to the sheriff to be executed on the thirtieth. It was not executed and Romine secured an alias writ issued on Sept. 20. No further order was made. The jury must have made a favorable report since Estlack, from whom they wanted to take an acre of land for the abutment, had appeared and consented, no further order was necessary. Clemans and Romine at once proceeded to construct the dam and built a saw and grist mill made of logs and used the old-style water wheel.

The dam was eight feet high and backed the waters of the river for a distance of seven miles, giving potential power which was very great.

Clemans and Romine operated the mill together until May 22, 1819, when Romine sold his interest to Jacob Coplin for the sum of $900. Romine then purchased John Hutson's mill on Gnatty Creek.

By this time the mill had become a community center, and Jesse Lowther, seeing this, took advantage of the situation, and laid off ten acres of his adjoining land into lots and streets for West Milford which was legally established by an act of the Virginia General Assembly on Jan. 15, 1821.

Jacob Coplin, who had bought Romine's interest in the mill, was a man of influence. He had owned a great deal of land, had been deputy sheriff, a justice and a member of the county court. However, he became indebted to several persons who sued him and had executions on their judgements in the hands of the sheriff.

William A. Rodgers arrested Coplin and threw him in jail. In order to get out, Coplin took advantage of the Insolvent Debtors Law, turned his mill over to the sheriff, and was released from jail on March 4, 1823.

The sheriff sold Coplin's half-interest in the mill for $250 to Joseph Johnson, who then owned the Bridgeport mill, and was later governor of the state. The deed was made to Johnson on Aug. 2, 1823.

Johnson, on Nov. 20, 1823, sold his interest in the mill to Holdridge Chidester for $500. The following August, Chidester, sold his interest to Warren Chapman. Chapman then operated the mill, along with his partner Clemans, until Sept. 18, 1825, when he sold to Clemans for the sum of $800. For the next 25 years, Clemans was the sole owner and operator of the mill.

In the meantime, he rebuilt, enlarged, and greatly improved the mill. On Sept. 29, 1853, he sold it to Olphrey L. Medsker.

Samuel Clemans was the son of John Clemans who came from Pennsylvania. His parents came to settle in 1787. Samuel Clemans was born in New Jersey. He built and operated the mill both as a partner and alone for 35 years in all.

His son, Lemuel Clemans, built the Clemans mill at Benson. He was succeeded by his son Clermont D. Clemans, and Clermont by his sister, Mrs. Belva Ward.

Medsker owned and operated the mill until April 10, 1857, when he sold it to Austin Shinn and George W. Golden for $4,500. Shinn and Golden continued as partners in the operation of the mill until Jan. 2, 1860, when Shinn retired and sold his interest to Golden for $2,450, and some years later purchased the Holland Mill.

Golden then continued alone in the operation of the mill through the trying days of the Civil War, or until Dec. 1, 1865, when he sold to Bennett D. Rider, and his father-in-law, John A. Williams, who was a farmer and a Methodist preacher, retired and sold his interest to Rider on Aug. 26, 1866.

After Rider purchased the interest of his father-in-law in the mill, he continued alone to own and operate it for nearly 28 years, before he sold it to John Pritchard, March 28, 1884, for $10,000. In all the years of his ownership, the mill was kept in perfect condition, with a first class reputation for good work and fine treatment, as indicated by the price received when sold.

Pritchard found the milling business either disagreeable or unprofitable, for he sold the mill to Wesley Post, Feb. 24, 1885, for about $2,000 less than he paid for it nearly a year before.

About a week after Post made the purchase, he formed a partnership with Thomas Marion Smith, and for $3,500 sold him a half-interest in the mill, one fourth of an acre of the original two-acre site, and the one-acre on the opposite side of the river, originally condemned for the abutment. Post retained one and three-quarter acres of the original site, and the residence thereon. At that time, a new patented roller process for making flour was being introduced, and Post and Smith were among the very first to make the necessary changes for installing it. As they needed a considerable sum of money to do this, Smith borrowed $950 from Sarah Owens, and to secure payment, he gave her a deed of trust on his half interest on Sept. 10, 1887, with O. Q. Queen as trustee.

The great flood of July 9-10, 1888, washed the mill away. Scotland G. Highland, the general manager of the Clarksburg Water Board in 1940, was then a young boy living within one mile of the mill. He wrote that he saw the mill leave its foundation, enter the main channel of the river, and strike the middle pier of the bridge a short distance below. The impact wrecked the mill. At the moment of destruction, he was standing beside Post and Smith and he observed that there were tears in the eyes of each.

Both of the owners were past middle age. Smith had all his life savings invested in the mill, and as he watched it being carried to destruction by the angry surging waters, he realized his fortune was all lost, and he still owed the debt the mill had secured.

Owens, the trustee in the deed of trust, sold Smith's

interest in the mill site and what was salvaged from its wreckage, to Wesley Post for the sum of $501, June 11, 1889.

Soon after his purchase of Smith's interest, Post rebuilt the mill, and equipped it with the roller process. The new mill had a daily capacity of 50 barrels of flour. Post employed Smith, his former partner, as his head miller. Smith continued with him in this capacity until he sold the mill, Sept. 21, 1896, to W. C. Burnside for $9,000. This conveyance included about 10 acres in addition to the mill.

Soon after Burnside purchased the mill, he added a steam engine and when the water was low he operated the mill with steam. He purchased western wheat by the carload which he hauled from Lost Creek, and ground into flour and feed, and then rehauled to Lost Creek for shipment to his customers in various places. Marion Smith was continued by Burnside as his head miller. After operating the mill for about seven years Burnside sold it and 2.77 acres of land to R. C. Helmick on January 11, 1903, for $750.

Helmick owned and operated the mill very much as did Burnside until March 1, 1904, he sold to the West Fork Milling and Lumber Co., a corporation, for $12,000.

This mill company lasted only one year and reconveyed the mill to Helmick for $10,000 and the payment of the company's debts. Three days later Helmick gave a deed of trust on the mill to Millard F. Snider, trustee, to secure a note given to Leeman Maxwell. About two years later, Snider, as trustee, sold the mill to Leeman Maxwell on Sept. 2, 1907 for $4,000. Maxwell operated the mill, only at intervals after he purchased it, until May 1, 1912, when it was run for the last time and finally abandoned. Edwin D. Steel was then operating the mill for Maxwell. Maxwell sold it to his son-in-law Louis A. Henderson, and he sold it to the City of Clarksburg (Clarksburg Water Board), Dec. 22, 1919, for $2,000. The city razed the mill in 1922 but still owns the site.

At the time the mill was washed away, there were two kinds of buhrstones in use. One was a native stone, and the other, a wheat buhr, was an imported French buhr. These were so heavy, they sank as the mill was carried away by the turbulent waters. Some years later, when Edward G. Smith established his "Dixie" homestead near West Milford, he secured the old buhrstones and placed them on his property as much prized historic relics and as a reminder of his labors in so important an institution.

In the early days of the mill, a "slope" about 40 feet wide, was added to the dam to enable timber and flatboats to be floated over it, and to permit fish to pass up and down the river. Much fishing was done at the mill, both above and below the dam and very fine large fish were caught. Sometimes flatboats were loaded with lumber and flour and floated to market in Pittsburgh and other points.

A tragedy occurred at the mill when William Wirt Patton, 10-month-old-son of Ebenezer Wilson Patton, fell from the arms of Ellen Parker, a nurse in the Patton home, while she was standing on the loading platform. As a result of the fall, the child died Feb. 21, 1849. No blame was attached to the woman as the fall was clearly unavoidable. Lucinda Earle Patton Highland, mother of the late Virgil L. Highland, Cecil B. Highland and Scotland G. Highland was a sister of the child.

There were probably many romances and pleasant associations connected with the mill, but the history of the mill and its impact upon the people of Harrison County remain as important factors in the development of the area.

We'd heard Rumors that...

'Cattlemen Had Disappeared Along The Turnpike'

BY JOHN RANDOLPH

If you ask folk around the area if they believe in ghosts, they will tell you that they are more scared of the "living." And we find that during the settlement here in the hills that was probably excellent advice.

Not only did these hills attract the good "farm folk," but it was also an excellent place for unsavory characters to find refuge.

In his book "Tales and Lore of the Mountaineers" William B. Price takes us on an adventure with Zeke Posten as he goes looking for his brother John. He ends up searching the hills in the central of our state for his brother.

"It was in the year 1854 that we Posten brothers planned to buy a large heard of cattle for the eastern market. My brother John was to cross the mountains and bring the cattle back by late fall. He left Staunton in September and hoped to return with the cattle in October, but the fall months passed and the mountain trails were threatened with snow and still he had not returned, nor had any word reached me as to his whereabouts.

"We had heard rumors that cattlemen had disappeared along the Staunton Parkersburg Turnpike from time to time, and so, toward the end of November, I started out in search of my brother. On my way, I inquired at inns along the pike. About one day's travel from Staunton, I found John's name on a register, and the innkeeper remembered John, as he had known both of us for several years. John's noon stop was also found, and his evening stop as well. In fact, it was easy to trace his movements for a couple of days, but after the third day, no registers had been signed.

"At the various places where John would probably stay all night, everything seemed to be in order. I began to think that John had met with foul play somewhere in the mountain vastness about the third day out of Staunton.

"Reluctantly, I turned back toward home and stopped at an inn for the night. At supper I was served smoked ham, which had a rather peculiar flavor, along with a fine meal of other foods.

"The weather had been cold, and, as was customary in that day, I removed my boots to thoroughly warm my feet and legs before retiring. As I sat by the fire toasting my shins, a small boy, sitting by the side of his mother at the far side of the far fireplace, whispered to his mother, ''Hairy legs for me to scrape tonight.' I heard this but paid no attention. Then the little boy whispered again, 'Hairy legs for me to scrape tonight.'

"Hush up, you little fool," scolded his mother unobtrusively.

"I began telling some big tales about my escapades, relating some gambling stories of the past few days and making a big show of myself as a wealthy and successful cattleman as well as a gambler.

"Pretty soon the innkeeper made a trip to the cellar and returned with a mug of fine cider. This cider, he said, had been pressed from frozen apples, and had a beautiful amber color. Only the wild seedling apples that remained on the trees after a hard freeze could be used this way. The juice was especially rich and delicious.

"By and by I said I would like to retire. In order to whet the appetite of my host, I asked the man to carry my bag upstairs. The bag was heavy, but not with gold or silver. It contained a heavy dragoon revolver and a Bowie knife with a ten-inch blade.

"After closing my bedroom door, I began to examine the room very carefully. The single window opened toward the road but was very high above the ground. A closet space beside the chimney held clothes. But no secret passages; only the bed seemed to be curiously made. Looking under it for a trap of some kind, I could see nothing.

"I was about to sit down on it when I had a feeling of danger. Clearly my brother's voice came to me, as it had back on the farm when any danger threatened, "Look out Zeke." Looking closer I discovered that the bed seemed to be fastened to the floor by the front posts.

"Finally, I picked up a chair and struck the bed a heavy blow. It fell through a trapdoor in the floor. The bed, covers, mattress, and all had been securely fastened to the bedframe. The chair crashed into the basement. As it did so, a cloud of steam came up through the opening, and furor downstairs gave me the answer. 'There he is,' yelled the old man. This was followed by a pounding of feet as they raced down the stairs into the basement. Loud cursing followed the discovery of the chair instead of the body. I hurriedly bolted the door, and drawing the heavy Colt revolver and Bowie knife from my bag. I waited for my hosts' next move.

"A faint creaking of the stairs and a sudden lunge against the bedroom door told me only too clearly that my life was in danger for sure. I was scared — really scared. Even now, when I compare that night's experience with later experiences in the War Between the States and the terrible battle at Gettysburg where men fell around men on every side in Pickett's charge. I think that night in the mountain inn was more terrifying.

"The innkeeper cursed loudly and tried again to break down the heavy door. I called to him and said that I was heavily armed and intended to shoot the first person or first thing that came through the door. I also told him that I would begin shooting through the door if he didn't leave. To emphasize my words, two shots were fired in quick succession. The balls passing high above the man's head knocking splinters into the room on the other side.

"The man continued to curse and threaten me with starvation if I didn't come out. To the cursings and threats I paid no heed. Fearing that they would try to smoke me out, I pulled the bed back up, closing the opening completely.

"The candle burned low, and finally my room was in complete darkness. I could hear voices in the room below, but they were spoken in a foreign tongue that I could not understand. The weather was cold and I had left my boots beside the fireplace downstairs, my feet were soon so cold that they seemed to be freezing. After a while, I took the covers from the bed and wrapped them around my feet, and by draping a heavy blanket around my shoulders, was able to be somewhat more comfortable.

"I have walked many a sentry post in the war, but that night was fraught with more real fear than the most dangerous sentinel duties.

"Daylight finally came and with it plans for my rescue. I first wrote a note and tied it to one of the heavy Colt balls. Then, as a traveler came down the road, I threw the ball towards him, but it was passed by unnoticed. After several such attempts to attract attention, a rider saw the flying object hit and strike the road and stopped to pick it up. As he picked it up, he pretended to examine the right front hoof of his steed. Placing the note in his pocket, he mounted and rode leisurely away. As he mounted his horse, he looked toward the upstairs window and saw me, but gave no sign of recognition.

"It was not long before he came back with three other men on horseback and stopped at the inn. Now I could hear voices downstairs, loud voices of the innkeeper and his wife; then some stern commands of men stating not loudly, but in deadly earnestness.

"Stand back against the wall with your hands up. Hes, tie their hands to those spikes in the wall."

"Soon someone came up the stairs and knocked on my door. "Who are you?" I asked.

"I am your neighbor, Bill Stone, from Staunton." I knew then that release was at hand.

"The door opened and I came downstairs, pistol in hand, happy to see men who were my friends. A search of the cellar was made revealing things too gruesome to mention. There were human thighs smoked and salted, others parts still in brine.

"Then we found an almost inaccessible glen at the base of a cliff where bones and gear littered the ground. It did not take a jury long to decide the guilt of the innkeepers, or their punishment. A large hoard of gold and silver money, rings, watches and other valuables were returned to the families of men who had disappeared at their ghastly inn on the Staunton and Parkersburg Turnpike.''

Bands, Beautiful Girls, Historical Displays Part of Harrison County Bicentennial Parade on Saturday

People in the central West Virginia area will want to set aside Saturday morning to see the Bicentennial parade in downtown Clarksburg at 10 o'clock.

The gala parade featuring bands, floats and beauty queens will begin at the Senior Citizens Center and proceed down Main Street to Second Street, onto Pike Street and end at the Post Office.

James Riddle, a 97-year-old Clarksburg resident, will be the parade marshall. He will be driven by a member of the Antique Auto Club of America in an antique car. Mr. Riddle was employed by the Baltimore and Ohio Railroad as a teletype operator and is an active member of Christ Episcopal Church.

The honorary parade marshall will be lovely Miss Terri Wells., a Salem College student.

High school bands from Bridgeport, Washington Irving, and Notre Dame will be attending. They will add that element only a band can give to a parade.

Floats are being entered by the Independent Order of Odd Fellows, Alderson-Broaddus College, Rosevelt-Wilson High School, and the Lumberport Historical Landmarks Commission. Trophies for Best Commercially-Made Float, Best Amateur-Made Float and the Most Historically-Significant Float were donated by FirstBank of Shinnston.

Many office holders are planning to participate including state and county politicians and nearly all county mayors.

For those who enjoy various sounds and colorful entries, there will be fire trucks from eight of the county companies.

The West Virginia National Guard plans to participate. There will be equipment from the Nathan Goff Armory which will represent basically civilian forces that began before 1776 when the farmers of Concord fired "the shot heard around the world" to modern day.

There will be many more entries. The Doddridge County Historical Society will attend. Smokey the Bear will be there from the Department of Natural resources. The Salernos will have their horse and wagon. The W. Va.. State Police and the Clarksburg City Police will start off the parade.

Other events Saturday are as follows:

11:15 a.m. - Street Fair featuring historical displays, crafts and food booths along Main Street.

11:30 - Court House Plaza, Welcoming from the Harrison County Commission; Parade float awards; Harrison county Week in W. Va. Proclamation by Gov. Jay Rockefeller; Remarks by the State President of the Sons of the American Revolution; School awards in art, history and essay contests; Remarks by the West Virginia Secretary of State.

3 p.m. - Reception for River City Brass Band, sponsored by the Stonewall Jackson Civic Club, at the Harrison County Senior Center.

8 p.m. - Concert by River City Brass Band, Robinson Grand Theatre. Tickets on sale at the box office.

Scheduled on the Bicentennial Calendar for May are the following:

May 13-20 - Harrison County Week in the State of West Virginia.

May 13 - Dorothy Davis' weekly Harrison County Biographical Series continues.

May 14 - Covered Bridges of Harrison County exhibit opens at the Clarksburg-Harrison Public Library.

May 20 - Harrison County Cities and Towns Development Series articles continue.

May 21 and 28 - Historical Harrison County Weeks begin for the following 17 weeks honoring present-day counties of West Virginia created wholly or in part from Harrison County of 1784.

May 22 - Akro Agate Glass Major Historical Exhibit opens in Harrison County.

Down The Old Clarksburg Road Through The Dark, Dripping Night

By WILLIAM B. PRICE

Our farm borders on the Old Clarksburg Road in one of the many watered glades on the Appalachian Plateau. Sometimes I think the only reward I get for farming is a good case of rheumatism which returns every year when the late October rains have stripped my country world to naked timber waiting for the snows that winter always brings.

Thus I was philosophizing as I milked one of my cows in the dusk of a late October evening, when I heard above the rain a strange wild laughter.

Stepping to the barn door I looked down the Old Clarksburg Road through the dark and dripping night but saw nothing.

Later that evening we just sat down to the table when there was a knock at our kitchen door. Before I could get the kinks out of my knees, Mary had bounced up and swung the heavy door wide. The lamplight fell on the figure of a tall, gaunt man soaked to the skin by the beating rain. I looked into the black eyes shining beneath the dripping brim of his old felt hat and knew the laughter I had heard had been born from the lips of the man who stood before us.

"My goodness! Come on in out of the rain, Stranger!" Mary exclaimed. As our visitor came through the door I welcomed him with a handshake. His long hard fingers started new rheumatic aches in every joint of my hand before he let it go.

"Your fire and your faces are as gold to the heart of a pauper," he said.

I watched the gaunt figure draw near our fire and was touched with sadness as he stood shaking his graying head slowly in the steam that went up from his pants legs. "Was that you I heard a-laughing down toward the creek ford a bit ago?" I asked.

He stretched out his long hand and felt the buckskin he had hung on a chair at Mary's invitation. I wondered if I'd offended him, but he chuckled, answering, "I was laughing, my friend, and standing in the middle of that muddy stream when I was doin' it. My jump was short and I'd landed not on

the bank, but in the water up over my boot tops. Ha-ha-a-a.''

"This 'as been a terrible day to be a-travelin' in," I said. "Where's your horse?"

Our guest straightened up. "My 'orse 'as been in my boots ever since I left the pike!" he said in his thunderous voice, and then laughed. The laughter stopped as quickly as it had started, and the stranger looked around the room as if searching for something he could not afford to lose. "Friend," he said, "am I on the right road to Morgan's Town?"

"Yes, you are," Mary spoke up, "an' a right muddy road you'll fin' hit!"

I knew now that my laughing stranger was no fancy. As we continued our meal I led him to talk of the needs for better roads. I found him to be a knowing man about roads and felt relieved until a heavy downpour of rain began. Then our guest pushed himself back from the table and glared wildly around the room until his black eyes fixed their stare at the far window. We waited for that unholy burst of laughter but it did not come, and then the old man dropped his head in silence.

"Come up to the fire and we'll talk," I said. I questioned him about news from outside and offered him my twist of light tobacco.

"I'm from down East, Friend," he remarked, breaking off a little piece of the twist. "I've been trying to get to Fort Henry, which you folks call Wheeling, on the Ohio. I've a new idea for a boat I want to build there. It will run by its own power and needs no wind or sail."

"Well, now, that's fine, Sir! Allus thought I'd like to build a steamboat myself, sometime," I replied, and waited to hear more.

"Mister, could yer name be Rumsey?" Mary asked him.

"Why, no, Ma'am," our guest answered, and I saw a gleam of fun in his eyes. "My name's as much a secret as my boat. Now when I set out to build a boat, it is a boat unlike the work of any living man." The drumbeats had started in his powerful voice again, and I found I'd been holding my breath to hear what would come next.

"Why, Sir," he continued, "that boat I'll build will travel on land as easily as upon the bosom of a river, and this trip convinces me that my boat is the very thing for roads in autumn storms."

"Lord, help us!" I said to myself, for as the stranger's words rolled like cartwheels around the room I saw his eyes burning with madness or fancy of some strange fever of the mind. So, I spat my cud into the fire and stood up, saying quietly, "Guess I'd better wind the clock," and attended to the task.

I noticed that the inventor took a big silver watch from his pocket and wound it with a key attached to a heavy silver chain.

"I reckon yer plumb tuckered, Mister!" said Mary, and then added, nodding to me, "Clint will show ye to yer bed."

When I awoke the next morning the stranger's boots were gone and also his buckskin jacket but I saw his hat still hanging on the drying peg.

"Clint," asked Mary from the table, "where do you reckon that inventor feller went off to?"

"Oh," I said, careless-like, "he's probly gone down to the creek to see if it'll do for his fancy boat."

"Clint, you know what I think?" Mary said, "We'll never see thet pore soul again. You were asleep las' night-aroud' midnight, I think hit wuz- when I heerd a light sound o' laughter from upstairs. I roused up some more an' listened, wonderin' if I'd better call ye. Then there wuz the sound o' light steps at the kitchen door, an' then I heerd a mincy squeak o' the hinges an' nothin' more, 'cep' the wind, an' after a few minutes a way-off sound thet might've been him or an owl, I couldn't be plumb shore which."

"Oh, now Mary," I argued, "I 'druther think he's gone on toward Morgantown than that some harm has come to him." I did not like to see my wife worried and upset, but as I sat looking at the old felt hat, now dry upon our jamb peg, I shared my wife's apprehension and thought it strange that any man would set out across country without protection for his head.

Mary pleaded, "I'll not tease you any more about being a man given to fancy, Clint, if you'll get some neighbors and look for thet pore soul." I agreed at once to do so.

We found his boots first. They were standing on the bank of the creek not over a mile from our house, and barefooted tracks led to the bank of the stream. We headed down stream and the body was where I thought it would be-lodged in the branches of a tree that had fallen into the stream.

We cut two sour gum poles and made a stretcher by pinning a horse blanket to them with thorns cut from a white thorn bush by the side of the stream. We carried the body to the dry floor of the barn and prepared it for burial.

In the stranger's pockets we found three silver dollars, two dimes, and three handmade nails. The big silver watch was gone.

That night, as the clock struck twelve, we heard a sound upstairs, like someone walking barefooted across the creaking floor. The kitchen door opened and shut very gently. Then that ghostly laugh came from the woods near the mill race rapids. The light of the moon, now full, seemed to grow dim, and an owl called from the hill by the graveyard. We looked out and saw a black cloud in the shape of a mountain gliding slowly across the moon. As the wind kept rising, the sighing of the great pine added to the somber sounds of the night.

We buried the Laughing Stranger the next day in the graveyard on a hill overlooking the creek. The death of this man was the main topic of conversation for some time; then nothing more was said about his mysterious appearance and passing. As Mary was treasurer of our church, we decided she should hold the money for a year and a day, and then have a small headstone cut giving the date of the stranger's death which we carefully marked on our almanac.

Another October day came, and there was preaching at the church. Mary and I went to the meeting that night. We had forgotten that it was just a year since our strange experience with the Laughing Stranger. Then, suddenly, just as we reached the creek ford, that horrible laugh roared out over our heads. The horses broke into a gallop. The sweat broke out between my shoulders, and I was glad to get into the house.

I was awakened that night by the old square clock as it struck the midnight hour. Listening, I heard the soft thudding of bare feet upon the upstairs floor. I nudged Mary awake and whispered, "Footsteps upstairs... listen... now they're going through the kitchen!"

The kitchen door softly opened and closed. Mary gave a faint groan and gripped my hand. The sweat again broke out between my shoulders. We held our breath and listened. Then a mournful laughter drifted up from the woods along the creek: "Ha-ha-ha! Ha-ha-a-a!"

"Clint," Mary said faintly.

"Yes, wife," I answered as gently as I could.

"Clint," she said again, more strongly. "I thank the good Lord we took him in and did for him."

"Yes, Mary, so do I," I told her, and prayed I could go back to sleep; but I heard the clock strike three before my nerves would give way enough to let me rest.

EPILOGUE

For 50 years the sturdy house stood beside the Old Clarksburg Road, and, for more than half of them, it was empty — after Clint and Mary passed away. The house was considered famous for its ghost of the Laughing Stranger. Passersby reported that laughter frequently sounded through its dusty rooms; and a lean shadow, some said, went in and out of the doorway when October's rains came pouring down. Sometimes, some claimed, a death's head looked out from an upstairs window.

Then one September day a farmer, who had bought the house along the creek, plowed up a big silver watch to which was attached a heavy silver chain. After that nothing more disturbed the abandoned house. The ghost of the Laughing Stranger had been laid to rest.

Joseph Johnson...

The Stick Pointed South, They Followed, And Arrived In Bridgeport In 1801

By PAULINE G. LeROY

When Joseph Johnson of Bridgeport became governor of the Commonwealth of Virginia in 1852, it was a noteworthy occasion for three reasons: he was the only governor of that state to come from west of the mountains; he was the last governor elected by the Virginia General Assembly under the old law before the Constitution of 1850 went into effect in 1852, and he was the first governor to be elected by the people.

Johnson came by his aptitude in politics honestly. His ancestors had been part of the New England political scene since their arrival from England in the 1620s, and three generations in the Wolcott line of his family had held the office of governor of Connecticut.

His grandmother, Abigail, the daughter of Gov. Roger Wolcott, had married Silas Wright, an East Indian silk merchant and schooner captain. Their daughter, also an Abigail, was courted by Aaron Burr, but chose instead to marry Joseph Johnson, a Revolutionary soldier, for which she was disinherited by her Tory father.

The Johnsons and their three small children moved to Orange County in New York after the war where Joseph Jr. was born Dec. 19, 1785. Before he was six his father died, just prior to the birth of William, the Johnsons' fifth child.

The widowed Abigail and her children moved to New Jersey and then, shortly before 1800, to Baltimore. During their stay in Maryland, the two older children were married and Abigail's third child, Martha or "Patty," who was said to be particularly attractive, was toasted as "the belle of Baltimore."

Abigail was intrigued with what she had heard of the western lands and so, forming a party consisting of her three younger children, Mrs. Catherine Winter, a widow from New Jersey, and her children, and a Mrs. Link, said to be Lord Baltimore's granddaughter, she set out in 1800.

Family tradition has it that, coming to a fork while they were on the trail, they set up a stick to determine whether to go west to Pennsylvania and the Ohio or south to western Virginia. The stick pointed south, they followed, and arrived in Bridgeport in 1801.

Sixteen-year-old Joseph found employment with Ephriam Smith, a well-to-do farmer and owner of a mill on Simpson Creek, who was in ill health. Joseph became Smith's farm manager and three years later married Sarah, one of his daughters.

Upon Smith's death in 1808, Johnson received the mill and 90 acres by written agreements with Smith's widow and other heirs which transferred to him all rights and title to the land.

In 1811 he was appointed constable of his district.

Johnson was the commander of one of two companies of riflemen from Harrison County that served in the War of 1812. Captain Johnson and his men were in Norfolk with the Sixth Regiment of Virginia Militia from Aug. 31 to Nov. 25, 1814, then from the latter date until Feb. 22, 1815, were attached to the militia's Fourth Regiment.

Having established himself as a leader, Johnson was elected to the Virginia House of Delegates in 1815, a position he would hold again in 1818-20, 1821-22, 1831-32 and 1847-48. During the earliest years he traveled on horseback over buffalo trails to get to Richmond.

Forty-two days after he took his seat in the General Assembly a bill he had introduced was passed which created a town by the name of Bridgeport.

The act provided for 15 acres of Johnson's land at "Simpson's Creek Bridge (at the location of the present cement bridge) to be laid off in town lots with convenient streets." Johnson, Matthias Winter (husband of Johnson's sister Martha), Benjamin Caplin, Peter Link, John Davisson, David Coplin, and Jedediah Waldo were named as the town's trustees. Johnson divided a portion of his farm into one-quarter lots and sold them for an average of $40.

From 1823 to 1827 he served in the United States House of Representatives. He was unsuccessful in his attempt to be elected to the 20th Congress, but served in the 22nd from Jan. 21 to March 3, 1833, in a vacancy created by the death of Philip Doddridge, then was elected to the 24th, 25th and 26th Congresses. His last term as a member of the House was from 1847 to 1849.

The Harrison County Court passed an order on June 16, 1828, appointing Thomas Haymond, Joseph Johnson and John Reynolds to lay off Clarksburg into streets and alleys under the Act of Assembly passed Jan. 16, 1828.

Matthias Winter served as Harrison County's sheriff from 1833 until 1836 when Johnson was appointed to fill the position. When he failed to qualify, Winter continued as sheriff until the following year.

Always concerned with education, Johnson was one of the trustees of the Western Virginia Education Society which was incorporated in early 1838.

Johnson joined 113 other delegates from 16 counties of present-day West Virginia and the Shenandoah Valley of Virginia at the Presbyterian Church in Clarksburg in 1841 for a three-day session called "the most important education meeting ever held on the soil of Western Virginia."

Presided over by George Hay Lee, a Clarksburg lawyer, and dominated by the clergy, the meeting had as its purpose the taking of "such action as would induce the General Assembly to enact laws providing for the establishment of a

Free School System," or, in the words of Dr. D. Alexander Campbell of Brooke County, "... schools for all at the the expense of all."

Meetings at Lexington and Richmond followed Clarksburg's and on March 5, 1846, "Twin Acts" which required counties to divide into school districts, to appoint a commissioner for each, and to elect a county superintendent, were passed by the legislature. The public school movement, superseded by the demands of sectionalism and the Civil War, stood still for 20 years, but the foundation for West Virginia's free school system was laid.

Johnson returned to Baltimore in 1844 as a delegate to the Democratic National Convention.

He had retained ownership of the mill on Simpson Creek and rebuilt it in 1849 to include machinery to card wool. Five years later, during his term as governor, he sold this business to Burton Despard.

As one of four representatives from Harrison, Wood, Ritchie, Doddridge, Tyler and Wetzel counties, Johnson attended the 1850 Constitutional Convention in Richmond.

Virginia's new constitution, as set forth by this convention, called for the governor to be elected by the people rather than by the assembly. It was adopted by Virginia's voters in the fall of 1851, a few months after Joseph Johnson had been elected governor by the assembly. Nominated by the Democrats as their candidate for governor in September, 1851, and defeating the Whig candidate, Johnson became the last governor elected by the assembly as well as the first elected by popular vote.

Gov. Johnson was described by contemporaries as a medium-sized man of agreeable manners, a persuasive stump speaker and of great political popularity among the people.

As a candidate for governor he was opposed by George W. Summers of Kanawha County, a superb orator and a favorite of the Whigs in western Virginia.

There were no joint debates during the campaign and Johnson's opponents made the charge that he did not dare meet Summers to discuss campaign issues.

Johnson replied, "I do not shrink from meeting Mr. Summers, for have I not met the lion of the forest and shaken the dew drops from his mane." This was an allusion to Philip Doddridge, whose reputation as a lawyer, scholar and orator no one in the West had exceeded.

At the conclusion of his term, Johnson returned to Bridgeport and his home, Oakdale, where he continued to be active in state and local affairs.

When John McManaway's St. Charles Hotel was opened in 1858, former Gov. Johnson delivered an address during the celebration, standing on a balcony that extended over the sidewalk from the hotel's second floor. (The St. Charles, a three-story brick building fronted 50 feet on Main Street and 125 feet on Fourth St. It ceased to exist as a hotel in 1917 at which time it was remodeled to accomodate retail stores. The building burned in the early morning hours of Feb. 18, 1955.)

On April 22, 1861, a mass meeting of some 1,200 Harrison County citizens, presided over by John Hursey, was held in Clarksburg. John S. Carlile, who had served as Harrison County's Union Party representative at the Virginia Convention in Richmond and denounced the state's secession from the Union, was the speaker. Upon his motion, those present adopted a resolution calling for a convention to be held at Wheeling on May 13 "to consult and determine upon such action as the people of North Western Virginia should take in this fearful emergency." Copies of the resolution, printed in an extra edition of Clarksburg's West Virginia Guard were distributed from Wheeling and Parkersburg to the Lower Potomac by horseback and by railroad.

Handbills, addressed "To the Southern Rights Men of Harrison County," appeared immediately throughout the county calling for a "solemn assembly" in Clarksburg on April 26 "to take counsel together and take such action as the circumstances then surrounding us may require."

Joseph Johnson served as the chairman of the secessionist meeting at which a long series of resolutions was adopted, wherein the participants voiced their support of the General Assembly, the Convention and the governor, their desire that the state not be divided, and their recommendation that "all citizens loyal to the commonwealth should at once in the manner prescribed by the laws of the land, organize themselves and stand ready to fight the battles of Virginia against her hostile foes."

When war came, Johnson left for Staunton where he remained until the conflict's end.

Gov. Johnson was a member of the Simpson Creek Baptist Church, which since 1834 had stood near the present-day Bridgeport Cemetery, and was used by three other denominations as well as the Baptists.

On July 4, 1868, Johnson and two other members were appointed "to concur with the Methodists either to buy or sell their interest in the Church property." On May 3, 1873, having raised a building fund of $600, the Baptists voted to build another church, a move opposed by Johnson.

The Clarksburg Telegram, on Jan. 8, 1876, published the following: "Gov. Johnson is passing his days calmly and happily at his home, Oakdale, near Bridgeport, where he is pleased to have his friends visit him and where they are always sure to meet with a cordial reception and agreeable entertainment, for the venerable governor, notwithstanding his advanced age, still converses with great zest and animation, and there is not one whose conversation is more instructive."

In February of the followng year, Gov. Joseph Johnson died shortly after celebrating his 92nd birthday. He was buried in the Simpson Creek (Bridgeport) Cemetery.

Col. Henry Haymond, in writing about him, said, "Gov. Johnson was a good conversationalist and having met all the prominent men of his time his recollection of passed events was exceedingly interesting.

"He had the respect and admiration of the people of his county and his private life was without reproach."

Although he had begun his life with comparatively few advantages, because of his mother's disinheritance and his father's death, Johnson's intelligence and ambition carried him a destiny far beyond that achieved by most other 19th century Harrison Countians.

Granville Davisson Hall...

If It Is Written In The Language You Should Understand The Book

By JACK SANDY ANDERSON

When I was a child, I sometimes heard members of my mother's family speak of Granville Davisson Hall. A few of them had known him personally and had supplied him with information that he incorporated in his novel, "Daughter of the Elm." Because of them I at an early age became much aware of Mr. Hall, and through the years often felt that I, too, had personally known him.

Granville Davisson Hall was born at or near present Salem, September 17, 1837, a child of William Patton and Fatima (Davis) Hall. Both Halls and Davises were Harrison County pioneers and were related to numerous other families that settled in the West Fork Valley during the eighteenth century. Mr. Hall was aware of his heritage, took considerable pride in it, and from it derived much satisfaction throughout his long and useful life. The ties that bound him to Harrison

County were always recognized by him; and for the county and certain of its old families he felt a fondness and closeness that lasted until his death.

When he was about four years old, his parents established the family in Shinnston, then a slow-growing village still dominated by its founding family, the Shinns. The Eighteenth century had not yet faded way, and Mr. Hall as a boy knew two Revolutionary War veterans living in the village, David Wamsley and Leonard Critzer. Being unusually observant, even as a very young child, he noted and remembered the virtues, the idiosyncrasies, and the foibles of his elders as well as of his peers; and from his observations learned much of human nature that later guided him in shaping his own destiny.

There are in every generation individuals born with the rare spark of genius. Such an individual was Mr. Hall. His genius, however, did not set him apart and cause him to live an isolated and lonely childhood, as so often is the case. Rather, he had a happy and golden childhood marked by participation in all the activities then common to ordinary boys in ante-bellum Virginia.

As a child and youth, Mr. Hall was closely associated with his father's many relatives. He especially enjoyed visiting his grandfather, John Hall Jr. (1777-1865), who maintained a cheerful and hospitable home a few miles from Shinnston. He also enjoyed visiting the home of his grandfather's sister Phoebe (Mrs. William Rhody Ogden) and her husband and family. The Ogden home was an affluent one, always open to a wide circle of relatives and friends. From William Rhody Ogden, Mr. Hall early in his life heard of the evils of slavery from one who had been a slaveowner and received the grim warning that sooner or later slavery would plunge the nation into a great and bloody conflict. Another relative he liked to visit was a great-uncle by marriage, Robert Mason (1781-1871), who lived an eccentric existence in the Bingamon country. The progenitor of a family later illustrious in Harrison and Marion counties, Mr. Mason owned an incredible amount of real estate, was considered fabulously rich for his time, but chose to live as he saw fit with little regard to the artificialities of social pretension.

Formal education in long-ago Shinnston was lacking in both duration and quality. Teachers were frequently little more learned than their students, and gifted teachers were as rare as the proverbial hen's teeth. Mr. Hall, though, was fortunate in having two superior teachers from whom he received inspiration as well as instruction. These were Isaac Morris, a Pennsylvanian whose family acquired a sizeable portion of the Shinn estate south of the village, and Emory Strickler, later a locally-famed physician. Much that he learned though, he learned on his own by studying at home. In later years he observed: "If one man makes a book and prints it in a language you understand, you ought to be able to understand his book." While most educators would not agree with this observation, it did work for Mr. Hall. Among the subjects he taught himself was shorthand, at that time referred to as phonography, which he mastered with relative ease and which was to be of great importance in his life.

Mr. Hall's early years were not free of physical labor, for he and his brother Van (1834-1887) had to help their father in his tannery and store. He also worked on nearby farms belonging to relatives and friends and always enjoyed working in the hayfields. Due to the persuasion of Dr. Strickler, he taught one term of school but discovered that the life of a pedagogue was not for him. It has been said that he and Van for a short time had an apothecary shop in the village.

As he reached maturity he decided that he must leave home to find the opportunities a little country village could never afford him. In March 1857, then in his nineteenth year, he went to Fairmont and from there traveled by train (the first he

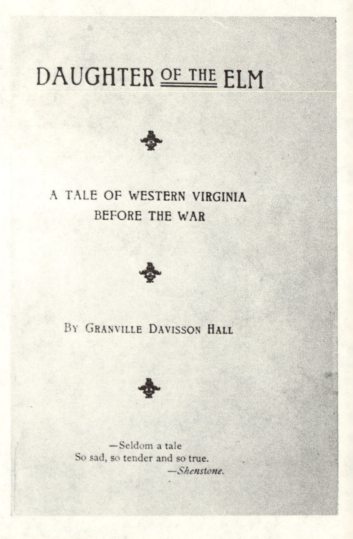

DAUGHTER OF THE ELM

A TALE OF WESTERN VIRGINIA
BEFORE THE WAR

By Granville Davisson Hall

—Seldom a tale
So sad, so tender and so true.
—*Shenstone.*

had ever seen) to Washington to find employment. Through the influence of John S. Carlile, a member of Congress from Clarksburg, he was hired as a stenographer for the Senate. At first he delighted in his job and being in the nation's capital where the atmosphere was both awesome and exciting. It was thrilling to meet the great men he had read about in the newspapers back home, great men who were desperately striving to lead the nation in a time that daily grew more anxious and dangerous. After several months, though, he tired of the monotonous routine of his job and returned to Shinnston.

In 1859 he was hired as a reporter by the well-known Wheeling newspaper, "The Wheeling Intelligencer," but had so much difficulty with his vision, which typhoid had weakened, that after a few months he was forced to quit. He came back to Shinnston and remained there until February 1861, when he rejoined the newspaper staff in Wheeling. During this short interval Mr. Hall's vision had improved, but the national situation had deteriorated to the point where civil war was not only inevitable but also imminent.

In his old age Mr. Hall once noted that his fascination for politics began in his boyhood when he found himself at the age of seven taking a deep interest in the Clay-Polk campaign of 1844. From then until he reached maturity he concerned himself with national politics and the leading political figures. When the Republican Party came into being, both he and his father (who had been a Whig) enrolled in its ranks and actively supported its principles.

Shortly after returning to Wheeling, he closely associated himself with some of the men whose zealous leadership resulted in the Restored Government of Virginia when the Old Dominion cast its lot with the Confederacy. He covered (as a reporter) the historic Wheeling Conventions and also the Constitutional Convention which met in November 1861, in Wheeling to create a constitution for the proposed new state of West Virginia. Mr. Hall's historically priceless notes on the debates of the Constitutional Convention many years later were purchased by the state and in 1942 were published in three large volumes.

When the new state of West Virginia became a reality on June 20, 1863, Mr. Hall was elected clerk of the first House of Delegates. He also served as private secretary to the first governor, Arthur I. Boreman, and in March 1865 became West Virginia's second secretary of state. In the election of 1864 he was honored by being elected a member of the Electoral College and cast his vote for President Lincoln. After serving one term as secretary of state, he declined renomination for that office and directed his attention to journalism. He purchased an interest in "The Wheeling Intelligencer" and assumed editorial charge of it until 1873. He then disposed of his interest and resigned from the editorial staff.

Soon thereafter he affiliated himself with the Pennsylvania Railroad Company and established his residence in Pittsburgh, where he remained for several years. In the 1880s he settled in Glencoe, Ill., one of Chicago's suburbs, which was his home for the rest of his life. He took part in Glencoe's civic affairs and for 25 years served as its village clerk.

It was in Glencoe that he had his writing career. He authored five books: "Daughter of the Elm" (1899), "The Rending of Virginia" (1902), "The Two Virginias" (1915), "Old Gold" (1907), "Lee's Invasion of Northwest Virginia" (1911). The one by which he is best remembered today is "Daughter of the Elm," a novel based on the activities of an outlaw gang that existed in the Shinnston area just before the Civil War. To the author's amazement, this novel was an instant success and aroused much comment and controversy in North Central West Virginia. Several editions have been published through the years, a fact that bears testimony to the book's continuing popularity.

Granville Davisson Hall died in Glencoe on Sunday, June 24, 1934. He was survived by his wife, the former Dolly Hancher, and two sons.

The Dyson House...
The Body Was Supposedly Hidden Upstairs

by JACK SANDY ANDERSON

Located on U.S. Rt. 19 a short distance north of Shinnston is Big Elm Farm. Here once stood a towering elm tree in whose shadow plotted an outlaw band which terrorized the West Fork Valley more than a century ago.

This band and its activities inspired Granville Davisson Hall (1837-1934) to write "Daughter of the Elm," a novel originally published in 1899. Much to the author's amazement, the book immediately became a best seller. Its popularity persisted, and through the years other editions have appeared.

My interest in "Daughter of the Elm" began in childhood. My father was closely related to some of the characters (the heroine was his great-aunt), and often I heard certain of his relatives arguing about the authenticity of incidents mentioned in it. Too, my mother's relatives occasionally spoke of Mr.

Hall, for some of them had known him and remembered when he had interviewed old-timers, including my mother's great grandmother, to obtain information that he used in his book.

At first Mr. Hall avowed, no doubt with tongue-in-cheek, that "Daughter of the Elm" was purely a work of fiction and was not intended to be a portrayal of reality. No one though, believed him, for it was too obviously based on persons and happenings still remembered in 1899 by a number of older people. Of course, he wove considerable fiction into its fabric to disguise identities, however thinly, and to give it a romantic appeal. Through the years fiction and reality have so blended that today it is nearly impossible to distinguish one from the other. For this reason, and to avoid offending anyone now living, I will refer to most of the characters by the fictitious names Mr. Hall gave them.

In 1785 David Wamsley (1755-1849), a veteran of the Revolution, acquired land that came to be Big Elm Farm. A tract of 400 acres, it was assigned to him by Samuel Merrifield, who had settled upon it in 1773. Near the gigantic tree that gave the farm its name he built his house, now one of the oldest in Harrison County, which is often referred to as the "Daughter of the Elm House." (Sadly, today this historic old house is in great disrepair and literally falling down.)

Wamsley and his wife (Sarah Delay) were the parents of

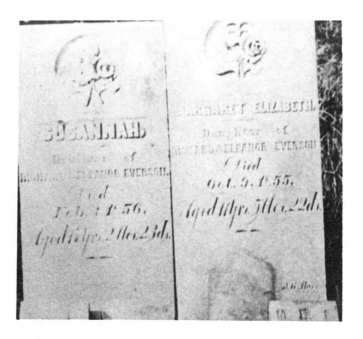

eleven children who grew to adulthood and married into some of the area's best-known pioneer families. Many of their descendants were and are among the leading citizens of north central West Virginia.

In the 1840s Nick Esmond (in real life, Richard Everson, my great-great-grandfather) purchased the farm. It was his son Harry who headed the outlaw band that flourished in the fitful years just prior to the Civil War. The farm was its main headquarters and soon took on a sinister reputation.

Although many crimes were committed, none of the band was ever brought to justice. Some of the crimes were the murder of a rich Pennsylvania cattle-buyer who made the fatal mistake of going to Big Elm Farm in search of a bargain; the burning of an insured saloon west of Clarksburg; robbery of a Shinnston general store; stealing horses from area farms; and a hold-up in the Mausby Covered Bridge at Gypsy. The hold-up proved very disappointing, for the victim (Joseph Tetrick) had only four dollars in a pocketbook, a knife, some tobacco,

and a bottle of whiskey instead of the large sum of money the outlaws thought he was carrying. They were so disgusted that they gave back everything except the whiskey.

Harry Esmond was a complex individual. Handsome and self-assured, he dominated his family and seldom was seen helping with the farm work. He preferred to keep his slender hands soft and to ride around the countryside on a fine thoroughbred horse. At times he was friendly and easy-going; at other times he was remote and quickly angered. A daredevil, he looked upon crime as a dangerous game that challenged his wit as well as a means of getting what he wanted without work. He was also a born leader capable of commanding loyalty from even cut-throats.

In December 1853, before the outlaw band came into existence, Harry was a prisoner in the Fairmont jail. In the cell with him was an expert locksmith. On Christmas Day, Harry decided he had been deprived of his freedom long enough and persuaded the locksmith to open the lock. This was soon done, and the two men slipped away.

Three years later Harry got into a fight while attending a horse race at Boothsville. He ignored a peace officer's order to stop, and a warrant was issued for his arrest. Not long afterward two or three Harrison County law officers were in Shinnston and saw him on the street. When they tried to arrest him, he fled toward the river, waded across, and ran into the thick woods on the other side. The chase was abandoned, and the warrant was forgotten.

When the Civil War erupted, Harry chose to side with the South and enlisted in the Confederate Army. He served bravely and fought at Gettysburg. After that battle he raised a company of cavalry and was its captain until the end of the war. His last years were spent in Pocohontas County where he lived under an assumed name and where his death occurred in 1903.

In 1917 Mr. Hall commented on Harry as follows: "Standing at this remote time on the border of the Great Divide, which nearly all my early friends and familiars have crossed, and recalling this one who did 'his bit' — not all discreditably — and has gone to answer for it, there come into my memory some reflections indulged by Fenimore Cooper in his farewell to the Hutters, in the last paragraph of Deerslayer: 'We live in a world of transgression and selfishness, and no pictures that represent us otherwise can be true; though, happily for human nature, gleamings of the pure spirit in whose likeness man has been fashioned are to be seen, relieving its deformities and mitigating, if not excusing its crimes.' "

Harry's brother Guy, supposedly the oldest of Nick Esmond's children, was also a member of the outlaw band. Although he was married and lived in Shinnston, he spent much of his time at Big Elm Farm. Two of his daughters, one of whom I vaguely remember, were my great-aunts by marriage.

The novel's heroine — the "Daughter of the Elm" was Loraine Esmond (in reality, Susannah Everson), one of Harry's sisters. According to accounts that have been handed down, she was an unusually beautiful girl noted for her gentleness and serenity. She fell in love with George Holmes, a young man associated with the outlaws. In the book they marry and settle in Kansas. However, in reality Loraine died in 1856 of fever (probably typhoid), and George was killed by the outlaws when they learned he was planning to quit the band. Three months after his disappearance his body was found in the river at Worthington. One of the Esmonds and Ray Harris, who had married Eloise Esmond, were accused of killing him and were arraigned before a justice of the peace who released them because of insufficient evidence.

One of the most feared outlaws was Lot Dyson. In 1929 Rev. L. F. Fortney referred to him in these words: "... for some years Lot Dyson lived in a fairly good log house located on the Uncle Nick Esmond farm, almost directly opposite from a coal bank just below what was long known as Brown's Hole, but back distant from the river and road some — I would say nearly 400 yards... the Dyson house was where the body of George Holmes was supposedly secreted (upstairs) for at least the first night after he met his death.

"I here stop to say that on that dark night when George was known to have crossed the high water in a boat, Albert Shore, who had recently married his second wife (Henrietta Martin, mother of Clara Jarrett), was standing with his wife on the upper portico and heard a gun shot which appeared to be at or near the Dyson house.

"I remember how Lot Dyson looked as if I had seen him yesterday. He was a large-formed man, very broad across the shoulders and deep-chested and with a red face and not inclined to look one in the eye. How may meals of turkey he took off our apple trees we never knew; but we knew where one monster gobbler was in a smart battle with him, but rather than be shot, we did not appear on the scene. After daylight father (Dr. Jacob H. Fortney) followed the large footprints through our river field and saw the gobbler's head where it had been wrung from the neck. The tracks went in a bee-line to the Dyson house. For years he was a trusted member of the Esmond band."

In "Daughter of the Elm" Dyson died in Webster County during the Civil War. This, however, is fiction. He lived to be an old man and was a respected citizen of the community where he died in 1900. It is interesting to note that his wife Catherine and George Holmes's were first cousins, for their mothers were sisters. Dyson and his wife, whose death occurred in 1907, are buried near Wallace in a small family cemetery which I visited a few years ago.

A Shinnston tavern, the Blue Boar (but in reality the Red Lyon), was frequented by the outlaws who used it as their village rendezvous. Jonas Blue, the proprietor, was their good friend and confidant. He and Guy Esmond had married sisters, and when Guy wasn't at his father's farm, he could usually be found at the tavern. Later this tavern was owned by Mr. and Mrs. John W. Carder. They razed it in the 1890s and erected a new building that they named the Carder House. Around 1926 this building was dismantled, and today a store occupies its site.

The Civil War brought an end to the outlaw band. Big Elm Farm and the Peter B. Righter farm on Coon's Run were both centers for Rebel enthusiasts. In fact, both places were said to have been recruiting stations for volunteers into the Confederate Army. In June 1861, Union soldiers successfully raided the Righter farm. Fearing that Big Elm Farm would also be raided and knowing that it had reasons other than political for not desiring arrest, the Esmond band dissolved, thereby bringing to a close a colorful chapter in West Fork Valley history.

In 1868 Nick Esmond sold the farm to Col. William Hood (1822-1899). Progessive and ambitious, he developed it until it became a showplace. Among his several children was Willa, the state's first woman pharmacist, who spent much of her life in Fairmont. In 1889 she married Dr. Emory Wallace Strickler and was the last bride to walk out under the great elm tree. Eventually, Col. Hood's granddaughter, Miss Hannah Hood, became the sole owner of the farm. After her death in 1976, Big Elm Farm was purchased by the Ten-A Coal Co.

The phenomenal popularity of Mr. Hall's novel aroused tremendous interest in the Big Elm and long-ago events. Newspapers in Fairmont, Clarksburg, and Shinnston printed articles about the outlaw band and its crimes. Local poets composed sentimental verses about the tree and its "daughter." People flocked from far and near to see the Big Elm and the old house where Loraine had once lived. There sprang into being the Great Elm Restaurant and a Big Elm Cigar. And a Shinnston photographer, Muta U. Swiger, took pictures of the tree and places mentioned in the book which were reproduced on postcards and widely distributed.

Unfortunately, the Big Elm began to die in the midst of all this interest. Some said it was dying of a plant disease, but others said it was because hogs had girdled the tree Still others said it was due to the fact that construction of the nearby streetcar line damaged much of its root system. Whatever the reason, by 1910 the nation's largest elm was dead. In May, 1917, the skeleton was cut down and burned.

Soon afterward Mrs. Mary Shinn Martin of Haywood passed by Big Elm Farm and saw that the famous tree was gone. When she returned home she wrote Mr. Hall: "Well, it is no more. They are making a brick road from Shinnston to Enterprise, and the Elm stood in the middle of the road. So it was cut down and burned. They say many watched it fall and burn; and many pictures were taken. And then as soon as the ashes were cold, they began to grab for them. A woman who lives near the palce told me they are going to put in a marker to show where the tree stood. Thus ends the Big Elm — but the story of the 'Daughter' will go on — and on."

Time, I think has proved Mrs. Martin right, for "Daughter of the Elm" does indeed go on and on and will continue to do so for many years to come.

A Shinnston Tavern Named "Blue Boar"

By JACK SANDY ANDERSON

Although more than 65 years have passed since the famed Big Elm of Shinnston disappeared from the local scene, it still lives in the memories of both those who remember when it towered majestically over the countryside and those who may never have seen the tree but have read Granville Davisson Hall's "Daughter of the Elm."

The elm itself, according to records, was the largest elm tree in the nation and was awarded first prize in 1876 at the Centennial Exposition held in Philadelphia. Near its base it measured 33 feet in circumference and was certainly a mature tree long before the settlers came into the West Fork Valley.

The story written by Hall employing the elm in its title is today a classic in Harrison County and has aroused the interest of people since it was first published in 1899. While the book concerning the Everson outlaw band which made the Big Elm Farm its headquarters in the years before the Civil War is allegedly mostly fiction, the fiction Hall used but thinly

conceals a very true and a very real series of episodes, people and places along the West Fork River many yesterdays ago.

One of these places was a rendezvous which Hall's outlaw band had in Shinnston proper known as the Blue Boar Tavern. It was here that many of the nefarious plans of the band were plotted and schemed and it was here that the Everson band had another base of operations.

In reality the Blue Boar was actually the Red Lyon Tavern, a name derived from a large sign which stood out front that had a picture of a red lion painted upon it and was also a pun on the name of the original owner, William E. Lyon. It was a large and commodious hostelry which stood on the corner of Main and Pike Streets and was frequented by travelers along the Clarksburg-Fairmont Turnpike. One of its early proprietors was Jacob Long, supposedly a friend of the Eversons and who was reportedly in on some of their escapades. The building passed through a series of owners until John W. Carder acquired it, did some rebuilding, and renamed it the Carder House.

The Blue Boar inspired many tales of the doings which went on within its walls. Some of the tales are more factual than others but all involve the Eversons, the Blue Boar, the Elm and the villianous activities surrounding them in the early days of Harrison County.

Granville Davisson Hall relates how Joseph Tetrick, called Joe Diedrick in the book, lived on a farm above the Everson home. He was a man of considerable means for those days. Occasionally he was involved in land transactions that ran into a good bit of money. Peter B. Righter owned a farm on Laurel Run, not far from Enterprise, which he sold to Mr. Tetrick. The amount of the purchase was in the thousands of dollars, and Uncle Joe was to go to Clarksburg where he kept his money in the bank, to draw out a payment for Peter B. Somehow the outlaws got wind of all this. The Eversons liked their congenial neighbor and refrained from attempting to rob him. Some of the band, however, had no such scruples and met at the Blue Boar plotting to steal the money. They proceeded to the long covered bridge at Gypsy, known as the Mausby Bridge, where they concealed themselves and impatiently waited for the unsuspecting victim to pass through on his way home with the money. Eventually Uncle Joe appeared but all that his searchers found were a plug of tobacco, a jack-knife, and a small bottle of whiskey. The disgust and keen disappointment the villians felt when they discovered Mr. Tetrick had chanced to run into Peter B. in Clarksburg and had given him the money was apparent when the outlaws returned everything except the whiskey to Uncle Joe and sent him on his way.

Another tale of the Blue Boar was related by teacher and folklorist Dr. Ruth Ann Musick in a folktale entitled "The Blue Boy Hotel" which took place in a two-story hotel on Main Street in Shinnston between 1870 and 1895. The hotel had not only a notorious past but also a saloon in the front and a poolroom in the basement. Behind the hotel was a huge barn where all the livestock was kept. Two brothers by the name of Bill and Melvin Everette were the owners of the Blue Boy and both were as notorious as their establishment.

Dr. Musick's account is as follows:

"These men would take in many guests during the year, most of whom were rich or well-to-do. If they had very large sums of money, Melvin Everette knew it, because it was a house rule for the people to tell how much money they had. He would get them into poker games, playing with a large sum of his own money so that the guests would keep playing. He often arranged to have a man or group of men come in and hold up the game. He would never be suspected because he played with a large amount of his own money.

"The two brothers also rustled cattle and hid them at a

farm at Adamsville until the brands were changed. Bill would then sell them to cattle buyers for a very reasonable price. But after each sale he would try to kill the buyer, take the cattle, and sell them again.

"After a life of swindling, cheating, rustling, and murder, Bill died around 1890. Every night, after Bill's death, Melvin would dream about all the money Bill had. In the dream, Bill was hiding his money, but Melvin never found out where. One night as Melvin was getting ready to go to bed, his brother's ghost appeared. Bill told him to go to the old abandoned Lucky Lady mine, and then he disappeared. Melvin ran to the mine and got the money packs. Before he could reach the entrance again, he was covered by a slate fall.

"The money was found beside Melvin's body. Inside the packs was a note, signed by Bill, saying that if anything should happen to Melvin the money was to go to Melvin's wife.

"Not wanting the hotel and unable to sell it, Mrs. Everett had it torn down. When the barn was torn down, the bodies and skeletons of the murdered people were found.

"When he heard what had been discovered under the barn, Aleza Driscal of Bluefield, whose daughter had disappeared while she was in Shinnston, came to town. Believing that his daughter had been killed by the brothers, he went to see Mrs. Everette and courted her. As a form of revenge, he took her out one night, shot her, and threw her body in the West Fork River.

"Every night thereafter Mrs. Everette would appear to Mr. Driscal. He would see her walking in the garden moving about in the house, and going down the street.

"One rainy night he decided to walk down near the river. Reaching the river, he began to cry from shame. The ghost of Mrs. Everette was always with him, walking alongside him. He jumped into the West Fork and drowned himself. The bodies of Mrs. Everette and Mr. Driscal were found the next morning by the riverbank where Mr. Driscal had jumped in.

"The ground was wet, and Mr. Driscal's footprints were clearly seen — down to the riverbank. And alongside his footprints was a set of woman's footprints, a set like those that could have been made only by the shoes Mrs. Everette was wearing."

The Blue Boar Tavern and the people who popularized it for so many years are gone today and a colorful chapter of local history has been closed. The tales which the tavern inspired, however, whether fact or fiction, continue to live today in the folklore of Harrison County.

Geography, Politics, Prevents Carlile For Satisfactory Relationship With Richmond
BY DOROTHY DAVIS

John Snyder Carlile was the last of the group of ambitious, bright lawyers who beginning circa 1815, left their homes in the Shenandoah Valley of Virginia to practice in Clarksburg.

Carlile's route to the West was circuitous for as soon as he had qualified as an attorney in 1840 in his native county of Frederick, the 23-year-old struck out for Beverly, the county seat of Randolph County, where he set up practice. Seeing more opportunity in a county just being formed. Carlile appeared at the first meeting of the Barbour County Court on April 3, 1843, and asked permission to practice in Barbour County. A month later he took the oath to practice in Harrison County.

Sometime after his first visit to Clarksburg, John Carlile met Mary Gittings, daughter of Micheal D. Gittings M.D., and married her in Clarksburg March 5, 1846. Carlile and his wife lived in Phillipi, where their daughter Mary was born

March 5, 1849. About the same time the citizens of Randolph, Lewis, Gilmer, Barbour, Braxton, Wirt and Jackson counties elected Carlile and three other men to represent their district at the 1850 Virginia Constitutional Convention.

The opportunity for an attorney in Clarksburg was attractive and Mary Gettings Carlile naturally liked the idea or returning to her hometown. So Carlile bought from his father-in-law Dr. Gettings on Aug.15, 1853, the mill on Elk Creek near Water Street and 60 acres of land on the hill to the east of the creek. There is no record of when the Carliles moved to Clarksburg or when he built the large brick house that stood facing west on the hill above the creek.

Always of independant mind and fearless in action, Carlile did not refuse when the fledgeling American Party "drafted him in 1854 to run for the U.S. Congress. He won and served in the body 1855-57. He ran for Congress on the Democratic ticket in 1857 and was defeated. He said he "would retire to private life strengthened in correctness of my political opinions.

His political opinions were that the Democratic Party "has allowed itself to be diverted from the principals of democracy as inaugurated by Jefferson and has accepted the sectional issue which the fanaticism of the non slave holding states has sought to bring about." In other words, the slavery issue was secondary to the preservation of the Union. During the 1850 Constitutional Convention Carlile had developed a prejudice toward Tidewater Virginia because of the machinations of Eastern Virginia to control the Virginia assembly. He held the view of many in Northwestern Virginia: geography and politics prevented people living in land drained by the Monongahela River and upper reaches of the Ohio River from having a satisfactory relationship with a government in Richmond.

Union men met in Shinnston January 19, 1861, and nominated Carlile and Charles Lewis as their candidate in an

THIS TABLET IS ERECTED TO KEEP BEFORE
FUTURE GENERATIONS THE VIRTUES AND
COURAGE OF THE PEOPLE OF HARRISON
COUNTY, WHO, AT A TIME OF GREAT CIVIL
COMMOTION, ASSEMBLED IN MASS MEETING
ON THE 22ND DAY OF APRIL, 1861, IN THE
COURT HOUSE THEN OCCUPYING THIS
SPOT, AND TOOK ACTION IN THE ADOPTION
OF RESOLUTIONS, CALLING ON THE
PEOPLE OF NORTH WESTERN VIRGINIA, TO
APPOINT DELEGATES TO MEET IN
CONVENTION AT WHEELING ON THE 13TH
DAY OF MAY, FOLLOWING, TO CONSULT AND
DETERMINE WHAT ACTION SHOULD BE
TAKEN IN THE EMERGENCY CONFRONTING
THEM.
THIS PROCEEDING WAS THE INITIAL
MOVEMENT THAT FINALLY RESULTED IN
THE CREATION OF THE STATE OF WEST
VIRGINIA FROM THE TERRITORY OF THE
STATE OF VIRGINIA.
THE MEETING WAS PRESIDED OVER BY
JOHN HURSEY WITH JOHN W. HARRIS AS
SECRETARY.
THE FOLLOWING DELEGATES WERE
APPOINTED TO THE WHEELING CONVENTION.

JOHN S. CARLILE
WALDO P. GOFF
JOHN J. DAVIS
THOMAS L. MOORE
SOLOMON S. FLEMING
LOT BOWEN
WILLIAM DUNKIN
WILLIAM E. LYON
FELIX S. STURM
BENJAMIN F. SHUTTLEWORTH
JAMES LYNCH
1914

election called by the Virginia Assembly to choose delegates to a convention to decide the secession issue. Voters in Harrison County chose Carlile and Benjamin Wilson states rights candidate, to report at the state convention on Feb. 13, 1861.

The week of Lincoln's inauguration was a stormy one at the convention. Carlile, spokesman for the Unionists, delivered a long, stirring speech during which he said: "The people that I have the honor in part to represent, have not been seized with this frenzied madness which has seized our friends in other parts of the commonwealth... We know we have the protection of our common Constitution; we know that the flag is ours; we know that the army is ours; we know that the navy is ours; we know that in any battle in defence of our rights; fifteen hundred thousand gallant voters in the non-slaveholding states will rush to our assistance... We cannot reconcile secession with our notions of Virginia's courage. We know that this Government we are called upon to destroy has never brought us anything but good."

After two more Carlile speeches and a vote by the convention to sescede, Carlile's boarding house in Richmond was surrounded by a mob who had a rope to hang him. Carlile and other men representing the Northwest slipped out of Richmond in disguise and on reaching Clarksburg, Carlile on April 22, 1861, addressed a mass meeting attended by 1,200 Harrison Countians. Carlile recommended that counties in Northwestern Virginia send delegates to meet in Wheeling on next May 13 to determine the course for the counties to follow. People at the meeting chose the following men to represent Harrison County: John S. Carlile, Waldo P. Goff, J. Davis, Thomas L. Moore, Soloman S. Fleming, Lot Bowen, William Dunkin, William E. Lyon, Felix S. Sturm, Benjamin F. Shuttleworth and James Lynch.

Carlile worked at Wheeling for immediate formation of a new state. At succeeding conventions in Wheeling delegates formed a "Restored State of Virginia" to be located in Alexandria, Va., and sent John S. Carlile to the U. S. Senate. The restored state government could give permission for a new state to be formed within its borders as required by the U.S. Constitution.

May 30, 1861, federal troops arrived in Clarksburg. Less than a year later Lot Bowen and John Vance, both Harrison County members of the legislature meeting in Wheeling, had resigned from the governing body and John S. Carlile worked in the U.S. Senate to scuttle the bill that would form a new state from the western counties of Virginia.

A man active in the swirl of events leading up to the formation of the State of West Virginia once said that the true history of the state could never be written. Carlile's son wrote that his father objected to the bill because his native county of Frederick was not included within the borders of the new state. John S. Carlile himself wrote that he worked against the bill because he objected to the radicalism reflected in the bill, meaning perhaps the clause that would emancipate slaves in the new state.

Carlile was in disgrace after the Emancipation Proclamation and after Lincoln signed the bill forming the State of West Virginia. He finished his term in the Senate in 1865 and lived two years in Frederick, Md., and one year in Baltimore. He returned to Clarksburg in 1868, the year he supported Grant for U.S. President and said: "My opposition to radicalism is well known. That I would have saved the Union party from it if it had been in my power, is also well known. So great was my opposition to the ultraism of Congressional legislation, and so sincere my convictions that rather than abide the one or surrender the other, I gave up my place in the Senate and for a time lost the confidence of my Union friends... The conservatism of Republicanism nominated Grant. The radicalism of Democracy nominated Seymour."

John Carlile's last years were tragic ones. He ran for the W. Va. House of Delegates in 1869 and lost. Creditors plagued Carlile. In 1870 he purchased 316 acres on the West Fork River in present Custer Addition and built a house called "Waverly" on the Mt. Clare Road. In 1878 the Carlile Waverly property was sold at a forced sale in front of the Harrison County Courthouse.

John S. Carlile died in Clarksburg Oct. 24, 1874, and is buried in the Odd Fellows Cemetery on South Chestnut St.. Frank Shuttleworth, son of Benjamin Shuttleworth, wrote of Carlile: "So many have forgotten that John S. Carlile was brilliant and perhaps the most forceful and talented speaker we ever had among us. Nature did much for him. Handsome and attractive in person, his speech on the platform or in conversation was inspiring, masterful. When Carlile was billed to speak, people came from afar, all sure of an oratorical feast."

All He Could See Were His Own Footprints Leading Up the Steps

During Civil War days, Charles Perry, a soldier in the Union Army, was often sent out to get supplies for the hospitals — butter, eggs, milk, chickens, and so on — and had many interesting experiences.

One morning when he started out to gather supplies, he came to a farmhouse situated near a small creek below Shinnston.

He rode up to the place, hitched his horse to the post, and knocked on the door. After a few minutes he decided no one was home, but as he was going down the steps, he saw someone peering out of the second floor window.

Charles went back up the porch and pushed open the door, gun in hand. There by the chimney stood a middle-aged lady, as white as a ghost. He asked why she hadn't answered the door, and she replied that she was afraid he would kill her, since he was a Union soldier. Remembering the face at the window upstairs, he asked if anyone else was in the house. She swore to him that they were alone, but he asked if he could look around. Although she said she would rather he left, he started upstairs.

Slowly he climbed the steps, expecting a Confederate soldier to jump out of a doorway to shoot him at any moment. He ventured first into one room and then another. Finding no one, he had almost decided that he had imagined the face at the window.

Suddenly, out of the corner of his eye he saw the figure of a young woman slide into an opening in the wall. The girl had long brown hair and a beautiful complexion. She wore a pink silk dress that fell in folds around her. As he turned toward her, the opening in the wall closed and, upon inspection, could not be found. Thinking it could be a passage to an inner room of the house, he closely examined the wood. There was not even a crack in the wall!

Bewildered, he went to find the woman he had spoken with, but when he returned to the first floor of the house, she was nowhere in sight. Searching the house carefully, he could find no trace of her anywhere. Knowing she could not have gone far, he looked around the farm, but could find no clue to her disappearance.

He rode to the nearest farmhouse, and a lady came out on the porch to greet him. He asked who lived in the farmhouse to the south, and she replied that the place had been deserted since an intoxicated Union soldier had come upon the house where the mother and daughter lived alone. The soldier had taken both their lives when they would not give him food and money! Shocked, he asked the housewife to describe the mother and daughter. Her descriptions fit the women he had seen exactly.

Charles rode back to the house in hopes of seeing the beautiful girl again. A strange feeling seemed to attract him to the place. Upon entering, he saw for the first time that the rooms were filled with dust and cobwebs, as if no one had been in the house for months. All he could see were his own footprints leading up the stairs.

The Brigade Had Borne The Name Before The First Battle Of Manassas

By H. KYD DOUGLAS

It was on the field of Manassas, a bright Sunday afternoon, the 21st of July 1861. The armies of McDowell and Beauregard had been grappling with each other since early morning, and, in their mutual slaughter, took no note of the sacredness of the day, nor its brightness. In Washington General Winfield Scott was anxiously awaiting the result of his skillful plan of battle, and General Joseph E. Johnston had come down from the Valley of Virginia, in reponse to Beauregard's appeal — "If you will help me, now is the time."

Hotly had the field been contested, and the hours passed slowly to men who had never tasted of battle before. Wavering had been the fortunes of the day, but it was evident the advantage was with the Federal Army, and, it seemed the day was lost. After changing position several times, without fighting, Gen. Jackson learned that Gen. Bernard Bee was hard pressed and he moved to his assistance, marching through the wounded and the stragglers, who were hurrying to the rear. It was then after 2 o'clock, and the general formed his brigade along the crest of the hill near the Henry House, the men lying down behind the brow of it, in support of the two pieces of artillery placed in position to play upon the advancing foe.

Gen. Bee, his brigade being crushed and scattered, rode up to Gen. Jackson, and, with the excitement and mortification of an untried but heroic soldier, reported that the enemy were beating him back.

"Very well, General, it can't be helped," replied Jackson.

"But how do you expect to stop them?"

"We'll give them the bayonet!" was the answer, briefly.

Gen. Bee wheeled his horse, and galloped back to his command. As he did so, Gen. Jackson said to Lt. Lee of his staff:

"Tell the colonel of this brigade that the enemy are advancing; that when their heads are seen above the hill, let the whole line rise, move forward with a shout, and thrust to the bayonet. I am tired of this long range work."

In the storm which followed Bee's return to his command, he was soon on foot, his horse shot from under him. With the fury of despair he strode among his men, and tried to rally and hold them against the torrent which beat upon them; and finally, in a voice which rivaled the roar of battle, he cried out: "Men, there are Jackson and his Virginians standing behind you like a stone wall!" Uttering these words of martial baptism, Bee fell dead upon the field, and left behind him a fame which will follow that of Jackson as a shadow.

It would be but the repetition of history to mention, at length, the movements of Jackson's Brigade that day. It was Bee who gave him the name of "Stonewall," but it was his own Virginians who made that name immortal. This brigade checked the victorious tide of battle, but to turn it back was no easy labor. Around the Henry House and its plateau the contest raged with renewed violence and vacillating success for an hour; and then Jackson led his men in their last bayonet charge, and pierced the enemy's center. The timely arrival of Kirby Smith and Jubal Early upon their flank finished the work, and defeat was turned into a rout. Gen. Jackson will be forgiven for his sentence in a letter to a friend: "You will find, when my report shall be published, that the First Brigade was to our army what the Imperial Guard was to Napoleon; through the blessings God it met the victorious enemy, and turned the fortunes of the day."

Thus, the story has been told from generation to generation of how Stonewall Jackson got his hame. It is not a matter of historical fact but one of historical folklore which allows historical fact to become blurred in the march of time. Others have written of the supposed origin of the name and have traced the legendary nickname back not to the stone bridge at Bull Run, nor to the stone fences of Winchester Heights, nor the phrase "There stands Jackson like a stone wall" of Gen. Bee; but to Jackson's original "Stonewall Brigade" so called because they were principally recruited in the stone-wall country, the Virginia valley counties of Jefferson, Clarke, Frederick, Page and Warren. The brigade had borne the name before the first battle of Bull Run and the Winchester Heights affair.

Gen. Jackson did not claim the title of "Stonewall" for himself, and it was some time before the name, by a metonymy that was altogether natural and proper was applied to him. The fact that the Stonewall Brigade lent its name to its stout leader and did not derive it from him may be found in various published items of the time. For example, in the Staunton Spectator of March 18, 1862, the following paragraph headed "The Stone-Wall" appeared: "General Thom. J. Jackson has moved the "Stonewall" from Winchester to Mt. Jackson, in Shenandoah County, where he will give the enemy fight if they pursue him to that place…"

In the same periodical, dated April 8, 1862, was printed another article entitled "The Stonewall Brigade" which read in part: "In every encounter of Gen. Jackson's men with the enemy, they have fairly earned the title won by their sturdy and unconquerable valor at Manassas, the "Stonewall Brigade."

In his last hours Stonewall Jackson was careful to explain to some members of his staff who hung upon his parting words that the honorable title belonged to his men and not to him; it was not personal and figurative like Andrew Jackson's "Old Hickory" as the newapapers persisted in making it, but the local designation of a corps of gallant fighting men.

Who was Stonewall Jackson, and of what stock? Although he was of sterling and respectable parentage, it matters little, for, in historic fame, "he was his own ancestor." And it was well enough that Virginia, who gave to the war Robert E. Lee, of old and aristocratic lineage, should furnish Jackson as the representative of her people. On the 21st of January, 1824, in Clarksburg, among the mountains of western Virginia, was born this boy, the youngest of four children; and with no view to his future fame, he was named Thomas Jonathan Jackson. It was a rugged, honest name, but is no cause of regret that it is now merged in the more rugged and euphonious one he afterward made for himself.

Every Night They Would Hear The Horses… 'A Ghost Story'

By RUTH ANN MUSICK

During the Civil War when West Virginia was often overrun by both Confederate and Union troops, a father and his two sons went off to fight in the army, leaving the wife and daughter at home alone. Before leaving, the three men took all of the money and buried it, never telling the rest of the family where, for fear the women might be forced by enemy soldiers to surrender it. The men, of course, believed that at least one of them would get back alive.

It so happened that all three men died in the war and none was left to return home. The lonely women continued to live in their remote country home. Every night they would hear horses galloping around and around the house, but when they looked outside, nothing could be seen. Finally, the mother could stand it no longer, so she and the daughter would walk to a nearby farmhouse to sleep each night, returning early in the morning to tend the farm. No matter how hard they tried, things seemed to go from bad to worse, and the two women were having a very difficult time making ends meet.

One evening when the two women were preparing to leave for the night, a peddler arrived and asked for a night's lodging. The women explained that they did not stay in the house at night because of strange noises, but he was welcome to sleep there if he wished. The peddler was quite tired and accepted their offer, telling them he had no fears.

As soon as the women were gone, the peddler prepared himself for the night. He covered the fire in the fireplace, took off his boots, and lay down on a cot near the fire. Soon he was fast asleep.

About midnight he was awakened by the sound of horses galloping down the road. He thought this unusual in such a remote area and at such a late hour, but he was even more surprised when they galloped up to the house and around it. He quickly went to the window, drew aside the curtain, and looked out into a clear moonlight night. He saw no sign of horses. He lay down again and soon dozed, only to be awakened by the same sound, louder and closer than before.

The peddler now began to be frightened, so he latched the door tightly and pushed heavy bureaus and other furniture against it. Again he lay down, feeling more secure.

Suddenly the galloping stopped and the door opened as easily as if it had not been barred. An old man with a long beard entered the room and sat near the fire, looking into the coals. The peddler noticed that the old man's throat was cut from ear to ear. He could not keep from asking, ''Old man, do you know your throat is cut?''

The old man answered without looking up, ''Yes, I know my throat is cut.'' And then he continued to look into the fire.

About this time a second man, younger than the first, walked through the door. He too sat looking into the fire, and he too had his throat cut. The peddler finally asked him the same question and received the same reply. Soon a third man entered the room, in the same condition, and he too sat staring into the fire. He gave the same answer to the peddler's question that the other two had given.

After some time had passed, the peddler asked who they were. The old man explained that they were the men of that particular household, who had been killed in battle by having their throats cut. He said they could not rest until the money they had hidden was back in the hands of the two women who needed it so desperately. They wanted to show him where they had hidden the money and asked him to give it to the wife and daughter.

The peddler promised that he would put it in their hands, and the ghosts proceeded to lead the way to the fence corner where the money was buried. But upon leaving, the three men warned him that if he did not give the money to the women to whom it belonged, he would never sleep another night, but would always hear the galloping horses. They also told him to tell the wife and daughter that they need not leave the house again, since they would never be bothered by the sounds of galloping horses after that night. Then the three men rode away.

The peddler kept his word and gave the money to the women as he had promised and was rewarded handsomely. From that time on, the women stayed in their home and never heard the sound of horses galloping around the house again.

McNicol China Exhibit To Be Held At Public Library

By William D. Gaston

Chances are, if you were born in the last one hundred years, at some time or place in your life you have eaten or drunk from a piece of McNicol china, be it in a restaurant, hospital, military mess hall, on an ocean liner, your first A.B.C. baby plate, or even if you attended a $100-a-plate dinner for the campaign fund for a candidate for President of the United States. McNicol Pottery Company made a durable ware for every walk of life.

The McNicol plant was located in Stonewood at the corner of Water and Woodland streets from 1914 to the mid 1960s. It employed between 200 and 500 men and women at it's peak

The McNicol Pottery Company was a producer of high-quality pottery from **1923** till **1954**. Located in Stonewood, it was a major employer at that time. Creative Building Supplies occupies this site today.

production during the war years. All that remains of it today is the main office, shipping platform, warehouse and packing sections. The room for making "slip" jigger room, decorating, tunnel kilns and machine shop, have all been demolished and are memories of the past now. But there are those of us who had parents, grandparents other relatives and good friends that are not about to let their untiring efforts and craftsmanship go unforgotten. There's was a way of life which contributed so much to the prosperity of our community, county and state.

An example of this proud heritage is now on display at the Clarksburg-Harrison Public Library's main entrance through the first week of October. The display is a small part of a collection belonging to Sherry and Gary Messenger of Clarksburg. The display consists of pitchers, cups, trays, creamers, tea pots, and an outstanding plate collection, among other interesting items. The display also has pieces that were made for The McNicol Company's own use, such as sample plates which have the color codes on them for the decorating department. To look at the many shapes and sizes that McNicol produced, one can only be amazed. Each piece of ware had to be decorated in comparison with it's size; and all of this was done by hand. Each piece had to be handled over 60 times before it ever left the factory. It is difficult to imagine what it must have been like to put thousands of handles on cups and pitchers that went through that plant. Most of the employees that had to do with production were paid by the piece. The decorators were usually the best paid, depending on the type of decoration. Some sprayed while others used a brush on items that required more skill. A lot of ware was decorated with gold. The rags that they used to wipe off excess gold were washed to retrieve the gold for reuse.

McNicol made so many different items that to collect even one piece of each would be nearly impossible. Perhaps the greatest difficulty in collecting McNicol china is the fact that there is no catalogue, and probably never will be one, that could list all the production items every made by McNicol. The company just made too many special order items that have

never been catalogued and many records were disposed of when production ceased in East Liverpool, Ohio and moved to Clarksburg in 1914. Because of discrepancies in immediately available records, and in order not to be misleading, the approximate life of the company in both East Liverpook, Ohio and in Clarksburg was from approximately 1877 to 1965.

Unlike glassware which is known by its cut, pressed, etched, or embossed design, McNicol used numbers, rubber stamps and decal monograms, among others, to identify special orders and without proper records or catalogues it is both difficult and rewarding to collect McNicol china.

It is very gratifying to hear the comments of people looking at the display. The "Oh's" and "Ah's" and "Oh, look at that one. My grandmother had one like that and she gave it to me!" And because Sherry Messenger's grandmother gave one to her from which she began a collection, the author and the Bicentennial Committee are grateful to her and her husband for sharing a part of that collection with us, and grateful to the many employees of McNicol whose hard labor made this community and Harrison County a better place for all of us to live.

Guerilla Warfare - They Said He Tried To Escape and They Shot Him to Death

By JACK SANDY ANDERSON

Many historians consider the Civil War the greatest tragedy that ever befell the American nation. It was a long and bloody chapter in our history that saw families torn asunder and friendships destroyed by the heated passions of the time. For four years the nation struggled to settle once and for all problems that had beset it for decades and to arrive at a clear definition of its destiny.

Few sections of the country experienced greater anguish in this war than did West Virginia. Thousands of its men saw service in the armies of the North and the South, and numerous battles and skirmishes were fought on its soil. Greatly adding to the anguish was the guerrilla warfare that flared sporadically from 1861 to 1865.

The West Fork Valley was the scene of several guerrilla incidents, accounts of which have been handed down through the years. There are different versions of these accounts and the ones I here relate are those that, for some reason or another, I like best.

One of the early incidents was the murder of George Seese in April 1862. A Southern sympathizer, he had been arrested by the Home Guards and was detained by them at Boothsville. They shot him to death and repoted that he had been trying to escape. Neither his family nor his friends, not a few of whom were loyal Unionists, believed this report. They considered his death a brutal, cold-blooded murder.

The Home Guard functioned as a militia to protect and defend the local area while most men of military age were away serving in the regular army. Southern sympathizers were closely watched, and those whose activities were deemed traitorous to the Union were arrested. However, early in its existence the Home Guard acquired a bad reputation, for it was evident that a number of its members were using it as a means of harassing and "getting even" with people they didn't like for personal reasons rather than political ones. Some whom they harassed and upon whom they inflicted hardship had been their friends in ante-bellum days. Apparently relationship did not matter much, either, for certan relatives of Home Guard members also suffered. In the Home Guard were men from the rougher segment of the area's population, men regarded as ruffians and bullies. Even several of the most ardent Union supporters, including some of my mother's family, looked upon the Home Guard with a degree of contempt and considered its members "cowards who didn't have enough guts to join the regular army."

Of course, the Home Guard members were important to the defense of the West Fork Valley and demonstrated their bravery on more than one occasion during the war. The bad reputation was only partly deserved, for most of the members were patriotic men trying their best to do their duty in a confused and unsettled time.

In late April, 1863, Confederate soldiers under Jones invaded the West Fork Valley and reached Shinnston, where they seized livestock, particularly horses, and food suplies. Soon thereafter members of the Home Guard arrested

Nathaniel Barnes and his son, who were accused of telling the Confederates where to find the neighborhood's best horses. The Barneses, who lived in what is now East Shinnston, stoutly denied the accusation, but were nonetheless sent to Camp Chase in Ohio, a place where many local Southern sympathizers were imprisoned. They both contracted disease and died.

During the night of December 16, 1864, Southern guerrillas murdered Henry Swiger in the Coon's Run community of Adamsville. A well-to-do farmer, Swiger was a Republican and a strong Union supporter. The day before he had sold some of his cattle in Clarksburg and had been paid a large sum of money which he had in his home. These facts were known by some of his neighbors, one or more of whom passed on the information to members of the guerrilla band. Around 10 p.m. the guerrillas forced their way into the Swiger home.

"Give us your money," one of them demanded of Swiger, who handed over $40, all he had in his pockets.

"You have lots more than this, damn you," snarled the guerrilla. "We want the money you got for the cattle."

Realizing that these were desperate and dangerous men, Swiger replied, "Very well. But I have to go to the attic to get it."

As he started to climb the stairs, sounds were heard coming from the attic. One of the guerrillas yelled out, "Shoot him! Shoot him!"

The loud sound of gun shots filled the room as three of the band fired pistols. Although struck by the bullets, Swiger was still standing. A guerrilla then grabbed a gun belonging to Swiger that stood nearby and discharged it at the unfortunate victim, killing him instantly.

It had been said that when the guerrillas heard the sounds coming from the attic, they feared they had unwittingly entered a trap and panicked, causing them to shoot Swiger. John Blackburn Swiger, the older of the two Swiger sons, and his friend, James Elmore Koon, were sleeping in the attic when the guerrillas invaded the house. Through a crack in the floor, they had been watching in horror the proceedings taking place below them. Their movements had made the sounds which so alarmed the guerrillas.

Word of the atrocity quickly spread, and the next day members of the Home Guard arrived at the Swiger home. From information given by Mrs. Swiger, who had recognized some of the guerrillas despite their attempt to disguise themselves, and by following tracks made by a horse ridden by one of the guerrillas, the Home Guard soldiers were led to the house of a known Rebel located two or three miles from Adamsville. A thorough search was made, and a membership roster of the guerrilla band was found on which was recorded the name of the house's owner.

Some of the Home Guard on this same day (December 17) decided to retaliate against Southern sympathizers by arresting John Short, a young man whose pacifist ideals had caused him to be labeled a Southern sympathizer and who had recently been released from Camp Chase. In the afternoon they found Short near the head of Laurel Run cutting corn in a field that belonged to his brother-in-law, Alfred Tetrick. He offered no resistance, and they marched him down the road. Not far away stood the home of another of Short's brothers-in-law, Harrison Tetrick, and the soldiers stopped there for supper. Short was confined in a small building near the main house, and Mrs. Tetrick slipped away while the soldiers were eating to beg him to escape into the woods back of the house.

"But I have done nothing wrong," Short told her. "I have broken no law. They cannot hold me. I will soon be set free."

As soon as the soldiers finished eating, they and their prisoner started down the road toward Enterprise. Alfred Tetrick was accompanying them, and he and Zimri Spencer were walking behind the others. Spencer, a zealous and influential member of the Home Guard, was Short's step-brother; and Tetrick was pleading with him to keep the other soldiers from harming Short.

As they neared the Union Church, a shot rang out and Spencer exclaimed, "There, by God, it's too late now! They've shot him!"

And, indeed, they had. Short's wound was mortal, and the soldiers left him lying in the road. Alfred Tetrick remained with him. He was soon joined by Mr. and Mrs. Harrison Tetrick, who had heard the gunshot, and James Harrison, a friend who lived nearby. Efforts to save Short's life were futile, and in a little while he died.

The last incident which I'll relate took place on Booth's Creek, not far from Monongah, early in 1865. William Russell and Samuel Vincent were serving in the Confederate Army and had come home together to visit their families, even though the risk was great of being arrested or killed by Home Guard members living in the area.

It was time to return to the army, and Vincent came to the Russell home to get his friend. However, one of the Russell children was sick, and the worried father wanted to delay their departure a few hours to see if his condition improved. Night came and the two men decided to wait until morning before starting out. Somehow, the Home Guard soldiers learned of the Rebels' whereabouts; and before daylight they surrounded the house and demanded that Russell and Vincent surrender.

Knowing they had no other choice, they did. Russell and his wife knew all the soldiers present, some of whom had been among their closest friends before the war, and invited them to breakfast. The invitation was accepted. During the meal, they assured Mrs. Russell that no harm would come to her husband or to Vincent as they were only going to send them to Camp Chase.

Soon after eating, the soldiers and the prisoners left. Minutes later Mrs. Russell heard gunshots but paid little attention and went on with her morning work. Not long afterward she saw a neighbor boy running toward the house. Sensing that something was terribly wrong, she opened the door and walked out onto the porch to meet him.

When the boy saw her, he began to sob, "Oh, Mrs. Russell, come quick. They're shot! They're shot!"

Icy fear gripped Mrs. Russell's heart as the boy led her to where the two Confederates lay in the road. They were beyond earthly help, and the grief-stricken woman sat down beside her dead husband and cradled his head in her lap.

A few months later the Civil War was over. However, the bitterness engendered by the guerrilla incidents remained for many years. Even today traces of it linger on.

The Sweetest Music I Ever Heard

By H. KYD DOUGLAS

In face and figure, Stonewall Jackson was not striking. Above the average height, with a frame angular, muscular, and fleshless, he was, in all his movements, from riding a horse to handling a pen, one of the most ungraceful men in the army. His expression was thoughtful, and generally clouded with an air of fatigue. His eye was small, blue, and in repose as gentle as a young girl's. With high, broad forehead, small, sharp nose, thin, pallid lips, deep set eyes, and dark rusty beard, he was not a handsome man.

His face in the drawing-room or tent, softened by his smile, was as different from itself on the battle-field as a little lake in summer noon differs from the same lake when frozen.

One night, at tattoo, this cry broke forth in the camp of the Stonewall Brigade, and was taken up by brigades and divisions, until it rolled over field and wood throughout the whole corps. The General came hastily and bareheaded from his tent, and going up to a fence near by, he leaned upon it and listened in quiet to the rise, climax and conclusion of that strange serenade, raising his head to catch the last sound, as it grew fainter, and until it died away like an echo along the mountains. Then turning toward his tent he muttered, in half soliloquy, 'That was the sweetest music I ever heard.'

Gen. Jackson's troops and his enemies believed he never slept; the fact is, he slept a great deal. Whenever he had nothing else to do, he went to sleep, especially in church. During the invasion of Maryland, or Sunday night he rode three miles in an ambulance to attend church in Frederick, and then fell asleep as soon as the minister began to preach; his head fell upon his breast, and he never awoke until aroused by the organ and choir. He could sleep anywhere and in any position, sitting in his chair, under fire, or on horseback. On a night march toward Richmond, after the battles with McClellan, he was riding along with his drowsy staff, nodding and sleeping as he went. They passed by groups of men sitting along the roadside, and engaged in roasting new corn by fire made of fence-rails. One group took them for cavalrymen with an inebriated captain, and one of the party, delighted at the sight of a man who had found whiskey enough to be drunk, sprang up from the fire and, brandishing a roasting-ear in his hand, leaped down into the road, and seizing the General's horse, cried out: 'I say, old fellow, where the devil did you get your liquor?' In an instant, as the General awoke, the fellow saw his mistake; and them bounding from the road he took the fence as a single leap, exclaiming: 'Good God, it's Old Jack!' and disappeared in the darkness. Yes, Gen. Jackson slept a great deal, but he was never caught napping.

Walking or riding the General was ungainly; his main object was to go over the ground, without regard to the manner of his going. His favorite horse was as little like Pegasus as he was like Apollo; he rode boldly and well, but certainly not with grace and ease. He was not a man of style. Gen. Robert E. Lee, on horseback or off, was a handsome soldier. It was said of Gen. Wade Hampton that he looked as knightly when mounted as if he had stepped out from an old canvas, horse and all. Gen. John C. Breckenridge was a model of manly beauty and Gen. Joe Johnston looked every inch a soldier. None of these things can be said of Jackson.

Akin to his dyspepsia, and perhaps as a consequence, was his ignorance of music. One morning, at Ashland, he startled a young lady from her propriety by gravely asking her if she ever had heard a new piece of music called "Dixie," and as gravely listening to her while she sang it. He had heard it a thousand times from the army bands, and yet it seemed new to him. Judged by the Shakespearean standard, who could be more 'fit for treasons, stratagems, and spoils?' And yet there was one kind of music which always interested and delighted him. It was the rebel yell of his troops. To this grand chorus he never failed to respond. The difference between the regular hurrah of the Federal army and the irregular, wild yell of the Confederates was as marked as the difference in their uniforms. The rebel yell was a peculiar mixture of sound, a kind of weird shout. Jackson was greeted with it whenever he made an appearance to his troops, on the march or in battle; and just as invariably he would seize his old gray cap from his head in acknowledgement, and his 'little sorrel,' knowing his habit, would break into a gallop and never halt until the shout had ceased.

Nathan Goff Jr. - Congressman, Banker

By DOROTHY DAVIS

Nathan Goff, Jr., son of Waldo Potter Goff and Harriet Louise Moore Goff, was born Feb. 9, 1843.

The second son and third child, Nathan was named for his uncle Nathan Goff with whom Waldo P. Goff had run a successful mercantile business in Clarksburg across from the courthouse and branches of the business in Morgantown and Buckhannon. Nathan, Jr. was born in the mansion his father had built for his bride in 1839 at 400 West Pike Street in Clarksburg and a stucture which a century later would be named "Waldomore" in honor of Waldo P. Goff's mother Zerviah Waldo Goff and Harriet Moore Goff's father, Thomas Preston Moore.

Young Nathan attended Northwestern Academy two hundred yards east of his home from the time he was school age until 1860, when he went, along with his cousins Meigs Jackson and Charles Lowndes, to school at Georgetown College in Washington. The chaos of the impending war caused Nate Goff to leave school after one quarter of instruction during which he had showed his brilliance with a record of first in a class of 30 in Greek, Latin, and English and first in a class of 35 in mathematics.

Waldo P. and Nathan Goff, both Whigs, were staunch Unionists. Young Nathan soon after arriving home delivered a Union oration and wrote for the Clarksburg newspaper: "Shall we, as Virginians... follow this damning scheme of ruin, war and devastation, as indicated in the program of the Disunion Party... Methinks I hear the voice of Virginia's noble sons arising in thundertones from the hills and vales of

our lovely land: 'Never — no never' '' And on May 23, 1861. fearful of being stopped by the Confederate Home Guards, Goff and a group of young Union men walked to Wilsonburg to catch a train for Wheeling to volunteer in the Union Army.

Nathan Goff, Jr. had risen to the rank of major when he was captured near Petersburg (W. Va.), Jan. 28, 1864 and placed in Libby Prison in Richmond on Feb. 10 in solitary confinement as hostage for Confederate Captain Thomas Armsey who had been captured spying in his hometown of Clarksburg and sent to serve a 14-year term in a prison near Boston. In a damp cell and given food consisting of a daily ration of ¼ pound of cornbread and ½ pint of black beans, Goff kept his sanity by reading Blackstones's ''Commentaries'' supplied by Waldo P. Johnson, a relative and former U.S. Senator from Missouri and a Confederate who could visit the hapless imprisoned youth.

Alarmed that their son Nathan's health was fast deteriorating and certain that the death a few months earlier of their firstborn Henry Clay Goff while serving in the U.S. Army gave them a good case, Waldo P. Goff and Harriet Goff in July left by train for Washington, where letters from Senators Van Winkle and Willey, Governor Boreman and B&O President John W. Garrett helped the Goff's secure an interview with President Lincoln. The president authorized the exchange of Armsey for Goff.

According to newspaper accounts in the 1860s, Nathan, Jr., was breveted a brigadier general for gallant service during the conflict. His biographer G. Wayne Smith noted that Goff ''did not deny the reports, and after some years had elapsed, he asserted that the rank was rightfully his.''

Matured by the war experience, 22-year-old Goff was admitted to the Harrison County Bar March 15, 1865. Eight months later he married Laura E. Despard, daughter of Burton Despard and Emily Smith Despard. Their son Guy Despard Goff was born in 1866 and a second son Waldo Percy Goff, in 1870. Nathan Goff, Jr. joined the law firm of Burton Despard and Edwin Maxwell. Goff ran on the Republican ticket for the seat held since the formation of West Virginia in the House of Delegates by his Uncle Nathan in 1866 and won. He returned to the legislature in 1868, the same year he was appointed U.S. Attorney for West Virginia.

In 1880 Goff began construction of his palatial residence that still stands in 1984 on West Main Street. Plans for the structure were drawn up by Philadelphia architects who supplied hardware, furnace, bathroom fixtures and experienced brick layers for outside brick work, but most material was gathered from Goff's own land. Goff supervised every detail of the construction of the two-story brick house with mansard roof of slate and an interior with rooms between 13 and 14 feet high. The Goffs moved into the house in 1883.

President Hayes appointed Nathan Goff Jr., Secretary of the Navy on Jan. 6, 1881, but after James Garfield was inaugurated two months later, the new president appointed Goff to return to his position as U.S. Attorney for West Virginia. Goff resigned the position to serve in the 48th, 49th and 50th sessions of the U.S. House of Representatives from 1883-1889.

Nathan Goff Jr. was unsuccessful in the 1876 and 1888 contests for the governorship of West Virginia. After the 1888 election Goff had won by 130 votes. His opponent challenged

some of the votes cast and was eventually seated even though Goff had traveled to Charleston and had staged his own inaugural parade.

Goff became a private citizen in 1889 for the first time for more than 20 years. He had inherited most of his uncle Nathan's estate reputed to be $650,000 and which included vast acres of land in Harrison County. Goff was president of the Merchants National Bank and president of the Clarksburg Gas and Electric Company. In 1890 Goff and four other Republicans bought the Clarksburg Telegram Company, Goff wrote for its newspaper: "In politics the Telegram will teach the Republican faith. I believe the policy of that great party to be essential to the development and prosperity of this country...."

With others, Goff in 1891 formed the Elk Hill Coal and Coke Company and the Commercial Coal and Coke Company. The same year Goff began negotiations with the B&O Railroad to move the railroad station from the East Pike Street area to Goff's Elk Hill Farm north of the city. Goff gave the land for the railway station and divided the area on both sides of the tracks into streets and building lots. In 1897 Goff, R. T. Lowndes, Charles M. Hart, David Davidson and Jasper Y. Moore formed the Clarksburg Bridge Company to build a bridge across Elk Creek to the Elk Hill Farm and the heirs of Waldo P. Goff gave enough land to extend Fourth Street to the new bridge.

During the early 1890s when Goff held no public office, he became a nationwide symbol of retiscent Southern Republicanism. His skill as an orator and his engaging personality made him among the first to be asked to speak at Republican functons in all leading cities. A Baltimore paper described Goff as "one of the brightest men in his party and in the country... in the prime of life, and the picture of vigorous, aggressive manhood." A New York newspaper reported: "Goff was received clamorously... This undersized man, with small bones and dainty hands, with his smooth, plump, boyish face, sparkling blue eyes and fine, closely cropped hair, was the sensation of the night." On December 16, 1891, President Harrison announced the appointment of Goff as a judge of the U.S. Circuit Court for the Fourth Judicial District which included the states of West Virginia, Maryland, Virginia, North Carolina and South Carolina.

Someone once said that in business anything Nathan Goff Jr. touched turned to gold. His good fortune is exemplified in his ventures into drilling for petroleum in the western portion of Harrison County. Not sure of the extent of the Wolf Summit oil field, Goff worked out a plan whereby he leased drilling rights to the South Penn Oil Company. If the wells drilled did not prove successful, the leases would revert to Goff. None of the drilling by the company produced wells and Goff went into drilling in 1895 as an independent operator. He produced gushers on Hall's Run and excellent wells on Big Rock Camp. In the next 10 years Goff's sales in oil amounted to more than a million dollars.

Much of the oil income Goff invested in Clarksburg buildings. In 1901 he completed the Elkbridge Building in Glen Elk at the north end of the Fourth Street Bridge; in 1903 he built the Oak Hall Building, an office and apartment building on West Main Street; in 1904 he completed the Waldo Hotel at the corner of North Fourth and West Pike streets; in 1911 Goff built the Goff Building, an office structure on West Main Street.

"The construction of the Waldo Hotel was an indication of the bent of Goff's mind. Naturally convivial and friendly, he could now entertain prominent and important guests in a magnificent style. The Waldo, named for his father, soon gained a fine reputation as a hospitable and luxurious hotel where the service was excellent in the best Southern tradition. For many years the hotel not only improved Clarksburg's hospitality, but it made money for Goff. During the years 1917-1919 the gross income from the 135 guest rooms and the dining rooms averaged $128,000 a year, while the net profit for the same period averaged almost $29,000 a year."

March 13, 1913, Goff resigned as judge of the United States Circuit Court after serving as judge for 13 years. On April 7, 1913, Nathan Goff, Jr. took the oath of office as U.S. Senator from West Virginia. He remained in the Senate until March 4, 1919.

After a long illness Goff's wife Laura Ellen died Oct. 28, 1918. At the end of June 1919 while at Lake Placid, N.Y., Nathan Goff was stricken with a partial paralysis of his right side. He returned to his home in Clarksburg to convalesce.

During his illness he was attended by his son Percy, who lived in the Clarksburg residence, Dr. Robert A. Haynes, and Miss Katherine Penney who had nursed Percy's son Nathan back to health after a serious illness. In late August Dr. Haynes told his patient he could go and come as he pleased.

Goff left for New York City where on Aug. 28 he and Miss Penney were married. They returned to the Clarksburg residence where they lived until the death of Nathan Goff Jr., which occurred on April 23, 1920.

After The Gun Barrel Was Found The Ghost Was Never Seen Again

BY WILLIAM B. PRICE

The old inn, a large two-story structure built of logs, had weathered to a gray color. The fibers of its gray poplar logs had loosened on the surface, and hornets, wasps and yellow jackets were collecting them for their nests.

By mixing such fibers with saliva, these insects' ancestors had, countless centuries before, made the first paper in the world.

While the insect workers busied themselves with their trade on a lazy May afternoon, a stranger carrying a small rifle approached the inn. On his right side, he carried a small pouch and powder horn by a strap hanging from his left shoulder. From a cord passed over his right shoulder, he carried a small satchel which rested against his left hip. The man's clothing was clean, but much worn. The innkeeper noticed that it had been darned in a few places, and that a patch covered a knee of the old gray trousers. As the stranger stepped up on the porch, a small dog ran up to him, sniffing and wagging his tail.

The innkeeper, a Mr. Ford, greeted his guest who, in turn, asked for a meal and a few days' lodging. The newcomer signed his name in the register as Steve Darton. Because sympathies were so sharply divided between the Union and the Confederacy, people in those days did not ask a stranger about his business. If they spoke at all about the war, they spoke in whispers. When the innkeeper served Darton his supper, he noticed that his guest ate with his rifle and the little dog by his side.

Early the next morning, Darton awoke to the songs of a thousand birds. Nature's woodland chorus continued its concert in full volume until dawn's chariot had driven the shadows of the night away. A few clouds, high in the eastern sky, were lined with silver and gold. The rest of the sky was blue as a woman's eye.

At the inn, word came through from the telegraph office that Jones' Raid was on, and everywhere people were hiding their valuables, food, cattle and horses. Down among the folks in the countryside, all was hate, suspicion and fear.

Darton ate an early breakfast and asked that a lunch be packed for him. He then took his gun, and, returned just in time for supper.

When it was observed that the newcomer had continued this pattern of movement for several days, folks at the inn became suspicious. Surely, this man's hunting in May was unusual. Besides, in the two or three days he had been out, he had brought back no game. It was also observed that he drank very little and ate lightly, that his gun was always by his side, that his black hair was usually well groomed though somewhat long, and that his penetrating gaze held anyone who looked straight into his face almost as if hypnotized. It was whispered that the new guest was most likely a spy on one side or the other.

One day word came that Jones and his raiders would likely reach the inn on the following day. The next morning, Darton left the inn before daybreak, without the dog. About noon, some soldiers stopped at the inn and asked for water. While they were filling their canteens, a big hog was observed in a lot not far from the well. One of the soldiers raised his musket and shot the hog. The other soldiers laughed and all then mounted their horses and rode away toward the east, taking the road to the left that led over the hill toward the Ohio River. After the soldiers were gone, the innkeeper's family dressed the hog and saved the meat.

That evening, the hunter did not return to the inn. It was thought he had probably joined the raiders. A few days later, old Uncle Jessie Davis said something about a lot of buzzards flying above the hill. Nobody thought much about it at the time, but then, an old man who kept the toll gate said that on the afternoon after the raiders had stopped at the inn, he had

heard the sharp pop of a small rifle near the top of the hill. This, he said, was followed almost instantly by a wild rebel yell. Then a volley was fired and all was still.

Months later, the skeleton of a man was found in the woods to the right of the road, looking north. There was no way to identify the person as only the bones and shredded clothing remained. These were buried on the hill where they were found. There was considerable speculation as to who the man was and how he had met his death.

After that, folks in the area would frequently hear, late in the evening, the pop of a rifle and a wild yell, followed by firing muskets and screams of pain. It was noticed that these sounds were heard at about the same hour. Sometimes a fleeting figure could be seen against the skyline.

Many years, later, the disappearance of the mysterious hunter was explained when the barrel of a squirrel rifle was found extending completely through the center of a pin oak tree. The gun had been dropped into the forks of the tree three

years before. As the tree grew, the barrel of the small rifle was completely surrounded by the tree.

After the gun barrel was found, the sounds associated with the lone hunter's death were no longer heard, and the ghost was never seen again. But the gun barrel can still be seen in the growing tree not more than four miles from Salem. The muzzle protrudes about eight inches from the tree on one side, and about one and a half inches of the breech end can still be seen at the other side of the tree.

Bridgeport - Named For The Port Or Passageway Via A Bridge
BY SHARON R. SAYE

At one time there were two covered wooden bridges across Simpson Creek in Bridgeport. The upper one was on the Northwestern Turnpike, or Rt. 50, and the lower one near the stockyards on the road from Rt. 50 to what was Davidson's Mill.

On June 18, 1811, upon a petition for a bridge across Simpson Creek, the County Court appointed commissioners to locate a site. The commissioners reported that they had selected a site about a quarter of a mile above Joseph Johnson's mill. The Court considered the report favorably and directed the commissioners to sell out the construction to the lowest bidder, and to advertise the time and place of sale in the "Bystander" for three weeks. The "Bystander" was the first newspaper published in the county — the first issue was published only one week before the order to advertise was made.

The Court further ordered that the sum of $150 be appropriated for the building, one half out of the levy for 1811, and one half out of that for 1812.

Not long after the bridge was built, Joseph Johnson, who then thought he owned the land around his grist mill and the bridge, laid off some of his land into lots for the purpose of establishing a town between the mill and the new bridge. To do so he secured an Act of the Legislature passed Jan. 15, 1816, chartering his town.

As he saw people crossing the bridge, he observed it was a port, or passage way, for all such persons and this gave him the idea to add to the word Bridge the word port, and that would give him the word Bridgeport, as the name for his new town. It is now, with the assistance of the late Michael L. Benedum, a very popular and prosperous town.

Bridgeport is actually more than 200 years old. Between 1771 and 1774, the families of Joseph Davisson, James Anderson, John Wilkinson, Andrew Davisson and John Powers settled along Simpson Creek after a difficult journey from Eastern Virginia. These early settlers built a fort; the

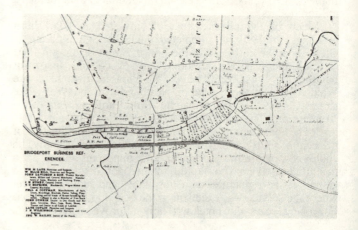

exact location is subject to controversy. One local historian puts the fort "near the site of the old Methodist Church (now converted into an apartment building) on Davis Street, just south of Main Street at the top of the hill. From the fort the men built a bridge across Simpson's Creek just above where the present bridge on U.S. Rt. 50 stands, and the rich bottom land on the southwest side of the creek was cleared for growing crops."

Other sources suggest the fort was built near the present Methodist Church on Worthington Drive; this location was chosen because of defensive reasons. The early settlers were often threatened by Indian attacks. Both sources agree that the crops were grown on the southern side of Simpson Creek and that the settlers built a pontoon bridge to connect the fort and their farm lands.

In the early days of the community, Joseph Johnson was its most distinguished citizen. He came to Bridgeport in 1803, was a captain in the War of 1812, elected four times to the State Legislature of Virginia and seven times to Congress. He was the only governor of Virginia from west of the mountains and served a four-year term. Johnson obtained passage of an Act of the Virginia Legislature on Jan. 15, 1856, which established the town of Bridgeport.

J. B. Sandusky, an outstanding businessman, had much to do with the history of Bridgeport, as did John Davison, James Hurry and Emanuel Benedum. Benedum was elected a justice and as such he was for a number of years a member of both the Board of Supervisors and the County Court. He was the father of Michael L. Benedum, whose successful career was told by Sam Mallison in a book of some 500 pages entitled "The Great Wildcatter."

Bridges and roads seem to have been particularly influential in Bridgeport's development. The first road connected the town to Winchester in 1786. The Northwestern Turnpike was opened in 1838 connecting Bridgeport to Clarksburg. This caused a shift in the town's center as settlers moved nearer the turnpike. It also brought a flourishing trade for taverns and hotels. The Baltimore and Ohio Railroad began serving Bridgeport in 1856 and brought a new influx of residents.

Presently the town has Benedum Airport which provides air service to many cities, and Interstate 79, which is a North-South route from Charleston to Erie, Pa.

Bridgeport's first school house was built near the present site of Simpson Grade School. Later this was replaced by a buff brick building in 1903 which still serves as a grade school. In 1923 a high school building was completed on Newton Street. This building served as a high school/junior high until 1963 at which time the new Bridgeport Senior High School was completed on Johnson Avenue. Bridgeport now has three grade schools, Johnson, Simpson, and All-Saints, one junior high school and the high school.

Through the generosity of Michael Benedum the town now has a Civic Center. Benedum also helped finance the building of the Methodist Church and donated funds for buying the land and for paving the city fire department parking lot.

Simpson Creek Baptist Church was founded in the early 1770s by Rev. John Sutton. It is the oldest Baptist church in West Virginia and reputedly, the oldest Protestant church west of the Alleghenies. One of the early members of the congregation was tried for witchcraft in 1787. While sick with chicken pox, Rhoda Ward was seen to spit up crooked pins. Rhoda denied any knowledge of the incident, and the church must have found her innocent since she continued as a member.

"Rhoda the Witch" exerts an unending fascination to children who find the facts dull as opposed to the legends. Some versions of the story have her burned at the stake, others that she was hanged. Children will tell you that she was

responsible for the tornado that struck in 1970 since it damaged the Baptist Church. Others hunt for her grave in the Bridgeport Cemetery despite rumors of dire punishment from Rhoda's ghost.

The town has not been without natural disasters. Floods in 1852 and 1888 washed away bridges. In 1926, a flash flood on Ann's Run inundated Main Street stores with two feet of water. In 1903, a fire severely damaged Main Street and would have been more destructive without a local minister's early alarm and a sudden wind shift which blew the fire back on itself. Tornadoes hit the area in 1944 and 1970. Civil War raiders passed through in 1863 and Emmanuel Benedum to save his general store from plunder put a "For Rent" sign in the window. When this did not stop the raiders he innocently asked if any of the soldiers had ever had smallpox. The raiders left the store untouched.

In 1887, the town was incorporated by order of the circuit court; its population numbered 247 females and 222 males and it covered an area of 178¾ acres. By 1930 the population was 1,200, but in the next 50 years the town's growth was phenomenal earning it the reputation as "the fastest growing city in the United States." The 1980 census reports 6,604 people within the city limits and an area of over 10,000 acres.

Bridgeport has a rich personal history due primarily to its citizens. Within its borders there is no particular industry as the town is mainly residential but the people of the town, as is true with so many of the areas of Harrison County, make the community of Bridgeport what it is today — a pleasant place to live.

Joseph Herbert Diss DeBarr - Designer Of The Great Seal Of West Virginia

By DOROTHY DAVIS

Perhaps one of the most fascinating persons to pass through the Harrison County area was Joseph Hubert Diss Debar. Born March 6, 1820, in Strasbourg, France, Diss Debar emigrated to the United States in 1842 and made his way west to Cincinnati. He became employed by John Peter Dumas and came to West Virginia as an agent for over 10,000 acres of land known as the Swan lands located on Cove Creek in Doddridge County. Due to the fact that Doddridge County had been formed from Harrison County in 1846, Diss Debar knew that much of the legal work concerning the Swan lands would have to be done in Clarksburg, the county seat of Harrison County. He had already engaged William A. Harrison of Clarksburg as his attorney when in the spring of 1846 he traveled to Parkersburg to catch a stagecoach for Clarksburg.

He stopped in Clarksburg at the North Western Hotel on Pike Street kept by James Carder, a structure which, as he saw it, was "a large wind-shaken, two-story frame with a long ell and double porches in the rear and ranked second because the other tavern kept by Mr. Bartlett was built of brick and adjoined the courthouse lot." Debar observed that "The denizens of Clarksburg are chiefly of Old Virginia descent, and constitute a somewhat exclusive conservative set with all the traditions and social prejudices, pertaining to an ancient moss grown aristocratic town, such as Clarksburg was reputed to be. With very few exceptions there was but very little actual wealth to back up their pretensions, which were by common consent founded upon antiquity of pedigree and superior culture and manner. Their language was uniformly correct, their conversation refined and their hospitality generous within their means."

In addition to Harrison, Diss Debar was soon friends with

Luther Haymond, to whom he carried, on arriving, a letter of introduction, and with other men in town. Sometime later Diss Debar sponsored a frog supper at the Carder tavern attended by John S. Duncan, James M. Jackson, Caleb Boggess, Lloyd Moore, U. M. Turner, Robert Johnson, Robert Sommerville, Granville G. Davisson, and Edgar M. Davisson. When the frogs arrived, the landlord refused to relight the fires that at the time had gone out. Diss Debar prepared the frogs in a salad which with the addition of various liquids was immensely enjoyed by the jovial company.

Diss Debar adds an interesting comment as to the after effects of the party: "A year or two later my friend Duncan, who had served a term in the State Legislature as a brilliant champion of the right of way for the Baltimore & Ohio Railroad, was again a candidate in competition with Col. Joseph Johnson, later governor of Virginia. It was the most spirited contest known in that section and decided in favor of Johnson by a majority of one vote magnanimously cast by Duncan for his opponent who on his part failed to vote for Duncan.

"A short time afterwards riding to Randolph County with Judge Edwin S. Duncan I was surprised to learn that it was my French frog supper that had defeated his son's election beyond a doubt. Three of the Judge's rural neighbors, staunch Whigs, incensed by John's lack of self respect in feasting on raw frogs, had remained away from the polls where their votes would have given them a decided majority."

Diss Debar sympathized with the abolitionists and unwittingly had occasion to meet the most famous abolitionist during the August 1859 term of the Federal Court of Western Virginia sitting in Clarksburg. Extraordinary interest had been generated from the case of the United States against certain parties indicted for the crime of abducting slaves from Virginia to the free state of Ohio via the "underground railroad." The trial was unusually tedious and the courthouse was daily crowded with citizens and strangers. Diss DeBar by this time well known as an accomplished artist and master of the caricature wrote: "Do you see that tall, bearded old codger," said a Clarksburg gentleman, Major James M. Jackson, to me, as I entered the courthouse. "I wish you would sketch him for me. He looks quite a character.

"I'll bet anything he is of your way of thinking," next remarked the major who knew my free-soil proclivities, but generously forgave them for the sake of my other merits. "He tries to look like a rock, but is as restless as a squirrel. Just watch him changing his hat from one hand to the other. This is the second day I see him here. No doubt an abolitionist, every hair of him, and he has a big crop of it."

"Since most readers have at one time seen his effigy, I shall not describe him further than by saying that he was one of those startling figures which once seen are never forgotten. When my sketch was finished I made a duplicate of it for Major Jackson, retaining the original of which the picture in this article is a faithful copy.

"Meanwhile the major, a philosopher and a wit, had endeavored to find out something about the odd looking stranger, but had only learned that he passed for a cattle buyer. This supposition was not conflicting with the man's seasonable costume, which consisted of a slouchy hat, a faded nankeen vest, a long gray linen duster and mixed jeans trousers.

"On the following day the kidnapping case was given to the jury for deliberation. After the adjournment of the Court I got into the saddle to ride about a mile to the residence of my lawyer, William A. Harrison, later to be judge of the Court of Appeals in the new state of West Virginia, and who like myself and a quartette of other citizens of Clarksburg and Shinnston, was a subscriber to the tabooed New York Tribune which has been proscribed by local authorities as a felonious

Courtesy West Virginia Department of
Archives and History

John Brown, from a drawing
made by J. H. Diss Debar

abolition sheet.

"Half way out I accidentally overtook the mysterious stranger and slackening my gait, cordially sympathized with his reflections upon the charm of the landscape and the fertility of the soil. Not accidentally, however, I failed to stop at Harrison's and, and continued alongside my new acquaintance.

"At last, in reponse to a particularly suggestive remark of mine upon the varied resources of this section of Virginia, 'Yes indeed!' he stated with a deep-drawn sigh, 'as fine a country as the Lord ever made,' but muttering in a solemn undertone, 'black with the curse of human bondage.!'

"I lost no time in intimating to him that he was in congenial company. Yet he did not deem it prudent to directly pursue that delicate theme though he lingered on the verge of it quite significantly while inquiring about the state of the roads, the number of inhabitants, slaves and cattle in certain sections of the country, notably the Great Kanawha Valley. I was singularly impressed with his rapidly developing idiosyncrasies among which scriptural forms of language and quotations were especially obtrusive. While meditatively dialating upon certain subjects, the pupils of his keen grey eyes would often contract to a suggestion of mental aberration, while any repression of his innermost feeling was betrayed by a flash of unusual fire from under those ominous brows.

"I learned very little more about my eccentric companion than that he had a farm in the Shenandoah Valley, and was looking out for young stock to winter. The sun was sinking behind the hills and I was going to face about when he reined up his steed, and taking out a pocket map of Virginia and Maryland (old edition) said: 'Let us alight a moment under this tree, so that I may make some corrections on this map by the light of your information.'' In his penciled tracing out of roads and streams under my direction he did not forget the underground route that figured so prominently in the kidnapping trial.

"Something tells me we shall meet again," said he sententiously as we parted with a hearty shake of the hand.

"Two months later the whole country was thrilled by the tidings of John Brown's Harper's Ferry raid. Being at Clarksburg again on business soon afterward, and meeting my friend Major Jackson, I was scarcely surprised when he pulled a pictorial weekly from his pocket and pointed to a well-known face on the title page, 'I told you there was something wrong about that old crank,' said the major, "But I never dreamt he was such a big game as that.'

"And, truly, it was brave old Osawatomie Brown that had come all the way from Maryland to watch the Clarksburg kidnappping case — and for other purposes —now mysterious no longer.''

Years later Diss Debar was asked to design the State Seal for the newly-created state of West Virginia. He originally suggested the motto "Libertas et Fidelitate" (Liberty out of Fidelity) expressing the concept that West Virginia became free and independent through her loyalty to the Union. The final design, however, was changed by Diss Debar into the well-known and publicized version which is still in use today. The State Seal is two and a half inches in diameter. A rock inscribed June 20, 1863, the birthdate of the state, a farmer, anvil, plow, woodsman's axe, a miner, a sheaf of wheat and a cornstalk are some of the symbols of the seal together with the Latin phrase "Montani Semper Liberi," the state's motto, meaning, Mountaineers (are) always free."

I Saw Him Standing in the Door... Millie I've Come for You, He Said

BY JACK SANDY ANDERSON

I have often thought that I inherited my great liking for tales of the supernatural from the great-grandmother whose house I now occupy. She not only liked them but also more than half-believed in them. In fact, on at least one occasion, she was certain that she had contact with the supernatural world.

Millie Elizabeth Tichenor (1852-1927) was not born in Harrison County, although most of her life was spent in it.

Her father, John Tichenor, a native of Monongalia county, was a grandson of a New Jersey Revolutionary War veteran who settled in that county before 1800 and a lineal descendant of Martin Tichenor, an English emigrant to America in 1644. For a time John lived on Long Run, one of Bingamon Creek's meandering tributaries, but eventually went to Ritchie County where both he and his wife died in the early 1890s.

In 1870 Millie Elizabeth married Lorenzo Dow Martin, a Bingamon native, and except for a few years spent in Ritchie County and at Big Elm Farm near Shinnston, she and her husband lived at or near Pine Bluff. In 1916 they built the house that for years was the home of their youngest child, Mrs. Mabel Martin Leonard (1886-1979), and that since November 1979 has been my home.

Millie Elizabeth clearly remembered the Civil War. Her father served in the Union Army and was stationed briefly at Grafton, where his wife and children came to be with him. It was there that Millie Elizabeth knew a soldier who gave up drinking because of a frightening experience. A habitual drinker, he was the despair of his wife. Nearly every cent he got quickly went for whiskey. On a certain evening he decided he must have a few drinks (his few inevitably became many) and demanded money from his wife. She had none, and he flew into a rage.

He then remembered some onions up in the loft which might be traded for a bottle or two. He proceeded to the loft, filled a sack with them, and started walking toward the town. He had gone but a little way when he heard a strange noise. Turning around, he saw a coffin coming toward him. He dropped the sack and began to run. Glancing back to see where it was, he discovered it was right behind him. By now the trip to town had been completely forgotten, and he ran terrified toward the safety of his home. When he reached the front porch, the coffin disappeared. Firmly believing this was a warning to quit drinking, he never again drank anything stronger than sweet cider.

One story that Millie Elizabeth enjoyed telling over and over again was about a young married couple in the neighborhood where she spent part of her childhood. They went to housekeeping in an old log house located at the edge of a woods a good distance from any other house. Before long they heard the sound of a crying baby. This went on night after night. They searched diligently but found nothing which would account for the sound. At first, afraid of ridicule, they told no one; but, finally, hoping somehow to find an explanation, they told some of their neighbors.

One of them, an old lady who had always lived in the area, told them that once years ago a cruel man lived in their house who had been suspected of having killed one of his several children, a sick baby whose crying annoyed him. When asked how the baby was after it had not been seen or heard for a few days, he replied that it had gotten better, and he had taken it to his sister in a remote county. However, no one believed him. A few weeks later, he and his family suddenly left, never to return. Other people living afterward in the house, the old lady said, had also heard the pitiful crying and seldom had anyone stayed long in what was considered a haunted place.

Certain that the baby had been killed and then buried somewhere near the house, she urged the couple to search for it.

"If you find the baby," she said, "and bury it in the cemetery, the crying will surely stop."

Shortly thereafter a group of men gathered at the house to help the couple search for it. A few hours of digging revealed, in the woods back of the house a baby's skeleton. It was placed in a wooden box and buried in the cemetery by the neighborhood church. After that, the crying was heard no more.

Millie Elizabeth and her husband had a delightful eccentric friend who often visited them, even after he had gone to the county seat to live. He believed fervently in the supernatural, especially witches, and had a repertoire of tales requiring hours to exhaust. Often told was a story about a dog he once owned. It was unusually pretty and more than just a dog. It was also very playful and liked to be teased. One night he played with it until he was worn out, so he stopped and went into an adjoining room. The dog followed, looked up at him, and in a small voice said, "Bob Thompson, Bob Thompson, devil me some more, or I'll nibble-nibble-nibble you."

Another story he usually told before ending his visit was about a witch he met somewhere in the Bingamon country. She changed him into a black cat, climbed on his back, and rode him through the hills all night long. He said he knew this was true because his hands and feet were so filled with briers the next morning that it took him days to remove them.

Millie Elizabeth's husband died March 21, 1926. After his death, her oldest child, Cora (Mrs. Fredrick Lincoln Sandy, my grandmother), nearly every afternoon visited her, for now Millie Elizabeth was an old and frail lady often in need of help as well as company. On an afternoon in early March, 1927, Cora had so much work to do in her own home (the Isaiah Shinn House, built around 1820) that she phoned her mother to tell her she was not coming and would see her sometime the

next day. Two or three minutes later Cora's phone rang. It was her mother, much upset.

"Come quick, Cora, I need you," she said, and hung up.

In a very short while Cora arrived at her mother's.

"What is wrong?" she anxiously asked.

Millie Elizabeth replied, As I turned from the phone after you called, I saw Dow standing in the door. He said, 'Millie, I have come for you,' and disappeared."

Did this really happen? I do not know, but within a week Millie Elizabeth was dead and at rest beside her husband in the Pine Bluff Cemetery.

The Fourth of July - Independence Day

BY DOROTOHY DAVIS

For more than one hundred years in Harrison County the holiday celebrated with the greatest preparation and with the most fervor was the Fourth of July. Christmas occurred when roads were muddy and winds were cold.

In the late eighteenth century the frontier was so unchurched that Christmas, for the first fifty years of the county, was little more than just another day.

This was shown in a letter written by George Jackson from Winchester to Clarksburg on December 25, 1803. He had reached Winchester on the way to Washington, D.C. He made no comment as to Christmas Day, saying only that his horse was lame.

On the Fourth of July the roads had dried out; the gardens were producing crops; the young Republic had still living patriots who had sparked and had written the Declaration of Independence and the U.S. Constitution, and veterans who had fought in the American Revolution. In Virginia, where militia laws existed, every male citizen trained as a soldier in units that mustered for parades. The customs followed on the Fourth of July from the founding of the county until the War Between the States (1861-1865) required that the militia parade with its bugles, fifes, and drums; that the entire town bring food for a community picnic; that a citizen read the Declaration of Independence after which the leading citizen of the town would deliver a patriotic oration.

In Clarksburg in the early years of the nineteenth century the Eleventh Regiment of the 20th Brigade of the Virginia militia paraded through the Main Street after which townspeople went with picnic baskets to Monticello Springs near the mill on Elk Creek at the foot of East Main Street hill. By 1823, when the Clarksburg unit of the militia was called "The Clarksburg Rifle Blues," the citizen who delivered the address following the reading of the Declaration of Independence was John George Jackson who had married a sister of Dolly Madison in 1801; had served in the U.S. Congress from 1803-1817; and was named judge of the first U.S. Court west of the mountains in Virginia in 1819.

After he had delivered the speech — which was largely a tribute to General Lafayette —Jackson sent one copy to John Quincy Adams to forward to Lafayette and a second copy to Thomas Jefferson with a note to Jefferson which read in part: "The Declaration of Independence, alike the immortal monument of the nation's glory and the fame of its authors, has been ascribed by the concurrent testimony of all contemporaries to your pen. As a post-Revolutionary man enjoying all its benefits and a friend to Liberty devoted to my Country, I tender you the homage of sincere gratitude. And I repeat the prayer expressed in the enclosed address that your end may be as happy and glorious as your life has been illustrious and beneficial to your country and to the whole human family."

In addition to printing a notice for the Clarksburg Rifle Blues under Capt. Eli Marsh to muster for the 4th Day of July,

"The Independent Virginian," Clarksburg's newspaper, in 1825 informed citizens that "men attached to the company commanded by Capt. Alexander L. Patton will attend a company muster at (West) Milford on the 4th day of July next at 10 o'clock armed and equipped with a sufficiency of ammunition to celebrate the day."

Ten years later in Clarksburg the citizens assembled after the parade at 12 noon in the courthouse, where the Declaration of Independence was read by Richard W. Moore followed by an address by Daniel Kincheloe. At 2 p.m. citizens went to Randolph Academy to partake of a sumptuous dinner.

The same day in 1835 people in the Bridgeport section of the county traveled to the spring between the residences of Humphrey Faris and Meshack Ross, where Dr. Benjamin Dolbeare read the Declaration of Independence and Capt. Augustine J. Smith delivered a "neat and appropriate oration." John Horner, president, presided with the flag of the Union flying over the heads of the assembly.

In Shinnston in 1835 "a large and respectable company of citizens were marched by Col. J. S. Martin to the front of Mr. Black's tavern, where the citizens had assembled in honor of the day." Dr. Flowers led an appropriate prayer. His son then delivered an oration followed by Joseph S. Morris and W. K. Shinn whose speeches were equally appropriate to the subject they spoke upon. The company sat down to an elegant dinner prepared by Mr. Black.

At Rock Camp (near Sardis) in 1849 "ladies and gentlemen assembled at the sugar orchard of Capt. Isaac Smith near the mouth of Little Rock Camp Creek. Andrew Davisson was chosen president; Felix R. Coffman, vice president; John B. Davisson, secretary; and John W. Stout, marshall. The gentlemen were then paraded and marched to a convenient shade where they were arranged in military order, the rifle men in front. The ladies were then paraded and escorted by the marshall and brought in front of the first platoon, when by order of the Captain the rifles were discharged in regular order amid the cheers of the company. The procession was marched to the stand and the Declaration of Independence was read by Samuel D. Smith. The orators of the occasion were James L. Smith, Mathes J. Orr and Allen Martin. Dinner being announced and the procession being formed with the military company in front, the audience marched in regular order to the tables. The president took his seat at the head of the table, the ladies occupying one side and the gentlemen the other, the tables being loaded with an abundance of provisions. After dinner a number of toasts were offered and received with applause.

Each Fourth of July celebration was ended with volunteer toasts, which were usually short patriotic statements of political beliefs such as "Henry Clay, the great American Regulator. May he be our next president!" Sometimes someone would throw a bit of levity: "May the pretty girls of Old Harrison (County) soon find husbands to the satisfaction of their minds."

The War Between the States ended a bit of the color of the Fourth of July celebrations because the Virginia militia laws ended with the war. No longer was a military company waiting for an excuse to march. The Fourth of July remained the big celebration of the year with picnics and orations the order of the day and by the end of the century, fireworks in the evening of the Fourth were popular.

Community celebration of the Fourth of July ceased during the years 1915-1930 as the automobile replaced the horse as a means of locomotion. Now citizens could drive to a sequestered spot a distance from their hometown and near a stream where the children could swim. They carried a picnic dinner in baskets and at noon spread a white linen tablecloth on the ground where food was placed after which feasters sat on the

ground near the tablecloth to dine. The age of the picnic table at set recreational areas was not born until the mid-1920s, one of the first in the county being Laurel Park where the Sidebottom family operated a dance pavilion, a park for picnicking, and a bathhouse and swimming area foe the public.

July 4th Celebration Has Dual Meaning for County
By MYRA LITHERLAND

As July 4th, America's 208th birthday, draws near, it's hard to believe that Harrison County is only eight years younger than the United States.

And just as our country marked its 200th birthday with a year-long Bicentennial celebration in 1976, our county is observing its anniversary with a full roster of events throughout the year.

The schedule is diversified, overflowing with events and activites certain to appeal to almost everyone. They're not only entertaining, but educational as well, in that they highlight Harrison County's rich history from its creation in 1784 to the present.

This year's Bicentennial celebration didn't just happen, though. It's the product of the labors of many hard-working, dedicated people, including the Harrison County Bicentennial Committee.

The committee was formed last year, drawn from a cross-section of county residents. They began to meet mid-year on a monthly basis, "kicking around ideas" for the upcoming celebration after obtaining financial assistance from the Humanities Foundation of West Virginia, a state program of the National Endowment for the Humanities.

Other assistance had been provided by Consolicated Gas Transmission Corporation, along with the people of Harrison County.

As plans for the celebration were being formulated, Bostonian lawyer James Pool and his family were relocating to the Clarksburg area, because he and his wife - a West Virginia native who is also an attorney - thought "Beacon Hill isn't the best place to raise a family."

Once here, while he awaited certification to practice law in the state, Pool says he found himself with a little "time on his hands." Consequently, when approached by Merle Moore, director of the Clarksburg/Harrison Public Library, about accepting the job of historian-in-residence (the position had recently become vacant) at the library, he took it.

Onto the position was tagged the job of Harrison County Bicentennial project director.

While Pool was being recruited, so was Lloyd Leggett, a Weirton resident, to fill the position of historian-curator at Waldomore, open because of illness. The job also would involve Bicentennial committee involvement.

With the addition of Pool and Legett, the Bicentennial committee, chaired by John McCuskey began to establish a course of action.

On Valentine's Day 1984, Pool began his first day of work. Leggett had been on the job at Waldomore a month.

The pair immediately set to work on their "part-time/full-time" job of organizing Harrison County's Bicentennial celebration.

"Here we were, a boy from Boston and a boy from Weirton, planning Harrison County's celebration," Leggett said, leaning forward in his chair in the booklined office on the second floor or Waldomore. "It probably worked better that way," Pool added. "We could be completely impartial about the whole thing because we aren't natives of the county."

And the two began an objective study of the history of the county.

Pool pointed to the files jamming the top of his desk. "All this is material related to the Bicentennial," he said. "Almost everything anybody would want to know about Harrison County is in here."

After "getting a handle" on the county's history, the pair took up the reins of the celebration, and set a deadline of February 29 for ideas from the committee.

Plans were finalized and on March 14, the first event of Harrison County's Bicentennial celebration - a kickoff reception at Waldomore - took place.

Just as our July 4th, or Independence Day, observances - commemorating the formal adoption by the Continental Congress of the Declaration of Independence, drafted to justify the Resolution of Independence approved by Congress on July 2, 1776 - stem from our pride in America and her accomplishments, so do our county's observances.

The first anniversary of the declaration was observed in Philadelphia by the adjournment of Congress, a ceremonial dinner, the ringing of bells and fireworks.

As years went by, Americans observed Independence Day - in a swirl of red, white and blue - with parades, public oratory, military displays and fireworks, patriotic programs and pageants.

Later, family reunions, picnics, games and sports, backyard barbecues and beach parties, usually accompanied by the traditional pop of firecrackers, highlighted July 4 holiday activities, much as they do today.

And Harrison County's celebration is just as enjoyable and full of activity.

The day following the Waldomore reception, the Bicentennial Art, Essay and Historical Research contests began in Harrison County Schools.

On March 18, the first in a series of captivating monthly articles on Harrison County history was published in area newspapers - articles James Pool says will "make anyone who reads all of them almost an expert on Harrison County."

The first of many local club and organizational meetings carrying an historical theme was held March 21, and the following day, March 22, an aviation history mini-exhibit, only the first of many such exhibits, opened at the library.

And March 25, another "first" was launched with a weekly series of bicentennial biographies on people contributing to the development of Harrison County, published in area newspapers.

Two days after that, the Harrison County Cities and Tours Development Series began its monthly publication in the papers, followed by the Bicentennial Folklore weekly publications. The tours offer guidelines to five separate self-guided visits to historic sites in both Clarksburg and Harrison County, and give complete directions to each area, along with brief descriptions.

Each tour can be taken at leisure, and its routing makes it easy and convenient to visit all the historically-significant areas of both the city and county.

On May 12, a parade, street fair and a special concert performed by the River City Brass Band of Pittsburgh highlighted Bicentennial Weekend in Harrison County.

The list continues, with a burgeoning schedule of exhibits, workshops, special programs - and even a film festival - planned for the rest of 1984.

And who are some of the people, in addition to James Pool, Lloyd Leggett and John McCuskey, who have been instrumental in making Harrison County's Bicentennial celebration such a success?

Again, the committee is composed of a cross-section of county residents. It includes, on the Bicentennial Weekend Committee, Harrison County Senior Citizens Center represen-

tatives Delores Christopher and Candace Snyder, and from the Quota Club, Bernice Life; on the Weekend Parade Committee, Floyd Fullen and Jeanne Kalaycioglu; the Commemorative Committee, Edward Forinash and William Lear; Bicentennial Park Committee, James Pool and Gary Weiner; Oil and Gas Historical Exhibit Committee, David Cotton; and National Figures of Harrison County Historical Exhibit Committee, S. J. Birshstein.

Merle Moore chairs the Acro/Agate-Glass Historical Exhibit Committee. This exhibit was the subject of an interesting article by Edwin Sweeney, Clarksburg Exponent staff writer, published in both GOLDENSEAL, the state magazine of the West Virginia Department of Culture and History, and in the June 24 edition of the Clarksburg Exponent-Telegram.

The Bicentennial Pageant Committee chairmen are David Spelsberg and Robert Balhatchet; Fort New Salem Living History Committee, John Randolph and Dorothy Davis; Harrison County School Participation Committee, Pauline LeRoy and Beulah Cornwell, and the Historical Tours Committee, Barbara Highland and Lloyd Leggett.

Connie Huffman and Susan Maxwell chair the Bicentennial Souvenir Program Committee; Publicity Committee, Ann Harvey, Edwin Sweeney and Charles Miesner; Present-Day Harrison County Liaison Committee, Wanda Ashcraft; Historical Harrison County Liason Committee, Sharon Saye, and on the Community Involvement Committee, Madeline Phillips, Mary Ann Kersting and Charles Forsythe.

The Oral History Presentation Committee chairmen are Lloyd Leggett and Dr. Charles Righter; Local History Workshop Committee, George Ashby Short and Lloyd Leggett; Bicentennial Biography Committee, Helen Weeks; Historical Preservation/Restoration Committee, Laura Goff Davis and Ralph Pederson; and the Genealogy Workshop Committee, Vivian Sue Moore and Lloyd Leggett.

On the Mini-Exhibits Committee, Merle Moore and Lloyd Leggett; Social Committee, Friends of the Clarksburg-Harrison Public Library, represented by Joe Nutter. The Friends, in addition to their many other fine contributions to the county and community, provide refreshments at the multitude of functions held at Waldomore.

Ann Williams and Thomas Martin chair the John W. Davis Day Committee; Bicentennial Art Exhibition Committee, Karen Bowers and Paulette DePolo; Bicentennial Antique Show Committee, Jack McBee and Fred Kyle; Bicentennial/Italian Heritage Festival Program, Rosalyn Queen and Merle Moore; Bicentennial Finance/Fundraising Committee, John McCuskey; and heading the Bicentennial County Folklore Committee, John Randolph and Harry Berman.

It's quite a list.

But let's go back to the crux of celebration, Harrison County's birth.

Just how did it happen?

Harrison County was formed by an act of the Virginia Assembly in 1784.

Formerly a part of Monongalia County, it extended from the Maryland line to the Ohio River, as far north as Marion County and South far enough to include all of the Little Kanawha and portions of the Great Kanawha River.

For two years, it was the largest county west of the Alleghenies, and over the years its boundaries changed numerous times, until 1871, when the present boundaries were established.

Many notable people were products of Harrison County, including CSA General Thomas Jonathan "Stonewall" Jackson and U. S. Secretary of State Cyrus Vance.

And in the county named in honor of Benjamin Harrison, Virginia governor and a signer of the Declaration of Independence, and in the city named for General George Rogers

Clark, at least 200 years of history-making events have occurred.

The Bicentennial Committee planned its celebration around those events and the people who made them happen. The schedule is full, from its beginning at Waldomore to its close to be marked by a final reception in the beautiful old mansion.

It's an historic year for Harrison County, a year of pride and patriotism.

So next Wednesday, as we countians celebrate another Independence Day, complete with all the trappings that make it so enjoyable, we have yet another reason to celebrate - Harrison County's birthday.

As in 1976, this is a Bicentennial year - a banner 200th birthday year for the county.

Fang-Like Marks in Back of Neck Give Clue to Mysterious Death of a Stranger

BY JOHN RANDOLPH

These West Virginia hills and valleys, with hanging fogs and deep shadows create a perfect setting for all kinds of stories. Many of these stories started even before the white man had seen his new home.

The Indians, using this area as a special sacred land, told tales of their ancestors. These Indian tales were heard by early settlers who in turn handed their versions along.

The settlers, who to a great extent were Anglo-Celtic (English, Irish and Scots) began to settle here in the latter part of the Eighteenth Century. They brought with them a variety of tales and stories that reflect their culture.

Because these hills resembled those of their homeland, the tales lived on and have been collected throughout the passing generations.

William B. Price, a teacher and educator in Harrison County, spent a great deal of his adult life collecting and telling the "old tales." Before his death in the mid 60s and while he was teaching at Salem College, his collection called "Tales and Lore of the Mountaineers" was published in 1963.

I especially remember sitting with him, while the smoke of his old pipe circled around his head and his eyes flashed.

"Prof" Price related to us his tales. I would speculate that his work was some of the purest "folk history" ever collected in West Virginia. He was a scholar of folk lore before his time; a special man, trying to preserve a dying culture.

As a small tribute to William B. Price, let me share one of his favorite tales as he wrote it in his book, "The Smallpox Victim and his Ghost."

A stranger came to the farmhouse one afternoon and called from the road "Hello!"

"Hello!" the farmer's wife answered from the cabin door.

"I am a sick man," said the stranger. "I'm covered with some kind of rash."

The woman came closer and suddenly realized that the man probably had smallpox — that dreaded and often deadly disease of the old days. In those days smallpox victims were isolated in an unused cabin kept prepared for such emergencies. The woman directed the man to go to the cabin and told him that food and medicine would be left in springhouse as soon as her husband came in from the field.

Food was taken to the man every morning. It was not too long until he was able to come outside the cabin and he told the farmer that he had been helping to build the new road known as the Northwestern Pike. When he seemed sufficiently recovered, the stranger was told that fresh clothes would be brought and that he was to clean himself up and burn the old clothes; then he could go back to his road work. Clothes were left for him near the cabin as promised.

It was the next day — sometime in the afternoon — that the farmer chanced to come by the isolation cabin. To his horror he found the man hanging by the neck from a rope tied to a branch of an oak tree in the yard. The farmer immediately sent word to his neighbors, asking what they thought he should do.

As the corpse was being prepared for burial, the farmer noticed two marks on the back of the man's neck. He thought they looked like the marks of a snake. As there was very little swelling, they said nothing about it at the time. The more the farmer thought about the dead man, however, the more puzzled he became. There was something about the position of the body that he did not like.

After the man was laid out, the farmer took a good look at him but saw nothing unusual except those two fang-like marks at the back of the neck. He remembered a small child that had been bitten by a rattlesnake some years before. The fang marks were nearly three inches apart on the child's neck. The girl had died in a few minutes after the bite. If those were fang marks on the dead stranger, how did the man hang himself, or did he hang himself?

The farmer went to the spot where the body had been found swinging from a big oak tree near the cabin. The branch was too high to be easily reached without standing on some kind of support. There had been nothing there upon which he could have supported himself while tying the rope. Many small spouts or branches grew upright on the limb, these had not been disturbed. Had a murder been committed?

The man was buried on a knoll back of the house and the neighbors went to their homes.

When the farmer told his wife about his suspicions, she recalled that the stranger had carried a small bag when he appeared at the gate. A search was made in the ashes in the fireplace of the cabin. The ashes of the burned clothing were easily identified, but no signs of the bag could be found. The stranger was a topic of conversation in the neighborhood for some time, but nothing was said by the farmer or his wife about the suspicious circumstances of the man's death.

It may have been a month or so later that one of the neighbor boys was passing the old cabin where the sick stranger had stayed — just at dusk. Chancing to look toward the big oak tree, he saw hanging from the same branch the stranger had hung from, an object swaying to and fro. He immediately walked into the yard and toward the tree only to see the figure fade slowly from his sight. "I'm imagining things," the boy thought to himself, and left the place in a hurry. After that the figure was seen by several of the folks as they passed the place in the evening, or at night. For almost a year the ghost of the smallpox victim was the talk of the neighborhood.

The one afternoon the farmer saw the figure in broad daylight. He went to the cabin and, upon looking inside found the body of a man lying on the floor. By his side was a small bag which the farmer's wife identified as the same bag carried by the sick stranger. On the wrist of the body now lying in the cabin were the fang marks of a large snake. The snake was soon found in a cubbyhole beside the fireplace.

Piecing the evidence together, the farmer and his wife concluded that the newest stranger-visitor had caused the death of the first man by holding the snake to his neck. He had then hanged the body to the tree to make the death appear a suicide. Perhaps a sudden appearance of the farmer had forced the intruder to leave more quickly than he had planned without the bag of loot. Perhaps he had not even found the bag. Now he had come back to get the coveted treasure, found it in the cubbyhole, reached into get it, only to be bitten by the instrument of the murder he had committed nearly a year before.

Johnson Newlon Camden - Developer of West Virginia's Natural Recourses

BY NEVA WEEKS

One of the most important persons in the early oil industry in West Virginia was Johnson Newlon Camden. Born March 6, 1828 at Collins Settlement, Lewis County, the second son of John Scrivner Camden and Nancy Newlon, he was named in honor of a maternal uncle, Johnson Newlon. Early in life he showed a great love for field and stream which gave him much pleasure and marked him as a sportsman in later life.

Much of his young life was spent in and around Sutton, where his father purchased much land, and was greatly impressed with the fact that his father and other relatives were office holders.

When he was fourteen years of age he went to Weston to become an assistant in the Lewis County Clerk's office, where he learned the business of keeping county records.

Late in 1843, the youthful Camden, now nearly 16 years of age, went to Clarksburg, and entered the Northwestern Academy, a new school just opened to the youth of Trans-Allegheny Virginia. The academy was chartered in 1842 by the Legislature of Virginia and supported by private subscription and donations. As a two-story brick building nearly completed in 1843, the school was placed in the hands of the Methodist Episcopal Church, which had already voted to accept the responsibility of its conduct and management.

Johnson took up his studies and with the exception of a month's vacation with his parents, remained at the Academy until spring 1845 at which time he went back to Sutton and secured a position as Deputy Clerk of Braxton County.

On June 1, 1847, Camden was admitted to the United States Military Academy and withdrew in 1849, not finding it to his liking. He later studied law and on Nov. 11, 1850 was admitted to the bar in Braxton County. Not finding much success at this venture, and as a result of his training at West Point, he was employed by the Weston and Gauley Bridge Company as a surveyor.

In 1852, he again had another chance at his chosen profession. In May, he was elected Nicholas County Prosecuting Attorney but only served one year.

On June 22, 1858, at St. Matthews Protestant Episcopal Church in Wheeling, he married Anne Gaither Thompson, daughter of George Thompson and Elizabeth Steenrod Thompson. They soon made their home in Weston where he was appointed director of the "Lunatic Asylum West of the Allegheny Mountains," more commonly known today as Weston State Hospital. Camden entered politics again only to be defeated or to withdraw from various races.

In ensuing years he had many occupations — banking, wholesale mercantile business, and in the extraction of oil from cannel coal. His main interest was in the development of West Virginia resources.

Johnson N. Camden soon went into the oil business again with great success near Burning Springs, and soon saw that sizable profits were to be made in the oil business at Volcano and other places.

According to information in Festus P. Summers' biography of Camden, "The Creek Sand Diggings were not far away, and they drew Camden's attention. Soon after the famous Karnes well was struck, Camden leased an acre and a half of land from W. P. and J. C. Rathbone. He formed a company known as Camden, Byrne and Company and began drilling for oil. In January 1861, they struck oil and gas in such large amounts that the drilling tools were blown from the well. The oil spurted out far into the air, and thousands of barrels of valuable oil were thus wasted. Some of it was saved, however, by borrowing barrels from the Karnes well and by using open barges.

"Camden realized at once that there was a great future in the oil business. He purchased a hundred acres of land near the well at a cost of $100,000 and then sold part of his holdings to others at more than he had paid for all his lands. He also signed contracts to have the drilling for oil done without cost to himself. When the Civil War came, most of Camden's partners left for military and political service, but Camden remained with the oil business. By the end of the war, he and his remaining partners had control of the oil fields of the Little Kanawha Valley.

"In 1866, Camden entered the oil refining business. He bought most of the West Virginia wells producing crude oil in order to be sure of supplies for his refineries. Later his property became part of the Standard Oil Company holdings, and Camden became the chief representative of the company in West Virginia. As part of the Standard Oil interests, the Camden refinery at Parkersburg produced most of the kerosene used in the South and West."

As he continued with his various business deals, he was also in and out of politics and in 1881 he was finally elected to the United States Senate. As a senator, he took a great interest in the construction of railroads. He wanted railroads to connect small towns so that people could travel from place to place. He was instrumental in getting railroads from Weston to Buckhannon, Glenville, Clarksburg, even though some of them were narrow gauge railroads. He urged the building of a railroad from Wheeling to Charleston. Several years later following his term as senator, Camden turned his attention to the coal business. The first "coal boom" occurred in the 1890s as a direct result of the building of a railroad to Fairmont. Harrison County had seen the need of a railroad for many years and Camden supplied the money to make this a reality in 1889. While he worked at the coal business, he never let up on the building of railroads.

In 1891 Camden sent a "substantial check" to Gov. Fleming to meet payments for damages incurred to property in Harrison County in building the railroad from Fairmont to

Clarksburg. When Fleming presented the check, he was refused the money. He wired Camden for currency. Angered, Camden remarked, "I will establish a bank in Clarksburg which will cash my check or those of any reponsible party." This was the beginning of the Traders National Bank and was situated where the Union National Bank now stands. The Traders Bank was destroyed by fire in 1911.

For many years Camden kept his interest in politics. He served for several years as a Democratic National Committee-man from West Virginia while at the same time he was still working in rails and getting more deeply involved in coal.

From 1892 to 1900 all business was at a low ebb. Camden tried to keep things going concerning his business holdings, but nothing seemed to be making much progress or money, and by this time he was getting along in years. He resigned from several positions of industrial prominence including presidency of the Northern Coal and Coke Co. and also the presidency of the Monongah Coal and Coke Co.

Camden was commonly regarded as a man of great wealth. As a result, he was constantly asked for support from churches, civic groups, educational institutions, and miscellaneous foundations, both within and outside the state. For 40 years he was viewed by the Protestant denominations of West Virginia as a veritable combination of Midas and godfather. In 1902 he wrote facetiously: "I try to give help to some extent in West Virginia especially to churches of all denominatons and rather flatter myself that I am piling up a pretty long list of credits as against a long list of debits in the Great Ledger." He refused several institutions of learning, even his own Protestant Episcopal Church that asked for a donation to help support a religious center to be maintained in the interest of students at West Virginia University.

Camden often overlooked factors of age and health but the close of autumn 1907, found him sick at heart as well as of unsound body. On Dec. 6, 1907 one of the worst mine explosions of all time brought disaster to his pet mining project, Monongah. The number killed was 359 and although the mine was under lease to the Consolidation Coal Co., Camden felt the full force of the catastrophe.

In 1908, he wintered in Miami and he wrote that he was having "good days and bad days." He took a fishing trip not far from Miami and became over tired and caught a cold from which he could not recover. He started home and got as far as Baltimore where he was placed under the care of specialists but failed to respond to treatment. He died on April 25, 1908. The same day his remains were moved to Parkersburg where they were interred in the Camden Mausoleum in the Odd Fellows Cemetery. The burial service was simple and brief, a fitting acknowledgement of the passing of a plain man who developed the natural resources found beneath the ground in such great abundance.

Greenbrier River bridge and Sharps Tunnel.   PCHS

'Soon As Silver Run Tunnel... There Was The Woman In White'

BY JOHN RANDOLPH

With the coming of the Baltimore and Ohio Railroad, a goodly number of strange stories were born into West Virginia Folk Lore. "The Phantom of Silver Run" is a ghost story as was collected by William B. Price and is one of the stories in his book "Tales and Lore of the Mountaineers."

I have asked different people where the Silver Run Tunnel is located and most people conclude that it was the original tunnel on Long Run, just over the Doddridge County line outside Salem. I can't recall hearing "Prof" Price telling us where he thought it was, however, it was one of his favorites

and he repeated it on various occasions.

One night late in June around midnight I was sitting outside the Baltimore and Ohio yard office in Grafton. Lazily I watched the clouds floating above me and listened to the other railroad men talking. They, too, were waiting for train No. 1 to come roaring in from the West before checking out the freight trains on the eastern division.

Occasionally, strains of "Sweet Adeline" or "In the Evening by the Moonlight" broke the silence of the night as a few of the men tried to harmonize. Most of them, however, just talked or took advantage of this lull to snatch a short nap.

This was the summer that Halley's Comet streaked across the western sky. Some people thought it was an ill omen; some thought that it predicted the immediate end of the world; others thought that it was a magnificent spectacle. We began to tell stories of death tokens and premonitions.

An old engineer was usually among the yard office gang. Most of the time he was silent, appearing to be lost in thought. On this night however, his attention was caught by the tales of ghosts and death tokens.

As soon as there was a lull in the converstation, the old engineer said "Boys, I've got a true tale to tell you — one that you'll find hard to believe. But it's true, I tell you. It happened to me.

"I was a young engineer at the time that it happened. I was very proud to have the westbound express as my run. I had been on that train for a year, and up to that time I had made a record for my train.

"I well remember that night. When the train pulled into the station, the heavy fog, combined with the smoke and steam from the many engines in the yard, gave an eerie and unreal atmosphere to the terminal.

"The shouting of men servicing the trains with ice water, inspectors inspecting coaches and air brakes, passengers arriving at the station, greetings and farewells, laughter and tears — all were a part of the vibrant life and spirit of the railroad of that period.

"That night comes back to me more vividly than any of the hundreds of nights in more than 40 years of my life as an engineer. The engineer from the third division stepped down from this engine; the hostlers uncoupled it and moved it to the roadhouse area; then they coupled my engine to the train.

"The west-bound mail was put on, the fireman took his place, and the conductor gave me the signal to go ahead. The train pulled slowly out of the station as there were several swithces to pass, but once on the road the engine responded to the touch of the throttle like a living thing.

"Soon the river with its smoke and fog was far behind. As we climbed into the hills, I watched the half moon dodging through fleecy clouds like a silver shuttle. As we sped through the warm night, I had a feeling of exhilaration — a feeling that the engine and I were akin.

"We stopped at Clarksburg, and there was the usual hustle and bustle as the mail and express were unloaded along with passengers, trunks, satchels and other luggage. Then we were on our way again.

"The half moon was nearing the top of the mountain as we neared the Silver Run Tunnel. Suddenly I saw in the distance a woman in a white evening gown standing on the track. I stopped the train as quickly as possible, the brakes screeching and moaning. I thought that the train would hit her before I could bring it to a complete stop, but she glided down the track without an apparent movement. The fireman and I leaped from the engine and ran toward the woman. She faded from sight into the fog which obscured the track.

"The conductor jumped from his car and ran down to the engine to find out what happened. I told him about the woman who was standing on the track in front of the on-rushing train. We walked down the track, searching for a sign that would indicate that someone or something had been there. There was nothing.

"We boarded the train and continued on our way west. The moon had set; the air was still balmy, but it was no longer exhilarating. I was uneasy and depressed, and I was glad to reach the end of my run.

"The return trip, which was always made in the daytime, was without incident, but I couldn't get the woman in white out of my mind.

"Since my run was every other night, I asked the engineer who made the next run if he had any unusual experiences on his trip. However, he assured me that nothing out of the ordinary had happened at any place or any time.

"By the time of my next run I had begun to convince myself that I had imagined seeing the mysterious.

"I boarded the engine with little or no apprehension. Again we left in a fog and climbed out of it as we raced into the hills. We made our stop at Clarksburg, and were soon approaching the Silver Run Tunnel. There stood the woman in white. The light of the train and the moonlight clearly revealed her golden slippers as she stood with one foot on the rail. I would see that her hair was as black as a raven's wing,. I thought I saw a jeweled pin sparkling at the neckline of her dress.

"We stopped the train. The fireman and I, followed by the conductor, and ran down the track. Again the figure disappeared.

"The conductor was as much puzzled as I. An express train cannot be delayed without good reason, so we decided to blow the whistle and go ahead if the apparition appeared on the track again. "I neither heard nor saw the woman in white again until a month later when the half moon was again hanging on the rim of the western mountain. As I approached the tunnel, there she stood at the same spot and in the same pose. I stopped the train, and then blew the whistle to go ahead. As the whistle echoed from the surrounding mountains, there came back with it the agonized moan of a lost soul.

"Eventually the tale reached headquarters, and I was called before the superintendent. He immediately took a dim view of the whole proceedings, and I was taken off the express and given a freight run on the third division.

"Engineer O'Flannery was given the westbound express with orders to investigage the happening. For almost a month nothing had happened and folks began to think that I was a bit touched in the head.

"The nights were beginning to get cool and there was a hint of frost in the air. One night while I was waiting at the yard office, the fireman on the west-bound express, an old friend of mine, motioned for me to go around the building with him.

"'O'Flannery saw her too,' he said in a low voice. 'Last night the air was clear as crystal, and just as soon as Silver Run Tunnel came into view, there was the woman in white. O'Flannery pulled the throttle and applied the airbrakes. Fire flew from every break shoe as the train ground to a stop. O'Flannery jumped from the engine and ran down the track after the woman in white. However, she disappeared in a blanket of fog which disappeared as quickly as it had come. Imagine fog on a clear night like last night!

"'O'Flannery came back cussing. I could tell he was nervous. When he climbed in the cab he thought he saw the woman on the track again. And then he thought he saw her when I opened the boiler door. I don't think O'Flannery will be long for this run.'

"I happened to be at the station when O'Flannery left on his next run. He looked at me as he mounted the steps and said, 'I'll run her down if she shows again.'

"The next morning there was lots of excitement at the yards. As soon as the fireman got back from Parkersburg that afternoon I asked him what had happened.

"'Well,' he said, 'O'Flannery meant what he said about running her down. I could tell he was nervous. He had the throttle wide open as we came to the tunnel. To tell you the truth I was half scared to death. There was the woman. O'Flannery blew the whistle and the train rushed on.

"'When we got to Parkersburg, there was an awful commotion. Messages had been coming in to the western office from all the towers saying that there was something in white on No. 1's cowcatcher that looked like a woman. Every tower was alerted, as the train was slowing down for Parkersburg, several of the railroad men who were on watch said that they saw a woman in white sitting on the cowcatcher as gracefully as a queen on a throne. Suddenly the train entered a dense blanket of fog. When the train stopped at the station there was no sign of anything on the cowcatcher. There was not even a mark.'

"Poor O'Flannery was ill for a time. I heard that after making many inquiries — the railroad was interested by that time — it was found that a beautiful lady had disappeared from the train some 25 years ago. It was said that she was on her way to meet her intended husband. Some thought that she arrived at the station in Parkersburg, and then left in a carriage. Although there was an extensive investigation, she was never heard of again."

I became interested in the old engineer's tale and decided to do some investigating on my own. Years later some workmen who were digging a cellar under an old house near Silver Run came upon the skeleton of a woman.

After that, the phantom was seen no more but sometimes, when the moon hangs low over the western hills, and the midnight train blows for Silver Run, the dying echoes bring back the moaning cry of a woman's voice in the distance.

Lost Creek - A Friendly Progressive Town
By ALTON BELL

Along State Route 25, Half way between Clarksburg and Weston, nestled in the narrow Valleys of four lofty hills, at the intersection of three small streams — T. G. Lick, McKiney's Run and Lost Creek a tributary of the West Fork River — one finds a small village of white painted houses and some brick structures. Here a person finds some two hundred and twenty or more homes of loving dwellers of the hills.

The town was named Lost Creek because it grew up along a little stream meandering along the hills, flowing westward from a point some distance above Rockford. Peaceful looking most of the time, probably following a course on nine to ten miles in length, it can become a torrent of rising water as it rushes along to empty into the West Fork River, a short distance from the town of West Milford.

Very likely the stream, because of its size, was followed by hunters at an early date, as they traveled about on hunting excursions and scouting trips seeking new home sites.

Today one can notice dividing lines of our ridges that branched off from Indian trails open for travel to many points on the Ohio River.

Early settlers coming into Harrison County visited at the two forts located near the West Fork River — Richards Fort and West's Fort — when coming out to locate homes during times the Indians were less likely to be on raiding excursions or war path activities.

Not much was known of Lost Creek, Grant District, Harrison County prior to 1800, when a few families came to this area and established a church of the Seventh Day Baptist faith. Churches were built in three locations and today we find the attractive Brick Church, in beautiful surroundings, with a

LOST CREEK, W. VA.

history of more than 175 years, and a devoted congregation of friendly, good-willed, loyal members, dedicated to carry on the same high principals of the early settlers.

In 1878 the Baltimore and Ohio Railway began construction of a line to join Clarksburg to Weston, and later it was extended to Buckhannon, passing through this community. A "stop" was made by the company, referred to by the company as a station. the railroad marked the elevation of the depot at 1010 ft. above sea level, and one of the hills that can be seen from the town is 1500 ft.

Early life around and about Lost Creek was much like that of other rural frontier and pioneers villages. The good blue grass areas of the cleared land made it a choice place for the grazing of cattle, sheep, horses and other farm stock. Because of this early settlers to the region began to clear the bottom flats and hillsides, and raise animals to sell to eastern coast markets.

Even in 1925 Lost Creek, on the branch line of the B&O Railroad Division, was a leading cattle shipping center, sending cattle to the eastern market in Baltimore, north to Pittsburgh, and to Chicago.

The newly-built railroad enabled the people of this vicinity to send eggs, chickens, rabbits, and animal pelts to close markets. It is interesting to note that chickens were sold by the dozen, as scales were not common. One might receive a price of six dollars per dozen — this would be easy to buy one half dozen, one fourth dozen or even one third dozen.

Children could earn money by selling berries in the right season, walnuts, chestnuts, and hickory nuts, and also in the spring of the year they could dig many apple roots to sell. In the late summer the roots of Ginseng from the woods brought a fair price. During the winter months one could sell furs of animals caught in traps, snares or dead-falls.

In these early days wages for both men and women were not very high, probably fifty to seventy-five cents per day. A day's work was measured from sun up to sunset. Work was not easy to obtain for pay with wages, but many folks received food items in exchange for labor.

Before 1800 Levi H. Bond had a grist mill on the bank of Lost Creek, on property owned by Alton Bell. A part of the mill race and stones of the foundation are visible yet today.

The brick home occupied by Mr. and Mrs. Dana Bassell, in the center part of town, was built from brick made at the home site. Daniel Bassel helped in the supervision of the kiln work as he guarded the property, that was sometimes used by soldiers of opposing scouting parties in the Civil War.

At times Lost Creek has been a noisy place. Mining activities for coal began here about 1910, with a side track laid to the mine opening about one and a fourth miles away. Then in 1914 the Monongahela Valley Traction Company extended a line to give passengers and freight service to Weston and Clarksburg throughout the day. Later the street car was replaced by bus service as hard surface roads were built in the area.

These improved roads were first laid of native stone, and later surfaceed with concrete and black tar. this was a welcome pleasure as it made travel in private cars possible along the four highways leading from the town. In 1915 Grant District High School was opened for a fall term. Sometime later the school was renamed Lost Creek High School and remained so until 1965, when South Harrison High School was opened, joining the two senior high schools of West Milford, Lost Creek and Mt. Clare. To this school recently was added a Junior High School building, showing a quick growth in enrollment.

The children from this area are picked up by bus and transported to Lost Creek Grade School, West Milford Grade School and South Harrison High School, and some to special classes in other schools about the county.

Many of its graduates are in attendance at the college throughout the state and many go to other states for special courses of study.

At an early date young folks of the community completed a program in the public school system that used the five books of McGuffey's Readers, the five book series of Ray's Arithmetic, and Webster's Spelling Book, with courses in geography, West Virginia and United States history, grammar and penmanship.

After completing the advance book in reading and arithmetic the advanced pupils were permitted to go to the

114

Court House in the spring of the year for examination to qualify for a Teacher's Certificate. These certificates were rated as First Class or Third Class.

After a time the larger cities were able to establish a high shool that provided two or four year training courses, which later were organized into Normal Schools, for special training of teachers.

One-teacher schools sprang up in most rural communities of Harrison County when the county was first formed, as many of the pioneer settlers wanted educational opportunities for the young members of their family. A few communities organized an independent school district composed of a group of families in a rural vicinity willing to hire and select a teacher of their choice, while some schools were financed by private tuition, and many children were left out for parents were unable to supply the needed books for their children. In that day the slate and a special kind of pencil markers were used. They were later replaced by tablets, notebooks and fountain pens.

In the era following 1879 it was not easy to get an education; even up to 1900, schools were not close at hand to maintain a program of education, as the staff of superintendent, special teachers, janitors, cooks and bus drivers provides today.

Many of the pioneer families banded together to build a log structure often called a school house, but it served a duel purpose, as a church for worship and public meetings.

Harrison County even at an early date had sponsored the movement for free choice of religion, and churches of all denominations have been successful in establishing center's of worship of the people's choice in the wide area of the county.

In the vicinity of Lost Creek, the first settlers, a group of families from the Seventh Day Baptist Church of New Jersey, built a log church not too far from the cemetery at Sheets Mill, that was destroyed by fire. Next they came to the grounds near the town of Lost Creek where saved timber was used to erect a frame church on ground Daniel Bassel donated. In time the frame church was destroyed by fire and the congregation moved about a mile away and erected a log church that was later replaced by brick from a kiln the members worked. This is the Brick Church so well recognized today.

The Lost Creek United Methodist Church as it now stands was organized July 15, 1894, by Rev. A. L. McKeever, with a total of 25 charter members. The first church, a wooden structure, stood on land donated by David Lee Nutter. This building was destroyed by fire, and in 1912 a substantial brick structure was erected at the same site. In 1951, an addition was constructed to supply space for a kitchen, serving room, and quarters for individual Sunday School classes.

The Woman's Club of Lost Creek, was organized in 1929, with 22 members. They have been very active over the years and are a joyful working group in projects of various kinds.

In 1940, a group of men joined together to organize a Lions Club. In the first organization there were 36 original members. Today led by Harry Allman, they are very active and do many civic projects for the community.

There is also an active Senior Citizen organization, meeting at the Methodist Church each Wednesday, since organizing May 7, 1969, with 15 members. President today is Flo Latta.

The Town of Lost Creek was incorporated in 1946, with the aid of the local Lions Club. Eugene Alkire serves today as mayor and Patricia Bennett as recorder.

The town today has a bank, a post office, three service stations to accommodate automobiles; a Community Center building to house the Public Library and Fire Department equipment; four general stores, a restaurant, a real-estate office, a barber shop, a county feed store that suppiles the needs of local farmers; and a hardware store building which has space for the Village Pharmacy, a beauty parlor, a laundry mat. It also has a dentist, a medical doctor and veterinarian, whose services reaches out from the town in four general directions.

After the Volunteer Fire Department was organized, the Woman's Auxiliary was established to give help and aid for the department's needs and support for community activity in social and civic ways.

Harrison County Bands - Strains from Drum and Fife Carry Great Importance

BY DOROTHY DAVIS

The sound that catches best the spirit of parades, holidays and festive gatherings that have occurred throughout the history of the nation and Harrison County is that of the brass band.

One symbol of the American Revolution is the drummer and fifer marching with Old Glory waving above their heads, for music and the military fit hand in glove. The Continental Congress had authorized in 1775 two battalions of marines "including a band of fifers and drummers." Thomas Jefferson, called the godfather of the marine band, circa 1800 encouraged the addition of clarinets, French horns, oboes, a bassoon, and a bass drum and invited the marine band to play for presidential events, a custom continued by every president since 1800.

After Indian incursions ended in Harrison County in 1795, the fifer and the drummer were important men in Clarksburg at the April and October musters of the eleventh regiment of the Virginia militia which every county man past the age of 16 by law must join. Four years after the Virginia Assembly cut Doddridge County out of Harrison County in 1845, the adjutant of the new 180th regiment stationed in West Union wrote into the record of accounts: "Joseph Childers, fifer 1 day at April muster $2, October muster $2; Issac Stutler, drummer 1 day at April muster $2."

State militia laws ended with the War Between the States and by the second half of the 19th century, bands embellished with brass, wood-wind, and percussion instruments began to appear in Harrison County. Every town by 1900 had a band ready to play at church and community picnics and at family reunions and to march through the streets of the town on the Fourth of July. The first town band on record is the Stoey Band organized in Shinnston in the late 1850s under the sponsorship of Solomon S. Fleming whose son William H. Fleming and son-in-law David Edgar Foreman played in the band directed by Mr. Story. The tradition of a town band for Shinnston continued, for on January 23, 1877, M. C. Jarrett organized "The Shinnston Coronet Band" which had instruments played by Hugh and H. T. Shinn, Dorsey Shore, S. Long, W. T. Reader, Albert and John Knox, George Haught, Emory Stickler, C. T. Harrison and M.C., A. L. and M. J. Jarrett. A few years later the Jarretts had another band called

"The Royal Military Band" with one of its members Russell L. Anderson who by 1907 was directing his own Shinnston Band.

The history of the Johnstown Band shows how casually men who played musical instruments organized into a band. A young man attending the wedding of Sylvia Queen to Judson Thrash in Johnstown on July 2, 1900, said to someone: "Let's start a brass band." And start they did a band that was hired to furnish music in 1903 for a Democratic convention in Clarkburg and which for decades played for picnics and reunions. The band picked up new members Allen Queen, Bunner Palmer, Samuel Davis, Herbert Longenette and Carroll Palmer in 1924 and lasted until 1938, when the organization broke up. But bands have many lives. March 1951 Floyd Jenkins reorganized the Johnstown Band with Judson Thrash the leader. The band existed awhile, disappeared, and rose again in 1955 under the leadership of Ed Zeller.

Soon after the Belgians and French imigrants built window glass plants circa 1905 and settled in Salem, the men organized a band consisting of about 35 members. The Belgians and French eventually built a clubhouse where the band practiced every Sunday morning. The band gave concerts, marched in parades; and when a member of a glassworker's family died, the band marked at half cadence before the hearse to the town cemetery. Beorge Bourmark directed the band.

The organization lost members when the United States entered World War I and young musicians went into active service with the Fairmont National Guard Band. After the war so many glassworkers moved from Salem that the band broke up. Clark Siedhoff of the Salem College Music Department directed a Salem town band in the late 1920s. Some of the members of this band were Harrison T. Westfall and his son Leland, Victor Flowers, Ira Williams, Harry Davis, Howard Stutler, Bond Davis, "Doc" Jones, Clarence Stutler, Herschel Fox and sons Herbert and Aldine, and "Shorty" Flowers. When this band ceased to exist, Herschel Fox directed a smaller group in a Salem Community Band.

During the years Stealey was a municipality separate from Clarkburg, music for community gatherings was furnished by John E. Stealey who directed a band with the members his own children. And when the town was a municipality, Adamston had a band.

In the early 1920s after surrounding communities had in 1917 been brought into the Greater Clarksburg municipality, the city council hired a professional city manager, Harrison T. Otis. In June 1923 when the City of Clarksburg staged an elaborate homecoming, "The Clarksburg Telegram" announced: "The Greater Clarksburg Band and the Adamston Band composing 50 Union musicians have been employed to furnish music for Homecoming June 10-16." And the paper added: "The committee will also procure the St. Mary's High School Drum and Fife Corps under the direction of Father Constantine."

The 1920s was the heyday of the Greater Clarksburg Band. Mr. Otis started a playground system and hired the Greater Clarksburg Band to play regularly scheduled concerts at the playgrounds in each ward of the city. A bandstand was erected the day before the concert. Here the band sat and here guest soloists performed and young people skilled in dancing the "Charleston" flung their heels into the air as the band played such tunes as "Yes Sir, She's My Baby." Young and old milled around the playground or sat on the grass near the playgound during the summer evenings when the band played.

Most every community organization in Clarksburg at one time or another in the 1920s and the 1930s had a band whose members often were many of the same people. The musicians would play with a band and when the organization's interest in a band flagged the musicians moved to another band.

Herbert Fox, when interviewed recently told how the system worked. Fox said that Sylvan Ledoux came to Salem circa 1920 to ask Fox's father to play in a VFW band being organized by the Clarkburg unit. H. H. Fox told Ledoux that he had two sons who played too; so all the Foxes joined the band, This band journeyed to the Chicago World's Fair in 1933, where it played concerts. Fox said that the American Legion in Clarkburg had a band about the same time.

When a Mr. Holliday, who played in the Greater Clarksburg Band and who traveled once a week to Salem to give lessons, died in Clarksburg in the late 1920s, Herbert Fox went to Clarksburg to attend his teacher's funeral after which the Greater Clarksurg Band members, carrying their musical instruments, boarded the trolley and rode to Victory High School. There they formed ranks and marched ahead of the funeral procession to Greenlawn Cemetery playing a dirge as they marched.

August Smith was director of the Greater Clarksburg Band. He was followed by Clifford Selden who composed the song "Clarksburg My Hometown" for the 1923 Homecoming. In the newspaper account of Selden's death was the statement: "Selden adapted all music played by the Shrine Oriental Band." Henry A. Mayer was named director of the Greater ClarksburgBand after the demise of Selden. Mayer in the early 1960s started concerts that have become a tradition with Clarksburg musicians. Financed by the Union Performance Trust Fund of the Federation of Musicians to which members of Local 580 in Clarksburg belong, musicians travel to hospitals, nursing homes, and senior-citizen apartments in the county to entertain at Christmastime. Directed by Robert Swain, the musicians who made up the brass choir in December 1983 were: Donald Hamilton, alto sax; John Morgan, alto sax; Fred Ross, tenor sax; Phillip Waytt, baritone sax; Randall Hall, clarinet; Edward Propst, baritone horn; Louis Oliverio, trombone; Orlando Colombo, Donald Campbell and Richard Johnson, trumpets; and W. T. Kirkpatrick, drums

Horse Lovers Were a Part of Early Life at Lost Creek

BY ALTON BELL

Time was short as it often times was for people who were busy. Fall days passed into winter season and now spring had come to Harrison County farmlands. This was early spring, and so it didn't mean flowers such as the sweet scented roses, or birds in happy song, but it did mean green grass appearing on the hill slopes, damp areas of the meadows, and places on the other side of the fenced enclosures of the pasture land.

And now with the sun shining enough to assure time for spring thaw and fewer muddy tracks about the barn lots, men thought of getting out to field work. One and sometimes two horses were used to pull the farm sled that had just received a new set of hickory runners to check fence lines and repair winter damages.

The typical day's work on the farms of Elk and Grant districts was like that of other cattle, sheep and horse farmers, but to the large farm owners of southern and eastern Harrison County, men were thinking hay barns were getting bare and time was approaching to turn stock on open pasture range.

For sure the thoughts of Ira C. Post, Porter Maxwell, Aquilla Ward and Enoch W. Post were similar to those of many of their neighbors in the vicinity of the beef-raising area.

Enoch Post, one of the substantial farming residents of Elk District, made his home in the county since February 1859 when he settled on Rooting Creek. He was born in Lewis County Jan 6, 1838, and his wife, Sarah F. Hottspillar Post, was born in Rockingham County, Virginia on May 12, 1844.

From the time of settlement in the western part of Virginia the mode of travel depended on good horse flesh. In the days of the Ceasars ruling Rome travel was by chariots drawn by the speedy-prancing and dashing horses. The first fire trucks and ambulances were pulled by spans of trained horses that

recognized the call to duty as the warnings were given for service call of bells sounding or horns tooting.

It has been said man's friend, well-used and tried, has been his pal, a horse. The horse can be trained to come when called and put in service on many different occasions.

The color of a horse is only in its coat. The true character of the animal is in its strength, durability, temper, and grace or gracefulness of its charm. Most horses have a keen mind to sense danger, kindness in treatment, difficulty on icy roads, slippery rock, swampland and a very keen sense to locate quicksand and water holes in a strange pasture. They can see well at night and have saved many lives of riders lost on public highways or in woods.

As has often been said, the love of nature, the green templed hills, narrow valleys, sparkling streams rushing along so gleefully, make Harrison County a restful homeland to its people.

Enoch Post and a relative, Ira Post, who lived some three miles apart in 1881, introduced the Percheron breed of horses into Harrison County in the section along Elk Creek, Gnatty Creek and Rooting Creek, going out to Hacker's Creek, to Bridgeport and near Philippi; in general the greater part of eastern Harrison County and neighboring farms.

They bought from Mark W. Dunham, the noted importer, who bought such breeds as English Bay, Clydesdale, English Coach and French Draft from Virginia, Illinois and Yorkshire, England. They bought one stallion, "Martine," number 1261, paying $1800 and "Vidocq," a half-blood, for $700. The following September 18, they bought of Crumpacker, Winters and Company of Westville, Indiana, the stallion "Armand," number 11855. Finally they purchased the much prized beauty of strength and grace of carriage. This was a stallion of dapple-gray, "Tallyrand," number 1852 and costing $3,500, with a filly named "Rose" costing $700.

These men of Harrison County and neighbors on surrounding farms like the ones from the "Lengend of Atri" loved their horses and opened a new branch of progress to the farmers of this area. This was raising good stock horses for home usage and outside markets. The gas and oil boom that opened up in this vicinity needed draft horses, and teams were in demand for the years that followed.

It is interesting to note Riding Clubs and Academys for care and hire of horses for enjoyment today use lightweight animals, these stallions bought by the Posts were draft breeds as the weights show: Martine weighed in at 1,650 pounds. Armand weighed 1,850 pounds, Tallyrand weight 1,600 pounds and Vidocq weighed 1,30 pounds .

Porter Maxwell owned land on Peel Tree Run and joining Ira Post devoted much of his time and acreage to beef cattle raising. He had a need for many teams of horses which were often purchased from the neighbors who raised colts for sale. When a good team was spotted, Mr. Maxwell was never slow in buying the pair and saw they were well cared for and most carefully trained.

Porter Maxwell had fields designated for yearling cattle, two-year-olds, three-year-olds and occasionally cattle of older groups. He raised cattle to supply beef for the markets of Baltimore, Pittsburgh, and occassionly Chicago. The tenants on his farms were treated as neighbors to be helped and many advantages were given to them for family enjoyment and improvement. It may and should be said, the men working as tenants with Mr. Maxwell were taught to be thrifty, to pursue their work in all interest and deep concern. He believed the land owed men a living but thought they must work to receive the reward of that gift.

Porter Maxwell lived a dedicated life to his helpers, friends and family in a span of days from his birth, April 13, 1845, to the time of his death on, Oct. 13, 1928. Any traveler stopping at his home was received as a friend, and all neighbors for miles around were welcomed as his friends, for a friendly chat or counsel in business matters.

Porter Maxwell lived before the handy invention of the hay baler or balers on equipment of farm machinery today. He would have enjoyed the convenience of this man saving machinery. Much of the bottom of Porter Maxwell's property was used to produce crops of grasses for mixed hay. The grass was first cut and cured, then put into stacks and hay barns for storage. But when winter days came with wind, snow and sleet men worked through the day with teams pulling wagons to put hay out on the ground for herds of cattle for as much as five to seven hours per day.

A grandson, Dr. Issac H. Maxwell II, who lives at Lost Creek today, is on daily call to go for miles around to help those who graze cattle, and dairy farmers.

These early men were lovers of the hills, dales and valleys where they worked the land for enjoyment and a good living. They were taught to recognize the part animals played on the farms in a man's life.

Dr. Maxwell, II followed the lessons his elders taught him in animal care and used this wisdom as a background for his study at West Virginia University and in getting a degree from Ohio University as well. His care and devotion to service for forty odd years shows Dr. Maxwell to be one who loves farm animals, his neighbors, friends and people in general.

People of Harrison County and adjoining areas have had a friend and helper in Alvin D. Bassel, who lived at Lost Creek from 1866 to 1926. He was a son of David and Margaret Bassel. The Bassel home was north of the town of Lost Creek on State Rt. 25. The David Bassel farm has been a landmark to many travelers along the highway, as it was a farm of good grazing and bottom land to produce good hay crops. For a number of years Alvin Bassel twice a year held a Sale and Exchange Auction at the two large barns on his property. Here farmers could buy stock as needed in the spring of the year and sell their surplus stock at the fall season.

Alvin Bassel loved to deal in horses and two favorite stallions he kept for service were a light riding and buggy horse, White Stockings, a draft stallion of Clydesdale breed, and at times a favorite of the Morgan breed. He often traveled to county fairs across the state to exhibit horses and take part in races.

The Ghost Had Waited For All These Years

BY RUTH ANN MUSICK

It was a cool summer night. As my great-grandfather sat on his back porch overlooking the railroad tracks, little did he know he was about to see the town ghost — the man on the railroad tracks.

My great-grandfather had moved to the county just two weeks before. As he sat on the back porch of his new home this particular night, he noticed an old man walking on the railroad tracks. He did not think this was strange, since hobos often waited to jump the train. But this man tonight was different.

As grandfather observed him, the hobo kept taking a drink of something out of a bottle. After a while he sat down on the tracks and kept drinking from the bottle. It was obvious that the man was drunk and soon would be insensible. If he were aware of what was going on even now, he would move away from the tracks, because the 9:15 freight train was due in five minutes. But the man sat there without moving an inch, and he continued drinking from the same bottle which, it seemed, would never run dry.

At this point my great-grandfather was getting a little worried. My great-grandmother had joined him on the porch and she too was aware of the scheduled train. She urged her husband to go help the man.

The tracks were about a fourth of a mile from the house, and my great-grandfather started to run down in the direction of the man. He had only about four minutes to reach him.

He ran faster, and in the distance he heard the train's warning whistle. Would he be able to reach the man in time? He told himself he had to. He began to shout, "You fool, get out of there before you're killed!" but the man paid no attention whatever to the warning.

Great-grandfather heard the train drawing nearer. He knew it would soon reach the spot where the man was sitting. Since the engine was so high, the engineer would not be able to see him and would not bring the train to a stop.

It was already too late. The train was right there, and a horrible death was about to occur before my great-grandfather's eyes. But much to his amazement, before the engine struck the man, the old hobo had disappeared into thin air!

At first my great-grandfather thought he was seeing things and waited for the train to pass to prove to himself that someone had really been sitting there. However, there was no trace of anyone. He was positive he had seen a man. His wife had seen him too, for she had suggested that he go down and help him, now he was gone!

Great-grandfather returned home quite shaken up and told his wife what had happened although she had watched the scene herself. They both were disturbed over the matter and decided to keep it a secret. After about a week the mystery troubled them so much that they told their landlord about the strange night.

Expecting to be called silly or crazy as they revealed their story, they were surprised when the landlord instead listened intently, with a serious look on his face.

A long time before an old man, whom no one had ever seen before, appeared in the town. Being wary of strangers, the people refused to give him food, shelter or even a job. The stranger got drunk, and for the good of the town he was driven away.

The only thing the stranger knew how to do was jump trains, so he sat down on the tracks waiting for the next freight. When the train came, the man on the railroad was mangled to pieces.

Every year at the time of his death, this man would return and wait for the train. Whenever people would try to ride past the tracks on the anniversary of his death, the horses would buck and would go no farther. No one had ever succeeded in getting past the tracks on this particular date. My great-grandfather was the only one ever to go near them on that strange night. He thought he saw a man in trouble and tried to help him.

A year after the incident, my great-grandfather waited to see the man on the railroad tracks appear again. It was 9:10 — five more minutes and the train would pass. There was no sign of the hobo. At last the train passed and no man appeared.

No one has seen the man on the railroad since. Some people believe that great-grandfather satisfied what the ghost had waited for all these years — a person with a human heart to help someone in need.

T. M. Jackson - Traders Bank President

By MRS. CREEL CORNWELL SR.

The man largely responsible for building the springboard from which industries related to coal and gas were launched in central West Virginia was Col. Thomas Moore Jackson.

Col. Jackson was long and prominently identified with important industrial and business enterprises in his native state and city. He was a representative of a family whose name has had much prestige in the history of Virginia, especially that part of the Old Dominion that now constitutes West Virginia.

James Madison Jackson was the father of Thomas Moore Jackson. His wife was Caroline Moore Jackson.

The James Madison Jackson house was located on East Pike Street on a rise of land above Elk Creek.

Family tradition has it that after Caroline Moore married J. M. Jackson she wanted to be closer to her sisters, Mrs. Waldo P. Goff, and Mrs. Luther Haymond. Her husband sold the home and purchased a cottage six blocks away on West Pike Street. He remodeled the structure which grew into the Jackson mansion at 528 W. Pike. Until it was razed after World War II it stood where the new addition to the Clarksburg Post Office is now located.

T. Moore Jackson was born June 22, 1852 in Clarksburg. He received his early education in the public schools and at the Northwestern Academy. He attended Bethany College. Afterwards he entered Washington and Lee University where he took a special course in civil engineering and constructive engineering. He graduated from W&L in June 1873, with high honors, with a degree in civil engineering.

From 1874 to 1875, Jackson served as chief engineer of the Middle Island Railroad in West Virginia, and from 1875 to 1879, he was chief engineer of the Western and West Fork Railroad. In 1879, he was appointed first assistant engineer of the Iron Valley and Morgantown Railroad, later becoming chief engineer. He resigned this position to accept that of chief engineer of the Tunnelton and Kingwood Railroad in West Virginia where he remained until 1881, when he was appointed engineer in charge of mines at Wilsonburg, Clarksburg, Flemington, and Gaston.

Jackson had been engaged in mining engineering in various parts of West Virginia and Pennsylvania since 1875 and as a geologist he opened and developed many of the coal, oil and gas properties in central West Virginia.

In 1881 he was elected surveyor of Harrison County. A year later he was appointed chief engineer of the West Virginia and Pennsylvania Railroad. He held this position until 1885 when he resigned. He was retained, however, by the company as consulting engineer for many years.

In 1884, he was married to a Clarksburg native, Emma Lewis, daughter of Judge Charles S. Lewis, who had been a member of the Virginia Legislature and served as a member of Congress prior to the Civil War.

Jackson had a variety of interests many of which became valuable assets of Harrison County in later years. The first telephone line was assembled in Clarksburg in 1884, eight years after Alexander Graham Bell successfully talked over his "miracle."

Jackson and Charles L. Hickman originated the system which was the first telephone service in West Virginia. H. U. Crumit, Clarksburg's first telephone lineman, said the fist two lines consisted of something like broom wire tied with string insulators to buildings or to poles where the lines crossed railroad tracks. It ran from the Ruhl-Koblegard Wholesale Grocery Compay in East Clarksbsurg to the telegraph office at the Baltimore and Ohio passenger station in East Clarksburg, and from the Hart Machine Shop to the B&O Station.

Telephones were wooden boxes about eight inches square by three inches deep with a calfskin drumhead stretched over one side of the box. In the center was a small hole with wire stuck through and fastened to a button, the wire being stretched taut. When someone wished to attract the attention of a person near the other telephone, he tapped with a lead pencil on the drumhead. After the party being called tapped in answer the conversation began.

Jackson became fascinated by telephones after talking over the line between Pennsboro and Harrisville. Hickman interested Jackson, John Koblegard, Col. J. C. Vance, D. P. Morgan and H. C. Wells in establishing a central office in Clarksburg. The oganization the men formed was chartered July 10, 1885, as the Clarksburg Telephone Co. Stock, sold by the company for $25 per share, financed a switchboard, installation of telephones, and later the extension of the service to Weston, Shinnston, Bridgeport, and West Milford.

On Nov. 18, 1890, the Central District Telegraph Company won a franchise to operate a telephone system in the city. This company which had offices in the Odd Fellows Building, and the Clarksburg Telephone Company sold out, in February 1891 to the Bell Company which, after a few years, moved to the Oak Hall Building, where the switchboard grew to five sections of magnet board. In 1896 the Bell System built long distance lines from Uniontown to Clarksburg via Morgantown and Fairmont. In 1906 the same company constructed an East-West long distance service through Clarksburg. By Sept. 7, 1907, increasing numbers of subscribers made necessary the installation of a common battery switchboard.

Another of Jackson's interests was the creation of a better water works program for Clarksburg. In 1887 he was made assistant engineer of the Clarksburg Water Works and was also engineer in charge of geological maps of West Virginia and Pennsylvania, working on the coalfields of these states.

For 100 years residents of Clarksburg depended on wells for their water supply. Many of the wells were private; some were accessible to the public. The most widely used wells in the center of town were located near the house occupied by the Link Family at 216 West Main Street, and a well on the plaza of the courthouse which was used continuously from the days of the early settlement until the second decade of the 20th century. A tin cup tied to the pump served all thirsty shoppers.

Water Works comissioners — R. T. Lowndes, chairman, Jackson, and John B. Hart employed John W. Hill, consulting engineer of Cincinnati, to design a water works system that when completed consisted of six miles of cast iron pipes, two pumps having a capacity of 750,000 gallons, and a battery of two 70 horsepower boilers with an 80-foot brick stack. Water pumped directly from the West Fork River through the mains of the system reached the homes of patrons on April 10, 1889. Harvey W. Harmer recalls 20 years or so of muddy water piped into Clarksburg homes. Careful citizens boiled water before drinking it.

The oil and gas industry attracted Jackson's interest based upon both his geological and engineering training. He became a pioneer in the early development of these industries in Harrison County.

The Harrison County Oil and Gas Company incorporated Sept. 15, 1887, by Charles M. Hart, Charles J. Goff, John C. Vance, Burton M. Despard, Richard T. Lowndes, Nathan Goff, and Jackson, is the earliest drilling company metioned in county records "for the purpose of boring for or otherwise obtaining petroleum or other oil and natural gas and buying and selling oil and gas and constructing and maintaining lines of tubing and piping for transportation of petroleum or other oils and of Natural Gas for said company and for the public generally."

Dr. I. C. White and Jackson drilled several wells, all of which proved to be dry holes near Quiet Dell in the 1880s. The first successful venture of the two men was a well drilled to 975 feet in 1890 on the farm of I. L. Marsh at Brown.

White and Jackson, who held leases in Monongalia, Marion, and Doddridge counties as well as in Harrison County, sold out to the South Penn Oil Co. organized by Standard Oil Co. in 1889 to operate in Pennsylvania and West Virginia.

In 1889, Jackson went to Morgantown as chief engineer of the water works and natural gas plants there. In that year the chair of civil and mining engineering was established at West Virginia University and Jackson was chosen to head the department. He remained in this position until 1891, when the School of Engineering having been firmly established, he resigned against the protests of WVU, to takeup the active practice of his profession.

After leaving WVU, Jackson served as chief engineer of several railroads, among which was the narrow guage road from Clarksburg to Weston, afterwards known as the West Virginia and Pittsburgh branch of the B&O.

The first coal boom occurred in the 1890s as a direct result of the building of the railroad to Fairmont. Harrison County businessmen had seen the need for the road years before Johnson N. Camden supplied the money to make the road a reality in 1889. R. T. Lowndes, Col. Benjamin Wilson, John L. Ruhl, and A. G. Smith had financed construction at the Fairmont end of a projected railroad in the early 1880s and after years of working to find ways to complete the project, finally abandoned the plan.

When Camden became interested, property owners asked exorbitant prices for rights-of-way. He turned the problem over to Gov. A. B. Fleming who condemned the land needed by the railroad and appointed B. Tyson Harmer, M.S. Brooks, F. A. Robinson and Edmund Denham to the jury which set a fair price.

The Fairmont road proved so lucrative that the Camden interests contemplated a road to run from the Ohio River north of Parkersburg to Belington. Jackson, who had interests in the Temile Coal Co., near Lumberport, favored a road which would run past his mine.

Being prominent in the development of coal, oil and gas in central West Virginia, and realizing the importance of a more direct route to the Ohio River for these products, Jackson undertook and was directly responsible for the building of the West Virginia Short Line Railroad from Clarksburg to New Martinsville. He formed a company to build the road with himself as president; J. H. Allen, vice president; C. Sprigg Sands, treasurer; Thomas G. Brady, secretary, and J. Phillip Clifford, attorney. One evening at the dinner table in the Jackson home during discussion of the 60-mile line, Mrs. Jackson asked her husband why it was not called the "Short Line." From then on it was the Short Line.

A Jackson employee boarded a train for Charleston where he filed a map and the legal requirements with the secretary of state, then went to Martinsburg where he filed similar papers with the federal clerk. The Camden interests did not realize the road was being considered until after Jackson was ready to start construction.

The builders of the Short Line planned to run the rails in Clarksburg to the site of the terminal building some distance behind the residences of R. T. Lowndes and Nathan Goff Sr. who objected to the trains being so near their homes. At the time a law existed whereby if the "fact were accomplished" the owner of the right-of-way desired by a common carrier could not prohibit the installation of tracks. So the contractor moved the equipment and 100 workers after dark, graded for the road on the Lowndes land and laid the track before daybreak. The first train ran over the Short Line in 1899.

Regular operation began in 1900, the first passenger train ran in March 1901. The trains used B&O track to the railroad station in Glen Elk. Jackson served as president of this railroad until its purchase by the B&O.

Another venture of Jackson's led to the establishment of a bank. In 1891 Sen. J. N. Camden sent "a substantial check" to Gov. Fleming to meet payments for damages incurred to property in Harrison County in building the railroad from Fairmont to Clarksburg. When he presented the check and was refused payment, Fleming wired Camden for currency. Angered, Camden remarked, "I will establish a bank in Clarksburg which will cash my check or those of any other responsible party."

This was the beginning of the Traders Bank. The incorporaters of the bank were Dr. Fleming Howell, Dr. D. P. Morgan, and Jackson, all of Clarksburg; Col. William Hood, Shinnston, Joseph E. Sands and C. Sprigg Sands, Fairmont; and Capt. J. Hurry, Bridgeport. They began business in May 1891 in a building that had formerly housed a shoe store. On March 3, 1894, they bought the Shuttleworth property on the southeast corner of Main and Third streets for $12,000, razed the building and built the Traders Block with rooms for the bank, an opera house, and a number of stores — all occupying a space of 75 feet by 180 feet. The structures cost $100,000 when completed. T. Moore Jackson was president and Charles Sprigg Sands was cashier. Officers of the bank reported resources of $1,445,704.33 on April 30, 1902. The Traders Bank was a partner in the merger with the People's Banking and Trust Co. that in 1905 formed the Union National Bank. The Traders building was destroyed by fire in 1911.

Jackson was also one of the chief promoters of the Traders Hotel, the building of which gave the city an up-to-date hotel and it was through his efforts that the Jackson Iron and Tinplate mills were established in Clarksburg.

In July 1901 the Jackson Sheet and Tin Plate Co., capitalized at $300,000, was incorporated by Ingraham Grove of Cleveland; G. C. Moore of Columbus, Ohio; and C. S. Sands, Fleming Howell, L. S. Horner, and Jackson of Clarksburg. The company purchased 10 acres of land north of East Pike Street and invested $45,000 in five buildings worth $80,000.

About 1903 the Jackson Iron and Tin Plate Co. opened for business in the manufacture of tin plate. Declared bankrupt in 1904, the company was purchased by the bondholders at public auction for $62,000. The following April 1905, the bondholders sold the company to Pittsburgh capitalists who sent J. R. Philips of Pittsburgh to operate the plant and renamed the concern Phillips Sheet and Tin Plate Co.

Another interesting event took place in December 1902. During that month, the local horse fanciers formed a corporation known as the West Virginia Fair Association and purchased a tract of land east of the city in the Nutter Fort area, land the incorporaters labeled "New Fairgrounds." Officers of the West Virginia Fair Association who bought part of the White Farm south of the Buckhannon Pike for the new project were Jackson, president; B. B. Stout. vice president; A. D. Parr, secretary, and W. H. Lewis, treasurer.

This group was formed because the then existing fair group was interested in agricultural and mechanical developments and the newly-formed one was interested in horse racing. Thus for several years the county had two fairs.

In 1910, Jackson organized and was made president of a company to build the Clarksburg and Northern Railroad to extend from New Martinsville, by way of Middlebourne and Salem, to Clarksburg.

Construction began on this road in 1912 and the grading was completed between New Martinsville and Middlebourne. All seemed to be going well when Jackson returned from New Martinsville to Clarksburg where he suffered a severe heart attack which caused his death on Feb. 3, 1912.

Practically his entire life was spent in his home town and he did much toward its development as an industrial center. His ability as a civil engineer and his great knowledge of geology enabled him to realize the importance of the vast oil, gas and coal areas in central West Virginia and to develop them for the establishment of manufacturing industries.

The Oil and Gas Industry Developement, Vital to Strong Harrison County Economy

by J. ROBERT HORNOR

The history of the development of the oil and gas industry in Harrison County is of more recent vintage than much of what we consider as being history today. It has been only 94 years since the first commercial oil well was drilled in Harrison County. I say, only, because it is a relatively short period in which so much took place.

In that 94 years communities have grown overnight to fairly good size cities and just as quickly returned to their original size. Thousands of individuals have come in and out of our county to seek, in one way or another, their fortunes in the oil and gas industry.

We were fortunate, I believe, in that our development as a whole was carried out by men and companies with vision, knowledge and skill. We did not experience that waste and dissipation of the oil and gas that took place in other fields. That is the reason, I am sure, that our wells have produced as they have, and having been properly drilled and operated, many are still valuable for deeper tests, or for gas storage pools which is a most valuable asset for any gas utility today.

The greatest period of activity in our county was from 1898 to 1915, but before starting into the development of the industry in Harrison County, it might be of interest to give a short summary of the early history of the oil and gas industry.

The story of petroleum is the greatest romance in industrial history. It is the story of a discovery and development which more radically reshaped human affairs and more completely effected human behavior than any other event of the past 125 years. This discovery transformed vision into reality, annihilated distance and made personal comfort commonplace. It took men with imagination, courage and ingenuity. Men knew about petroleum long before there was an oil industry. Ancient peoples in many parts of the world found oil seeping from the ground. They used it for medicine, for waterproofing, for caulking boats and occasionally for fuel. The Bible and ancient Greek and other histories contain references to petroleum under various names. Medical scientists described it and named it petroleum, meaning rock oil. It is also believed that the pitch with which Noah coated the ark was a form of evaporated petroleum.

Early settlers in the Kanawha Valley drilling for salt found the well contained gas, which they were to use to heat the brine furnaces. The petroleum was considered a nuisance and allowed to escape into nearby streams and rivers. It was not until 75 years later that this area was leased for oil and gas and developed on a commerical scale.

Some say the oil industry was born because people wanted to read more. They needed better and cheaper light than just candles or whale oil. A Pittsburgh druggist named Samuel Kier applied to petroleum the method of refining coal oil and his experiments were successful. As a result, the Seneca Oil Company was founded. That company hired Col. Edwin Drake to supervise the drilling of the first successful well for the sole purpose of producing petroleum, in Oil Creek district, Venango County, Pennsylvania. This week came in August, 1859. The depth was only 69½ feet and oil filled the hole to the surface. A pump was installed and the well produced 300 barrels per day. The price of crude oil then was $20.00 per barrel. Drake had demonstrated that oil could be found in large volumes by drilling for it through rock and the oil industry as an industry was born then and there.

In connection with early salt wells, a boring was sunk here in Harrison County in 1835 on the Righter Farm on Shinn's Run by Abraham and P. B. Righter to a depth of 745 feet, in which a light flow of gas and a strong stream of fresh water was encountered. This is now known as Saltwell, and the water is still flowing from the top of the hole and, also, a small amount of gas escapes in the bubbling water. There were several other salt wells, or so called mineral wells, drilled in the county about 1870, one at West Milford in the Lowther Settlement.

The Rathbone Family is associated with the earliest beginnings of the petroleum industry in Western Virginia and in recent years one of the descendants, V. J. Rathbone, was president of the Standard Oil Company of New Jersey.

On one of their farms in Wirt County, the Rathbones decided to drill their own well after seeing the success of the Drake well. In July 1860, at a depth of 303 feet, they struck oil. The well produced 100 barrels a day for about four

months, then gradually declined. This was the first well drilled in what is now West Virginia, for the sole purpose of obtaining petroleum. Thus the Rathbones inauguarated the Burning Spring Field. This started a real influx of people and drilling. The population in the spring of 1860 was twenty adults and by August of that year increased to six thousand. The excitement compared to the Gold Rush in California. Leases bought and sold for as much as $100,000 and the seller even retained a one-half override. Three to four hundred wells were drilled and averaged two hundred barrels per well.

In 1863, the destructiveness of the Civil War descended on the Burning Springs Oil Region. The Confederate troops under General William E. Jones, had not intended to destroy the oil stores and production machinery, but once they reached the area the opportunity for destruction could not be over-looked. They destroyed 150,000 barrels of oil, besides the wells, barges and storage tanks. It must have been spectacular as well as calamitous.

For some forty years after 1870, the history of the oil and gas industry was chiefly the history of the Standard Oil Company and the fight against it. Standard Oil was the most dominating and most controversial factor in the industry throughout the world, and it shaped the course of events for two or three generations of oil men. It was the overwhelming need for some degree of stability in oil that opened the way for the formation and rapid growth of Standard Oil.

Those were the days when free enterprise meant freedom to do almost anything short of murder. There were few laws regulating business conduct, and the few that were, were regarded with contempt.

John D. Rockefeller bought refineries to control markets and with these companies he got some of the industry's ablest and most progressive leaders. No one outside of Standard's top management knew for sure the extent of Standard's influence. Between 1875 and 1900 Standard Oil controlled as much as eighty percent of the domestic trade in petroleum products.

About 1888, Standard Oil decided it had better get into the producing business to insure a crude supply for its refineries and a gas supply for its markets in the cities in Ohio and Pennsylvania where gas was starting to be piped for industrial and domestic use. This move would also enable Standard Oil to control the supply to market and the prices paid for and received for its products.

This was the background when West Virginia was coming into its own. I will now try to follow through in chronological order the commencement of operations by individuals and companies in Harrison County.

Dr. I. C. White and T. Moore Jackson were two of the early pioneers in the oil and gas industry in West Virginia who joined resources to discover oil and gas. Jackson was a well-known and respected business man, who along with his oil and other ventures, organized and built the Short Line Railroad between Clarksburg and New Martinsville.

Dr. White, the first geologist to apply in a practical way, the anticline theory of oil and gas, made a number of studies of fields and well locations in the Pennsylvania area, noting that the great gas wells were all near the crowns of anticlines. He generalized that the oil fields of Pennsylvania would extend down into West Virginia and prove even more prolific there than in Pennsylvania.

In 1884 and 1885, with J. M. Guffey of Pittsburgh, Dr.

White took up nearly 500,000 acres of oil and gas leases in West Virginia. These leases extended south-westward across the northern part of the state, including Harrison County, to the Little Kanawha River and covered practically all the great oil pools which were to be developed in this part of the state. Guffey did not receive the financial support he expected and the leases were surrendered. One can imagine their disappointment later when the area was proven productive.

Dr. White, in 1888, however, decided to undertake oil development on his own account, and in connection with, Jackson, a large number of leases were secured through Monongalia, Marion, Harrison and Doddridge counties. The first test well was located near the town of Mannington and on the 12th day of October, 1889, oil in paying quantity was found in the Big Injun sand. This well marked the opening of the northern West Virginia oil fields. Dr. White eventually sold all his working interests in the producing properties to South Penn Oil Company and returned to the study of geology and later became the first head of the State Geological Survey.

The first successful well drilled in Harrison County was drilled by Dr. White and Jackson on the I. L. Marsh Farm at Brown in 1890. It produced a small quantity of oil from the Dunkard Sand at about 975 feet. The well was drilled through the Big Injun to a total depth of 1867 feet, but no other oil was found. Dr. White and Jackson drilled several wells in the Quiet Dell area, which had gas shows, but were not commercial. One well on Suds Run is still producing gas for domestic purposes.

In 1889, the South Penn Oil Company was organized by Standard Oil Company in Pennsylvania as its operating and producing company in that state and in West Virginia.

The South Penn took thousands of acres of leases which it gradually drilled as it came south from the early Pennsylvania fields. It was not until January 1898 that it drilled its first well in Harrison County in the Jarvisville area and found oil in the fifth sand. This was the start of the great Wolf Summit and Salem oil fields.

This brings into our history Michael Late Benedum, one of the county's most famous citizens. One day in about 1890, Benedum started out for Parkersburg to see if he could obtain a position with the Baltimore and Ohio Railroad and chanced to meet John Worthington of the South Penn Oil Company on the train. Worthington was impressed by Benedum and put him to work as a leasing agent. By 1892 Benedum had made quite a reputation in the oil fields. In 1895, he was sent to Cameron as a chief official of the South Penn Oil Company. In early 1896, Benedum took some 5,000 acres on Fish Creek, south of Cameron. He paid a high price — too much, South Penn thought, and told him he could keep the leases and pay for them from his own pocket. He quit South Penn to develop the acreage, which was very productive and Benedum got into a drilling contest with South Penn. Eventually, he sold out to Standard for $400,000 and shortly afterward started drilling in Oklahoma and Texas and because of his success, acquired the name of "The Great Wildcatter."

In September 1898 the Hope Natural Gas Company, organized in Oil City, Pennsylvania. Its stock was held by National Transit Company, a Standard Oil subsidiary. The immediate purpose of the company in West Virginia was to transport natural gas to the West Virginia state line for distribution into Ohio and southern Pennsylvania. It first purchased from South Penn, eleven wells and some 29,000 acres then under lease in Wetzel County.

South Penn continued to unload a substantial number of wells and properties to Hope. Standard's policy was that companies with essentially oil producing functions should be relieved of gas wells accumulated through exploration and purchase. Hope also acquired the Flaggy Meadow Gas

Company property and the Carter Oil Company transferred to Hope its wells and acreage in the Sistersville area.

The Reserve Gas Company also transferred a large number of its wells and acreage to Hope. These were all Standard Oil concerns and with these additions, including properties of the Mountain State Gas Company in Parkersburg and the Home Gas Company in Mannington, Hope became the major gas company in northern West Virginia.

In 1907, its field offices were moved to Clarksburg and were located on the top floor of the Empire Bank Building. The main offices were in Pittsburgh. In 1929, Hope purchased all the wells and properties of the Clarksburg Light and Heat Company, and in 1940, moved the main offices to Clarksburg.

Nathan Goff Jr., took an early and active interest in the oil and gas development in the county, organizing the first company of record, in 1866, "The New State Oil Company." This coming shortly after the formation of the State of West Virginia was an appropriate name. It was organized to bore for, excavate and sell petroleum and rock oil in West Virginia. It soon died a natural death, although it was thought some leases were acquired in Pleasants County. This must have been on the strength of the Burning Springs excitement.

Goff purchased two tracts of land about 1888, one of 683 acres on Hall's Run of Ten Mile Creek and a 1,200 acre tract on Big Rock Camp near Brown. In 1892, Goff leased all of this acreage to T. Moore Jackson for a royalty, and under the terms that a well would be started within 60 days. The lease was to be cancelled in three years if oil was not found in paying quantities.

Jackson assigned ½ interest to South Penn and ½ to Ten Mile Oil Company of which he was President. A well was started in the fall of 1892. Upon completion of the well, the South Penn called it valueless and attempted to cease further exploration under the terms of the contract. Litigation followed with a compromise that South Penn would drill another test well. This well proved to be dry and the lease-contract reverted to Senator Goff in 1895.

Goff and Burton Despard then started development. Their first well came in at 200 barrels per day. They drilled seven wells in 1899 and 18 wells in 1900 on the 700 acre Hall's Run tract alone. The settlement there became known as "Oilville."

The wells on the Hall lease were very productive and in 1900 Goff sold over 295,000 barrels of oil from this tract.

On the Rock Camp tract, Goff drilled his first well in September 1900. All together, from 1899 to 1915, Goff drilled 53 oil wells, which were all good producers.

Goff also drilled a number of wells on his Oak Mound farm and the Elk Hill farm in North View. In 1912, he persuaded the Owens Bottling Company to build on his Oak Mound farm and furnished the plant gas from his own wells. His income from his oil and gas ventures was in turn reinvested in real estate. He constructed the Elk Bridge Building in 1901, the Oak Hall Building in 1903, the Waldo Hotel in 1904 and the Goff Building in 1911.

The Carnegie Natural Gas Company was orgnized in Pittsburgh in 1884 to supply gas to the Carnegie steel plants and eventually moved into West Virginia in the search for additional gas reserves.

In September 1895, the Philadelphia Oil Company of West Virginia was organized and began drilling operations in West Virginia. Eventually, there developed the Pittsburgh and West Virginia Gas Company and these two companies operated under the parent Philadelphia Company in Pittsburgh.

These three companies, Carnegie, Philadelphia Oil and the Pittsburgh and West Virginia Gas Company, drilled hundreds of wells in Harrison County to supply gas for their West Virginia and Pennsylvania industrial and domestic markets.

The Eureka Pipe Line Company was also a familiar name

to everyone in the industry. It was chartered in West Virginia in December 1890. This Standard Oil subsidiary eventually laid a network of oil gathering lines over practically the entire northern area of the state. It built and maintained a tremendous tank farm at Morgantown where most of the oil was transported and stored for shipment to the different Standard refineries in Cleveland and along the eastern seaboard.

W. Brent Maxwell was an independent operator and drilled over 50 wells on his Lynch and Turner farms at Laurel Park and on his farm where the Veterans Administration Medical Center now stands. The Turner and Lynch farms have produced over six billion cubic feet of gas and about 150,000 barrels of oil.

R. T. Lowndes also independently drilled over 100 wells on his Lowndes Hill, Davisson Run, Craigmore, Myers and Patterson Fork farms. Lowndes always liked to use a green dogwood stake to mark his locations to insure that he would get a good well.

In 1904, the Clarksburg Light and Heat Company was organized by J. P. Alexander, E. R. Davis, F. B. Haymaker, John Koblegard and B. F. Robinson, and shortly thereafter, from what I can gather, it was purchased and reorganized by the National Transit Company, a Standard Oil subsidiary, with Hope Gas Company officials as officers. E. Strong was president, Christy Payne, general manager and John B. Tonkin, treasurer. In 1929, it was purchased by Hope Gas Company.

Early Developement of The Oil & Gas Industry In Harrison County
By J. ROBERT HORNOR
PART II

Prominent citizens during the early days prior to 1900, along with Nathan Goff Jr. were instrumental in the development of the oil and gas industry. These included J. F. Osborne, T. S. Spates, R. T. Lowndes, Charles M. Hart, John B. Hart, Charles G. Goff, Burton Despard, John C. Vance, A. S. Smith, Edwin Maxwell, M. G. Sperry, Frank G. Bland, C. E. Parr, Virgil L. Highland, O. C. VanDevender and George Duncan.

Some of the early companies these men were associated with were: Clarksburg Gas Co., organized in 1871, 40-year franchises to establish gas works, sales were for street lighting; Clarksburg Natural Gas Co., organized in 1884; Harrison County Oil and gas Co., organized in 1887; Mountain State Oil and Gas Co., organized in 1889, listed J. B. Hart as vice president; Home Oil Co., organized in 1899, drilled several wells in the Clarksburg area.

Several of the companies supplied coal gas, then natural gas for domestic use and street lighting and others were formed to prospect for oil and gas.

The first oil and gas lease on record was dated July 3, 1887 from J. H. Hitt to the Harrison County Oil and Gas Co., covering 37 acres in Simpson District. The wording of the lease is interesting: "Granting the exclusive right to mine, bore and excavate and produce petroleum rock or carbon oil

and gas or other valuable and volatile substance." An interesting sidelight is the fact that this language would also conservatively cover the coal on these lands under the phrasing of these leases.

Ed and George Trainer organized the Trainer Oil and Gas Co. and developed considerable oil and gas in the early Salem days. They also had a gasoline plant during World War I. The Trainers sold their properties near Salem for $360,000. Over the years the Trainers were generous contributors to Salem College.

Dorsey Cork became actively engaged in the oil and gas business around 1900, selling gas in Mt. Clare and Lost Creek. Later he, with Orlandus West, drilled a number of wells at Erie and near the Maulsby Bride between Clarksburg and Shinnston.

About 1912, with Sam Bowman, Cork drilled ten wells at Wallace during the excitement there. The first well made about 100,000 barrels per day and Cork was there each day to turn the well into the tanks and make sure that the well produced and the oil was sold and moved.

With Thorn Koblegard of Weston, who was interested in the Mt. Clare Gas Co., Cork drilled three wells on the Bailey farm west of Jane Lew. These wells all had open flows of between 18 million and 19 million cubic feet per day. Cork always regretted that he did not participate with Mr. Koblegard, T. A. Whelan and Oscar Nelson in the purchase of the Raven Carbon Plant at McWhorter, which eventually was one of the first units of the United Carbon Corp.

Another company with which Cork was associated was the Vesper Oil and Gas Co., organized with West and a Mr. Zeising of the Grasselli Chemical Co., John W. Davis and Sam Bowman. Their drilling was mostly in the West Milford area. The company was sold in 1920 to DuPont interests for $565,000.

It is estimated there have been about 5,000 wells drilled in Harrison County. There were some notable and interesting wells:

The first well drilled by Dr. White and Jackson at Brown in 1890 is the starting point. This was a Big Dunkard sand well. I might add that Harrison County has to date over 24 different producing horizons. One does not find gas in every sand in every well, but it is unusual not to have two to three pays in one well. Just to show how close success and failure can be, the next well was drilled just west of Brown by South Penn in 1900 on the Whiteman farm and came in at a rate of 4,000 barrels per day from the Gordon Sand.

This was the largest producer in the United States at that time, but its reputation was short lived. In September 1900, the South Penn drilled in the famous Copley well in Lewis County. This well came in at about 8,000 barrels per day. Unable to supply enough tanks to carry off the oil from this gusher in the beginning, the oil ran into Sand Fork. The stream was filled with oil for eight miles below, within the ten foot banks. It was estimated there were 25,000 barrels in this pond. Guards were maintained to keep the crowds away.

The next well was another South Penn well drilled on the Jacob McConkey farm near Good Hope. It came in in February 1901, with an open flow of 36,000 MCF from the Fifth Sand.

The next well was the A. Talkington No. 2 drilled by South Penn in 1902 near the border of Wetzel County. This was a Gordon Sand well with a production of 2,400 barrels a day.

In 1908, South Penn drilled a well in Northeast Harrison County, the Copenhaven No. 1, which produced almost 3,500 MCF from the Cow Run Sand.

In 1909, the largest oil well ever drilled in the state was drilled by the Philadelphia Oil Co. east of Shinnston, The E. E. Swiger No. 1. It was actually tested at 12,000 barrels per day. This production came from the 50 Foot Sand. By 1963 this pool had produced over 5 million barrels of oil. There are still 67 wells producing there now.

About 1905, the Grasselli Chemical Co. drilled its Hardway well just south of Lost Creek. It came in with an open flow of 40,000 MCF. This is the largest gas well ever drilled in the county. This gas was found in the Gantz Sand and the company laid a six-inch line to its plant at Anmoore on the basis of this well, which produced for years. It eventually drilled over 300 wells in the county.

In 1918, the Hope Gas Co. drilled the deepest well in the world at that time on the Martha Goff farm on the eastern edge of Harrison County. It was a real achievement, going to 7,345 feet where the tools were lost. The well now is part of the company's Bridgeport storage field.

In 1941, the Hope drilled the C. S. Gribble well just east of Lost Creek. This was the first well drilled with rotary in the state and was drilled to a total depth of 10,018 feet. Gas was found in several deeper horizons than ever reached before in this area. I mention this well because it was a significant step and a milestone in West Virginia oil and gas history.

There are two principal geological structures transversing the county on a northeast -southwest axis, the Wolf Summit and Chestnut Ridge anticlines. From drilling in other parts of the state on similar structures, I will go out on a limb and predict that much more gas will be discovered in the county in the deeper horizons.

There is an old phrase that drilling wells is like playing poker. One never knows what is at the bottom of the deck until the last card is turned. This holds for wells. One never knows whether gas or oil will be found until one reaches the sand. The sand may be there but there may be no oil or gas.

Salem was a typical boom town, from all I can determine, with wooden boardwalks and stepping stones, flare lights and along the main street from one end of the town to the other, gambling houses, saloons and hotels, the most famous being the "Mountain State Hotel" across the street from the railroad station. There was a dice table in the lobby, electric lights and an electric piano.

Next door was the famous "Comique," where were found ladies of the evening and floor shows. It has been alleged the establishment had the finest entertainment day and night.

There were, of course fights and brawls continuously by the men coming in from the wells after pay day. Actually, pay was practically nothing compared to today's wages. There was no overtime.

Drillers made $5 per day, tool dressers, $4: team of horses with drivers, $5; roustabouts, 60¢ per day; and meals were 50 to 75¢ per day.

Salem College was founded in December 1888 and during the early part of the boom a group of hoodlums attempted to burn the college, but the president of the school, who could shoot as well as preach, drove the mob away.

In 1902, a fire which started in a printing office burned out the entire center of town. This gave the town a new start in rebuilding. When one drives though the community one will see that several of the brick buildings bear the date 1902.

Due to the oil and gas boom Clarksburg was also expanding. The 1902 City Directory listed 25 saloons, seven barber shops and a picture of F. J. Welch's Tonsorial Parlor on Third Street, which advertised that there were seven barbers to serve patrons. It also stated there were 14 hotels and numerous rooming houses. Among the 14 hotels listed was the Traders at the corner of West Main and Third and Walker House across from the Gore Hotel which was famous for its bean soup. Also listed were 10 lumber companies. It is presumed, according to the directory, that Clarksburg businessmen were well dressed because there were six merchant tailors listed.

A Cable Tool Rig

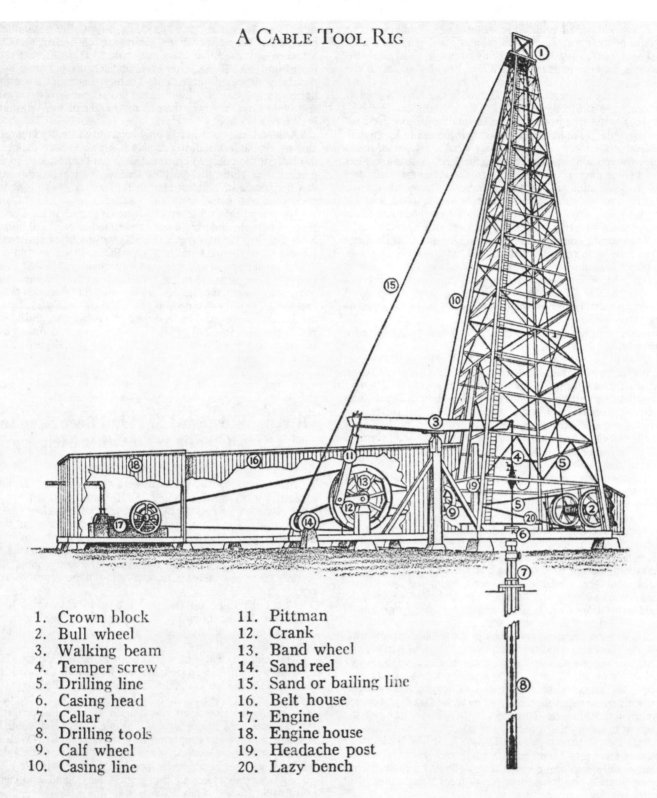

1. Crown block
2. Bull wheel
3. Walking beam
4. Temper screw
5. Drilling line
6. Casing head
7. Cellar
8. Drilling tools
9. Calf wheel
10. Casing line
11. Pittman
12. Crank
13. Band wheel
14. Sand reel
15. Sand or bailing line
16. Belt house
17. Engine
18. Engine house
19. Headache post
20. Lazy bench

Cable-tool drilling is done by raising and dropping a string of tools on the end of a cable. The up and down motion is imparted by the walking beam. The tools are pulled from or lowered into the hole by winding or unwinding the drilling cable on the bull wheel. Casing is raised or lowered by the casing line and calf wheel. The cuttings are removed from the hole by the bailer, which is raised and lowered by the sand line and reel.

Glass industries and other plants were building here because of the cheap fuels from oil and gas.

From 1900 to 1920, the following companies and individuals were actively engaged in drilling for oil and gas in the county:

Marshville Oil and Gas Co., Cambden Gas Co., Norwood Gas Co., and Bridgeport Gas Co.

Usually the first people on the scene of a prospective new field were the lease men and it was their job not to let anyone know what they were there for. They would, of course, try to pick up as much acreage as possible for their companies. Next would come the rig builders and teams to grade the roads and haul in the equipment. This meant timbers of tremendous size, rig sills and walking beams, headache posts, band wheels, manila cables, wire lines, casing, pipe, boilers, steam engines, tanks and drilling tools. Nails by the carload were required.

Then would come the drillers to rig up and start drilling. These men were really specialists and the good ones were in demand and could very easily make or break a contractor with fishing jobs. Tours were 12 hours or longer, depending on whether one's relief arrived through the mud after climbing up and down hills or through woods and sidling paths for miles to reach the location.

Good rooming houses or a farm house were usually available.

Then there was the tool dresser who had to get along with the driller or he would be doing a lot of extra work. Casing gangs were usually made up of farm boys with a leader who would let them all know when and where the next well to be cased was located. Sometimes they would be out for two or three days waiting for a well to be drilled in or for their next job. It was very dangerous work climbing and handing in the derrick or on the end of the walking beam on a cold icy night, with oil and gas blowing up in the rig.

Teaming was most difficult and the horses bore the brunt of the teamster's wrath. Roads were rivers or lakes of mud and horses would be in the mud up to their collars. Sometimes roads were so rutted that mud would run through the casing on the wagon. It took six months to drag an engine bed plate from Salem to Sedalia, a distance of about 10 miles. Now it can be driven by truck in less than 30 minutes. The major companies finally had to go into the teaming business to insure horses and teams would be available when needed and for fair prices. Eight horses were usually hitched to pull a boiler wagon. One could never take a single horse and buggy. Everyone used a wagon because of the rutted roads.

There were tremendous losses in some fields from fires, boiler explosions, windstorms and nitroglycerine explosions. A Mr. McKay and his wife were going up Buckeye to shoot a well one morning. There was an explosion and no one ever knew what happened because there was nothing left. William Goe formerly a superintendent for the Hope Gas Co., became owner of the Marietta Torpedo Co. which did most of the shooting in the northern part of the state.

Mr. Fitzpatrick was a well known figure in the industry and was known to have caught a shell loaded with glycerine when it started to come out of the well with a flow of oil, saving himself and the drilling crew from being killed. Bid Carson and his son were also well
-known employees of the Marietta Torpedo Co. Some communities would not allow the glycerine wagons to travel their streets.

National Supply, Oil Well Supply and Star Rig and Reel and Supply Co., the latter owned by Charles Smiley, were the major suppliers of oil field equipment in the area.

Aside from its many uses in homes and factories, natural gas has become an important industrial raw material especially in the rapidly growing petro-chemical industry. Natural Gas and hydrocarbons extracted from it are combined with other substances to make such products as plastics, symthetic rubber, fertilizers, medicines, detergents and refrigerants. It has been estimated that there are some 25,000 different uses for natural gas. It has even brought back the gas light as a popular source of illumination. There are actually more gas lights in use today for illuminating lawns, patios, driveways, and other outdoor areas than at the height of the "gaslight era" a century ago.

Although natural gas has only relatively recently emerged as a major modern industry, today it supplies more than one third of all the energy consumed in the United States and 17 percent throughout the world. Moreover, all indications are that the period of greatest growth for natural gas as a prime residential and industrial fuel lies ahead.

Natural gas has achieved phenomenal growth in the United States where the industry's sales amounted to over $10 billion last year. It goes into more than 50 million homes where it powers more than 200 million appliances. Pipelines and gas mains extend for an aggregate of more than 1,000,000 miles into every corner of the nation. Although production has easily quadrupled over the past 20 years to well over 20 trillion cubic feet a year, demand for natural gas in the United States, by far the largest single market, is expected to increase drastically between now and 1990. This is quite a projected future and Harrison County can be expected to play a real part in the growth of the industry.

It Was Whispered She Had Been Seen In The Company Of Other Men

By RUTH ANN MUSICK

Ezra Gordon was a hard-working carpenter, slightly eccentric, thrifty, and religious. Until his recent marriage to Sarah Garlow, he had seemed a confirmed bachelor. There was considerable gossip about the marriage, and it was generally agreed that Sarah had married Ezra for his money.

Ezra built a house for his bride on five acres of ground he owned for several years. All went well for a few months, but Sarah soon tired of the house, and living in the country irked her.

About that time oil companies began extensive drilling operations in the area and a nearby town became their headquarters. It rapidly changed from a sleepy village into a boomtown, with all the evils of fast growth and excess money.

The change had little effect upon Ezra Gordon. His services were always in demand and he had all the work he could handle. Such was not the case with Sarah. The happy life of the town had a special lure for her, and she made frequent trips, often returning home late at night. It was whispered that she had been seen in the company of other men, so it came as no surprise when Ezra reported that Sarah had run off with an oilfield supply salesman. Ezra then quickly settled his business, sold his house to Joe and Mary Blake, withdrew his money from the bank, and disappeared, leaving all who knew him feeling sorry for him.

Joe and Mary Blake felt sorry for him too, but their sorrow was overshadowed by their pleasure in acquiring his house. They had bought it at a bargain price, and it was just what they wanted. The day they moved in, they worked all day long setting up furniture, cleaning, polishing, and making plans.

Sleep came quickly that first night, since they were tired and worn out from moving. At about midnight, however, they were awakened by the sound of a dragging chain, but when Joe went to see what it was, he found nothing at all, although he looked everywhere.

The following night, the sound was repeated. At midnight, the clock struck twelve clear, deliberate notes. Mary awakened. The clock had been a gift from her family. But now, she thought, it seemed to have a peculiar sound, louder than she remembered it. Her thoughts were interrupted by a noise. A clanking sound like a chain being dragged outside the bedroom door caused her to scream, "Joe! Joe!"

When Mary told him the noise had seemed to go downstairs, Joe ran down to investigate. He wasn't sure whether he opened the door or whether it came open by itself. One thing was sure, he had heard a clanking sound like a chain being dragged, but it was dark and he could not see anything.

The third night Joe and Mary climbed the stairs with apprehension. Sleep did not come this night. It was pitch dark outside. The low rumble of distant thunder warned of an approaching storm. A jagged bolt of lightening lit up the room. Together they glanced at the clock. It was five minutes before twelve.

Slowly the clock ticked. In the stillness of the room, each sound seemed deafening. Another bolt of lightening lit the entire room. It was now one minute before midnight.

The clock struck. Slowly, deliberately, the notes sounded one through twelve. At the precise moment the twelfth note ended a dragging, clinking sound was heard outside in the hall. It seemed to come from a bedroom into the hall. Slowly it passed their door and clanked down the stairs. It seemed to

drag along the porch and then drop to the ground. They heard it clink as it touched the stepping stones in the yard.

When Joe and Mary went downstairs, the front door stood open. Joe gazed intently into the darkness. Another flash of lightning streaked downward. The house trembled from the peal of thunder that followed. Then came the rain.

Joe and Mary quickly withdrew to the kitchen. There they huddled together, too upset to sleep, and they could do nothing more until the storm subsided.

With the gray light of dawn, the rain stopped. Joe went upstairs. He carefully examined the rooms and the stairs, but found nothing. His search then led to the porch, his wife at his side.

"Look, Joe," said Mary, pointing to a corner of the garden.

Joe's gaze fell upon a sunken depression in the ground. He glanced at Mary. They crossed the wet grass to the garden and examined the depression. It was about five feet long and no water stood in it. Joe got a spade. The soft, wet earth came out in huge clumps. In a few minutes his search was ended. There in a corner of the newly acquired garden lay the body of Sarah Gordon in a shallow grave. Her skull had been crushed by a heavy blow from a hammer or hatchet, and locked to her leg was a chain with which her husband had tried to keep her at home.

Joe and Mary sold the house at a much lower price than they paid for it. Several people tried to live in it, but they were unable to do so. They were all disturbed by the sound of clinking, dragging chains, pulled by the ghost of Sarah Gordon as it made its way from her room to her shallow grave in the garden. Uninhabited by mortals, the house became weather beaten, and it was eventually torn down to make way for the expanding town that had been the undoing of Sarah Gordon.

The Rolland Brothers - Helped Make County World Center For Flat Glass

By GALE PRICE

The natural resources of Harrison County in many ways shaped its development and its future. Almost from its beginning, Clarksburg was an industrial city. The creeks and rivers that powered Harrison County's dozens of early grist mills also provided the power for other local industry. However, it was another source of power that made Harrison County an industrial center in the 20th century. Natural gas, found abundantly in Harrison, Lewis, and Doddridge counties, fueled the glass industry, and Harrison County was the world's leader in glass production through the 1950s.

In 1898, the Rolland brothers came to Clarksburg from Pittsburgh to work in the glass industry. Work was plentiful as over half a dozen glass companies had sprung up in the county. Demand for glass, and the cheap, clean burning natural gas brought them into being. All were small companies, where glass was handblown and the blower, not the cutter, was the center of the industry.

The Rollands, Aristide J., Charles, Eugene, Ernest and Albert A., came south as glassworkers, not glassblowers. Yet they were able to establish the largest locally owned glass plant in the county, one of the two to lead the area in flat glass production through the golden age of Clarksburg, and the only flat glass producer still operating in the area.

In 1907, Aristide J. Rolland was recorded as a glassworker, boarding with his brother Charles, Also a glassworker, in Northview. Ernest Rolland did likewise. Eugene Rolland, then the secretary of the Lafayette Window Glass

Company, also boarded in Northview. Lafayette Window Glass Co. was located on Railroad Street in Northview, no doubt on land now owned by the Fourco Glass Co.'s Rolland Plant. In 1911, Eugene Rolland became president of the Lafayette Glass Co.

The Rollands future lay with another small Northview glass company, though. In 1915 they purchased the Peerless Window Glass Co., and from it formed the Rolland Glass Co. Glass was still hand-blown at the Rolland plant, yet they were experiencing considerably more success than their competitors. They expanded, taking over the buildings occupied by the Lafayette Glass Co., the Pearlman Zinc Company, and the American Sheet Glass Co.

In 1918, the Rollands bought the Norwood Glass Co., on the corner of Water and Plainwood streets in Norwood. They dissolved the Norwood plant in 1934, by which time the Norwood plant had a large neighbor: Pittsburgh Plate Glass, Works No. 12.

In the early 1920s the Rolland plant was modernized. Dorothy Davis in her ''History of Harrison County'' states, ''Older citizens of the county may remember seeing strong-armed men, engaged in the hand-cylinder method of making window glass, gather molten glass on the end of a blowpipe, stand on a platform, and swing and blow the molten glass until it extended into a cylinder about six feet long in the pit below where the workmen stood. Then the ends of the cylinder were cut off; the cylinder split, reheated in an oven, and flattened with a wooden tool; passed through the annealing lehr, cooled, and cut. It was skill and hard work that enabled them to

produce the highest quality hand-made window glass and with low fuel costs, making their own repairs, and working their own long hours, they met the competition of the tank systems which prevailed in other states. The sheet drawing method was first introduced in 1923. Continuous drawing machines produced perfectly flat glass in quantity without the many operations involved in flattening glass from cylinders. The days of the glassblower were over and the golden age of the glass industry was about to begin.''

Molten glass is produced in the tank from a mixture of sand, soda ash, limestone, dolomite, aplite, saltcake, arsenic, and carbon. The molten glass is drawn out of the tank in a continuous stream. The glass is cooled, rolled out, and hardened as it passes through a series of rollers. Sheets of glass, unmarred by the ''bullseye'' of the glassblower of an earlier time, are broken off at the end of the drawing machine. Then the glass goes into the hands of the cutters. Cutters cut, sort, and grade the glass, using their skills and judgement to produce a quality product... or so it was in the golden age of glass production in Harrison County.

The Rolland Glass Co. did well. In 1935 it joined with one of the local competitiors, the Adamston Flat Glass Co., and also the Harding Glass Co. of Fort Smith, Ark., and the Blackford Window Glass Co. of Vincennes, Ohio. Together these four companies began to prosper and build the name they had chosen, the Fourco Glass Co.

Prosperity continued into the sixties, with drawn glass providing the need of the nation and with Harrison County the world's center of flat glass production.

Then time caught up with West Virginia's glass industry. Cutting machines were installed to replace the men who cut glass by hand. The machines worked only marginally well with drawn glass, as the machines could not anticipate quality irregularities in the product. However, a new means of producing glass had been developed, the "float glass" method. The float method produced glass of a consistent quality, glass that could be easily handled by the cutting machines.

Fourco built a new plant in Taylor County, just outside Harrison County, that employed the float method. Other float plants were built elsewhere in the country. In 1973, PPG closed the Pittsburgh Plate Works No. 12. The old Adamston Flat Glass Plant was run irregularly through the seventies by a variety of owners. It is now closed. The Rolland works of Fourco Glass is almost silent. The new float plant of the company founded by the Rolland brothers remains, one of the area's major employers.

From the beginning to the end, the Rollands were a part of Harrison County's industrial boom. They began in the glass business in Northview when glass was blown by hand, their company thrived in Harrison County's industrial heyday, and although Clarksburg is no longer the world center of glass production Fourco Glass today remains as a symbol of the important place of the glass industry in the History of Harrison County.

Ira Hart - The Only man in Harrison County to Build a Suspension Bridge

By GALE PRICE

The Hart family has a long and interesting history, a history that predates their coming to Harrison County. One John Hart was a signer of the Declaration of Independence. A monument in the public square of his home city, Hopewell, N.J., attests to this fact.

John Hart's youngest son, Daniel, moved to Randolph County in 1794. His fifth son, Elmore, was born at Beverly, lived for a time at Philippi, and established a permanent home at Clarksburg in 1836.

Elmore Hart demonstrated the mechanical talents of the Harts, as a manufacturer of a wool carding machine and as a bridge builder. In 1854 he constructed the Maulsby Bridge across the West Fork River between Clarksburg and Shinnston. It was the only large bridge in the county to survive the flood of July 10, 1888.

Elmore Hart's son, Ira, was perhaps the finest representative of the family. He proved a craftsman and inventor with even finer talents than his father, an astute businessman, and an idealist in the tradition of his ancestor, John Hart. Ira Hart built the first covered truss bridge in northwestern Virginia in 1846. The bridge, which spanned Elk Creek, did not survive the flood of 1888.

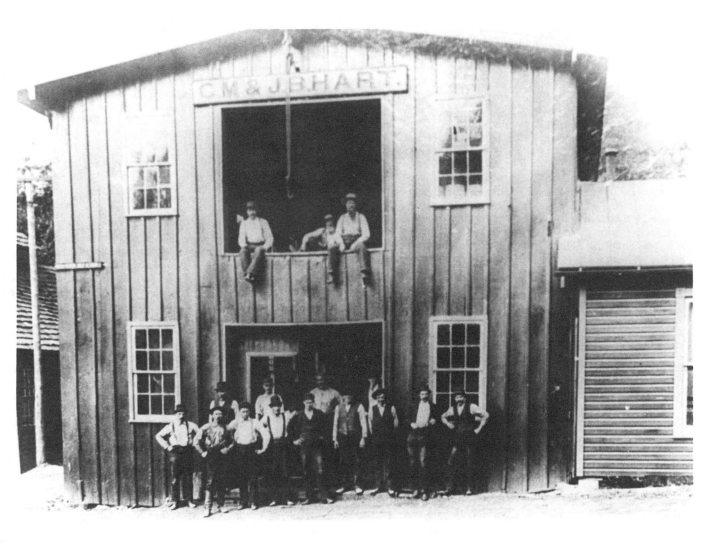

Ira Hart was the only man in Harrison County who ever built a suspension bridge. His suspension bridge, built in 1852, spanned the Elk River at Sutton. A story, demonstrating Ira Hart's business acumen, was told about that bridge:

"When the cables for the bridge were ready to be put in place, Mr. Hart went to the courthouse, court then being in session in Sutton. He invited everyone present to come down to the river and see how he was progressing with the bridge. He had, however, prepared a full barrel of mint julep; on the outside of the barrel dozens of nails were driven and on each nail a tin cup was hung. When they arrived at the barrel, all were invited to help themselves to its contents. It was but a short time until everybody was feeling fine and happy. Mr. Hart then said, "You know, men, these two cables support the bridge and it is necessary to have them stretched across the river. Will you help do this? They all agreed and were then asked to pick up the handspikes on which the cables rested. These spikes were four feet long and placed ten feet apart. With a man on each end of the spike the first cable was soon on its way across the river, many of the carriers wading waist-deep in the water…" Thus Ira Hart got his bridge cables strung across the Elk River at the mere cost of a barrel of mint julep.

Ira Hart's other accomplishments included the invention of a patented threshing and cleaning machine, a machine that was for some time produced by Aultman & Taylor of Mansfield, Ohio. Ira Hart founded the Hart Brothers Machine Shop in 1852, its original name being "Ira Hart's Machine Shop." There he produced the first circular milling saws ever made in West Virginia. He made the first steam engine produced in the state outside of Wheeling. He manufactured the first locomotive ever made in the state.

Ira Hart demonstrated both farsightedness and a well-developed sense of social justice in his political opinions. He stood against slavery in ante-bellum northwestern Virginia, accepting his neighbors' opinions of him as some impractical visionary. He stood loyal to the United States, not to Virginia, as the Civil War came. He lived to see the end of slavery and to see his political ideas on the ascent, a well-deserved reward for the outspoken descendent of a signer of the Declaration of Independence.

Ira Hart died while still in his prime, unfortunately, killed by being thrown from a buckboard by a runaway horse. He died Aug. 9, 1879. His sons, Charles M. Hart and John B. Hart, were left with the family enterprise.

Under their active leadership, the business flourished. The firm was incorporated under the name "Hart Brothers Machine Shop" in 1896. John B. Hart was the corporation's president, with Charles M. Hart as its secretary-treasurer.

Meanwhile, the Harts were bringing their foresight and intelligence into other enterprises. In 1887 Charles M. Hart started the Clarksburg Electric Light Company, insisting that electric street lights would be more effective than gas lights. In 1887, he also was among the original partners in the Harrison County Oil and Gas Company, the earliest oil and gas drilling company mentioned in county records. In 1901, he was one of the original partners in West Virginia Mine Supply Company. Adding politics to his experiences, Charles M. Hart served in the West Virginia House of Delegates from 1907 to 1909.

Always looking for opportunity, Charles M. Hart purchased the old Harrison County Courthouse for the price of two dollars in 1888. His purchase left him with the obligation to clear the building from its site, so that a new courthouse could be erected there. To prove profitable, it would be necessary to get more out of the materials of the old building than the cost of tearing it down. The Hart brothers, sons of the man who persuaded Sutton's citizens to help string his bridge, were equal to the task. They realized a reasonable profit on a

task no one else in Harrison County would take on.

John B. Hart, meanwhile, was making his name by involvement in other civic enterprises. In 1887 he was one of the three water works commissioners who contracted for the building of Clarksburg's first public water system. John Hart was one of the original stockholders in the Robinson Grand Theater. He was the developer who turned 70 acres of the J.I.S Stealey farm into four hundred lots, building the neighborhood of Stealey.

The Hart Brothers Machine Shop continues in operation today, owned by the descendents of Charles M. Hart. It is but one of the surviving legacies of one of Clarksburg's intersting families.

Coal Changed the Countryside in the Brown's Creek Area

BY ALTON BELL

The early settlers, hunters and explorers of western Virginia around the year 1791 kept along the West Fork River using small skiffs or canoes. In time they moved out to explore streams emptying into the West Fork as we know it today. Men on hunting parties and some of an adventurous nature no doubt tried to push small boats past the mouth of such streams as Brown's Creek, Lost Creek, Gnatty Creek, Buffalo Creek and others in the southern part of Harrison County but found it necessary to abandon the boats and walk along the banks of the streams.

These first visitors or explorers are with us today in the form of the names they left such as Brown's Creek, T. G. Lick, Kicheloe Creek, and Isaac Creek.

The first large stream early visitors camped upon when traveling south from Clarksburg was one of clear water, abundant fish and large turtles which is today called Brown's Creek. This stream drains a beautiful valley, narrow in places but surrounded with rolling hills and fed by large streams causing it to be an attractive area for settlement by our early pioneers. The clear air, welcome sunshine, and a valley of good length invited the attention of men who brought their families to plan for homes at an early date. Such family names as Lowther, Blake, Norman, Lynch, Bassel, Haselden, Mills and Maxwell have had a part in making the area along the stream delightful and prosperous.

Fortunately this area was picked as a line of travel by the stage coach that moved from Clarksburg south to Weston, the leading town in that section.

It is difficult to measure the extent of the vision of these early pioneers in settling and even building a farm and erecting a house. However we are assured each dweller looked to the wooded hills around him to be a source of fuel supply to heat cabins and cook food. So newcomers brought an axe, a grub hoe, and one or two pots of different sizes to cook hominy, meat, and vegetables that they could find.

As time went on and the new settlers grew tired of cutting wood, we can suppose someone found a black vein of soil or rock-like material that the people of Ireland and Scotland were familiar with and used for a fuel. Harrison County had hills and uplands with mineral wealth for men to use.

At an early date and until after the close of the Civil War most every farmer exploring his farm found a vein of coal and made an opening to have his own supply of fuel. This is not to say on every farm there was a coal bank, but most rolling hills led upward to a lofty peak or flat point, under which lay veins of black diamonds.

The farmers along Brown's Creek were very fortunate. They lived to farm and graze the land, but shortly after 1900 coal mining came with a resounding boom to the area and many changes came about. When the Baltimore and Ohio

Railroad passed through Mt. Clare new hope was born. The name of the train station was changed from Byron to Mt. Clare which is the section of downtown Baltimore where the main shops of the railroad were located.

It was not until about 1910 that persons in Harrison County were aware of the hidden resource of two veins or seams of coal under most of the hills in the vicinity of the peaks or knobs of hills with an elevation of 1,500 feet or a few hundred feet less. It was a spectacular and welcome sight to see coal at hand and a market willing to buy the good grade of Redstone coal found in the area about Mt. Clare, and a short distance from Clarksburg.

Now that the B&O was pushing through the valley along Brown's Creek, trains needed fuel. This was the age of the steam locomotive. A tank for storing water was placed at Two Lick along the river, a mile below Mt. Clare and a tipple was erected on the Lynch property to supply coal to power the engines pulling cars from Clarksburg to Weston, Pickens and Buckhannon. The fuel box on the engine held enough coal for a round trip but much water was needed by the engines and that was supplied along the line at different places. The need for engine coal however, kept the small Lynch mine in operation until steam engines were discontinued.

The coalfields in the vicinity of Mt. Clare have been mined by many small independent operators as well as by large companies. Due to a lack of records and available reports all of these operators are not known, but one operation, known as Interstate, West Fork and Two Lick built structures for equipment and living quarters for their employees in the area. Another operator was a company from Marion County which located in Hutchison Hollow, with other branch operations along the railroad line and proceeded to build coke ovens that turned out as much as 40 tons of coke in one burning. Some of the other mines of notable size were Freeport Coal Co. and

Marshall Coal Co. in Florence Hollow and Rhonnie Hollow; J. B. Smith on Alpha Hill; and Colliers Coal Co.

A number of men were employed in the mining operations at Mt. Clare during World War I. At that time some 12 mines operated along the railroad track for about three miles. Men went into the hill to face danger each day and to produce coal or the nation's industries which were producing equipment for the army.

Safety rules were not always enforced and this was a time for changing from an oil lamp burning kerosene to a mining light fueled with carbide. Unfortunately the electric light and daily charged batteries came along some years later, as did helmets, hard-toe boots, rubber boots and suits came with improvement of safety conditions.

Just as the opening of coal mines meant more workers moving into Mt. Clare the economic growth got a good boost also. Many places of business sprang up. Merchants, a barber shop, feed stores, shoe repair shop, restaurant, boarding house, recreation hall, a theater and coal company stores issuing scrip on the employees wages, made buying and dealing in the establishments of the valley a pleasure.

Two veins or seams of coal are found in the Mt. Clare region. Near the hilltops veins of coal and occasionally some iron are found as well as a trace of limestone. There is sandstone of good quality, and potters' clay. The stones in the archway at Spencer State Hospital were quarried at Mt. Clare from one huge piece of stone loaded on a flatcar and shipped to Roane County around 1891.

Veins of coal at Lost Creek and Mt. Clare, near Clarksburg, and Wilsonburg and other points around Harrison County have coal beds ranging from five through seven feet. In a few places the veins reach a thickness of 11 to 13 feet. Coal ranges from 100 to 400 feet under the surface of the ground. The Redstone vein lies above the Pittsburgh, and

133

under these two lies a second Pittsburgh vein and in some areas a Clarksburg vein. The Pittsburgh vein in some locations is of a high sulphur rating, but both veins burn well, with a marked degree of combustion, for smelting industries and the heating of furnaces in homes and office buildings. The Redstone vein is in much demand for processing such products as tar, coke, oil and even saccharine.

The prices of land in Harrison County have fluctuated. Due to the surface of the county's rolling and hilly upland, when much improvement has been evident the average price for agricultural land has balanced while good mineral acreage is most often costly.

The people who have lived in the valley along Brown's Creek look to the future not back to what they have passed. This kind of optimism leads people to want expansion, new opportunities for themselves, and members of their family. This little valley has offered a wealth in minerals and other resources of the land in abundance. These dwellers of the valley at various times have made adjustments to changing times and ways that appeared less attractive to their views of economy but they have made a stand and Harrison County is better for their presence and independence.

Flora Felt the Air Getting Heavy and Knew It Was A Matter of Time

BY RUTH ANN MUSICK

When my father first started working in the Pitcairn mine, the men had horses to pull the coal buggies instead of machinery as they have today. The horses were the men's best friends, and it was a sad day when they were taken out of the mines.

My father started working on the midnight shift when he first entered the mines, along with another buddy, Flora Santa. In those days a miner had to use a pick and shovel to dig out the coal, and it was hard work, especially if one ran into slate or sulphur balls. When the buggy was loaded it would be pulled up the mine shaft by a horse, and unloaded. The horses were often slow, and it usually took several hours to make the trip.

One night, when my father finished loading the buggy, Flora said he would take the load down to the tipple. It was supposed to be my father's turn to make the trip, but Flora said, "You're not as strong as I am, boy. You sit here and take it easy, and I'll make this trip for you."

My father was tired, so he didn't argue with Flora. To reach the tipple, Flora had to pass a section that had had a cave-in just a few days before. As Flora reached the section, the horse started whinnying. Flora cursed the horse under his breath for making so much noise. Then he heard a rumbling sound coming from overhead. Now he knew why the horse was making so much noise. The ceiling was caving in.

When Flora opened his eyes, he found that he was still alive. He was half covered with slate and he was almost choked from the rock dust that was in his mouth, but he was alive. With the help of his free hand, he was able to get out from under the slate pile. The horse too had lived through the cave-in. Dazed, Flora got to his feet and started walking in the direction of the tipple. He walked for a long time, but seemed to be getting nowhere. When he came back to the caved-in section, he knew he had been walking around in circles. He sat down on a lump of slate and waited for someone to come and rescue him, but then he realized that nobody would come for him, because nobody knew that he was missing or hurt. My father wouldn't think anything had happened to him because he knew it usually took two or three hours to make the trip to the tipple. The men at the tipple would think that he and his buddy were still working up in their section. Flora was a goner and he knew it!

Flora felt the air getting heavy and knew that it was only a matter of time before the oxygen would be used up. He laid his head against the side of the ribbing and prepared himself for death. The he heard a deep, far-off voice say, "Get up, Flora. Get up, Flora."

Flora opened his eyes, but there was nobody in sight — nobody but the old horse. Thinking that he was only dreaming, he closed his eyes again. Just as he was about to give up, he felt something hot against his face, and the same voice said, "Get up, Flora. I'll show you how to get out of here."

When Flora shut his eyes again, the horse put his head against Flora's shoulder and turned him over on his side. Again the deep voice said, "Get up, Flora. Get up, Flora, and I'll lead you out of here."

More dazed than ever, Flora managed to get to his feet and follow the old horse. It was as if some spell were compelling him. When Flora came to his complete senses, he was at the tipple. He didn't tell anyone how he got out of the cave-in, because he knew no one would believe him.

Years later, when the horses were all replaced with machinery, Flora quit the coal mines. And he didn't quit because he was ready to retire. He quit because he knew that a piece of machinery could never take the place of an old horse.

Art Show Set By Bicentennial Art Committee Will Honor Miss Whipple Feature Other Artists

Paintings of Harrison County artists are being sought for an art show honoring Miss Elizabeth Whipple, artist and teacher, which is being planned by the Harrison County Bicentennial Art Committee.

The show, to be held at Waldomore, will open for a two-week period at 2 p.m. Sunday, Aug. 12. It will continue during library hours until Saturdy, Aug. 25.

Artists are asked to submit no more than two paintings for exhibit. They must be more than 45 inches square and must be brought to Waldomore by Sunday, Aug. 5. All work will be juried by Paulette DePolo, Visual Arts chairman of the Clarksburg Art Center, and appointees of the Bicentennial Art Committee.

One room at Waldomore will be devoted to the work of Miss Whipple, with much of it being loaned by her sister,

Mrs. Louise Timberlake of Ohio. Other paintings are to be loaned by the Clarksburg Art Center, Salem College and private collectors. Former students and others who own paintings by Miss Whipple are asked to loan them to honor this fine artist who gave so generously of herself to the cultural life of Harrison and surrounding counties through her teaching.

The show will be hung by John Randolph, professor ar art at Salem College, who will also conduct an evening critique for participating artists at Wladomore on a date not yet decided.

Of special interest will be a "One Woman Show" featuring the work of Rosemary Bever, which will be on display on the second floor of the Clarksburg-Harrison Public Library at the same time that the Harrison County Bicentennial Art Show is on exhibit at Waldomore. Mrs. Bever was a close friend and associate of Miss Whipple for many years.

Among those loaning paintings for the show are members of the Harrison County Water Color Society. The committee hopes that other groups and individuals will be equally generous in loaning paintings so that this show can be truly representative of the best of Harrison County art.

Members of the Beta Chapter, Alpha Delta Kappa, international honorary for women educators, will be hostesses for an informal reception at the library on the opening afternoon of the show. Mrs. Diantha Hilton, will serve as chairman of the reception committee.

Persons who would like to loan paintings by Miss Whipple or exhibit their own work, may call Paulette DePolo, 842-4502, or Karen Bowers, 623-2931, co-chairmen of the Harrison County Bicentennial Art Committee.

Like other Bicentennial activities, the Harrison County bicentennial Art Show is sponsored by the Harrison County Bicentennial Committee and the Clarksburg-Harrison Public Library and is funded by the Humanities Foundation of West Virginia, a state program of the National Endowment for the Humanities, and by the Consolidated Gas Transmission Corporation.

Dr. Susan Dew Hoff - First Woman Given Medical Practice License In West Virginia

By NEVA WEEKS

The first woman doctor to be given a license to practice medicine in West Virginia was Susan Dew Hoff. She was born near Summersville on Nov. 24, 1842, the daughter of Dr. William H. Dew, who practiced medicine in Nicholas County and later in Harrison County for 40 years. Her youngest brother was Dr. Rush H. Dew of Salem. She also had a nephew in medicine, which accounted for the strong atmosphere in which she was reared.

By the time Susan was eight-years-old, she began to help her father, running errands, holding bandages, handing him instruments — learning by doing. As she grew older she was more and more interested and was learning all the time. Her father explained every process to her, and lectured her on every subject. He took her on calls and afterwards talked over the case with her. On one occasion she said, "I do not think any graduate of a medical school ever had as many lectures as I did." Dr. Dew wanted her to go to medical school, but this was not an easy thing to do in that day with most medical schools closed to women. So young Susan continued to help her father and study under him. In 1869 she was married to James D. Hoff and for several years her time and strength were given to her home and family with whom she lived on a farm near West Milford.

After the death of her father, his patrons, knowing of her familiarity with medicine, came to her for medical advice, but it was against the law for her to prescribe for them although she felt that she was perfectly competent to do so.

Mrs. Hoff had inherited her father's medical library and she also had access to the library of her brother. One year after her father's death when she was 42 years-old and the mother of four children, she confided to her husband that she thought she would study up and take the State Board Medical examination. He said, "You can't do it Susan," and her brother teased her about it and told her to take up midwifery because he did not think she could do it. To both she replied: "I'll show you whether I can do it or not." After studying intensively for three years, she wrote to the State Board of Health asking for an appointment to be examined as to her eligibility to practice medicine in the State of West Virginia. She explained that she had never gone to medical school, but her father was Dr. William H. Dew. There was nothing unusual about this for many others had tried it, but this time it happened to be a woman. Maybe they said to themselves: "She'll more than likely fail anyhow."

In due time Mrs. Hoff received a letter from the secretary of the board giving her the date of examination and saying in part: "We will make no difference on account of sex or condition in life but will carry out the law." She immediately answered and told them she would be there on the date named unless unavoidably prevented, and added "If I fail this time I will try again."

On the appointed day she said goodbye to her mother and her four children, the youngest of whom was seven and the oldest 15, and was driven by her husband behind his fine driving team to Clarksburg, a distance of 12 miles, to take the train for Wheeling. The examination, which was both oral and written, lasted a whole day and until 11 o'clock of the next morning. She passed with the best of grades. The examiners congratulated Mrs. Hoff and her husband. Dr. E. C. Myers, president of the State Board of Health, in congratulating her on her success said; "You are the first and only woman who has ever come before the board and you have passed one of the best examinations of anyone who has ever been before it."

When Mrs. Hoff told Dr. Myers that she did not intend to practice medicine, he told her it would be a crime for anyone as competent and well-prepared as she was not to practice medicine. She had taken the examination to prove to herself that she could pass it.

On the way home from Wheeling Mr. and Mrs. Hoff stopped at Salem to visit her brother and tell him that she was a full-fledged doctor and he thought she was joking. He said "Doctor nothing," and she showed the certificate that she had received.

She did not try to build up a practice but her father's old

patrons kept appearing and having gradually acquired a practice in spite of herself, she looked after it faithfully for 36 years. Dr. Hoff was always treated courteously by the profession in general. There were always those who scoffed and were afraid to trust a woman.

Dr. Hoff practiced medicine for 36 years. She was known to have never refused a call — for those years she rode horseback and went through all kinds of weather. She learned that doctors found themselves in strange situations sometimes and often she gave a good lecture in place of medicine. She would often remain at a patient's home until the patient was making a recovery, and she never lost a case of pneumonia or typhoid fever.

The charges that Dr. Hoff made for her services were liberal. Her office calls were $1 and that included the medicine that she furnished. For her maternity cases the charge was $5 within a mile of her office and after that a dollar a mile was added. She never sued but one man who was considered able to but refused to pay. Many of her less-fortunate patients never paid anything.

Dr. Hoff did not belong to the Harrison County Medical Society but was a member of the State Medical Association and in 1907 was named by the governor as one of the delegates from West Virginia to the Convention for the Prevention of Tuberculosis which was held that June in Atlantic City.

Dr. Hoff joined the Methodist Episcopal Church South, when she was 12 years old. She was always interested in her church, and also community affairs, schools, divorce, young people, good roads, and women's suffrage. Her three daughters and one son were not only devoted to their mother but were justly proud of her unusual achievements.

After her retirement, Dr. Hoff kept busy with things that she enjoyed. Her eyesight was failing but with the aid of self-threading needles and brightly-colored material, she was able to piece quilts.

Dr. Hoff was one of a kind. She lived a very interesting, useful and wonderful life. She had an independent, pioneer spirit that caused her to forge ahead in the face of almost unbelievable obstacles, and to succeed in her chosen profession at an age when most women of her time considered themselves old.

She practiced her profession for nearly 50 years in the West Milford vicinity. When she died Jan. 2, 1932, at the age of 90, she was buried beside her husband in the Odd Fellows Cemetery in West Milford.

He Lost the Horse But Saved the Medicine
BY EDWARD F. HOOD

Erasmus Fogg, alias Dog Fogg, was born in the early 1860s at Jimtown, a small post office that at that time was situated at the mouth of Scott's Run in Monongalia County, a short distance below Morgantown on the opposite side of the river.

A typical man of the woods and streams, he was an expert on herbs and turtle hunting with a technique all his own.

As a turtle hunter his equipment consisted of a short metal tapered spud with a hook in the same piece above the point on the end of a six to eight-foot pole and a burlap bag, what we call a coffee sack, and is known as a croaker sack farther south.

The doctor in the spring prowled his favorite small streams and swamps prodding and tapping from the bank as he moved slowly along. Turtles go deep in the mud for cold protection but come up as spring advances. The doctor could tell immediately when he tapped a turtle and, according to his claim, could accurately tell its size from the tap. The hook on the staff was then used to bring the turtle ashore. They were in

a more or less hibernating stupor and fat. These the doctor sold — cleaned or as was — to his trade.

His forte or year-round main source of revenue however was his herb business. The doctor had a trade slogan — "Man never had a disease but Jesus made an herb to cure it and I know 'em all."

He prowled Cheat Mountain and other heavily forested areas collectng his favorite herbs and carried them in a long leather case like a piano tuner or traveling dentist used.

One day Doc Fogg called at the office of Hugh Jarvis in the Union National Bank to talk with the banker. During the converstation Mr. Jarvis remarked that he wished to purchase some herbs and at the same time extended his hand toward a bundle of herbs in a container near his chair. Doc Fogg jumped up and yelled: "Good God, no Hugh! Leave them alone. That's women's herbs!"

The doctor was versatile in his practice. Shortly after street cars started running to what we called the "New Fair Grounds" (Norwood), the doctor came aboard the car.

In those days when a doctor called on a contagious case, such as diptheria, scarlet fever or smallpox, he always used a protective coat. My father, Dr. Thomas M. Hood, had an old what we called a "macintosh" that was hung in an isolated part of the barn. We children were afraid to go within touching distance of it. With this in mind, I asked Dog Fogg if he ever treated any contagious diseases.

"Son", he said, "I have treated every contagious disease known to man except bubonic plaque and leprosy and I ain't dead yet."

I then asked him what preventative he used to escape catching the disease and his answer was "Just before I go in to see one of them cases, I take a big rub of snuff and I ain't caught nothing yet."

At that time infantile paralysis or Pilio had just been identified. I asked the doctor his idea on the disease. He said: "Son it's a kind of bug that floats around in the air and is liable to lite any place."

With the years of work on this devasting malady since that time by the best brains in the world, we must admit that Dr. Fogg was not far afield in his diagnosis.

Around 1903 or 04 I was working for the Williams and Davison Wholesale Hardware. Auto and truck deliveries unknown. Wholesale houses like breweries prided themselves on their delivery teams. Jim Teter was head teamster for the Williams and Davisson company and drove a pair of prize winning dapple grays. Jim's idea of treating a rusty nail in a horses hoof (there were plenty of them before hard surfaced roads) was ink (any kind) and turpentine. One of this pair picked up a rusty nail. After the Teter treatment failed. Dr. Truman E. Gore was called. He took a short look at the horse. "Lockjaw (tetanus) in advanced state. he said. "Nothing can be done. The horse was still on his feet at the barn, which was located on the lower or west end of Clark Street. Quite a number of people had gathered. Here came Doc Fogg pushing through the crowd with his herb case in hand and announcing in a loud voice; "When all others fail they always send for Doc Fogg. I can cure this horse — no cure, no pay."

I advised him we would have to see J. M. Williams, known as Billy Williams, and one of the finest and most likeable characters that made Clarksburg's jobbing center.

Fogg immediately went to Williams' office and repeated his "No cure, no pay" offer. Williams, who had already written the horse off on the advice of Dr. Gore, had Fogg repeat his offer and then accepted. Whereupon, Doc Fogg asked for an order on the drug store to get "just a few things to make my herbs work."

In those days it was the practice of all jobbing houses to go out and buy for a customer articles o their wholesalers' line. There was no wholesale drug store here. To serve that demand we had a printed form known as a "buy out order." Williams gave Fogg a "buy out blank. Fogg went to a drug store and obtained a gallon of grain alcohol.

He returned to the sick horse that was still on his feet and said Gentleman, I am going to cut a leader in that horse's jaw and he will get well." Then he pulled out a Barlow knife and slashed the horse high on his jaw. Several minutes later the horse fell over and died. In the excitement Fogg disappeared plus a gallon of White House, plus herb case. The first of the month Williams and Davisson Hardware Co. received an invoice from the drug store for one gallon of alcohol.

Billy Williams went through that four-story wholesale hardware house like a brush fire to find the employee who had clipped the company for a gallon of White Horse. When he finally got the facts he laughed until he was red in the face and charged it off to a typical Doc Fogg "professional call."

Melville Davisson Post - Attorney, Writer

by JACK SANDY ANDERSON

One of West Virginia's most famous writers was Melville Davisson Post, a Harrison County native who became known throughout the nation for his fiction. Born into a well-to-do family having a long and illustrious past, he was reared in an atmosphere of tradition. Post was fully aware of this tradition, and from it drew material that he wove into the fabric of his stories.

His father, Ira Carper Post (1842-1923), a native of Upshur County, was a son of Isaac and Emily (Carper) Post and boasted a lineage that went back to colonial and Revolutionary War worthies. A congenial person who enjoyed friends about him, he maintained a hospitable home that attracted frequent guests. Well-educated for his day, he was a good conversationalist and could discourse intelligently on many subjects. Shrewd but fair in his dealings with his fellowmen, he managed wisely his holdings and left a sizable fortune to his children.

The Bible was ever a source of inspiration and guidance for him, and there were few people in the locality who had a greater command of Biblical knowledge. In his children he inculcated a high regard for decency and honor, and his unfaltering belief in an ultimate justice at work in the world so impressed his son Melville that he used this theme for his Uncle Abner stories.

Post's mother, Florence May Davisson Post (1843-1914), was a daughter of Melville and Martha Juliet (Coplin) Davisson. Mrs. Post's ancestors had been among Western Virginia's first settlers and had played an important part in conquering the frontier, thereby bringing about a civilized society in what had been a forbidding wilderness less than a hundred years before the birth of their famous descendant.

One of her great-grandfathers was Daniel Davisson (1748-1819), proprietor of Clarksburg, officer in the Revolution, and sheriff of Harrison County; in the early part of this century she organized a chapter of the Daughters of the American Revolution in Clarksburg and named it in his honor.

Ira and Florence Post spent the first years of their marriage in an unpretentious frame dwelling on Raccoon Run in Harrison County's Elk District. Of their five children — Maude, Melville, Emma, Florence, and Sidney — the three oldest are definitely known to have been born there.

None of the family is certain just when the Posts moved into the brick mansion they built a short distance away on the Clarksburg-Buckhannon Turnpike; but it was in the 1870s, for in it their second son, Sidney, was born in 1878. Templemoor, as this handsome old Victorian mansion is called, was one of the finest country residences in the state when it was built and is still an impressive house.

Melville, who was known to his relatives and friends as Mel, was a small boy when his parents went to Templemoor to live, and it was there that much of his childhood was spent. His first playmates were his sisters Maude and Emma, and together they passed many hours filled with childish pleasure as they explored the wonders of Templemoor's fields and wooded hills.

Often they visited their Davisson grandparents, who lived nearby in a two-storied log house dating from pioneer days. Melville Davisson and his wife were always glad to see them, and could usually be persuaded to tell stories of the long-ago. How the time would then fly! And, occasionally, Grandmother's mother, old Great-grandmother Coplin — she who had been born Prudence Davisson (1788-1876), daughter of the

"RANDOLPH MASON" Near by was the home of the late Melville Davisson Post, author of many novels, but particularly noted for his stories concerning the strange points of law, woven about the fictitious character, "Randolph Mason."

legendary Daniel Davisson —would be there to conjure up the past. Indian times seemed very real as she talked; and when the three little children went home in the evening, they did not tarry along the road for fear Great-grandmother's Indians might be lurking in the dark shadows.

As he grew older, Post liked to slip away by himself. His mother often found him busy at work with paper and pencil writing stories which she seldom got to read, since he usually destroyed them when they were finished. Or he would saddle one of his father's spirited horses and ride alone over the countryside, not returning for several hours.

Although he loved the country, Post did not like the practical side of farming. The routine of managing a farm was not for one whose interest chiefly lay in the imaginative world of a creative mind. To him, such a way of life amounted to little more than drudgery, and he early decided against it. Realizing this, his father adroitly maneuvered him into going to college. Post had attended the academy in Buckhannon and had decided he had no desire to continue his education in a formal manner. He informed his father of his decision. Mr. Post did not argue or try to force him against his will. Instead, he pointed out that since he chose to stay home, he must assume an active share in running the farm and assigned to him the task of looking after the cattle. There were many cattle scattered over a wide area; the winter chanced to be unusually severe; and, before it was over, Post nearly froze his feet. He learned his lesson, and when the next term came around, he went to Morgantown to enroll in West Virginia University.

College for him was not much of a challenge, for his keen mind quickly absorbed the subject matter to which he was exposed. He felt much of it was of little — if any — value, and in after years wrote that he "was given a degree by a college of unbeautiful nonsense."

He took an active part in university life: member of Columbia Literary Society; captain of Co. C, Cadet Corps; co-editor in 1890-91 of the student publication, "The Athenaeum"; and director of an amateur theatrical production of "Richard III," which partly financed the University's first football team.

College training provided Post with the academic background necessary for one who desired to live in the realm of ideas, and without it his development as a skilled, competent writer could hardly have taken place. Morgantown at that time was far from being a city, but to a country youth it doubtless afforded a sophisticated atmosphere which gave him a larger view of the world.

In 1891 he received his A.B. and a year later, without difficulty, the LL. B. Within a decade he had become a famous author, and in 1901 he was invited to be the speaker at the Alumni Dinner. An indication of his popularity is the fact that 270 guests sought admission, 100 more than anticipated.

Post's choice of the legal profession was due to various factors, none of which was paramount. His analytical mind with its rare capacity to unravel involved situations naturally drew him toward it, as did his fascination with the motives determining human behavior. It was a respectable profession to which a gentleman could belong, and also one that could become fairly lucrative.

Shortly after graduating from law school, he was admitted to the bars of the Supreme Court of West Virginia, the United States Circuit Court of Appeals, and the Supreme Court of the United States. He entered the law office of John A. Howard in Wheeling and remained there for several years. Later, around 1901, he associated with his friend, John T. McGraw, in Grafton.

Had he chosen to continue his practice, he no doubt would have attained considerable success, for he showed much promise as a young lawyer. However, early in his career,

while practicing in Wheeling, he began writing in earnest and created that amazingly unique character, Randolph Mason. The phenomenal success of "The Strange Schemes of Randolph Mason" in 1896 proved that people were interested in his writing and that his pen could provide a more-than-comfortable livelihood. The die was cast. There would be no further hesitation. He was a writer, and he would remain one as long as he lived.

Post achieved success while still a young man and mounted its lofty summit without having to undergo the hardships so often the lot of aspiring writers. His childhood ambition realized, he must have felt a deep sense of personal accomplishment. Yet, there was a restlessness about him that somehow eluded explanation — it was as if he were searching for something his success could not give him. While on a voyage to Europe, he discovered the source of his restlessness, and in a moment of revelation that for which he had been searching was found. Love, in the form of a strikingly beautiful young widow, came into his life. Trite though it sounds, the old adage about opposites attracting is more valid than one ordinarily supposes, and he lost his heart completely to the gay, vivacious Ann Bloomfield Gamble Schoolfield, of Roanoke, Virginia.

Theirs was one of those ideal romances seldom experienced in real life, and on June 29, 1903, they were married in Philadelphia. To them was born one child, a son named Ira C. Post II, who died on August 19, 1906, when he was 18 months old.

Post and Bloom, as she was known, traveled a good bit during the first years of their marriage. They were frequent guests in the home of her brother-in-law and sister, Mr. and Mrs. John DuBois, of DuBois, Pa. The glittering society life of the East attracted them for awhile, and they went to Bar Harbor and Newport, where they rubbed elbows with the millionaire elite. But it was England they most enjoyed. An ardent admirer of the English, Post considered them a superior people who had developed a way of living unequaled by any other nation. He began to adopt many customs of the English gentry and to wear clothing made by fashionable London tailors.

Resplendent in diamonds and pearls, Mrs. Post was presented at the court of Edward VII. An account of her presentation and a large picture of her dressed in elaborate court attire appeared in "The Wheeling Register" of June 30, 1907. For a time Post and she leased a house and entertained the nobility and intelligentsia in baronial style.

Next to England, Post preferred Switzerland. The breathtaking beauty of its majestic mountains filled him with awe, and as he gazed at their snow-crowned peaks, he marveled at the overwhelming splendor the Creator had wrought for human eyes to behold. Friendly but independent, the Swiss impressed him favorably, reminding him not a little of the hill people he knew so well in his native West Virginia.

Although both of them loved Templemoor and were often there, they decided in 1914 to build a home of their own. The nouveau riche of the period were feverishly erecting mammoth monstrosities in assorted styles of exotic architecture, most of which were as tasteless as they were expensive. None of them held the slightest appeal to the Posts, who wanted something simple, classic, and yet different —something that would reflect their own taste and express their own individuality. The chalets they had seen dotting the rugged mountainsides in Switzerland had fascinated them, and they decided to have one built on a hill near Templemoor.

The site selected had been inhabited by Indians, and on it were stones that had once been used for grinding ochre to make the red and yellow pigments with which Indians painted themselves. Thus, Post named it "The Hill of the Painted

Men.'' Workmen of exceptional skill were sent by John Dubois, who also furnished the wood. Weeks flew by as the sound of hammer and saw filled the air; and, at last, like a transported Alpine jewel, The Chalet stood in solitary grandeur. Its basic furnishings were French, but scattered about in delightful profusion were lovely and costly accessories from all over the globe. Unfortunately, this splendid house is no longer standing, for it was destroyed by fire some years after Post's death.

Mrs. Post was not destined to live long in her beautiful home. Within a comparatively short time after its completion, she became ill and died Dec. 17, 1919, in a Philadelphia hospital. Stunned by her death, Post was for many months like one lost; but as time slowly passed, he adjusted and was able once more to derive meaning from life, although things were never quite the same again.

His remaining years were often lonely, but he kept busy with his writing, traveled extensively, and on occasion entertained relatives and friends. On a favorite horse he could be seen riding up and down the area's country roads or across the fields of the Post property. Polo was, as it had been for a long time, his favorite sport; and now and then he would invite a small group of young men from Wesleyan College at Buckhannon to play with him. The late Arthur V. G. Upton, for years superintendent of Harrison County schools, was once included and recalled long afterward the thrill of being a guest at The Chalet, where the atmosphere was cosmopolitan and the cuisine superb.

Armed with his high-powered rifle, Post would go hunting for small game, especially groundhogs, in the hills near his home. He owned several cars — a Franklin of ancient vintage, a Stutz, and a Ford — and frequently drove over the rough dusty highway to Clarksburg where he transacted much of his business.

He maintained an interest in politics and government but would not accept a position that carried with it time-consuming responsibilities. Before his marriage, however, he had given serious consideration to political life, and in 1892 had been a Presidential Elector and secretary of the Electoral College.

In the spring of 1930 it was obvious that Post's health was failing, and on June 10 he fell from his horse and began to hemorrhage. Rushed to St. Mary's Hospital in Clarksburg, he was found to be suffering from varicose veins of the esophagus and cirrhosis of the liver. At first he responded to treatment and improved, but within a few days he had a relapse and his condition steadily worsened.

Death came at 4:58 in the morning of Monday, June 23. Two days later his funeral, a simple Episcopal service, was held at The Chalet. He was buried between his wife and son in Clarksburg's Elk View Masonic Cemetery.

Throughout his writing career, Post wrote many stories and articles that were printed in serial publications. His books were: The Strange Schemes of Randolph Mason (1896); The Man of Last Resort (1897); Dwellers in the Hills (1901); The Corrector of Destinies (1908); The Gilded Chair (1910); The Nameless Thing (1912); Uncle Abner, Master of Mysteries (1918); The Mystery at the Blue Villa (1919); The Sleuth of St. James's Square (1920); The Mountain School-Teacher (1922); Monsieur Jonquelle (1923); Walker of the Secret Service (1924); The Man Hunters (1926); The Revolt of the Birds (1927); The Bradmoor Murder (1929); and The Silent Witness (1930), published posthumously.

The countryside in which he grew to manhood played a major role in his development, and in many of his stories he described it with a sensitivity that reflected the love he felt for it. His varied interests took him thousands of miles from home and gave him a certain sophistication, but his heart was in the land of his birth and to it he always returned.

Shinnston's Short Opera House
Part of Town's Long Tradition

By GEORGE ASHBY SHORT

The planned restoration of the Robinson Grand Theatre in Clarksburg during this Bicentennial year of 1984, into a center for the performing arts marks a fitting tribute to the long and illustrious history of the opera house or theatre as a cultural vehicle in Harrison County.

As early as 1820 the Thespian Society of Clarksburg advertised the performance of four different plays and the earliest opera house or theatre was located on the second floor of the W. P. Holden Building on the southwest corner of Third Street and Traders Avenue. The May 15, 1886, edition of the Clarksburg News described the Music Hall, as it was known, located in the Holden Building as follows:

''The Hall is handsomely furnished with opera chairs, and will seat 260 comfortably. A neat little ticket office is met with at the door, which, on this occasion, was presided over by Mr. B. M. Despard. The arrangement for gas is perfect, the entire hall being regulated from the stage, which has a row of jets overhead as well as the footlights. Two handsome chandeliers illumine the front of the house, and the dressing rooms are also provided with gas. The stage is 13 by 17 feet, on which is placed an elegant Hardman piano. Across the front is a guard chain, which adds to the appearance. The scenery which was appointed in Chicago, by Sosman & Landes, consists of four scenes, a parlor, kitchen, wood and street scene. The drop curtain which is simply immense, represents two partially draped curtains, back of which is seen a view of a small village with a river covered with boats, with the hills in the distance. Taken all together, it is as beautiful a little hall as any in the state, and it is to be hoped the company, which has expended $1,500 in fitting it up, will be amply repaid for the outlay.''

The early opera houses in the county were for the most part usually second story halls which made use of space of otherwise limited value. This approach to providing a location for local thespian talent continued until 1893 when Thomas Moore Jackson erected the Traders National Bank building on the southeast corner of West Main and Third streets, where the Union National Bank is now located. The Traders block contained not only an imposing banking institution but also a modern hotel and opera house.

Beginning in 1893 and continuing for nearly 20 years, thousands patronized the Traders Opera House as well as the excellent bar adjoining the theatre when the men gathered during the intermission only to be sent scurrying back to their seats by a large gong which hung in the bar as a reminder of the main purpose of the evening's entertainment. The Harrison County Herald in its November 7, 1982 edition described the opera house in the following terms:

''The seating capacity of this city theatre is 704. The house is up-to-date in all respects suitably provided with all the essentials of a first class playhouse. The stage is of large dimensions and with 18 sets of scenery as command affords every advantage for the production of performers are fully met by the dressing rooms of good size, situated on the stage floor... The people of Clarksburg are liberal patrons of the drama, and it is a rare thing to find any vacant seats whatever the character of the performance may be.''

The Traders Opera House burned in 1911 but that was not the end of the opera house or theatre in Harrison County. Between 1919 and 1920 several more would open in the area. The ''Victoria Opera House'' on West Pike Street next to Waldomore was erected the same year as the fire by Mrs. Lee Haymond and J. Carl Vance and was subsequently renamed the ''Palace'' in 1915 and later known as the ''Gillis'' in the early 1920s. In 1912 the Clarksburg Theatre Company built a $40,000 theatre on the north side of Pike Street and appointed Reuben Robinson as manager. When the theatre officially opened on Feb. 5, 1913, Claude Robinson had replaced his brother as manager and the illustrious history of the "Robinson Grand Theatre" had begun.

The following years saw the appearance of a number of theatres in the area beginning with the "Orpheum" in 1913 which operated until 1929; "Moore's Opera House" which opened on June 10, 1918 offering entertainment at a cost of ten cents for adults and five cents for children and operated until it was converted into store rooms in 1956; the "Odeon" or the "Bijou" existed during the second decade of this century on West Pike Street and operated successfully as "Marks Orpheum" until 1952; and the "Ritz" theatre which seated 1,-200 persons and stood at 404 West Pike Street on the location occupied since 1975 by the Clarksburg-Harrison Public Library.

Other areas of Harrison County have developed opera houses as sites for both cultural entertainment as well as general meeting places. The Lumberport Opera House was built in 1904, and Salem built a brick Opera House on the west side of Water Street after the fire of 1901 destroyed the frame building used as a theatre prior to that time.

The earliest opera house in Harrison County to be used for that specific purpose, however, was built in Shinnston, at the corner of Pike and Station Streets on the southwest corner where today the yellow brick "Short Apartments" now stand on the original stone foundation of the opera house.

It was in the year of 1889 that my father, a young energetic builder, decided the town of Shinnston needed a theater and general public meeting place and also space where the fraternal orders of the growing community could hold their meetings. He took it upon himself to build the Short Opera House. The top floor was rented to the two lodges, the IOOF and the K of P. Lena E. Poling, in her History of the City of Shinnston, described the early years of the Opera House as follows: "The most famous house of entertainment in Shinnston was Short's Opera House. It was located at the corner of Pike and Station streets... a variety of programs played the Opera House. Most are well remembered not only for their entertainment value but also for the excitement which surrounded some of the performances. One such example was a performance of the Dramatic Society on March 28, 1901. An open air concert by the First West Virginia Infantry Band preceded the performance. The drama presented was entitled 'The Confederate Spy.' "

Short's continued for 17 years after its opening to be the site of local entertainment as well as the stopping-off place of road companies until the tragic fire of Feb. 28, 1906. Two pictures were shown in Mrs. Poling's book taken the morning after the tragic fire, one of the smoldering remains of the Opera House and the other of the little two-story shop in the rear of the Opera House, which had been built originally as C.A. Short's carpenter shop and office and which he had vacated in 1896 when he established his planing mill on lower Station Street. At the time of the fire it was occupied by Howard Harmer and his plumbing shop on the first floor and the Shinnston News on the second floor, operated by Bill Meredith who had taken it over when he came to Shinnston in 1902.

Although we have always had and still have a good picture of C. S. Short's first carpenter shop, we never had a photograph of the Opera House except in the background of

these other pictures, the main one being an early photograph of the corner of Pike and Mahlon streets before Mahlon Street was laid out. It was taken before 1895 when the grade school was built and Mahlon Street was opened. The main objects in the photograph are the Fleming house and the Walter Hursey house, but in the background is the best image I have ever seen of the Short Opera House and by examining it with a reading glass the name and the date of construction can be seen along with the two lodges that occupied the top floor.

Taking all the information able to be obtained from the three available photographs, I have produced a very close replica of the largest building in Shinnston at that early date. The drawing related to the times when the old stepping stones were at each street crossing along Pike Street and the telephone pole is proof of the arrival of the new service in 1896 when the railroad came through town. At the extreme left of the drawing is the two-story plumbing shop and printing shop which stood where the Ashby Apartments now stand.

Only a short time ago a friend and I were sitting at a local restaurant reminiscing about the next road show that was put on in Shinnston after the big theater fire. It was three years after the burning of the opera house that the Shinnston Opera House Company was formed and the contract for a new opera house was given to C. A. Short with the understanding that he would arrange for a road show for the grand opening at the completion of the building. He made a special trip to New York to engage the then-popular ''Red Mill,'' a musical comedy. The then very modern opera building had a balcony with a peanut heaven, an orchestra pit, box seats at either side, full footlights and curtain lights, a curtain loft and dressing rooms.

He was saying he will never forget the beautiful stage in the Dutch setting with the large red mill in the background and every time the windmill turned another beautiful girl would step out of the mill onto the stage, which was filled with red and yellow tulips. He and I were both about five years old at the time.

This building, on Walnut Street was used for many important events until many years later, under a different management, the name was changed to the ''Rex'' and it was then used almost exclusively as a movie house. I know it is nice to settle down in a comfortable seat in your own living room and watch your favorite movie, but fifty years ago the seats in the balcony of the opera house had their pleasant moments too. Sometimes I start wondering which was the most fun.

John W. Davis - Lawyer, was Intelectual Without the Flaw of Austerity

By DOROTHY DAVIS

''In this soil rest four generations of my people... laborers all who played in simple fashion their appointed parts in the life of this community,'' stated John W. Davis on Aug. 11, 1924, in his speech accepting candidacy for the President of the United States.

John Davis, son of Caleb Davis, a clockmarker who lived in the Shenandoah Valley of Virginia, migrated to Clarksburg in 1816 and with his brother Rezin set up a saddle and harness business in the town in 1819. John Davis was a justice, sheriff of the county and a ruling elder of the Presbyterian Church. In 1824 a Clarksburg newspaper advertisement said the Davis saddle shop was located three doors west of the courthouse, a shop where John Davis ''manufactures a general assortment of ladies and gentlemen's saddles, bridles, collars, harness, fire-

buckets... which will sell as low as can be procured on this or the other side of the mountains, either wholesale or retail.'' In 1854 John Davis' wife, Eliza Steen Davis, wrote her son, ''Your father is still in the shop from daylight until 9 o'clock at night. For some weeks he has been posting books so that he does not go to bed before 12 and sometimes 2 o'clock at night. Poor man, he has a hard time of it.''

The son who received the letter about John Davis' hard existence was John James Davis, born in 1835, who in 1854 was attending the law school of Hon. John W. Brockenborough at Lexington, Va., and from which he would be graduated at age 20. Voters in 1861 elected John J. Davis to the House of Delegates of the Virginia Assembly, but the secession of the state from the Union prevented his taking his seat. Instead he was chosen one of the twelve men from Harrison County, ''the discreetest and best,'' to the First Wheeing Convention in June 1861. John J. Davis married Anna Kennedy of Baltimore in 1862, the year before he was forced out of politics temporarily because of his opposition to the new-state movement. In 1869 voters sent him to the West Virginia House of Delegates and in 1870 and again in 1872 to the U.S. House of Representatives. He was president of the W. Va. Bar in 1901. He died March 19, 1916.

The John J. Davis house was one of the fine homes of Harrison County. Along with the estimate of costs for the house, the contractor wrote John J. Davis in 1874: ''When you come to think about the size of this house, it is a whale. It will be an honor to any man to live in such a house.'' the stately home stood on the southwest corner of South Third Street and

without the fault of pretention; he enjoyed success but demanded immunity from praise. He was never abstruse, never deceptive, and never employed argument to cloud or confuse an issue. He wa always direct and explicit. Integrity was a naturally dominant element of his character.''

Davis won election fom the First W. Va. District to the 62nd and 63rd sessions of the U.S. Congress, where he was a member of the judiciary committee. During his second term in Conress President Wilson named him solicitor general of the United states and in 1918 President Wilson appointed Davis as ambassador of the United States to the Court of St. James in London.

The Democratic Party nominated John W. Davis July 9, 1924, on the 103rd ballot of the convention to be its candidate for the office of President of the United States.

Members of the Harrison County Bar unveiled a bust of John W. Davis at the opening of the Harrison County Court in december 1954. the citation during the ceremony read, in part: ''John W. Davis, one of Clarksburg;s most distinguished citizens, has argued more cases (140) before the United States Supreme Court than any other lawyer in the nation's history except for possibly Daniel Webster.'' John W. Davis died March 24, 1955.

John W. Davis - Presidential Candidate

By DOROTHY DAVIS

Four days after the Democratic Party, meeting in convention in New York City, had nominated him on July 9, 1924, to be its candidate for U.S. President, John W. Davis stated that he would travel to Clarksburg for his formal speech of acceptance. Immediately Dorsey R. Potter set out from Clarksburg for New York City to coordinate plans for the Clarksburg homecoming. July 18 Mr. Potter telephoned the Clarksburg homecoming committee that is had less than a month to make preparations. The hierarchy of the Democratic Party had set Aug. 11, 1924, for the big homecoming celebration.

Citizens began work on arrangements which included housing in private homes for the overflow from the Gore and Waldo hotels, decorating public buildings and homes with swaths of bunting, organizing parades, choosing a spot for the acceptance speech to be followed by a display of fireworks. The City of Clarksburg started construction of a raised sidewalk with molded cement balustrades where the grounds of the John W. Davis mansion joined Lee Ave.

Davis' sister, Miss Emma Davis, lived at the residence until her death. After the Second World War the property was sold to the former Union Protestant Hospital. The house was dismantled and the site was used as a parking lot. The parcel was later purchased by the Chesapeake and Potomac Telephone Co. which now has offices located in its building there.

All was ready at 9:15 a.m. on Saturday, Aug. 9, 1924, when a special train carrying the nominee pulled into the B&O Station in Clarksburg. Louis A. Johnson of the Clarksburg law firm of Steptoe and Johnson was the first to shake the hand of Davis, and the Homecoming Chairman Samuel R. Bentley and City Manager Harrison G. Otis, escorted the candidate to a platform for speeches of welcome before Davis walked through the throngs to join his friend John C. Johnson, 83 years of age, and be driven to the Davis home on Lee Avenue.

Sunday Davis left his home only to attend services at the Central Presbyterian Church on West Pike Street. Sunday afternoon a band esconced on the platform of the B&O Station in Glen Elk awaited the arrival of U.S. Sen. Thomas J. Walsh of Montana, who would deliver next evening the speech of notification of nomination. The band escorted Sen. Walsh and

Lee Avenue overlooking the courthouse. Davis liked trees which he planted in grand style, and two of which, a larch and an Empress, still in 1984 live on the Lee Street edge of the site.

Perhaps it was the birth of a son that caused John J. Davis to begin building a mansion, for Anna Kennedy Davis gave birth April 13, 1873 to her first child and first son, John William. The boy grew up in the Davis mansion, attended a preparatory school near Charlottesville, Va., and Washington and Lee University, where he graduated in law in 1895. He and his father formed the law firm of ''Davis & Davis.'' In 1899 he served in the West Virginia House of Delegates and on June 20, 1899, he married Julia McDonald, whose girlhood home was ''Media'' near Charles Town, and returned to Clarksburg with his wife to live in his father's home. In July 1900 Julia Davis gave birth to a daughter Julia. August 17, 1900 Julia McDonald Davis died.

John W. Davis plunged into work and late in life said of this period: ''Whatever professional success I have had is due primarily to the training in the rough and tumble of the Clarksburg bar. It was sometimes rough and, as I look back, I did a good deal of tumbling, but it was healthy discipline for all of that.'' In 1912 he married Ellen Graham (Nell) Bassel, a Clarksburg woman.

A contemporary of him during the decade and a half John W. Davis practiced law in Clarksburg said of him: ''He was intellectual without the flaw of austerity... much less disparagement of the opinions of the lesser endowed; he was dignified without loss of friendy interest; he was scholarly

his wife to the residence of George L. Duncan on East Main Street, where the two would be entertained during their stay in Clarksburg. Sunday evening the Greater Clarksburg Band presented a homecoming concert in the Carmichael Auditorium. Among the up-and-coming politicians who arrived in Clarksburg Sunday was Cordell Hull of Tennessee, retiring chairman of the Democratic Committee, and his wife.

Monday morning, Aug. 11, while a band from Huntington played in the street on Lee Avenue, citizens gathered on the spacious lawn of the Davis mansion. Late in the morning, Davis left his home, drove to the Elks Club for a meeting with the Democratic Executive Committee and then walked to the Waldo Hotel for luncheon. In the afternoon notables, bands and floats paraded through the business district of the city.

In 1924 Goff Plaza between East Main Street and Buckhannon Avenue was vacant land where each spring circuses performed followed in late summer by week-long sessions of Chautauqua. The site was chosen for the platform from which Candidate Davis standing in open air would deliver his speech on Monday evening.

Alas! no one knew that the elements would interrupt the well-planned program. A few drops of rain fell at the beginning of the speech delivered by Sen. Walsh. When the representatives of the Cincinnati firm hired to display fireworks from atop Pinnickinnick Hill at the close of the evening event saw storm clouds rolling in, he decided to fill the terms of his contract before he was rained out. A loud, colorful array shot into the blackening sky as Sen. Walsh spoke. James Rodney, chairman of the fireworks committee, jumped into his automobile, drove to the foot of Pinnickinnick Hill, and ran to the top to stop the ill-timed fireworks.

Davis walked to the podium just as torrential rain began to fall. Louis A. Johnson raised an umbrella over the speaker's head; the crowd chanted ''Go on, John;'' newsmen worked steadily under upraised boards held over their heads; someone wrapped a piece of cloth around the shoulders of the speaker. At the end of the acceptance speech the storm ended as abruptly as it had begun. Yet woe was not over, for cars parked on newly graded land near the platform were held fast in mud for hours. The acceptance speech traveled by radio throughout the United States. The C&P Telephone Company carried Davis' voice out of the hills over two different circuits, one running through Fairmont and Morgantown to KDKA in Pittsburgh; the second through Grafton and Cumberland to Altoona. At midnight on Aug. 11 C&P Telephone Co. trucks packed the equipment used to project the voices of the speakers to the audience in Goff Plaza into trucks which carried the paraphernalia via Rt. 50 over the mountains to Washington so that Calvin Coolidge could use the same mechanism to reach the ears of the crowd which would gather

to hear his speech later in the same week, a speech accepting the nomintion of the Republican Party as a candidate for the Presidency of the United States.

When older Harrison County citizens recall the John W. Davis Homecoming, the first comment is "Remember the rain?" Then they describe the revelry and the openness of the occasion. After the parade on Monday afternoon any citizen could call at the Davis residence and one citizen recalled that at age 10 she stood in the kitchen of the house and wondered why someone did not stop the youngsters who chased one another in and out of the back door. The number of reporters from metropolitan newspapers and national political leaders who filled the hotels brimful was mind boggling to the natives. Jennings Randolph, Salem correspondent for the "Clarksburg Telegram" as a Salem College student, had in summer 1924 graduated to a job as fulltime reporter on the newspaper. His vivid memories of the homecoming caused him to spark a celebration of the fiftieth anniversary of the nomination in 1974.

Observance of the sixtieth anniversary of the John W. Davis Homecoming will be a major event of the Harrison County Bicentennial. Julia Davis, daughter of John W. Davis, and her husband, William McMillian Adams will travel to Clarksburg for the anniversary luncheon on Aug. 11. Sen. Randolph will preside at the luncheon.

Davis' speech is excerpted here as follows:

"You will understand with little explanation on my part, the feelings which have led me to fix our meeting at this spot in the hills of West Virginia. These are the hills that cradled me and to which as a boy and man I lifted up my eyes for help. In this soil rest four generations of my people — artisans, tradesmen, farmers and a sprinkling of the professions, laborers all who played in simple fashion their appointed parts in the life of this community. Among them now lie those who gave me life, and to whose precept and example I owe all that I have ever been and all that I can hope to be. These witnesses who surround us are the companions of my youth and manhood. With them most of my days have been spent, and when circumstances have called me elsewhere, they have followed me with a regard and affection that had laid on me a debt of gratitude greater than I can repay. Twenty-five years ago they first called me to their service as their representative in the legislature of this state, and since that day, in public or private life, I have fought with them unceasingly the battle for Democratic ideals and Democratic principles. Of their own free will and motion they presented my name to the Democratic convention as one deserving its consideration. Better than all others, they will know whether what I shall say to you today is in keeping with the convictions I have expressed and the action I have taken in the past, and more than any others they will resent anything I may say or do that shows their confidence misplaced. It is in the presence of these hills, these graves, these witnesses, that I wish to hear your message and give you my reply."

Ernest T. Weir - Industrialist

By LLOYD LEGGETT

Seventy-five years ago a book was published on "The Natural Resources and Industries of Central West Virginia" compiled and edited by Douglass B. Williams. One of the major industries mentioned was the Phillips Sheet and Tin Plate Company which was located in Clarksburg and which was described as one of the major economic industries of Harrison County.

The Phillips Sheet & Tin Plate Co. is the largest manufacturing enterprise in central West Virginia. The well-built works of the company are an exemplification of the latest and best American ways and means of manufacturing tin plate and kindred products. The plant, located at Clarksburg, W. Va., turns out, most advantageously, not only the best quality of tin plate, but terne roofing, enameling material, galvanizing stock and all grades of uncoated plates. The company will soon operate two plants, the one at Clarksburg and one at Weirton. The plant at Weirton is now in course of construction and will be one of the largest and most thoroughly equipped factories in the country.

The organization first came into being in April 1905, and in a short time that has elapsed, this well-managed company has grown so rapidly, so substantially, that it has obtained national recognition, and is one of the leading independent manufacturers of tin plate in the United States.

The excellent showing made by the Phillips Sheet & Tin Plate Co. at last proves that the tariff has not destroyed competition, nor created conditions in which it was impossible for independent manufacturers to succeed. The two plants of the company will produce per annum over 1,500,000 boxes of tin and terne plates. One million one hundred thousand boxes of this will be tin plate, a quantity sufficient to make more than 347,600,000 ordinary sized cans. Of terne plate, which is used almost entirely for roofing purposes, over 300,000 boxes a year will be made. Its output of black plates and sheets for metal ceilings, for enameling and for galvanizing purposes will amount to more than 10,000 tons annually.

The general offices of the Phillips Sheet & Tin Plate Company are at the works in Clarksburg, but branches are maintained in Pittsburgh, New York, St. Louis, San Francisco and Portland, Oregon.

The present operation of this company's mills, situated at Clarksburg, on the main line of the B&O Railroad in the eastern part of the city, means steady employment to more than 900 men, the greater number of whom are skilled workmen whose earnings are very large. The mills, since the time they were started, have operated steadily and many extensive improvements have been made which have increased production.

The use of natural gas is of considerable advantage as more uniform results can be obtained in the heating of the raw material and in the anealing of the plates, the softness and

pliability being a most important feature of the manufacture of tin plates and the excellence of the products made by this company is partly due to the correct use of natural gas.

The officers of the company are men who have been identified prominently for many years with the sheet and tin plate industry.

In the iron and steel trade but few men are more favorably known than E. T. Weir, the present president of the company. Much of the success attained by the enterprise is due to him for the diligence, zeal and intelligence he has displayed in its management, having had active charge of the company's affairs since its organization.

Ernest T. Weir was born on Aug. 1, 1875, in Pittsburgh, Pa., the son of James Weir and Margaret Manson. His proudest boast was "I was born a commoner. I'm still a commoner. No one has ever given me anything." His father died when E. T. Weir was fifteen. He helped support the family by taking a $3-a-week job as an office boy in the Braddock Wire Co. Alarmed at the ever-increasing wire production in Pittsburgh, Weir decided that there was no future in the wire business. "I concluded that at the rate we were going, we would in a few years have made enough wire to last civilization for a long time." In 1899, he left the wire industry and became chief clerk at the American Tin Company. In 1903, Weir became plant manager, and then superintendent of the Monessen Tin Plate Mills (a subsidiary of the American Tin Plate Co.) but he eyed larger responsibilities and soon became associated with J. R. Phillips, of Pittsburgh. This association was eventually to lead Weir to become president of the Phillips Tin Plate Company and chairman of the board of National Steel.

The story of Weir's elevation to the presidency of the firm is an interesting one: About 1903, the Jackson Iron and Tin Plate Co. opened for business in the manufacture of tin plate. The plant, located in the eastern section of Clarksburg, was known as the Tin Plate Mill. It opened up with great hope and ran into financial difficulties and closed down for a time. Several financial sources in Clarksburg were interested in this institution and after some maneuvering, a certin Mr. J. R. Phillips, an experienced operator, was prevailed upon to take over the mill and operate it. He had, as his private secretary and assistant, one Ernest T. Weir. Of course the finaicial institutions in Clarksburg had assumed certain obligations and made certain commitments in order to persuade Phillips to take over. All of the business of transfer had been taken care of, and the name changed to Phillips Sheet and Tin Plate Co., and the mill started and the future seemed rosy when an accident occurred that threatened to upset the entire picture. It so happened that Phillips was asleep in a Pullman car, in the yard at Harrisburg, Pa. The car had not been pushed entirely in the clear. A train pulled through on an adjoining track, sideswiping the above-mentioned car and killing Phillips.

Clarksburg then had a tinplate operation on its hands with no guiding head. It was then that Weir, after much conferring and the promise of all necessary assistance, agreed to attempt to manage the mill. That was the beginning of the meteoric career of Weir.

When he became president, Weir decided to expand. His first idea was to build and operate a few other similar plants in the area. He chose the community known as Holiday's Grove (later incorporated in 1947 into the present-day city of Weirton) for his second site. The general offices of the Phillips Sheet and Tin Plate Co. were moved to Weirton in February, 1910. A month later the "Daily Telegram" reported E. T. Weir as having attended a meeting of the Clarksburg water and sewerage board and added, "The presence of Mr. Weir is an indication that he has not left the city as a citizen and will continue to have his residence in Clarksburg."

The name of the company was eventually changed to the Weirton Steel Co. which incorporated in 1918 with a capitalization of $30 million. This company formed the foundation upon which Weir created the second largest steel company in the country, National Steel Co.

Realizing the vast profits to be made in the coming auto industry, Weir sought and got contracts with Detroit, including a major contract with Henry Ford. And he raised the capital necessary to expand production and fill these contracts by selling stock directly to the public.

"I went to the opposite side of Wall Street from J. P. Morgan and Co.," Weir stated. "I wanted $40 million for 25 years at a time when that money looked like the national debt. I got it not from Wall Street but from Main Street."

In September 1929, Weir joined forces with the Great Lakes Steel Corporation of Detroit, and the M. A. Hanna Co. to form National Steel. Following the stock market crash, one month later, while other steel companies were cutting back production, Weir boldly planned expansion — a $25 million plant in Detroit to be followed by a $40 million plant in Gary, Ind. National Steel was the only major steel producer to show a profit in every year from 1930 to 1935.

Insisting the cure was infinitely worse than the disease, Weir became an outspoken critic of the New Deal. Claiming that his workers were fully satisfied with their own company-sponsored union, he refused to comply with Section 7a of the National Recovery Act, which called for free elections for union representation within plants. Taken to court by the government, Weir emerged triumphant when a federal district judge in Wilmington, Del. declared Section 7a null and void as applied to a manufacturing plant. It was one of the New Deal's earliest setbacks in the courts, and before the government could appeal this ruling, the U.S. Supreme Court, in a separate case, declared the National Recovery Act unconstitutional in 1935.

In 1939, the Weirton Steel Company found that, with

modern methods of producing steel, the Clarksburg plant was so unprofitable that it was forced to leave the city and consolidate all work at the plant in Weirton. Thus ended the 35 year relationship between E. T. Weir and Harrison County and the impact which the individual had upon the economic development of the area during that time.

E. T. Weir died June 26, 1957 in Philadelphia, but in Weirton his spirit still lives.

When National Steel annouced its plan to "dump" the marginally profitable plant at Weirton, the citizens of Weirton cried "foul." Weir had considered Weirton Steel the keystone of the National Steel Corporation conglomerate. How could this happen?

While debate was raging in Weirton as to whether the employees should buy out the plant or not, E. T. Weir was once again heard. The union magazine "The Independent Weirton" published an article with advice from E. T. Weir himself. Weir was depicted looking down upon Weirton from above advising the employees to buy out the plant from National Steel. His advice was taken. The steel mill was bought by the employees and today it stands as an outstanding example of the individualism of its new owners, reminiscent of the same rugged American individualism of its founder, E. T. Weir.

A Rembrance of Marbles and Glass Past

by EDWIN SWEENEY

For most of the first half of this century there was a small factory in Clarksburg which produced millions of glass marbles for shipment throughout the United States, Mexico, and Central America. The output sometimes reached two million a week. The company was Akro Agate, producing a colored, marbelized glass that once had a thriving market. In addition to common playing marbles, Akro also pressed cheap novelty glass which brightened homes during the Depression. Articles bearing the Akro tradmark — the letter A with the figure of a crow — now are collectors' items, some bringing many times their original price of less than a dollar.

Akro Agate was organized in Akron in 1911 and soon found a ready market for its marbles among the younger generaton. Like other Ohio glass firms, Akro was lured to West Virginia by the availability here of glass sand and inexpensive natural gas. The young company moved to Clarksburg in 1914, locating in a building in which glass lamps had been manufactured. It flourished here until shortly before its demise in 1951.

The factory off South Chestnut Street is now abandoned and not many people remember that it was once a booming operation. However, there are at least two men who do. Raymond Rowe, once Akro's maintenance foreman on 24-hour call, and Ralph Heatherington, its one-man sales department. They quickly bring the plant back to life when they begin reminiscing.

"I was pretty young when my father started hauling freight for Akro," Rowe recently told me. "He had a grocery store at 779 West Pike Street and delivered groceries in a wagon. One of his customers was Horace C. Hill, who started with Akro in Ohio and then came here when they set up in an old plant that made kerosene lamps and chimneys. Mr. Hill engaged my father to take wooden crates of marbles over to the B&O Railroad depot where a lot went to Mexico and Central America." Raymond Rowe himself went to work for the company within a few years.

Heatherington, who will be 91 in July, knows the details of the company's beginnings in Akron. It was there, he says, that Gilbert C. Marsh joined with George T. Rankin to form Akro Agate in 1911. Marsh was already a successful businessman, whose Wagner Shoe Company had outlets in Akron, Youngstown, and Canton, Ohio, while Rankin was a young physician.

"They initially purchased clay marbles from a factory operated by M. F. Christensen and later moved into the manufacture of glass marbles," Heatherington says. Marsh and Rankin bought the marbles in bulk or packaging and resale. This limited packing and shipping operation was successful into the early 'teens, and evidently the change to manufacturing came when they moved to Clarksburg.

The two founders acquired new partners along with their new factory. According to Harrison County records, they were joined in the initial Oct. 1, 1914, West Virginia incorporation by John M. Rowley, E. E. McGalliard, and Hill. That charter itself was dissolved April 1, 1921. Akro Agate was rechartered on March 4, 192t, by N. O. Mather, J. M. Neal, G. L. Keller, R. H. Nesbitt, and W. L. Wilkie. The Ohio founding partners remained in until their deaths more than 20 years later.

Raymond Rowe picks up the story of Akro from about the time of its rechartering. "I had been around there since I was a youngster," he says. "I went to work in 1926 and stayed to the end — for 24 years. I started in the packing room and went to the hot end after a year and a half. When I began, the glass was hand gathered, and this lasted into the late '30s when we motorized.

"In the beginning, the glass was melted in big clay pots. There were four to a chimney. It had to be pre-heated until it was rosy. Each pot weighed about a thousand pounds. The glass was gathered in what they called monkey pots, about 12 inches wide and 18 inches high. To get the glass from the large pot we used an iron rod about an inch round and six feet long."

This part of the operation will sound familiar to anyone knowledgeable of basic glassmaking. Rowe then went on to describe the special work done only at the marble factory. "We had to keep turning the rod to keep the glass on it so we could get it into the rolling machine. This device had two sets of rollers which kept the glass turning through a feeder to make it round. It then traveled about 30 inches and came out an orifice as marbles and dropped into a bucket. By then they were not hot enough to stick together.

"The buckets were taken to a grader," Rowe continues. "This was a machine with two round cylinders, eight feet long, which separated the marbles according to size. They were stored in six-foot-tall bins."

Rowe is a man who knows marbles. "Of course, marbles always look round but they were never perfectly round. If the glass was too hot or the machine was going too fast, the marbles lost their shape. Akro had a patent on striped marbles. other plants tried to duplicate them by making their glass hotter, but the just couldn't do it." The temperature was critical, but the process itself was a simple one. "In hand gathering we used basic glass and mixed in a wad of different colors for striping. We had to fill the furnace every half hour."

It was Rowe who brought the Akro operation up to peak production. When he went to the maintenance department he modified the equipment with longer, smaller rollers to produce up to 2,000,000 marbles per week.

"One man could put out about 7,500 to 10,000 marbles in a an eight-hour shift," he recalls. "I made from $8 to $10 per day. That was when I was doing piece work for two different sizes, zeros and ones. Ones were the most popular size for playing marbles. We also made twos, which were ¾ of an inch thick; fours that were of an inch, and sixes, which were an inch.

"The ones were used as lithograph balls, to clean press type. They were also used for reflecting letters in road signs and for cleaning out sewers."

Each type of marble had its own use, and Rowe notes that the company was quick to exploit new markets for its basic product. Back in the '30s there was a popular game on the West Coast called Chinese Checkers that involved marbles," he remembers. "It took two years to get to the East Coast but when it did we shipped out all the marbles we could make. Our marbles went all over the country and a lot of them went to Mexico — to Vera Crux, Mexico. I remember hearing one man say that this 'Vera Cruz' must be an awfully rich woman because she bought a lot of marbles.

"It was in the early '30s, too, that we started making a lot of pressed ware. We got our molds from the old McBride Glass plant at Salem and from the old Brilliant Glass in Weston."

According to Gene Florence's 'Collectors' Encyclopedia of Akro Agate Glassware,' Brilliant Glass, under the 'Westite' name, had made a line of children's dishes, marbelized towel racks, and ashtrays, among other items. After purchasing the equipment Akro Agate went into a similar line of production.

"When we bought these molds and started making our own wares, we began marking them with our Akro trademark," Rowe recalls. "We decided to go motorized. We had a press that had an air-operated plunger which pressed a pattern on the glass before it went onto a conveyor belt and slowly moved for about 50 feet through the annealing furnace. When it came off the conveyor it went onto a trap and was moved to the packing room.

"Much of our pressed ware was made from cullet. That was the glass discarded by other companies. A lot of cullet came from the Jeanette Glass Company in Jeanette, Pa. It was made at about the same temperature as ours and could be mixed easily. We also got glass from other plants closer to home.

"Ralph Heatherington was our crack salesman," Rowe continues. "We had a type of glassware that was inexpensive and moved well, and he kept the orders coming in. At the peak of production Akro employed 80 to 100 people. It was a successful operation, but after the major stockholders died their relatives were led to believe that the operation could be changed from making dimestore ware to specialty, higher-priced glass."

Heatherington, who went to work at Akro in 1929, recalls

the sales line well. He says the popular items included "Mexicali" jars for women's powder, sold for 40 cents a piece whosesale and $1.50 retail; ashtrays, whosesale at 50 cents and marked up 100 percent; and toy tea sets, which were $12 per dozen wholesale and $16 retail. What had been a small production of flower pots was expanded to a full range of garden containers in varying sizes.

One of the most successful lines was the Akro toy tea set in production during World War II. Earlier, the diminutive dishes had been made of metals such as tin. Lamps, bathroom towel bars, and glass holders were among the other items which Heatherington took orders for.

Akro Agate became a family affair for the Heatheringtons' when his wife joined the firm. She, the former Ruth Prendece, was going to business school in Clarksburg when the company began looking for a Spanish-speaking person to translate Latin American orders. Ruth Heatherington knew the language and was hired for the job.

Toys were always a big factor in Akro's success. As a major marble manufacturer, the company had been ready when the Chinese Checkers craze swept the country. The Parker Brothers game featured a playing board that used 60 small marbles, 10 of each color. Through the early 1940s this game and the tea sets accounted for much of the firm's production, which had by then grown to $2 million annually. The general run of glassware was sold to the F. W. Woolworth Company and similar stores all across the United States.

As often happens, changes came to Akro Agate with a change in sales and management personnel. Rowe thinks the changes were for the worse. "Ralph left the company, and a new fellow took over," he says. "He set out to change the type of glass we were making. But Akro had been set up to produce inexpensive glass from cullet and was not geared to compete with the specialty glass which was being made around the state."

'Around 1940, Libby Owens decided to make glass cloth. They set up a laboratory in Clarksburg and had a chemist here experimenting on making it at Akro. They were here for three months trying to develop it but the heat had to be so much hotter for their kind of glass. We tried it but it was burning up our equipment."

Other factors combined with changing management ideas to contributed to the decline of Akro Agate. The development of plastics undermined the toy tea set business, and hurt the glass industry in general. Some people felt that efforts by the American Flint Glass Workers to unionize the Akro work force further crippled the company.

Basically, Rowe feels that it was the new unfamiliar product line that killed the Clarksburg company. "When our new glass could not be marketed the way marbles and pressed ware were," he says, "the company went into a decline and never recovered."

Akro Agate was going downhill by 1948, when founding partner Rankin died. Toward the end of that year, founder Gilbert C. Marsh also died. The company continued production after the deaths of the two men, but was not able to show sufficient profit for the heirs to justify the operation. On June 30, 1951, the board voted to shut down. Shortly afterwards, the plant and machinery were sold at public auction.

"I was the last man there," Rowe said. "I stayed until the sale and got my last check. A lot of us think the company could have made it if it had kept making the kind of glass that sold."

Nowadays, Rowe mostly has only his memories of Akro left. Like others there, he treated the company's wares as part of the job and he saved few items. "I don't have but a few pieces of Akro," he notes. "We just never thought too much about it then, but now there is a big market for it. People are quick to pick it up at auctions."

Two people who have picked up a lot of Akro glassware are Dean and Mable Elliott, a retired Clarksburg couple. They have one of the most comprehensive collections, parts of which were lent to the Clarksburg-Harrison Public Library for an exhibition in 1980.

Elliott has not updated his inventory recently, but at last count it exceeded 1,000 pieces. He frequently receives inquiries about the glass. "It's not grand or expensive but in its own way it is attractive," he says. "it brings to mind the Depression and what those hard times represented.

"To me, two of the most interesting aspects are the texture of the glass and its color. It has a satiny feel. The variety of deep colors is most attractive. It comes in all colors. I like the deep reds, greens, and blues, and the marbelized quality of the glass.

"We have the apple, which was originally a powder jar," he continues. "We have several varieties of powder jars — the colonial lady, Scotty dog, glass bells, some of the Mexicali jars — and planters and flower pots in all shapes and colors. We have the glass baskets, dozens of ashtrays in several colors, marbles, several doll dish sets in their original cartons, bowls of various sizes." Elliott's list goes on and on, finally winding up with "two floor lamps and three table lamps and many of the cornucopias."

Like other collectors, the Elliotts are aware of the significance of the markings on their pieces. "Among the rarities," Elliott says, "we have a few pieces that in addition to the Akro A and crow have 'Akro Agate Co., Clarksburg, West Virginia.' They also made a lot of ware for the Jean Vivaudou Company. These pieces have 'Vivadou' of 'Jean Vivaudou' stamped on the bottom, but theh were made by Akro. These were apothecary jars."

Elliott goes on to note a few other items, some of them unusual. "We have some of the oxblood and lemonade pieces which are a deep red and a deep yellow, and were used for children's play dishes. We have a few pieces of translucent glass, but Akro didn't make much of that. We have some pieces that are questionable as to authenticity," he concludes.

Akro Agate glassware grows more scarce and more valuable to collectors all the time, for there is no possibility that any more will be made. Rowe remembers that the old factory and equipment were sold separately, and neither was ever brought into successful production again. "An outfit that made tire pumps and steel castings for Chrysler took over the plant," he recalls. "They were there for three years but I don't think they ever got the castings to pass inspection.

"After we closed, a company in Pennsboro bought the marble machines and set to making marbles. They weren't having much luck and they called me. I told them their glass was too hot for the machines. They never could get the machines into production like they were for us."

After 33 years, Rowe and Heatherington are among the declining number of people once directly associated with the Akro Agate Company. Otherwise, the small factory in Clarksburg is remembered through collections such as the one Dean and Mable Elliott have. Such collectors seek the A-and-crow trademark move avidly each year, as items once shrugged off as playthings and dime store trinkets come to be seriously regarded as important vestiges of West Virginia history.

Richard Tasker Lowndes - A Banker, Man of Varied Business Interests

BY DOROTHY DAVIS

At the time of his death at Waldomore July 23, 1930, Richard Tasker Lowndes was rounding out a century of Lowndes history in Clarksburg.

R. T. Lowndes' father Lloyd Lowndes as a young man had left his Georgetown, D.C., home with his brother Richard and traveled west to Cumberland, Md., where the brother stayed. Lloyd Lowndes came on to Clarksburg in 1832 and established a store on the north side of West Main Street just east of Third Street. He soon purchased the Hewes Tavern on the northeast corner of West Main and Third streets, married Maria Elizabeth Moore, second daughter of Clarksburger Thomas P. Moore, and set up a mercantile business and residence in the brick Hewes building. The site had the label "Lowndes Corner" for a century.

Before her death in 1847 Maria Moore Lowndes gave birth to four sons: Charles, born in 1841, who died in 1865; Richard R., born in 1843; Lloyd, Jr., (1845-1905) who would become lawyer, banker, congressman, and governor of Maryland; and Clarence who died at age three months in 1847.

Lloyd Lowndes' early years as businessman coincided with the availability of land at low cost because of the passage by the Virginia Assembly of laws to remove from the county books through sale of land purchased by speculators who by the 1830s were delinquent in paying taxes. With a store and residence across the street from the courthouse, Lloyd Lowndes was in a good place to buy extensive acreage in Harrison County at the same time that as a businessman he was winning the respect of fellow citizens: "Lloyd Lowndes built a reputation for integrity second to none in the community and the name Lowndes has ever since stood as a synonym for honesty and fair dealing."

Lloyd Lowndes' son Richard graduated from Northwestern Virginia academy in Clarksburg and attended business college in Philadelphia. As a youth he worked many a hot summer day in the hayfield at the foot of Lowndes Hill as a laborer for his father. He went into business with his father, was a prime mover in organizing in 1866 the Annual Fair of the Central W. Va. Agricultural and Mechanical Society and served as its president for many years. He was a member of the first board of organizers of the Clarksurg Gas Company which evolved into the Clarksburg Gas & Electric Company. When his father died in 1897, Richard Lowndes was ready to take over and expand the business foundation his father had built.

In the 1880s Richard Lowndes and Ira Hart developed vast timber tracts in Doddridge County. They built the Middle Island Railroad from their timberlands to connect with the B&O line at Smithburg. They were known for fine poplars converted into choice lumber much of it used in the manufacture of chair seats. Around 1885 Lowndes began floating logs from Braxton County down the West Fork River to his sawmill near Clarksburg.

Lowndes' big dream was to build a railroad down the West Fork and Monongahela rivers to the Pennsylvania border to connect with the Pennsylvania Railroad and thus form competition for the B&O Railroad and give Lowndes better rates for his several thousand acres of coal he hoped to develop. The company he and others incorporated secured rights-of-way and did some grading. A faithful old Irishman who had worked for Lowndes on his timber road up Meat House Fork in Doddridge County was set to work grading near Fairmont. He and his mule and cart worked there for years under a plan to hold the right-of-way to the annoyance of the B&O. The dream ended in the 1880s when the B&O and the Pennsylvania railroads entered relations which prevented competition.

The woolen mill Richard Lowndes owned and operated on Point Comfort where Elk Creek joins the West Fork River was severely damaged during the flood of 1888. Logs in the swollen waters crashed into the brick warehouse near the mill releasing into the water boxes of finished goods along with pounds of wool from the mill. Lowndes directed workers to retrive wares from the waters as far north as Fairmont and to tie the material to trees. Then wagons carried the stock to Clarksburg where blankets, yard goods, skirts were washed in the river and laid in fields near the mill to dry after which they were brushed in factory machinery, folded and packed for shipment.

In 1882 Nathan Goff Jr., resigned the presidency of the Merchants Bank for a federal judgeship. Richard Lowndes resigned as president of the West Virginia Bank and accepted the appointment as president of the Merchants Bank, a position he held to the end of his life. In 1896 Lowndes founded his

Old Mill Dam, Clarksburg, W. Va.

own private bank under the name of Lowndes Savings Bank and Trust Company. In 1905 he took in George L. Duncan and his Lowndes nephews as stockholders.

"Why I Don't Marry," the title of Richard Lowndes' oration for graduation from Northwestern Virginia Academy in 1859, was a portent of his future, for Lowndes did not marry until he was 53 years old. He wed his first cousin May Goff on February 5, 1896, in Christ Episcopal Church with Dr. David H. Greer, bishop of the Episcopal Church residing in New York City and a close childhood friend of the couple, officiating. May Goff Lowndes had inherited her father's home Waldomore which after 1896 became known as the Lowndes residence.

In the late 1890s Lowndes and Goff interests incorporated the Elk Hill Coal & Coke Company; in 1899 Lowndes, Charles Goff, C. M. Hart, and George L. Duncan organized the Independent Oil Company to develop 900 acres of oil and gas on Raccoon Run near Bristol in Harrison County.

Painstaking and methodical, Richard Lowndes gave earnest thought and attention to the minutest phase of business. He watched over every detail when he erected structures which he built for the future. He manufactured the brick for each building on the site of the work. He tore down in 1897 the small wooden store his father had built in the 1830s and by 1882 in its place was a three-story brick department store building; he removed the old Hewes Building on the corner of Main and Third streets in 1901 and erected a three-story structure for his bank on the first floor and dry goods wares on

the second and third floors; in 1902 Lowndes built a hardware store building between the bank and the department store thus giving a combined length of 91 feet for stores and bank; In 1916 Lowndes and others built a power station on West Pike Street for the Clarksburg Gas and Electric Company. The power station was conveyed to the West Penn Public Service Company in 1923 when Lowndes went out of the public utilities business; the Lowndes store buildings were sold to Parsons-Souders Co. in 1927.

Other than his keen business sense and devotion to duty, the reason for Lowndes' becoming the economic pulse of the county was that he showed the same compassion for fellow citizens as had Lloyd Lowndes who when a disastrous frost wiped out on June 5, 1859, the corn which stood knee-high all over the county, sent immediately for buckwheat seed which he doled out at low cost from his Clarksburg store to any farmer who came for it.

Two incidents show Richard Lowndes' identity with his fellowmen. One day at the same time executives who had traveled from out-of-town to Clarksburg to confer with Lowndes arrived at offices in the Lowndes Bank, an aged man came to see Lowndes about a problem. Lowndes delayed the meeting with the executives for a few minutes with the words: "An aged man is here worried with a problem. I shall return as soon as I help him." In 1928 or 1929 when the bank examiner told the officers of the Lumberport Bank, "You'll have to close," D. Ray Rogers went immediately to see Lowndes: "When I told R. T. Lowndes about the plight we were in, he said to me, 'You can have anything you want' and I walked out of his business with $10,000 to shore up the Lumberport Bank, but I was too late. I had to wait at the bank until Mr. Lowndes returned from his noonday meal, and when I stepped off the streetcar in Lumberport, the bank examiner was chipping off the letters spelling the name of the bank from the front window."

Richard Lowndes was a devout and active member of Christ Episcopal Church. He gave personal supervision to the erection in 1925 of a parish house which he gave as a gift to the church. He was a liberal donor to the social organizations of Clarksburg.

May Goff Lowndes, who was critically ill at the time of her husband's demise, died at Waldomore August 3, 1930, eleven days after the death of her husband.

Charles Ashby Short - Setup Shinnston's First Pump Station & Water Works

By GEORGE SHORT

Charles Ashby Short was an orphan when he arrived in Shinnston in 1883, at the age of 20, and through pure persistence was able to obtain a job with Lafayette J. Rowland and Ferdinand Richardson by offering his services for two weeks on the condition that he could prove that he was worth it. Charles was not two years old when his father, John Short, was killed in what the community termed a cold-blooded murder by the Union Home Guard because he would not join either side in the War Between the States.

When he was 11-years-old, his mother, Mary Ellen Tetrick Short, died of typhoid fever, a great killer in the early days of Harrison County, leaving Charles and his sister Samantha Jane to be reared by their uncles: Charles by Marshall Tetrick and Samantha by Joseph Tetrick. Young Short worked hard on the Tetrick farm, 1½ miles north of Shinnston, handling horses, oxen and doing general farming work to earn his keep.

In 1885, after two years working in the planing mill, Short was made a foreman and sent, at the age of 22, to the south branch of Booth's Creek to build a brick house. The house still stands ½ mile north of the Shinnston exit of I-79. He worked for Richardson and Rowland three more years, until 1888, when he went out on his own to build homes. This was his life-long ambition. His first efforts resulted in a house on Rebecca Street directly across from the Shinnston Baptist Church. He worked and lived in this house while finishing it, but when he completed it he had to have a shop and place to store his material, so he bought the lot at the southwest corner of Pike and Station streets and built a two-story shop on the Pike Street end of the lot next to the alley. The other end of the lot was later occupied by his other dream; the Short Opera House, built in 1896, and designed to fill a much needed void. Also in this year he formed a company, including his cousin Everal Whiteman and Irvin Hartley, and built a planing mill on lower Station Street which proved to be a thriving operation. Then, just before the turn of the century, Whiteman left the firm and it became Short & Hartley.

In 1896, when Short moved his shop to the new big planing mill, it left the little shop to be occupied by Howard Harmer and his plumbing shop while the second floor was taken over, in 1902, by William Meredith and the Shinnston News. In 1894, Short had the contract to design and build the brick Shinnston Grade School on what is now Mahlon Street. The property was owned by David Shinn, who did not think it was a proper place for the school and refused to sell the land to the school board. Short was so sure it was the right location that he went to the Harrison County Court and had the property condemned, and made an enemy for life. On his deathbed he confessed to Charles that he was right. The next year Short built the Enterprise School from the same plans as the Shinnston School. In his time he built 14 different schools.

He was very active in the Methodist Protestant Church at Shinnston and was a trustee for 37 years and a trustee for the state conference to hold the bequest left to the MP Conference. He built the MP Church on Main Street in Shinnston in 1897, and the ME Church on Main Street that was replaced in 1980.

Short and his brother-in-law, Robert R. Hardesty, and Hugh Martin started the Shinnston Water Co. to get better fire protection and also to get a water supply for the residents of Shinnston by putting two large tanks on the hill behind the town and setting up a pumping station at the lower end of Charles Street. The river water was not too bad at that time, as the mines were not dumping large quantities of waste into the streams. This development also called for sewers in the town so Short ordered a carload of pipe. His partner questioned the wisdom of this, but Short pointed out to the citizens that they should enclose all of the open ditches into which they had been dumping water. In the middle of the year he had to order a second load of pipe. As workmen were installing a sewer at the home of David Shinn, Short reportedly said, "David, if you just let us put a line from the old well out there to the porch and into the kitchen sink with a little pitcher pump at the sink, the women won't have to go out in the cold in the winter to get water." Shinn responded, "Oh, Charley, you are going to make things so easy that the women won't want to do anything." Mrs. Shinn saw to it that her husband installed the little pitcher pump.

When natural gas was first found in the Shinnston area and the big companies started piping it out of state, some of the local people did not like to see the gas taken out, especially since they had to pay a high price to get part of it for local use. Short, Hardesty, Martin and Sam Edwards formed the Home Natural Gas Co. They drilled and developed a well field on Cunningham's Run in the Peora area, piped it into Shinnston and laid a line parallel to those of the larger companies.

Everyone had a chance to connect to the line of his choice. This company continued until the late 1920s, when it was joined with a similar company operated in Lumberport by the Hornor interests. The new company was called the Shinnston Lumberport Gas Co. which continues to operate today.

C. A. Short married Minnie May Smith, who was a direct descendant of Aaron Smith and Sarah Allen Smith, who were among the early settlers of Harrison County. Their forebears settled on lower Simpson Creek, in 1772, at the sight of Smith Chapel. They had three children.

Short was one of the original founders of the Farmers Bank of Shinnston and of the Peoples Bank that was taken over by the First National Bank of Shinnston. He built a business block on Pike Street and several other buildings.

Politically, Charles Short was always a Democrat. He served on the Shinnston City Council and was a candidate for county office on more than one occasion. Perhaps his biggest mistake in politics was the fact that he always ran on the Prohibitionist ticket. It was never successful in the state.

During the Depression when 4,747 pieces of property were being sold for 25 to 50 percent of their original value, Short, like many others in a similar position with little cash flow, closed his business and made an assignment of his assets to his creditors.

Short entered a new career as a bridge repairer for the West Virginia Department of Highways for many years and during the balance of his life estabished himself as an authority on covered bridges. He built many coal tipples and raised over 400 houses of all sizes.

During the Harrison County Bicentennial Year his work remains as a symbol of his energy, talent and ingenuity. He was a master builder.

On A Summer's Eve - There is No Better Concert Than a Chorus of Whippoorwills

BY JOHN RANDOLPH

On warm summer evenings, on the front porch after the chores were done, our family used to gather to share stories. In some cases, it may have been talk about the events of the day or the repeat of a good family tale that was some child's favorite.

Today we call it oral history, but when I was a child growing up on Indian Run, it was the entertainment of the day. Oh I don't think we ended up on the porch every evening for the radio shared some of our evenings. But, to sit and hear the whip-o-wills call to each other and the soft gentle tones of the adult voices, helped speed little minds to a high degree of imagination.

I can visualize Old Ed sitting on the edge of the big L-shaped porch with his feet dangled down over the front steps; us kids playing "bottom bump" up and down the steps, while the other adults found their favorite "settlin' " place.

Talk of the weather, the days chores, decisions about when the beans needed to be picked or how many old hens to butcher, all were discussed. But it wasn't until someone said,

155

"Do you remember when...?" that we "young'uns" would settle into someones' lap or squeeze in between someone on the old glider, because story time was about to begin.

"Reminds me of the time that a bunch of us guys was working up on the knob," began Ed. "We had just started cutting timber on the north slope when one of the boys found a little pile of bones in a hollow tree. We all went to see what they was but they didn't appear to be the bones of any animal we knew, the head was too round and the front feet looked more like hand bones than of feet bones. Old Sye Green said he'd figure them to be a baby painter (panther), but there was one or two of the fellows wasn't so sure they weren't human.

"Well we went on working and in a couple of weeks we pretty well had cleaned the knob off. They told us that the new owner was planning to make it into sheep pasture so we ended up having to remove the stumps too. We sure did work.

"There was a yell down over the hill and up ran Gus Gum."

"I found another holler tree,' said Gus, "and another pile of bones, sure does look like that other thing we found except its bigger. What ya think it is anyway?"

"Well this time we figured that maybe we should sack up this bunch of bones and take them down home and ask if anyone could tell what they was, seemed powerful funny that we'd find two sets of bones so close together.

"Old Maggie Sims came by as the discussion was taking place on the Gum front porch about the bones. Gums lived down there in the old Bennett place along the road, you know."

"Well, she got all upset and swore that they was childrens' bones."

"You found two different ones?" she asked.

"They'll be one more I tell you, one more!"

"Well she was right. There down next to the road, below the lower gap there was another old tree. When the boys cut it down, it was found to be hollow clear up all the way to the top, and they found another skull along with a few other bones, all of them look real old. All gray and pretty well dried away.

"Some of us took these and went to old Maggies who seemed to be the only one who knowed anything 'bout the story. She told how before, her great grandpa had lost four children and his first wife to the Indians, they lived in a house up on the knob. He had gone hunting and when he returned he found the youngest child laying across the fence scalped and the rest of the family gone. He tracked the Indians up the trail but lost them about halfway up the valley. Some time later he and his brother found his dead wife, poor soul, but they never did find the three little boys. I think we have found them dear Lord."

"The men were shocked, scared, mournful and mighty glad the job was over." How did the little boys get in the trees: Did the Indians kill them? Did they hide there? All the questions started at once when Old Ed finished his story. Moma interrupted.

"Enough now," she said, "bed time, go wash your feet and get upstairs."

We sauntered off mumbling about having to go to bed so soon, although we were all yawning with every step and as I lay there on top of the covers listening to the night sounds, I wondered to myself if Ed's story was about my valley. Was it about some family that lived here? And what did we do to make the Indians so mad? And just as I drifted off to sleep, I wondered if those night sounds really were Indians out there?

You could hear the adults begin to come in off the front porch.

"Want anything before you go to bed?" Moma asked, "there's still a little coffee on the stove."

And the tones of the voices blended into the hoot owls and the whip-o-wills. Still, yet today when the work is done and the evening is calm, the front porch is a favorite gathering place. We don't tell the tales like Ed did nor do we sit there as often as we used to, but it's still one of the most pleasant places in the world and there's no better concert than a chorus of whip-o-wills mingled with the voices of loved ones.

From Fort Nutter: It Became One of The Counties Thriving Communities

By LLOYD LEGGETT

In the mid to late 1700s, the fort was very important for settlers living in the Ohio Valley and inland areas including Harrison County. Many of today's communities were built on the site of a former forts. The area in which a fort was located was considered safe for it offered defense from Indians and provided a focal point for trade and frontier civilization. Fort Nutter was no exception.

Fort Nutter was built by Thomas Nutter in 1772. He was aided by his brothers John, Matthew, and Christopher Nutter.

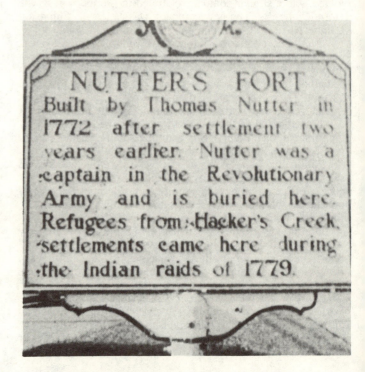

This fort, which was situated on the eastern bank of Elk Creek, served the pioneers mainly as a refuge.

When Thomas Nutter passed away, his sons, Elasia, Erwin and Christopher, inherited the Nutter estate which included the fort and much of the surrounding land.

Portions of the original Nutter Farm eventually fell to Thomas C. White, who sold 40 acres to a company that built the Fairground Park and the remainder of the land was purchased by the Jacobs Realty Company and Prunty Realty. Prunty Realty sold the land in lots.

When a community grows to a certain size (only a community itself determines the specific size) the need for some form of local government is felt to provide the basic community services. Police, fire protection, medical, garbage collection and utilities are more effective when based at the local level. The community around Fort Nutter continued to grow and the above mentioned services were desired by its population.

In May 1923, the Harrison County citizens living around the area of Fort Nutter voted to incorporate their community. They named it "Nutter Fort" in honor of Thomas Nutter.

seven days a week, 24 hours a day. This has reduced the crime rate in Nutter Fort to near zero. The maintenance department consists of five full-time workers along with three full-time workers in the waste department. These workers maintain the water and sewer lines, streets and the numerous other projects that keep the city operating and up to date. The office consists of three clerical workers to keep the city operating.

The volunteer fire department consists of men and women. The department has improved its equipment each year with the most recent purchase being a ladder truck.

Two banks in the county have located branches in Nutter Fort.

Approximately 91 acres were annexed by the city. Six new townhouses have been constructed, a motorcycle and mower sales company has started construction on a new building.

Nutter Fort continues to be a forward looking city. Its people desire, and usually receive the best services and protection. The future of Nutter Fort continues to look bright as new businesses move in and the population continues to take pride in the community.

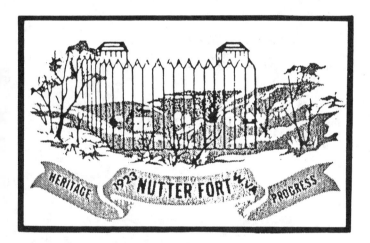

They chose the typical city government of mayor-council. The elected officials of Nutter Fort are the mayor, five council members, and a recorder. A city coordinator is appointed and serves under the mayor and council. In 1923, the first town election was held and Ralph Richards was elected as the first mayor of Nutter Fort. He served from 1923-1925.

The water system for the city was built in 1923. Sewers were added in 1927 and street lights were added in 1928. The citizens organized a volunteer fire department on May 25, 1927 called "the Fire Brigade," and elected J. S. Skidmore to serve as the first fire chief. In the early 1940s, a Works Progress Administration project financed the hard surfacing of most of the streets. A special levy election in May 1946 made possible the construction of the Municipal Building.

In the past ten years tremendous progress has been made in Nutter Fort improving facilities, expanding boundaries, improving streets and alleys, putting in additional recreational facilities, remodeling the Fire Department and Municipal Building, and attracting new business to the area. Revenue sharing made it possible to pave the streets and most of the alleys with asphaltic concrete.

In 1977 the town began its own waste collection service by purchasing mechanical equipment and waste containers.

With all the renovation going on, the police department has to keep up with the city's growth. The city has grown from one police officer to a chief and five full-time officers working

The Bicentennial Committee, Library Honoring 'Top 10' Nationally-Known State Natives

By MYRA LITHERLAND

In the bright, airy, booklined expanses of the Clarksburg-/Harrison Public Library, there's a "Top 10" currently being touted.

The compilation has nothing to do with rock groups, pop singers or country music performers, but the names on the list are fully as familiar to most Harrison Countians as those of today's superstars.

Each person represented is a native of West Virginia — 10 of them, to be exact — who has gained national prominence in his or her particular field of endeavor, and their individual lives and achievements are the focus of the National Figures of Harrison County exhibit, sponsored by the Harrison County Bicentennial Committee and the Clarksburg/Harrison Public Library, with funding by the Humanities Foundation of West Virginia.

Additional funding comes from a state program of the National Endowment for the Humanities and by the Consolidated Gas Transmission Corporation.

The "Top 10" personalities come from all walks of life and several different eras, but although their areas of expertise are wide-ranging, they all have a common denominator —they all hailed from West Virginia, and many from Harrison County.

The selection was far from easy, according to James Pool, project director of the Harrison County Bicentennial, because the area has produced many illustrious people.

Through a "process of elimination," however, members of the exhibit committee reviewed the information available and ultimately made their selections.

"There were several whom we considered, but didn't select — Nathan Goff was one," Pool explained.

"But we had to bear in mind the exhibits and the material we had at our disposal. With some, all we had were books to display and we wanted a little more variety. We just had to work with what we had.

"I think the combination has worked out very well, though, because the end result is a representative sampling," he concluded.

Members of the National Figures of Harrison County Exhibit Committee are Merle Moore, co-chairperson; Lloyd Leggett, co-chairperson; Regina Hardman, Carolyn Sirk, Virginia Orvedahl and Gale Price.

The unusual exhibit, featuring displays of photographs, historic memorabilia, video and audio presentations, is situated on both the upper and lower levels of the library and will remain open to the public through October.

In the library lobby, the location of each display is diagramed on a large board.

The outstanding West Virginians highlighted in the presentation are:

MELVILLE DAVISSON POST, West Virginia author who created the mystery novel characters, " Uncler Abner" and "Randolph Mason", thought by some to be the forerunner to the famous "Perry Mason".

At one point in his life, he was the highest-paid fiction writer in America.

Post earned his law degree in 1892 and practiced law for some years in Wheeling and Grafton., but in his early years as a lawyer began writing, and in 1896, his "Strange Schemes of Randolph Mason" was published.

He introduced "Uncle Abner" in the June 3, 1911, issue of the "Saturday Evening Post", in a short story.

From that point, his creative mind enabled him to author story after story that the reading public enthusiastically recieved.

The Post exhibit, situated on the ground level of the library, features various books, photographs and memorabilia dealing with his life.

SENATOR JENNINGS RANDOLPH, popular United States senator, well known not only for major pieces of legislation, but for a career that has personified all that a senator should accomplish.

Because of his activities on behalf of those in need, he earned the title of "Humanistic Senator".

A native of Salem, he was born in 1902, the son of Ernest and Idell (Bingman) Randolph, he was a graduate of both Salem Academy and Salem College in the 1920s.

After sucessful careers as an educator, author and public relations director, in 1932 Randolph entered into politics with his election to the U.S. House of Representatives as a Democrat. He served seven successive terms before being elected to the U.S. Senate to complete a three-year term in 1958. Two years later, he won a full term and has been subsequently re-elected since. The senator plans to retire this year, upon expiration of his term of office.

The Senator Jenning Randolph exhibit, located on the upper level of the library, features a vast array of fascinating photographs which trace the senator's life and career.

THOMAS JONATHAN "STONEWALL" JACKSON, brilliant Conferedate commander during the War Between the

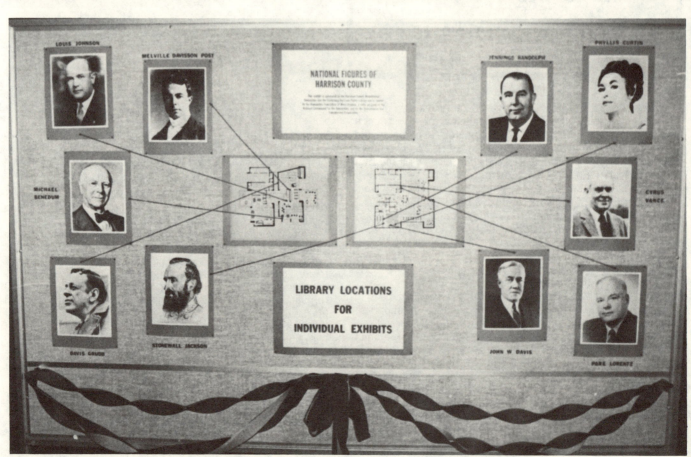

States.

Jackson was born Jan. 21, 1824 on main street in Clarksburg, the son of Jonathan and Julia Beckwith Neale Jackson.

His illustrious carrer ended in death, when wounded by his own troops at the battle of Chancellorsville in 1863, he succumbed to pneumonia.

Jackson was a gentle commander whose tactical brilliance was not only a great asset to the Confederate cause, but his battlefield innovations are still studied to this day.

The Stonewall Jackson exhibit is one of the most interesting of the group, and a delight to Civil War buffs. I features such items as a Confederate bond, Dated Feb. 20, 1863, which contains $35 coupons — one of which has been clipped — and a map outlining the general's movements during the 1861-1863 period of his military life from his departure from Virginia Military Institute in Lexington, Va., from where he left his teaching post at the onset of the war, to the return of his body for burial there.

In addition, the display offers a wide variety of fascinating photographs.

DAVIS GRUBB, Outstanding West Virginia novelist.

Grubb was a native of Moundsville, and from early childhood was well-aquainted with river lore and the legendary rouges and rascals of the region.

He chose literature as his career at the age of seven, and ultimately became the author of a variety of intriguing macabre literature which has delighted readers.

In his novel "The Night of the Hunter", it is believed that Grubb patterned his main character after Harry Powers, the heartless killer of two women and three children at Quiet Dell.

The Davis Grubb exhibit features and array of memorabilia, highlighted by his first attempt at writing a book he authored as a 7-year-old. Grubb not only wrote the book, but illustrated it, as well, right down to his renderings of newspaper front pages.

PHYLLIS CURTIN, world-famous operatic soprano.

Born in clarksburg, the daughter of Vernon and Betty Smith, she debuted at Town Hall in New York in 1950.

Selected as Woman of the Year in 1968, the gifted Phyllis Curtin has acclaimed as one of the most talented singers in the world. Her creative energies were recognized in 1959 when she was selected as one of 10 concert artists to receive a grant from the Ford Foundation program for stimulating creative developement in music.

The Phyllis Curtin display features a multitude of photographs tracing her life and career.

PARE LORENTZ, nationally-known writer, film critic and producer.

Born in Clarksburg in 1905. Lorentz gained wide recognition from his movies. His greatest triumph has been to make documentary films of such high quality that they have been shown on commercial movie screens around the country.

In conjunction with the National Figures exhibit, a series of Lorentz films is currently being shown each Thursday at both the library and Waldomore. They will continue until October 25.

MICHAEL LATE BENEDUM, oilcatter, businessman and philanthropist.

Born in Bridgeport in 1869, he drilled his first well on Whiskey Run in Pleasants County in 1896.

Other strikes occured in Oklahoma and Illinois. He discovered the Caddo Field in Louisianna, the Tuxpam Field in Mexico, the Tropical Oil Fileld in Columbia, Big Lake Field which opened the most sensational strike, the Yates Pool west of the Pecos River in Texas.

He was best known for his large gifts and the benevolence directed through the memorial to his son, the Claude Worthington Benedum Foundation.

JOHN W. DAVIS, Democratic candidate for President of the United States in 1924.

Davis, born in Clarksburg in 1873, was a corporate lawyer, ambassador, presidential contender, New York millionaire and world renowned figure.

Elected as a member of the United States House of Representatives from 1911 to 1913. Davis also served as solictor general of the United States—during which he argued more cases before the United States Supreme Court than any other lawyer with the possible exception of Daniel Webster—and ambassador to Great Britian prior to his unsuccesful campaign. Davis overwhelmingly defeated by Calvin Coolige's 15,700,000 popular votes and 382 electorial votes against his own 8,400,000 popular and 136 electorial votes, failed to carry any state in the Union and did not carry his own precinct.

The Davis exhibit contain a fine exhibit of photographs taken in Clarksburg on August 11, 1924, when Davis delivered his acceptance speech in the city.

LOUIS A. JOHNSON, whose career in both the armed forces and government posts earned him worldwide praise and respect. Today, The Veterans Administration Medical Center in Clarksburg bears his name.

Born in Roanoake Jan. 10, 1891, he migrated to Clarksburg, where, in 1914, he formed a partnership with Philip Steptoe to establish the firm of Steptoe and Johnson.

Johnson was elected to the West Virginia house of Delegates a year prior to his entering the armed forces in 1917. During World War I he served overseas and was decorated a commander of the Legion of Honor in France.

He was one of the organizers of the American Legion, ultimately being elected national commander in 1932.

In addition, he served as assistant secretary of war, and was appointed a personal represenative of President Roosevelt in India. While there, he formed a lasting friendship with Jawaharial Nehru, leader of the country.

Johnson was engaged in pastwar corporate activities when President Harry S. Truman appointed him secretary of defense, a post he held until late 1950.

The Louis A. Johnson Exhibit contains a wide array of memorabilia from his long career, and includes letters from both Nehru and John W. Davis, following the candidates campaign.

CYRUS ROBERT VANCE, a lawyer-diplomat best known for his service as secretary of state under former President Jimmy Carter.

Vance was born in Clarksburg in 1917 and served as secretary of the Army and special represenative of the president in both the Cyprus incident of 1967, and in negotions with Korea in 1968.

Vance, who expressed the desire to be a "stay at home" secretary of state, logged 295,225 miles of travel during the first two years in office.

He was honored by the American Institute for Public Service in 1980 with the Jefferson Award for " the greatest public service by an elected official".

The Cryus Vance exhibit features an interesting collection of material featuring his life and career.

Gov. Howard M. Gore - Known As Road Building Governor of West Virginia

BY NEVA WEEKS

A farmer, a stockman, a businessman and a governor — Howard Mason Gore was born Oct. 12, 1877, in Harrison County, about three miles north of Clarksburg in the Rt. 19 north area today known as Gore. He was the son of Solomon D. Gore who came over the Alleghenies in the Fall of 1846. His ancestors on his mother's side of the family had been farmers in that region since the Revolutionary War period.

He was graduated from Clarksburg public schools and in 1900 he received a degree in agriculture from West Virginia University. During his life he was a banker and owner/operator of the Gore Hotel in Clarksburg but his chief interest was always in farming.

On Sept. 30, 1906, he married Roxie C. Bailey of Taylor County. She died approximately five months later. He never remarried.

After the death of his father on Nov. 19, 1907, Gore took over the management of the farm. He became nationally known for his methods of cultivation and his development of beef cattle.

During World War I he was Assistant Food Administrator for West Virginia and in 1920, he was named to the state Board of Education, a post he held until he was inaugurated governor.

In 1921 at the request of a national farm organization, he did some special work for the U.S. Department of Agriculture in Washington. After completion of that project, he was made chief of the trade practice division of the Packers and Stockyards Administration. He later helped organize and build the Union Stock Sales in Parkersburg and also the Weston Stock Sales, as well as helping in other cities with their livestock sales companies.

After learning of Gore's good work, President Coolidge appointed him Assistant Secretary of Agriculture on Sept. 17, 1923. He still held the post when he made the race for the Republican nomination for governor in 1924. Soon after he was nominated in May, Agriculture Secretary Henry A. Wallace died. At Coolidge's request, Gore returned to Washington as acting head of the Department of Agriculture. His friends ran his campaign for election as governor.

A short time after he was elected governor in November 1924, the President named him Secretary of Agriculture. He continued in that position until the very day of his inauguration as governor on March 4, 1925, and he left the Cabinet of President Coolidge to become "the road building governor" of the State of West Virginia. He arrived in Charleston by train from Washington at 6:45 a.m. and was taken to a downtown hotel, where he waited until time to participate in the noon parade. More than 25,000 persons witnessed the parade.

Because the state capitol was under construction, the inauguration of Gov. Gore took place on the balcony of the

capitol annex on the site where the capitol burned in 1921.

Judge Frank Lively, president of the state Supreme Court, administered the oath of office. The new chief executive kissed the Bible used in the oath-taking ceremony and bowed to a huge crowd, and they gave him a burst of applause. He looked out at those who had jammed the streets and dotted the old Capitol grounds. All that was left of the old Capitol was a yawning chasm that was once a basement and the two brick-encased vaults. Boys climbed trees on the old capitol grounds to get a glimpse of the new governor. He then adjusted his glasses and read a brief inaugural address. "You ask what is my policy and what is my program," he said. "I have no policy save the rule of right and reason. My program is to apply these principles to the solution of each issue as it comes before us for consideration." Through the remainder of his address he let it be known that he wanted to be close to the people.

Throughout most of Gore's term, construction of the new state Capitol continued at the new location in the East End of the city. The completed West Wing was formally received by the state Capitol Building Commission on April 24, 1925. State departments started moving in immediately. The governor had served scarcely a year when the temporary Capitol in downtown Charleston caught fire and burned to the ground. There were no serious casualties but it was the second Capitol fire in state history. The first one occurred six years and two months earlier on Jan, 3, 1921.

Gore continued and expanded the highway construction program started under the previous administration. Funds were made available under the $50 million Good Roads Amendment passed in 1920. In 1928, before Gore left office, the people approved another road bond issue of $35 million and additional revenue was gained through an increase in gasoline tax.

Gov. Gore may be the only governor who won a legislative appropriation by making senators cry. A Clarksburg newspaper carried an account of Gore's method of getting the appropriation after he made a personal visit to the coal fields and "found little children so weak from hunger that they could not stand. He found expectant mothers undernourished and the old and feeble in an equal state of want and misery."

Gov. Gore returned to Charleston a sick man. He contracted a severe cold on his trip. A few days later he had pneumonia and for a time physicians feared for his life.

He sent word to the state legislature then in session and asked for a special appropriation to help the deplorable conditions in the mining camps. But the legislature took no action. By this time he had lost patience with the legislature and told them what he wanted. Running a high fever and weakened, the governor staggered from his room and started to the legislative chambers. On his way he met a group of senators.

Aghast at the governor's appearance, they asked him why he was out of bed. He immediately told them that he had been unable to impress the legislature, which was near adjournment, with the fact that he wanted relief for the starving people of the state.

With tears in their eyes, the senators told Gov. Gore to return to his bed and rest easily. Before midnight the relief measures had been passed. Toward morning the report came that the governor had passed the crisis and would recover.

In 1931, Gov. William G. Conley appointed Gore as Commissioner of Agriculture, a post that he held for several years.

Through the remaining years, he continued with his main business interests and was appointed to the Public Service Commission by Gov. M. M. Neely, a term that lasted until May 31, 1947.

Gov. Gore's hobby was flowers. Knowing that and also of his fondness for his mother, friends in the state Agriculture Department named a newly-developed carnation "Mother Gore."

At 2 a.m., on June 20, 1947, the 84th birthday of the state, Gov. Gore died of a heart ailment in St. Marys Hospital, Clarksburg. He was 69. The body of the 17th governor was entombed in a mausoleum in Elkview Masonic Cemetery, Clarksburg.

Sirus Orestes Bond - Teacher, Was The 6th President of Salem College

MRS. CREEL CORNWELL SR.

Sirus Orestes Bond, whose active career was one of close and constructive association with education in his native state culminating in his becoming the sixth president of Salem College, was born Aug. 12, 1877 on a farm in the Hacker's Creek section of Upshur County. He was the son of Levi Davis Bond and Victoria Arnold Bond. His father passed his entire life in Upshur County where he was an exponent of progressive farming, giving special attention to the breeding and raising of full-blooded Hereford cattle. His father and he were among the first to introduce this breed of cattle into West Virginia.

Dr. Bond was a grandson of Brumfield Bond, one of the early settlers of Harrison County, and as a boy lived what might be termed a typical life on a West Virginia farm until he was ready to attend Salem College. His formal education began in a rural school near the farm. The school term was four months. In his last year the term was increased by state law to five months. In addition to these years of elementary schooling, he attended a number of what were called "select" schools. In these spring terms such subjects as higher arithmetic, advanced grammar, and advanced history were taught. The advanced arithmetic used was *Ray's Fourth Arithmetic,* which was considered difficult and introduced algebra and some geometry.

Bond made up his mind he would like to become a school teacher. At the close of this advanced term, he and three or four other boys agreed to meet at the school building two

nights a week and review the subjects on which they would be required to pass examination if they wanted to teach. The plan of work was that each boy should prepare a list of questions covering a given subject. One of the boys found an advertisement for a book, *1,001 Questions on Elementary School Subjects*. He ordered it and they drilled very thoroughly on those questions and also on the ones they themselves had prepared. In the latter part of August when the teachers' examinations were held, this young man went to a neighboring county where the salary was four dollars per month more. He took the examination there and received a Class I certificate.

Later having been notified of the certificate, Bond contacted the trustees of a rural school about 2½ miles from his home. The teacher had already been hired. The trustees, however, told him that there was another school farther down the creek that had no teacher. They said it was a rather difficult one to teach. The last two or three teachers were unable to finish the term because the older boys could not be controlled. Bond wondered whether at 18 he could be called a man-teacher. In any case, he acepted the school and taught his first term at lower Jesse's Run in Lewis County.

After the close of the first year's school, Bond attended Salem College for the spring term. He repeated that the next year and then attended college for a full year. That summer he accepted an invitation to be the teacher of a two-teacher school and remained there for two years, going to college each spring term. Then he attended his second full year and continued until he received a degree in 1904. At that time arrangements were made and shortly after commencement day Bond and Venie E. Hagerty of Sardis were married by the president of Salem College Dr. Theodore L. Gardiner.

During the years 1904-06, Bond was principal of the Shinnston Schools, where he taught high school subjects to the advanced students. The next year he was principal of the East Side School in Fairmont. He received his AB from West Virginia University in 1909. From there he went to Mingo County in the southern part of the state where he had charge of the Lee District High School. At the end of the term he returned north. He secured a position as principal of the schools at Flemington. There he originated and organized the first school fair ever held in West Virginia.

After three years at Flemington, Bond resigned and went to Columbia University where he spent two years. At the end of the first year he received a master's degree in 1913, and during the second year he completed the resident requirements for a doctorate.

The second year at Columbia a group of young men, expecting to go into the administrative work in the schools, prevailed upon Dean James E. Russell to teach a class in school administration for teachers. The group was limited to ten. The course was so practical that three of the ten men later became presidents of liberal arts colleges. Three became administrators of colleges primarily for teachers, two later went into the Bureau of Education in Washington. One succeeded his father as dean of the Teachers' College of Columbia and later became its president.

The summer following Bond's return from Columbia was spent as the previous summers in conducting the summer teachers' institute in West Virginia. This service was continued every summer for 12 years in 45 counties.

This same summer, 1914, Bond was asked to take the presidency of Glenville State Normal School but this plan did not materialize. Bond went to the State Normal School at Shepherdstown in 1915 as a teacher and superintendent of district schools.

In spring 1918 Bond took a teaching position for the summer term at Salem College. He was to receive a small stipend for the term, the amount of which would be determined by the number of students attending.

On the Sunday evening that Bond arrived in Salem the Salem College president's secretary called to say that the president had to leave town due to the illness of his father, and Bond was to open the school the following morning.

The newcomer had no thought in mind that he was beginning a service that would continue through the next 32 years.

The president did not return for some weeks. When he did, he attended a chapel program and spoke, giving a sort of overview of the things he had accomplished in his 11 years at Salem. There was no evidence that he meant to give anyone an idea that this resignation as head of the college was in his mind. The next evening he called Bond to his office, told him he must return to his native Michigan and asked the new teacher to continue in charge of the school and manage it following his resignation.

Bond made plans to remain the following year. An agreement with the board of directors gave Bond a yearly salary of $2,400, $600 of which would be returned to the college as rent for the president's home.

The earlier years of Bond's administration could be called a fortunate beginning. Now the college had its first dean and its first coach. There was a great demand for the training of teachers but the darkest days of the college were still ahead. World War I came to an end. Soldiers sought an education but had little money. The college debts increased.

Many teachers wanted to take further college courses, but needed to continue teaching in their communities. Dr. Bond came up wth the idea of extension courses. Classes were organized in Clarksburg four nights a week and he taught the classes. Since there were no paved roads between Salem and Clarksburg, he traveled to Clarksburg on the 5 p.m. train and returned to Salem on the midnight train. The extension work which was begun in 1919 continued for many years as an opportunity for teachers.

In 1922-23 the graduating class was the largest that the college had known. Twenty-five students received BA degrees, eight young women received home economic certification and 22 received the standard normal diploma, 53 were given short normal certificates and six received diplomas in voice and piano.

By 1925, however, Salem College had continued to grow and President Bond stated that it was the duty of the college to train for leadership. In 1924-25 there were 902 students enrolled. The graduating class numbered 179 persons. A number of physical improvements were made by friends of the college. The graduating class painted the gymnasium, several citizens gave flowers and shrubs, and the Busy Bee Barber Shop placed a large clock in Huffman Hall.

When the college was first established, Salem was a little village of not more than 500 or 600 persons, but by 1932 it was a small city of 3,000. The demand for education changed the total enrollment of the college from 200 to 1,000.

The year 1932 brought heavy financial losses. The gymnasium burned on March 11. March was also the month that the banks closed. This affected the college greatly. The seven years following 1929 were the most difficult years that most small colleges faced, but Salem survived adversity and grew under the steady leadership of Dr. Bond during the Second World War.

Commencement for 1944 proved to be one of the most interesting ever held. The speaker for commencement morning was Eleanor Roosevelt. Her subject was "The Value of Christian Colleges" and the attendance was the largest for any commencement. On the evening preceding the commencement day exercise an alumni banquet was held at which President and Mrs. Bond were honored for his 25 years of service.

The 1944-45 school year seems to have been a demarcation point for Salem College. It marked a change in outlook from one of discouragement to hope. The financial condition of the college was good. The year closing May 28, 1946 was one of transition from wartime to peacetime conditions. Many returning soldiers enrolled and the years from 1947 to 1951 were termed the Golden Age of Dr. Bond's administration.

The progress of those years is reflected in a number of ways. The enrollment grew to 1,200 in 1951. After the war ended the government agreed that a considerable amount of equipment belonging to the Armed Forces might be distributed to various colleges according to their special need. Salem College secured a large quota including 25 house trailers to accomodate student-veterans who had families.

On commencement day 1951 at the close of his annual statement President Bond said, ''I like the expression that comes from the Bible — 'A thousand years in His sight are but as yesterday when it is passed, and as a watch in the night.' To me the 32 years which I have served here seem like a pleasant dream during a watch in the night. I have already thrown the torch. It has been caught by a young man on the Pacific Coast... the morrow's new president of Salem College —K. Duane Hurley.''

So closed the administration of the sixth president of Salem College, Dr. Sirus Orestes Bond.

Dr. Bond's second love was livestock raising. This he retained from his Hacker's Creek youth. It was a major interest throughout his life and he was the oldest continuous breeder of Hereford cattle in the state. His father established the first Hereford breeding farm in the northern part of West Virginia in 1884. When his father was ready to dispose of the cattle because of age and ill heath, Bond and his brother formed a partnership which continued for 37 years. When the brother died in 1937, the younger son took over the interest and the business continued as Green Acres Herefore Farm. Bond had more than 70 years of active contact with the registered Hereford cattle business.

At the time of his death Dr. Bond was 81-years-old. He had lived a life of unselfish sacrifice for the benefit of his fellow man.

The Legend of the Haunted House Lives in County

BY RUTH ANN MUSICK

On a hill in Harrison County stands an old abandoned house. It is a pretty, white house, with a large yard, and in the summer it is surrounded by many kinds of flowers. This house has been empty for a little over a year.

It is not a spooky-looking place that everyone would be afraid of, but for some reason none of the families who have bought it have lived there more than a month, in spite of its beautiful location. Some people believe the house is haunted.

This legend was probably strengthened one rainy night when Lee Harris, a traveling salesman, was passing through that section. He had a flat tire just down the road from the house. Seeing a light in the window, he decided to ask the people who lived there if he could use their telephone to call a repair station.

A very beautiful woman opened the door. Her hair was golden blonde and waved down her back; her eyes were as blue as the sky on a bright spring day; indeed, the man was enchanted by her many charms. She was joined at the door by three small children, bright-eyed and much like their mother. The salesman called a repair shop and found that a bridge had been washed away, and no one could come to fix the tire until the next morning.

When Lee explained where he was, the man did not believe that a woman and three children were in the house; he told the salesman to get away from the place as soon as possible — to sleep in his car, if he had to. Lee could not understand this because the woman treated him so nicely. She offered him a cup of coffee and told him he could spend the night in her house — and he accepted her hospitality.

He had a very comfortable night until about 12:30, when he heard the children screaming. At first he thought they were having youthful nightmares and would soon go back to sleep. But the screaming persisted, and he decided the woman could use some help in getting the youngsters quieted.

When he got downstairs, he was amazed at what he saw. It was the same beautiful woman he had encountered just a few hours before, but she looked entirely different — thin, rough, and almost ugly. Her once beautiful bright eyes were darkened and glassy with a look of torture. The children, now wearing ragged clothing, were not even clean, and they were crying from hunger.

Lee spoke to the woman and asked why she didn't feed the youngsters, but she only kept on screaming at them and begging them not to cry, as though she hadn't heard him speak to her at all. He walked over and touched her arm, trying to keep her from the children. When he touched her flesh, he found it was cold, as if in death. Could it be that all of them were dead? Lee used all his strength in trying to keep her from harming her offspring, but nothing he did seemed to stop her.

Finally she led the little ones out the back door. Lee followed them, sorry for the children and curious. He saw the woman line them up according to their ages. She took the smallest, who was about two years old, and led him by the neck to the well. Lee rushed to her but it was too late; she had murdered the little boy, once bright-eyed and happy. Lee

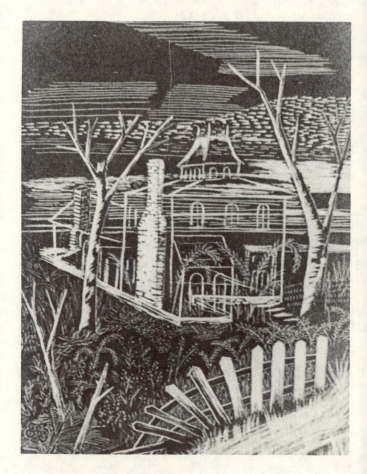

turned to the other children but with all his power he could not move them from their positions. The woman took the next child, who was about four, and proceeded to do the same with her; the five-year-old was next. After this she knelt by the well and began praying to God to look after her beautiful children. She did love them so, but she had no money and could not bear to see them tortured by starvation.

The woman then rushed into the house and cut her wrists. She died on the kitchen floor. Lee went upstairs to get a blanket to lay over her, but when he returned, the body had disappeared. He looked everywhere, but it was gone. There was only the stillness of the early morning and the sun coming through the window.

When the man from the service station finally came that morning, he was surprised to find Lee in the house. He said the house was haunted — that everyone who moved into it heard the voices of children screaming as though they were in pain. Lee asked about the lovely woman, but the repairman didn't seem to know anything about any woman living in the house with three children.

Lee did not tell the man about what he had seem, but he felt he had learned the real story behind the haunted house — and perhaps he had.

Michael Late Benedum - Oil 'Wildcatter', Remembered His West Virginia Heratige

BY SHARON R. SAYE

If there is any key to the career of Michael Benedum it might be faith — faith in himself, his fellowmen, his country and his God. His life was not an endless series of successes; he faced bankruptcy twice, nearly lost his arm in a milling accident, and he and his wife suffered the loss of their only child during World War I. But he still had faith. Benedum, himself, said, "I've had no ulcers because I've had confidence, faith and patience to carry me through. If half-way up an obstacle I'd meet a streak of bad luck I kept right on going 'til I was over the top."

Benedum was well aware of where he had learned these valuable lessons. In his dedication of the Benedum Civic Center in 1956 he spoke of his hometown. "This is home. It is where the foundation was laid for all that I am or ever hope to be. Here is the anchor to which I have been moored for eighty-seven years. No matter how far away I have gone, I have always been securely fastened to that anchor by the chains of faith and sentiment."

Bridgeport was a small rural community when he was born on July 16, 1869, the youngest son of Emanuel and Caroline Southworth Benedum. He was named for the family doctor who delivered him, Dr. William Michael Late. Emanuel Benedum was an important member of the Bridgeport community and was affectionately known as "Squire." He was a local general store owner and cabinetmaker. By the 1880s the Benedums were forced to sell the store to pay debts brought on by a worsening economy. Emanuel had dreamed of sending Michael to West Point where he could become another Stonewall Jackson, but at sixteen Michael was forced to take a job at John Davidson's mill to help the family's financial situation. Even years later Emanuel was deploring this lost opportunity. "Mike would have made a great general," he'd say.

By the age of twenty Benedum was managing a mill in Lumberport when tragedy struck. His shirt sleeve caught in the cogwheels of the machinery and his right arm was dragged up to the shoulder into the gears. It took an hour to dismantle the machinery so Mike's arm could be freed. He returned to Dr. Late for treatment, but it was many months before he could work.

A chance encounter on the train to Parkersburg in 1890 when Benedum courteously offered his seat to a harried middle-aged gentleman changed the course of his life. The man was John Worthington, General Superintendent of the South Penn Oil Company, a subsidiary of Standard Oil. He offered Mike a job in the oil business. "Is there a future in it?" asked Mike. "Oh, yes, there's a future." replied Worthington. "Thank you, sir; I'll do it." Thus began a career in the oil business so unique that the American Petroleum Industry named him "The Oil Man of the Century."

South Penn employed him to obtain oil leases from West Virginia farmers; with his farming and milling background, intelligence and charm he managed to obtain leases that Worthington thought were impossible. Benedum took advantage of his opportunities; he learned the oil business thoroughly from experts and made friends throughout the industry. He met Joseph Clifton Trees, an engineer, and formed what was to be a life-long partnership when they drilled their first well in Pleasants County. His leases on 1,500 acres near Cameron proved to be a bonanza. When South Penn realized the potential in the Cameron area they tried to break Benedum financially, but he fought back, a gallant, twenty-seven-year-old independent against one of the nation's largest corporations. He won. He sold the leases to Standard for $400,000 only one year after buying them for $7,500.

At his brother's behest, he invested part of the new money in pottery and glass manufacturing and in the First Citizen's Bank of Cameron. The companies and bank failed. Joe Trees told him, "You were a fool to gamble with such dangerous things as banking and manufacturing. You should have put all your money in a safe business like oil." Undaunted, Benedum started over, but this time he put his faith in what he knew best, the oil business.

Trees was not the only partnership Benedum formed at this time. While obtaining leases for South Penn he met a farmer, John W. Lantz, from near Blacksville. Invited to dinner he was impressed with Sarah, the only daughter. They were married on May 17, 1896; a son, Claude Worthington Benedum, was born in 1897. Claude enlisted in the Army Chemical Warfare Corps in World War I and died of pneumonia on Oct. 18, 1918. His death devastated both his parents who established the Claude Worthington Benedum Foundation in 1944 in his memory. Michael left a substantial portion of his estate to the foundation; seventy-five percent of the activity of the foundation must be used to benefit his native state of West Virginia. Over four million dollars is distributed to institutions and organizations every year in memory of Benedum's son.

In 1904, Benedum and Trees trusted their wildcatting instincts despite advice from John Worthington that the Illinois area was "no good." A chance meeting with a geologist in a hotel lobby who swore that Illinois was "oil country" confirmed their hunch. They leased 50,000 acres and hit gushers that produced 2,000 barrels a day. Eventually they netted eight million dollars from the Illinois fields that were "no good."

Benedum and Trees were explorers and gamblers, forever drawn to the next challenge. They struck oil in Oklahoma, Louisiana, Mexico, California, Colombia, Rumania and Texas. Texas is a classic example of Mike Benedum's faith. Having hit it big in the Ranger and Desdemona fields, Benedum bought out his associates and formed the Transcontinental Oil Company. Within months his new empire was in a state of collapse. He forged ahead, looking for new fields. He felt an obligation to the people who believed in him. "A

wildcatter can't quit, no matter how enormous the odds against him. The oil's there waiting, but it won't show itself unless you seek it and seek it strenuously.''

In 1924 only Benedum had confidence when Frank Pickrell came to him with a deal to drill wells in West Texas. Despite its reputation as the petroleum graveyard of Texas, Benedum formed a company and began drilling in the Big Lake area. When six of the eight test wells were dry and the remainder only produced 12 to 15 barrels a day it looked like another failure. But Benedum wouldn't quit; he drilled again at Santa Rita and discovered the great Permian basin where over 10 billion barrels of oil were produced in the next thirty years.

Despite his travels and wealth he never forgot his hometown of Bridgeport. He funded several major projects including the Bridgeport Cemetery, the Bridgeport United Methodist Church and the Benedum Civic Center. The exterior of the Civic Center is a replica of Mike's birthplace and is built on the original site on Main Street.

Benedum always emphasized what he received from his hometown and state rather than what he gave. At the dedication of the Civic Center in 1956 he spoke of both the past and the future. ''No doubt some of you wonder why I say that I was possessed of as much real wealth when I left Bridgeport as a boy of 21 as I am today. I left here to find my destiny with the rich heritage of a good name, with a solid foundation of religious principles instilled in me by my parents and other good people of this community. No boy ever left any background of greater material wealth with more; many have gone forth from palaces with much less... I cannot see this community today through the same eyes that most of you do. You look upon it as the modern, progressive and rapidly growing city that it is, but I see it through the eyes of the boy who swam and fished in Simpson Creek, who drove cows where your modern airplanes now land, and who hoed corn where business houses now stand... I pledge you that I will continue to try to keep the faith and when the race is finally over I shall hand the torch to the next generation of my family, confident that they will hold it high.''

Michael Benedum never retired and was looking for oil in Cuba when he died on July 30, 1959. He kept right on going 'til the end.

Dolans Created Sunny Croft With Plow and Horses

BY JIM SCOLAPIO

It was a period of civil strife; Abraham Lincoln was President of the United States, and the topic of slavery was an issue; it was a time during which John Brown seized the federal arsenal at Harpers Ferry and West Virginia was still part of Virginia. Closer to home, it was the era when John S. Carlile was taking charge of the Unionist movement in the northwest and leading the spirit responsible for the Clarksburg Convention of 1861, which was one of the first steps in West Virginia's gaining her statehood. During this period a man from Ireland found his way to the United States. It was here in America that Patrick Donlan purchased land and raised cattle. After coming to the United States, Patrick settled in the Wolf Summit area. East of Wolf Summit, he also purchased 300 acres of land that would become a local area landmark.

The "Roaring Twenties," also called the Jazz Age, was a decade of prosperity for many Americans. It was a time of hope and promise; a time of the "Tin Lizzie" and the period in history when Lindbergh flew non-stop from New York to Paris in the Spirit of St. Louis. People of this time were also aware of sports figures such as "Red" Grange, the Galloping

Ghost, and boxers such as Jack Dempsey and Gene Tunney. On the golf course, Bobby Jones and Walter Hagan were setting record after record. The Jazz Age, the time of prosperity, ended in October, 1929, with the stock market crash. Thousands found themselves without work. Poverty and hunger spread faster than the plague. Fathers and mothers could no longer provide for their families. Hoovervilles and Hoover Ham became popular and the Bonus Army staged a hunger march to Washington. It was during this period in history that the grandsons of Patrick Dolan, James and John Dolan, Jr., were asking friends if they thought it was a good idea to build a golf course. While the friends expressed their approval, it is interesting to note that at this point in history, the opportunity to build a golf course was very rare. Due to the depression, the golf course might never have been built, but this was not the case for on November 7, 1932, ground was broken for a new nine-hole course in Harrison County.

A man from England laid out the course and gave the course its name. Jimmy Spencer, born in Epson, England, came to this country in 1908 and worked as a golf professional at New Britain, Connecticut. In the early 1930's, he came to the Dolan farm and laid out a nine-hole golf course. Spencer gave the name Sunny Croft to the 6,075 yard course. Croft is an English word which means a ''small farm.''

With plow and horses, many young men went to work carving the fertile soil and hillsides, creating a place where a game the Indians started would be played. The men who had families were paid under Roosevelt's New Deal Program, the WPA. The young future caddies were paid nothing. They were only granted the opportunity to carry the members' clubs for 25 cents. They were also promised life-time memberships which never materialized. The caddies worked long and hard. They could carry dirt many yards to build mounds which they would later shape into greens. They often lined up in rows in the fairways and walked back and forth picking up rocks and other debris that they found on the new fairways.

The course was originally designed for eighteen holes, and in 1938, construction of another nine holes was already laid out and underway, but due to the economic conditions of the time, only nine holes were constructed. The estimated cost of building the course was approximately $1,000 a green. After approximately a year, the greens were sown, and although people occasionally played on the unfinished course earlier, the course was officially opened when John Dolan, Sr. hit a ball off the first tee on May 30, 1934.

The first golfers played on hard greens since they lacked a proper base, and many times, they found themselves chipping with their wooden shafted clubs from behind a stubbled corn stalk. As time went by, improvements were made. Coral rock was brought from Buckhannon to base the greens, and the stubbed corn stalks became obsolete. The course's first water system consisted of a two-inch gas pipe, and the players often remarked that the water tasted of gas. The grass planted on the fairways and greens was Kentucky Blue, Susa and Pentcross, and the fairways were first cut with an old 1929 model Ford. Jim Dolan, however, wrecked the tractor over a hill on the number four green shortly ater the opening and Sunny Croft's first tractor had to be replaced.

Sunny Croft, like any other social organization, has its memories and stories which have been told and retold as the years have passed. This is especially true of those stories by and about those colorful businessmen of the past known as the caddies.

Mary, Queen of Scots, used the word cadet (pupil) for a person who carried her clubs. This word later became caddie. At Sunny Croft, one could find many of the Queen's cadets or caddies, some of whom were only in grade school and were sometimes smaller than the bags they carried. They came from such areas as North View, Mt. Clare, Wilsonburg, Salem and other surrounding areas. They would get up at 4:30 a.m. and

hitch a ride to the golf course where they flocked by the hundreds. They were ranked A, B and C and each had a number. When the caddie master called a caddie's number he would tote a bag for 25 cents a round, 5 cents of which had to be given to the caddie master. In the 1940's, caddies were paid 35 cents a round, and they gave the caddie master 5 cents. Often they would make enough money to go to a movie and buy a Coke for 5 cents. Besides carrying clubs, the caddies also had the responsibility of weeding by hand the greens so they would be playable for the day. Although the caddies worked hard and helped make the course what it was, they were not allowed inside the club house. They had to go to the outside window to get a snack or a coke. On Mondays until noon, the caddies were allowed to play golf using the members' clubs. There were caddie tournaments in which they could compete with one another and it was in this way that many of the better golfers of today developed their skills.

The caddies knew the players who treated them well and those who didn't. They often had an influence in a player's game as well as many tricks to use on the players. One story is told of a caddie who took a ball out of a player's bag without the player knowing it. The caddie asked the player if he would like to buy a ball; the player, not knowing, bought the ball. As it happened, the caddie sold the same ball three times. A caddie would sometimes plug a player's ball or step on it pressing it into the ground. After declaring it a lost ball, the caddie would recover it and later take it to town and sell it for 75 cents. Caddies would also hit a player's ball a number of extra yards without the player's knowing it, and in this way, the caddie would speed up play so he could return to the club house for another job. Also, hitting the ball further made the player feel better and as a result, he would request the same caddie his next round.

There are numerous stories by and about caddies which apply wherever the game of golf is played, but there are two dealing with the caddies of Sunny Croft which are unique to this Harrison County golf course.

On a Wednesday evening in 1936, the club professional, Joe Palette, bet Tony Martino a dozen golf balls that Tony couldn't play 200 consecutive holes. Tony, a eighteen-year-old caddie at the time, accepted the bet, and the 135 pound golfer started the next day at 5:30 a.m. to win the wager. Young Martino had a sandwich at one o'clock, and then he changed his shoes and socks. Afterwards, Dr. Marcus Farrell examined him and declared him in fair condition. Martino drank orange juice and ate chocolate bars as he hurried from one green to the other. Louis Martino, a cousin, kept score and Joe Loretta kept the ball teed-up ahead of him. Jim Pickens, Vince Martino and Roger Martino carried his clubs. The marathon attracted a large gallery which Martino played 229 holes in fourteen and a quarter hours. He finished his feat at approximately 7:45 p.m. His rounds were 43, 42, 39, 40, 43, 41, 40, 41, 39, 39, 39, 38, 44, 40, 37, 38, 39, 42, 39, 41, 39, 42 and 18 after finishing four holes of his final round.

Another story often told occurred on Saturday, July 10, 1948, when Harrison County and the Sunny Croft Country Club had the distinct honor of hosting perhaps the finest woman's athlete the world has seen. Mildred "Babe" Didrickson Zaharias was born June 26, 1911, one of seven children of a Norwegian ship carpenter. She showed promise of stardom as she became a three year All-American basketball player in college, and in 1932, took her athletic talents to the Olympic Games where she won gold medals in both the javelin and the hurdles. In 1930, she had begun her golf career and won her first golf tournament in Texas at the age of twenty-three. In the decade of forties, she set record after record of winning seventeen major tournaments in succession. She became the first woman from the United States to win the British Women's Amateur open. This 5'7" 145 pound professional was noted for hitting a long ball, and the great golf professional, Bryan Nelson, estimated that at the time only eight of the men professionals could outdrive her.

More than 400 persons from throughout West Virginia paid a spectator's fee of $1.50 that day in July to watch the 18 hole exhibition match in which the "Babe" and her partner, Alpha Lawson defeated Stanley Zontek and George "Red" Hopkins 5 up or by five strokes with four holes still to be played.

Sam Scolapio, Jr., received the honor of caddying for the "Babe" that day due to his seniority amoung the Sunny Croft caddies and he often recalls the dazzling eighteen hole exhibition which she put on that day. Wisecracking all the way around the course with her oponents, her partner and the specators, the "Babe" scored as amazing 67 on the Sunny Croft course with a 34 on the front nine and a 33 on the back nine.

After two putting the first hole for par, she commenced to put together a round three under par for the course. Playing from the men's tees, she amazed the gallery as she drove the ball over the 230 yards. On the 230 yard number two hole (currently number seven), she asked her partner, Alpha Lawson, what club he was was hitting. The Sunny Croft ace who was to card a 71 that day himself replied that he was hitting a 3 wood. The "Babe" then picked up her 3 wood and gently laid the ball on the green. She also hit a wedge into the number 4 hole (now number 9) on her second shot and on number 8, she drove over 230 yards and powered a 7 iron with a snappy back spin on the green and made the put for a birdie.

There was an interesting disagreement among some of the officials that day over an incident on the No. 9 hole (now No. 5). Driving from the top of the hill, the Babe's ball went out of bounds across the road. Some of the officials moved the ball back across the road and jokingly "teed" it up. The Babe said nothing about the tee, but asked where her ball had landed. She was told "across the road," but was assured by officials that it did not constitute a stroke penalty for during the exhibition, the players were able to tee the ball up in the fairway and the rough. Although she missed several short putts which prevented an even lower score, the "Babe" was

pleased with her reception at Sunny Croft as well as with the condition of the course, and she remarked that she hoped to return in the fall.

Unfortunately, the "Babe" was never to return to Sunny Croft. The demands of her professional schedule and the beginning of another type of battle prevented her. In 1950, the Associated Press named her the Outstanding Woman Athlete of the first half of this century, and in 1953, after surviving a cancer operation, she came back to win the National Woman's Open Championship. On September 27, 1956, however, after a fight against cancer that lasted more than three years, the "Babe" died.

This year the Sunny Croft Country Club is celebrating its fiftieth anniversary (1934-1984). The caddies are gone today, having been replaced by carts, but the stories they lived, including the "Babe's" visit in 1948, are still remembered and often heard again and again as golfers make their way down the Sunny Croft fairways.

Harvey Harmer - Covered Bridge Writer

By JACK SANDY ANDERSON

In 1852 Shinnston needed a wagonmaker. A leading citizen, Solomon S. Fleming, who that year became the town's first mayor, wrote to Front Royal, Va., then a wagonmaking center, to ascertain if a person could be found who might settle in Shinnston. Benjamin Tyson Harmer (1824-1890), a young wagonmaker, was informed of Fleming's inquiry, corresponded with him, and was persuaded to come to Shinnston.

On upper Main Street he and his wife the former Margaret Jane Shepler (1828-1915), whom he married in 1851, established their home, and next to it he built his wagon shop. An expert woodworker, Harmer also made coffins and so became the local undertaker. This was the beginning of a local funeral home bearing the same name.

Harmer did very well in his new home. Congenial and industrious, he soon made many friends and in a few years became one of the community's most respected men. His business fourished, and before long he was well-to-do. Although from the Valley of Virginia, he did not hold to the tenets of the Southern Democrats and joined the Republican Party. Like the majority of Shinnston men, he was a strong Union supporter during the Civil War. He took an active interest in politics, and in 1872 was elected president of the Harrison County Court for a term of two years. Previously, from 1869 to 1872, he had served the county as supervisor of Clay District.

Harvey Walker Harmer, the fifth son of Benjamin and Margaret, was a happy boy. As a boy he liked to explore the countryside with friends and one day discovered a "secret cave" near Eldridge Knob (I have searched for this cave but have never found it, although my father as a boy in the 1890s was once inside it). He liked to pick blackberries in the summer and by so doing was able to earn a little extra spending money. He also liked to work in the hayfield and to take care of his father's horses — tasks he told me he considered treats rather than chores. Now and then, he would assist his father and older brothers in the shop; and sometimes he helped his mother tack satin lining inside the coffins his father made of oak, cherry, or walnut wood.

Early in life, however, he decided that farming, wagonmaking, and undertaking were not for him. As far back as he could remember, he liked books; and before he entered school, he was able to read and to do simple arithmetic. His affinity for academic learning convinced him that he should

earn his living with his brain instead of his hands. At school, which was located but a short distance from the Harmer home, he performed exceptionally well and was considered an outstanding student. For the most part, his teachers were capable, if not brilliant, and from them he received adequate instruction that laid the foundation for his further education. One teacher whom he liked and for whom he had great respect was William B. Wilkinson. In his old age Harmer recalled Wilkinson as an excellent teacher but a strict disciplinarian. Wilkinson had taught the town's first free school and for a time was partner in the Shinnston pottery that produced the pitchers, churns, jars, and jugs so avidly collected today.

One of his closest boyhood friends was Richard Leslie Fortney, son of the widely-known and colorful Dr. Jacob Holmes Fortney. Located across the river from the town, the Fortney residence was a two-story house which he had built soon after 1848 for his second wife, Mary Lefevre Shinn, widow of Elisha Shinn of Pine Bluff. Highly intelligent, jovial, and easy-going, Dr. Fortney was a favorite of children and would entertain them by the hour with his repertoire of amusing stories. In 1876 the first bridge to span the river at Shinnston was built, and the stones for its abutments and piers were quarried from land belonging to Dr. Fortney. Harmer and Fortney spent much time together watching the workmen quarry the stones and proceed with the bridge's construction.

Like Harmer, Fortney became a lawyer; but he left Shinnston and established his practice in Washington. He married Grace Harrison, a niece of President Benjamin Harrison, and lived a cosmopolitan life. Among my favorite possessions is a picture of Fortney as a young man which Harmer gave me not long before he died; and on the reverse he had written, "My most intimate schoolday friend."

Even though the Harmers were newcomers, young Harmer as a child became deeply interested in local history. He spent hours in the company of old-timers who would tell

him their recollections of the long-ago. A few were children and grandchildren of the area's pioneers, and they often told stories that included accounts of Indian warfare. These he found thrilling and exciting. One of the old-timers for whom he felt a special fondness was my great-great-grandmother, Emily Shinn Sandy Martin. Harmer always referred to her as Aunt Emily and related to me many of the things she had told him, including some that, perhaps, she should have kept to herself.

To him the Civil War was not the faraway past, for it had ended just months before his birth. In childhood he often heard his family and neighbors tell stories about it. Particularly he liked to hear them tell about Jones's Raid in April, 1863, when the town was invaded by a band of Rebel soldiers who terrified the inhabitants and took from them their healthy horses, grain, and food supplies. Harmer thought the Civil War had been an exciting time, and he sometimes wished he had been born earlier so he could have lived through it.

Harmer continued his education in Fairmont at the state normal school which had a reputation for academic excellence and which was primarily concerned with preparing men and women for the teaching profession. In the 1880s, when he was a student there, Fairmont was steadily growing and increasing in prosperity as its coal industry expanded. As a large town, it offered many attractions for a young man. Harmer thoroughly enjoyed the cultured atmosphere of the school and associating with intellectual and refined individuals, some of whom became his closest friends.

For a few years he taught school. He once told me that he liked teaching and found it both stimulating and challenging. But he soon discovered that teaching would never provide him with a really comfortable living. He wanted more from life than bare existence, and decided to abandon teaching for law. He received his legal training at West Virginia University and graduated in 1892.

That same year he was admitted to the Harrison County Bar and established his practice in Clarksburg, where he had been living since 1890. This practice he was to maintain for a period of 65 years. Very early in his career he was recognized as a lawyer of superior ability and found himself supplied with numerous clients. With a flourishing practice came financial success, and Harmer by 1900 was an affluent man.

During his long lifetime Harmer held many positions of trust and responsibility: member of the House of Delegates, member of the State Senate, mayor of Clarksburg, secretary of the board of education, deputy clerk to the circuit court, member state board of regents for normal schools, supervisor of the United States census, referee in bankruptcy, member of the Joint Legislative Committee of Revision of the West Virginia Code, bank director, president of the Harrison County Bar Association, and vice president of the West Virginia State Bar Association. His religious affiliation was with the Methodist Church in which he took an active and important role. He held membership in the Independent Order of Odd Fellows and in the Sons of the American Revolution.

His contributions as a lawyer and public servant were truly outstanding, but today he is remembered best for his historical writing. Had it not been for him, much valuable county history would have been forever lost. His legal skill enabled him to do the intensive research necessary to obtain accurate information for his books. Moreover, he had sufficient command of the English language to set down in readable and interesting form the results of his research. His books contain numerous family history references, thus making them of value to students of genealogy as well as to the historically-minded general reader or the devotee of local history. His two books on county history were "Covered Bridges of Harrison County" published in 1956, and "Old Grist Mills of Harrison County" published in 1940. He also wrote a history of Methodism in Clarksburg, a manual for magistrates that had a wide circulation, and authored numerous articles.

Harmer was twice married but had no children. In 1901 he married Nellie B. Martin, whose death occurred in 1923. His second wife, whom he married in 1926, was Florence Stemple, who served as dean of women at West Virginia Wesleyan College. She died in 1960.

Harvey Walker Harmer died at his home in Clarksburg on Nov. 21, 1961. He was buried in the Shinnston Masonic Cemetery.

On the Door Was Written...'Tornado June The 23rd on Friday Evening 1944'

BY JOHN RANDOLPH

"I wish you boys wouldn't go out camping tonight," exclaimed Mamma, as she watched my older brother Bud gather up an old frying pan, the tent and various other "camping things" as she called them. "It's gonna do something," she said, as he tied his gear to the bicycle.

"But Mom, we're just going down Tenmile and if the weather gets too bad I'll come home," he said.

It had been so hot all day, the sun had poured all its strength on us and although there was a lot of work which needed to be done on the farm, we had taken it easy all day. "The old cow didn't even give her usual milk this evening," Mamma went on, "and I just don't like the looks of the funny red sky off east."

Supper had been over for a while and as we watched Mamma finish straining the milk and Bud getting ready to go camping, there seemed to be a great hush all around, there were not the usual evening noises and even old Spot had disappeared off under the house somewhere.

As Bud peddled his bike down the road, a flicker of lightning could be seen against the red glow and Mamma gave us instructions to bring in the porch furniture along with the rest of the clothes on the line; she was sure we were in for a storm. "Don't forget to close the chickens up," she said.

By now, the gas light in the dining room had been lighted and old Ed, the hired man, turned on the radio. It snapped and cracked so much with static, that he turned it off in disgust and mumbled something about he'd not be able to sleep tonight either. I cannot really remember too much more about the evening before being toted off to bed. We were all standing on the front porch looking at the curious red sky off in the east and there was quite a discussion about the awful weather someone must be getting. I, too, remeber that it wasn't too long after bedtime that there was fierce lightning and thunder and it stormed the rest of the night.

It was hardly light outside when I could hear a lot of talk downstairs. Old Ed was not in his bed across the room, and I could hear Mamma's voice. Another voice I didn't know was saying, "There's water everywhere! I reached from hill to hill."

By this time I was out of my bed, yanking on my jeans and looking out the bedroom window. The sound was like a big motor running, I was under the impression that the rain had stopped, as I opened the window and looked off towards the little meadow, all I could see in the pale morning light was water running. Downstairs I was confronted with the rest of the family and old Annie from up the road sitting at the kitchen table trying to hold a cup of coffee that Mamma was spotting cream in for her. She would sip the coffee, set it down, and start wringing her hands.

Her voice would start to pitch higher as she exclaimed, "I'm sure old Boyd and Maude are in there. I could see their heads just bobbing up and down, couldn't get very close to the house, but the waters runnin' through the winders. What are we going to do? They'll drown for sure."

Annie's older sons were still out, they had gone off to town the evening before and evidently had the same problem as everyone else. They couldn't get home. So Annie had fought her way down through the field to see if Bud would come and look about her neighbors who she was sure were possibly even swept away by the rushing waters of the "cloud burst." The only problem, for us anyway, was that there was no Bud. And I distinctly remeber hearing him say they were going to camp down in Rock Hollow along Tenmile Creek. I suddenly was scared.

I could easily see that Mamma was very unhappy and she turned to Ed for advice. I should explain that Pap was away working. He would not be able to get home now until next weekend.

"Well the water out of Bailey Holler is over the road now," said Ed, "and there's no going back up the run. I can try to get down to the Hursts but it's probably over the road at the bottom of the hill by now."

"It's times like this I wish that confounded telephone company would try to get us a line." said Mamma. "I hope you can at least get some idea of Bud's whereabouts."

Ed was off. I was warned to stay in the house. Annie continued to sit and wring her hands.

Well it wasn't long before Ed was back and announced that the water was over the road in all directions and we would just have to wait until it went down before we could contact anyone. At least we were safe and hoped Bud had time to get to high ground. Ed remarked that he had seen a lot of high water in these valleys, but had witnessed nothing comparable

to this. It happened so fast. Excitement and worry finally convinced Mamma that perhaps we could go see about this water problem.

So hand in hand, Ruth and I followed by the grown-ups ran out to the top of the hills. The water sure was everywhere. It looked as if it was nearly up to Hursts' house, down below, and someone shouted, ''Look at the pigs'' which went floating with the current.

Tree limbs, boards, old oil drums and all kinds of debris was bobbing up and down in the swift yellow water. We followed the road bank in every direction. There was no way for anyone to come or go until the waters subsided. The cattle in the field all stood down next to the bars. The old milk cow bawled in the barn lot and no one had thought about the chickens. The many chores finally got done. We youngsters were busy running from puddle to puddle and to all the little run-offs down through the yard and around the house. As the milk was being taken to the cellar, it was discovered there was nearly a foot of water in it. Mamma was just beside herself. Of course Annie was still fussing which didn't help much.

Before anyone was the wiser, noontime had arrived and as a dinner of potato soup and cheese sandwiches was being put on the table, Bud and the neighbor boy Ted came bursting into the kitchen. They were barefoot and had their overalls rolled up to their knees. They were somewhat of a mess.

''Where on earth have you been?'' was Mamma's first question. This was quickly followed by others before Bud had a chance to answer.

''We got washed out,'' he said, ''the water was in the tent before we knew what was happening. Ted and I tore up the hillside or I swear I think we would have been swept away. I'm sorry Mamma but we didn't save anything 'cept our clothes and bikes. We went up to the Hursts and slept on the back porch until we heard the pigs squealing. Mr. Hurst went down and knocked the pen apart and the pigs took off to the hills.''

''Did you see those other pigs wash down earlier?'' Ruth asked.

''Yes they must have come up from the creek,'' said Bud.
''How'd you get home?'' asked Annie.
''The waters are down some now,'' replied Bud. ''We went around the hill and waded across way up the hollow.''

''Well,'' Annie said, ''my family will think I've drowned, so I'd best get up the road if'n I can.''

Bud and Ted agreed that they'd better go with her to see the Swigers.

''Did you hear about the tornado down Shinnston way?'' Ted asked.

''Lord no,'' Mamma replied.

''Heard it on the radio just 'fore we came up here. Sounds awful bad,'' he replied as they took off.

''Quick turn on the radio,'' Mamma commanded. ''We're missing all the news. Why I've been so fussed I never thought about the radio.'' The day was filled with excitement. The milkman finally came by to pick up our can and said he hadn't had such excitement in years. Reports over the radio told of awful destruction by the tornado and how people all over the country had been washed out or water was up in their houses. Later in the afternoon we all walked up the run to see about the nieghbors. The poor Swigers had lost nearly everything. They were fine, but it really seemed strange to hear how the water was running halfway up and through their windows.

''Just open them up and let the creek go through,'' said the old man.

Up and down the creek there was litter everywhere. The stream was still up far out of its banks and even though we hadn't had water in our house, we lost all the first cutting of hay along with most of the cornfield and as Mamma put it, ''We are all going to suffer, I'm afraid.''

After the chores were done and supper was over we all sat on the front porch to listen to the running water and watch the moon come up in a cleared sky. I cannot remember being told to get to bed, so I suspect I got there with some help. After all we'd had a big day and yes a big night before on Indian Run. The big flood would be talked about for all the years of remembering into the future.

I happened to be at the State Arts and Crafts Fair in Ripley in 1979, where a tole-painting friend of mine said, ''John, I want to show you my piece of talking furniture which is for sale.''

She opened the door of a small wall cabinet that she had decorated. On the inside of the door was written ''Tornado June the 23 Evening 1944.''

I bought her cabinet.

Cecil B. Highland - A West Milford Boy's Dream Led to Successful Banking Career

By DOROTHY DAVIS

"The thoughts of youth are long, long thoughts."
Longfellow

The dreams of the youthful Cecil Blaine Highland stretched all the way to California, a state tied in with the boy's early drive for success and recognition. Highland's first visions of being a flamboyant cowboy soon changed to pictures of himself as rich with gold found in the West.

Born the fourth son of John Edgar and Lucinda Earle Patton Highland November 7, 1876, on a 140-acre farm one mile below West Milford, Cecil early followed the footsteps of a brother Virgil six years older than Cecil. When he was eight, Cecil watched Virgil earn $8 to pay for a cornet to play in the West Milford Eureka Cornet Band that traveled in summer to furnish music for the Central West Virginia Agricultural and Mechanical Society Fair in Clarksburg. Soon Cecil had the ten dollars for a permit to sell peanuts and lemonade at the fair. The profit did not start the boy to California, for he sold patrons of the fair his products three days before he recovered the cost of the permit.

The next venture did start Cecil Highland on the way to California. At 15 he recruited his younger brother Scotland as partner to sell door-to-door memorial plaques in the state of Indiana. The Highland boys painted angels on red velvet, attached a sentimental verse with lines like:

"I loved him, yes I loved him
But the angels loved him more
And they have gently called him
To yonder peaceful shore."

and put the whole business under glass.

One bereaved widow, on calling attention to a smudge of white paint on the eye of an angel, was told by the boys: "Oh, that is a weeping angel." The statement quickly brought a sale. The boys made money that carried Cecil Highland first to Iowa, then to Colorado, and finally to California.

By the time Highland reached California, all talk was of the gold rush in Alaska. Cecil caught the fever and embarked for Alaska, where he found men losing more than they gained in prospecting, something that did not bother Highland who later said, "I didn't lose much because I didn't have much." He returned to California and left for Arkansas to visit his oldest brother Charles Bruce Highland. Young Cecil learned to sing "I never knew what misery was Till I saw Arkansas" and persuaded his brother to return to Fairmont to start a men's clothing store with Cecil as partner. Cecil Highland had learned that no royal road nor gold street leads to success. He would return to West Virginia and give hard work a chance.

The mercantile business was far too mundane for a youth with a bent for dreaming. Cecil Highland sold out his share in the Fairmont store to his brother and went to Lexington, Ky., to a business school. Soon brother Virgil, who in November 1896 had won election to clerk of the Harrison County Court, wrote offering Cecil the position of deputy clerk. Cecil Highland left the secretarial school whose officials offered him before his departure a diploma if he would pay for it. He accepted the position as Harrison County deputy clerk and stayed on the job five and one-half years, at a salary of $30 a month, $25 of which went for board and room to his landlord Virgil Highland. Cecil made some money on the side moonlighting as a title abstractor and learned a craft that gave him new dreams and new openings.

His brother and partner had purchased 15,000 acres of coal lands in Wetzel County. Cecil Highland moved to Wetzel County and later wrote, "abstracted titles, wrote deeds, paid for coal, and made some money."

New Martinsville prospered at the turn of the century. Cecil Highland liked the town and the people. Now in his early twenties, he had the first big dreams since the childhood yen for California: He wanted to own the largest diamond in Wetzel County and he wanted to own the largest automobile in Wetzel County.

Still he kept one foot in Clarksburg. With forbears staunch Whigs and Republicans who had voted in Harrison County at every election since 1806, the Highlands naturally leaned toward The Telegram, a weekly Republican newspaper that

had started publication in 1867. Virgil Highland bought an interest in the newspaper in 1899 and by December 1902, when The Telegram took over control of the Clarksburg Daily Post, Cecil Highland had bought a one-seventh interest in the Daily Telegram.

Virgil Highland wanted to start a bank to be called the Empire National Bank. He asked his brother Cecil to sell subscriptions to the institution in New Martinsville. Soon the bank was over-subscribed and funds raised for the building with a percentage of the subscriptions for both capital and building having been sold in Wetzel County by Cecil Highland who was named a director of the bank that opened October 3, 1903, in the Oak Hall Building. The bank moved into the new Empire Bank Building on the northwest corner of West Main and South Fourth streets January 14, 1907. The Daily Telegram moved to the basement of the new building.

Meanwhile Cecil Highland pursued a busy career in Wetzel County. He was appointed chief deputy to the sheriff of Wetzel County from 1904 to 1908 during which time he was named receiver of the Bank of Smithfield, receiver of the Del Rio Oil Company in Ritchie County and of a large oil company in Calhoun County.

He was strongly involved in Wetzel County politics. In 1904 he had helped elect the first Republican sheriff in the county. To further the Republican Party and to counter cries of ''carpetbagger'' because of his out-of-county origin, Highland bought the weekly Wetzel Republican. His interest in politics carried him to the West Virginia Senate as representative from the counties of Marshall, Wetzel, and Tyler. As chairman of the West Virginia Senate Finance Committee, he helped enact the appropriations necessary to build the new Cass Gilbert state capitol.

In his early days in New Martinsville, Highland boarded in the home of Josephus B. Clark and met Clark's sister Ella Cox Clark whose father Josephus Clark was a prominent merchant in New Martinsville and whose chemist brother, Dr. Friend E. Clark, would be honored in the 1960s by having Clark Hall at West Virginia University named for him. Highland married Ella Cox Clark in New Martinsville on February 10, 1909, and established a residence first on Maple Avenue and later at 245 Virginia Street, which would be the official Highland residence in New Martinsville throughout the couple's lives.

Cecil Highland's political activities centered in New Martinsville; his business interests, in Clarksburg. The bridge between Harrison and Wetzel counties was the Short Line Railroad which Cecil Highland rode on Monday morning to his offices sometimes listed in the Clarksburg City Directory as ''Highland Brothers & Gore, Shoes and Hats, 128 South Third St. (1911); real estate, 602 Goff Building (1917); president, Empire National Bank, mgr. Clarksburg Publishing Co. (1941).'' In the early years Highland spent weekday nights at the Waldo Hotel, then he lived during the week in an apartment that adjoined his office in the Prunty Building; and

in 1950 moved to an apartment in the Empire National Bank Building. He traveled on Friday evening by train, or after circa 1940 by automobile to his residence in New Martinsville.

In the first decade of this century Franklin Earle Highland, the brother nearest of the oldest three to Cecil in age, operated a shoe store in Clarksburg along with a Mr. Sine and a Mr. Crawford who wanted his name listed first in the official title of the business. Cecil Highland settled the matter when he bought out Crawford. At the same time Howard M. Gore, later governor of West Virginia, bought Sine's share in the store. The business ''Highland Brothers & Gore'' operated more than two decades until circa 1930, when after Franklin Highland's death, the business was sold to Robert Pettrey.

Then in 1914 Cecil Highland bought Goff Plaza for $215,000. He said he spent a small fortune on water lines, sewers, sidewalks, streets, buried power lines, and the metal lamp posts that stand in 1984; but July 28, 1915, the first day the land went on the market, he sold $150,000 in lots. Highland had no partner in real estate ventures.

The closeness between Virgil and Cecil Highland continued in the years Virgil served as National Republican Committeeman from West Virginia 1916-1930 during which time Virgil ran an unsuccessful race for the U.S. Senate. During the campaign Cecil traveled many counties of the state electioneering for his brother. Cecil Highland was already in Florida with his son in 1930 when he heard that his brother Virgil was so slow recuperating from influenza that he would travel to Florida for a change of climate. Virgil was no better in Florida and left there for home accompanied by his wife and brother Cecil who then went with Virgil Highland to the Mayo Clinic in Rochester, Minn. Virgil Highland died at the clinic Aug. 9, 1930.

One day before his death, Virgil Highland had added to his will a codicil in which he named Cecil Highland to the list of executors of his estate, a large one, three-quarters of which was encumbered with debts. Virgil Highland had owned majority interest in the Clarksburg Publishing Company formed July 1, 1927, as a combination of The Daily Telegram and The Clarksburg Exponent.

The Great Depression deepened. Two of the executors of Virgil Highland wanted to liquidate the estate. Cecil Highland refused to consent to the sale thus blocking the action which required unanimity of the executors. Virgil Highland's widow and children took the case to court and succeeded in having Cecil Highland named sole executor after a decision by the West Virginia Supreme Court of Appeals that read in part: ''(one of the co-executors) states... that the estate is clearly insolvent. Cecil insists that it is solvent and if properly managed, will pay the beneficiaries several hundred thousand dollars.'' Cecil Highland discharged all debts without material loss to the estate.

In the darkest days of the battle over his brother's estate Cecil Highland in 1931 was dismissed as vice president of the Empire National Bank. He walked out through the front door as he vowed not again to use the front entrance until reelected to an office in the bank. A year later he was dropped from the elected board of directors of the bank.

After the 1933 bank holiday and after the sale of preferred stock and the reopening of the bank, Mr. Highland was elected a director. He used a side door to do business and to attend meetings. November 20, 1940, Cecil Highland was named ''active vice president'' of the bank. In January 1941 shareholders reduced the directorate from 12 to seven, adding Scotland G. Highland as a new director, and the board then met to elect Cecil B. Highland president on Jan. 14, 1941. After his election as president of the bank, he arranged for a photographer to record his use of the front door of the bank —

the first time he had walked through the portals in 11 years.

Long, long before the 1940s Cecil B. Highland's Wetzel County dream of big diamonds and cars had come true: He owned four large diamonds. He had built a garage and then had bought a twin-six Packard at a cost of $6,500. The automobile would not fit into the garage. Mr. Highland laughed at the joke on himself and hired workers to double the size of the garage.

Mr. Highland's enjoyment of his own error displays his rare sense of humor which was combined with an understanding of human beings. A realist, he accepted the fact that all humankind have imperfections. He liked to watch people, to give them a chance for better or worse as he tested their candor and veracity in many ways. He made allowance for minor foibles, and was pleased with an associate or employee who passed Mr. Highland's test of competence and integrity. Mr. Highland was pleased with himself if he caught serious flaws in others.

On February 6, 1957, Cecil B. Highland was working at his desk when he died of acute coronary heart disease.

Railroad Exhibit Now at Library

The Harrison County Bicentennial Committee announces the opening of the "Railroads in Harrison County" small exhibit at the Clarksburg-Harrison Public Library.

This exhibit features the locomotives, freight and passenger cars used in Harrison County throughout the long history of the railroad as well as the tools, china and early photographs of Harrison County. The Baltimore and Ohio Railroad is featured along with the B & O Terminal located in Clarksburg as it appeared during the years when the railroad was king.

The exhibit was presented by Linda and Randy Strogen who have been working with rail activities and railroad history for 12 years. Randy is director of the Monongah Division Historical Group. Linda is editor of the "Mountain State Rail News," a newsletter put out to rail fans about every six weeks for the cost of a self-addressed, stamped envelope. Both Linda and Randy and their eight-year-old son Chris are active with the Affiliation for B & O Historical Research. They are trustees for this organization. Two years ago Linda and Randy put on a convention for rail fans and brought 113 people from as far away as California and Colorado to Clarksburg. Linda is one of the only two women to hold the title of trustee for the A B & O S H R, a national organization. Chris has his own article in the Mountain State Rail News called "By a Junior Rail Fan."

The exhibit may be viewed during regular library hours and will run until December. The "Railroads in Harrison County" exhibit series is sponsored by the Clarksburg-Harrison Public Library and is funded by the Humanities Foundation of West Virginia, a state program of the National Endowment for the Humanities, and by the Consolidated Gas Transmission Corporation.

Stonewood Makes Rapid Growth From Meadow Land Start in 1910

At the close of World War II, residents of Stonewall and Norwood, adjoining communities lying east of Clarksburg, decided to incorporate as one town. The Elk Creek Development Company, with Howard White as manager, in 1910 named the land the company laid off in lots Stonewall Park; residents living near the new fairgounds had named their town Norwood.

The two communities invited the children enrolled in the local school to enter a contest to choose a name for the new muncipality. Sixth-grader Charles Childers of Norwood School won the contest with a word which combined portions of the name of each of the two communnities —Stonewood. The town was incorporated Dec. 17, 1947. Citizens vote biennially to select a five-man council and other officials.

Immediately after incorporation, town officials arranged with Monongahela Power Co. to install street lights and in 1948 assisted the citizens in organizing a volunteer fire department. The town financed a $235,000 water distribution system, completed in 1950, to furnish residences with water purchased from the Clarksburg Water Board. In 1952-53, citizens volunteered labor to build a cement block building on Southern Avenue. The fire department and the city offices are housed in the structure.

From current revenue, the city has blacktopped two and half miles of streets and has built a city playground. In 1965, with 50 percent of the $856,000 cost supplied by the federal government, the town installed a sewage interceptor system.

With a population of 2,100 and still growing, the citizens of Stonewood are a proud people. They take part in all general elections and town affairs. It is often said that the percentage of persons voting in Stonewood is higher than for any town of comparable size in West Virginia.

Stonewood for its size and population has grown tremendously in the last ten years. One can see this by viewing new construction and road paving. The town is proud of its police and fire departments.

In October 1975 ground was broken for a new city hall addition. It provides for a council chamber, a mayor's office and a street superintendent's office, with funding for labor coming from the the Comprehensive Employment Training Act.

Ground has already been been broken to install new water and fire hydrants in Wilson Addition. This service is being provided with the aid of FHA funds. Sewage lines have also been provided with federal and state EPA grants. The town believes that by developing this area and helping the 100 families who already live there, Stonewood will draw industry and new citizens to its boundaries. The total cost of both projects will be approximately $250,000.

Another project which Stonewood citizens are very proud of is the Fifth Street Project. This endeavor was undertaken to correct a mistake which happened over 50 years ago. In the year of 1975 it was noted that the street was on private property and had to be moved to its correct boundaries. City employees worked day and night to erect new barriers and make a number of landfills.

Along Route 58 Stonewood annexed over 30 acres for building new homes and encouraging industry. A new phase in home building and recreation took place. Financed by the Land and Conservation Fund and the Harrison County Commission, is was a new beginning for Stonewood. Homes sprang up, citizens were given low government loans, tennis courts, basketball courts became a reality. Today real estate is selling well and more people are becoming aware of Stonewood's goal to be an All West Virginia City.

In 1972 Pittsburgh Plate Glass, a major industry, left Stonewood. The citizens as well as the town suffered financially. The glass plant was considered the largest in the state of West Virginia.

The City of Stonewood knew that something had to be done. With the help of the Harrison County Commission, the town was able to let bids to rebuild the area and turn it into an industrial park. The park will be able to host industry from glassware to marbles. When completed this year the park will consist of over 30 acres of prime flat land.

Stonewood's famous landslide occurred in 1972 on Heavener and Powell Avenues. Becuase of underground mining in the early 1900s the earth began to move during heavy rainfalls. Houses were destroyed and many persons had to find new homes.

The State Office of Surface Mining with the cooperation of the State of West Virginia began reclamation of the area. Tons and tons of dirt and rock were removed and continued to be moved. The excess material was and is being used to construct a playground on Kidd Avenue.

City officials feel that improvements need to be made within the community and with needed land filled the future projects will be a reality.

Stonewood is proud of its recreational equipment. It has made use of many areas to build and add many recreational settings. At the present time it has two tennis courts, two basketball courts, children's equipment, public shelter, and a new playground under construction.

Wade H. Coffindaffer - Harrison County Prominent Educator and Teacher

By LLOYD JASON LEGGETT

Wade H. Coffindaffer, educator and teacher grew to prominence in Harrison County from roots which were deep-seated in the history of the county.

The Coffindaffer family lived in Harrison County for many generations. Wade Coffindaffer's great-great-grandfather, John Coffindaffer, was one of the pioneer settlers of the county, locating on Sycamoore Creek when this section was on the outside edge of the frontier.

He had been born and reared in Culpepper County, Va., and his son, Abraham Coffindaffer, also born in Virginia, was a young boy when the family moved westward into the unsettled wilderness of what was then western Virginia. Joseph B. Coffindaffer, son of Abraham, was born at the old homestead farm on Sycamore Creek and on Dec. 20, 1861, Coffinndaffer's father Abraham B. Coffindaffer, was born on a farm on Kincheloe Creek.

The Coffindaffer family had been quite active in the field of education. Abraham Coffindaffer attended the select schools of the day, and for 18 years of his career he gave part of his time to educational work, teaching 17 of those years in Harrison County and one year in Doddridge County. When he taught, the school year was limited to a few months, and the remaining months were devoted to farming. He was one of the more prosperous farmers of Harrison County, owning approximately 1,800 acres, and he served several times as president of the local board of education.

When he was 19 years old, he married Josephine Carter, a native of Harrison County. They had 11 children. Of those, nine became involved in the field of education as their lifetime work.

Wade H. Coffindaffer Sr. was born on his father's farm in Harrison County, Aug. 19, 1881. He attended seven terms of his father's school class and had only three other teachers in grade school. He decided at a young age to become a teacher, and he neglected no opportunity to improve his qualifications for this high calling. For several years he was a student at Salem College where he graduated in 1907 with the degree of bachelor of pedagogy. While he was a student at Salem he taught many subjects as part of his preparation for graduation.

Coffindaffer's teaching career consisted of 19 years in one-room schools throughout the county teaching at various levels. Among the early locations at which he taught were: Burnside, McPherson, Two Lick and Hog Camp. He taught high school in Salem. For nine years he was at Burnside, his "home" school, and had nine of his brothers and sisters as pupils.

Coffindaffer was married to Maxie Ford in January 1908, and they had six children.

In November 1922, he was elected for his first term as county superintendent of schools. The thoroughness with which he administered the school system during his first term was given approval in his re-election to office in 1926. He was successively elected for as long as the position was an elected one in Harrison County.

After Gov. H. G. Kump's administration inaugurated the county unit system, Coffindaffer, as the basis for local education, directed the setting up of the county unit system in Harrison County. In 1935, he relinquished the superintendent's post and became an assistant superintendent, a position in which he served until his retirement in 1954.

Of a total of 50 years in the school systems, Coffindaffer spent 14 years teaching in one-room schools, four years in a two-room school, one in Salem High School, and 32 years in an administrative capacity for the county.

At the time of his retirement more than 350 Harrison

County teachers honored Coffindaffer at a retirement dinner held at the Masonic Temple in Clarksburg. Arthur V. G. Upton, then the superintendent of schools, commented, "It has given me a great deal of happiness and pleasure to work with Mr. Coffindaffer. I started teaching in Harrison Coutny when he was superintendent and for the past 15 years have worked closely with him as my associate. He has done a great job in raising the standards of the elementary schools and his kindness and patience in helping beginning teachers has been outstanding."

A former employee of the school system and a long personal friend of Coffindaffer's said, "I never (after being hired by him) had to go looking for work... other school systems sought me out." He explained that Coffindaffer's secrets were a well-disciplined school and his personal ability to get academic success from his pupils.

Wade Coffindaffer died on April 18, 1960 after an extended illness.

A Dollar and Five Cents, Postage Extra, Seven Cents

By WILLIAM B. PRICE

Clifford was in the woodyard where he had been sent for stove wood, but instead of cutting wood he was working a dogwood stick trying to make a bow. As he worked he noticed an old Sears Roebuck catalogue lying on the ash pile. The wind was blowing the pages of the catalogue back and forth. Suddenly, Clifford noticed the picture of a knife at the bottom of a right-hand page — a pocket knife such as every boy wanted but few were able to own. It had a fine blade, to be sure, it also had a screwdriver, an awl and a pair of pliers. But the price of that knife was high. It was marked one dollar and five cents, postage extra, seven cents.

Clifford knew that unless he could earn the money himself he would not be able to get the knife, but he was not one to give up easily. Tearing the page from the old catalogue he ran into the house and asked, "Mom, is there anything I can do around here to earn a dollar and five cents and the postage?"

"Well! Well, now! What is this all about?" his mother asked. She was used to Clifford's brainstorms and was not too much surprised at this sudden interest in earning money.

Clifford showed his mother the picture of the knife and then ran to the woodpile where he worked industriously for 15 or 20 minutes. Then, taking a small armload of wood, he sauntered into the kitchen, and again asked his mother if she had something for him to do that would be worth the dollar five and the postage.

"Yes," said his mother, "if you will cut all the brush in the chicken lot, and around the garden fence, and burn it up all clean, I will order the knife for Christmas."

Clifford went to work in earnest. Brush and briars, tangles of grapevine, old rails and other debris were all piled up and burned until, at last, his mother declared the job finished. By now it was only two weeks until Christmas.

Clifford was so excited, he began bragging to all his friends about the knife he was to get for Christmas, and showing them the catalogue picture. "And it cost a dollar and five cents and the postage," he kept saying. At school, in arithmetic class, he went to the blackboard and put down $1.05 for the knife, 2 cents postage, 3 cents mail order, and 7 cents delivery postage. Then he added the amounts all up, getting a total of $1.17. After several days of this, the boys at school began calling Clifford "Dollar-and-five-cents-Clifford" and other names he didn't like. He had two fights, had to stay in at recess, and bawled three or four times.

Clifford carried and folded and unfolded the picture of the knife so much it was soon worn out. The only person to give him consideration was Uncle Charlie who said, "Vill Hifford, I'd like to have one ike it, too."

At school, the children practiced each day for a Christmas program to be given for the whole community at the church on Christmas eve. The play chosen this year was *A Christmas Carol* by Dickens. Clifford was chosen for Tiny Tim. The practicing went on each day until the teacher was satisfied with all except Clifford, who insisted on mixing up his lines with his thoughts of the knife he was expecting. For this, the children deviled him all the more.

By and by the time came for the program. The church was packed with an expectant audience. The reed organ began playing a few bars of *Holy Night*. Other songs were sung and then suddenly, silence!

The church door opened, and, with sleigh bells ringing outside, in came Santa Claus with his usual hearty laughter. Holding up his right hand, he said, "My good people, with your help, we will now see who has been good!"

A line of young women and girls was all ready to deliver the presents. Clifford sat with several boys of his own age on a seat just back of the big stove. On the next seat behind him sat his Uncle Charlie and his friends.

The packages were being delivered very rapidly. Soon Clifford's name was read, and a small package was handed to the eager boy. "Oh, boy! Oh, boy! Here it comes!" said he as he immediately began tearing and wrapping from the present. To Clifford's dismay, it was only a ten-cent harmonica. This he didn't want, and, suiting his actions to his feelings, he threw it over his head striking Uncle Charlie on the nose. Presents, presents, presents galore were passed out to almost everyone with Clifford receiving his share, but no knife appeared to gladden his boyish little heart. As Santa Claus read the last name he held up his hands and spoke his benediction, "God bless you all, with a very Merry Christmas!"

Some of the boys began teasing Clifford, "Where's your knife, a dollar-seventeen?"

Clifford jumped up and said, "I'm going home, that's what I'm going to do." With that he ran out of the church and across the yard through the deepest snow he could find and came stomping up on the porch at home. In the house he became as angry and ashamed as a small boy can get.

Clifford's mother had stayed home that evening with his baby sister, and she was not at all surprised to see Clifford come storming into the house.

"Mom, I didn't get my knife and I've made a fool of myself talkin' too much. I know what I'm going to do, I'm going to bed, that's what I'm going to do."

"Now look here, young man!" said his mother, "You'll get your knife in a few days, I'm sure. It has been ordered almost 10 days."

"Why couldn't I keep my mouth shut like Grandpa told me. I'll bet I do next time," said Clifford as he dodged through the door to the unfinished room where he and his older brother slept.

A few bits of snow had blown under the eaves and lay on the floor. The pouting boy was soon in bed, but doubled up cross-wise instead of the way one should sleep. As Clifford began to feel warm, he heard his brother come home with a lot of laughing, tell how Clifford had rushed out of the church after the program.

Then, after what seemed to be only a few minutes, he heard his mother call the boys out for breakfast — a breakfast of yeast-raised buckwheat cakes, country sausage, yellow butter, and hot sorghum cane syrup.

Nothing was said about the knife until about noon, when, from far up the road, there came the faint jingle of sleighbells as the mail carrier came up with the daily mail. The sleigh stopped at a couple of boxes up the road, and then dropped a small package in Clifford's mail box. Clifford soon had the package in his hands and began to yell, "Here it is, Ma, here it is!"

The package was opened and in his hands Clifford held the most perfect knife any boy could ever hope to own. "I've got it, Ma!" he yelled, "I've got it, Ma!"

Having seen the old-timers try the blade of a knife by feeling the edge with a thumb, he snatched open the blade and tried it on his thumb to see if it was sharp, It was. Blood began to ooze from the tiny slit in the thumb. This caused more yelling. "It's sharp, Mom. Just look at the blood, Mom! Just look at the blood!"

Clifford's father thought it was a fine knife and said, "What boy wouldn't be wild about a knife like that?"

When dinner was over, Clifford went down to the village where the boys were coasting to show off his knife. It was biting cold, so Clifford put on an extra pair of pants and an extra coat. Of course the boys all liked the knife. When Uncle Charlie saw the knife, he offered to trade his old knife for Clifford's new one, saying, "Vell, Hifford, hit am the icest hife hi efer thee." When Clifford started back home, he was as proud as a peacock.

About halfway home, Clifford noticed opossum tracks in the snow. "Oh, boy," he said to himself, "I'm in luck!" Following the tracks, he finally found where the opossum had gone into a groundhog hole not far from his grandfather's old barn. Clifford stopped up the hole securely, and returned to the road. The excitement of tracking the opossum had caused him to forget his knife for the time being. Now, when he felt in his pocket for his knife, it was gone. He felt in the front pockets of his outside pants, the outside pocket of his outside coat, the inside pockets of his outside coat, the outside pockets of his inside coat, the inside pocket of his inside coat, the front pockets of his inside pants and the hip pockets of his inside pants — but the knife was gone.

Clifford began to bawl. With the bawling, he began to take off his outside coat. Next came his outside pants. By this time he was angry with himself. Taking the outside pants by the galluses, he hit them against a telephone pole. Wump went someting in his outside pants. It was the lost knife. It had slipped through a hole in a pocket of his outside pants and had caught in an inside patch of his outside pants.

As Clifford held the precious knife in his hand, he looked up the hill to the spot where the opossum had gone to hole. Still carrying the knife in his hand, he went back to the hole and pulled the rock out of the hole, saying, "This will be a better Christmas for you, too."

Back home, Clifford went to the woodyard where the old catalogue had been thrown on the ashpile. The sun had melted a little of the snow where fresh ashes had been thrown. The wind was again turning the pages. Taking the knife from his pocket, Clifford gazed at it in admiration and said, "Just think, it only cost a dollar and five cents and the postage."

County's History Comes Alive Today at Fort New Salem Fete

This story is about Fort New Salem - the place and its people - a prized county possession. Outdoor living history museum, Folk Life Educational Center, college campus - all are terms that describe Fort New Salem. The fort, a part of Salem College, was conceived in the mind of founder-director John Randolph in 1970 as a place to teach heritage arts in an appropriate environmental setting. From the meager expectation of securing a single log-constructed building for the purpose, it soon became apparent that the project was to be bigger and more encompassing. Long before the official dedication in 1974 many people had stopped by the fort site to see what was going on and soon the usual comment was "I see you're getting your fort built."

Now the fort is celebrating its tenth year of operation, with 20 some odd and varied log structures, an ever changing and growing professional staff, master craftsmen, student workers and an active volunteer "Friends of the Fort" organization.

Programming now includes a great array of activities, under-graduate and graduate level degrees, workshops, luncheons, and dinner parties, school children tours and living history experiences, group tours, and general public offerings. Fort New Salem's entire program is geared to present a representative view of early Appalachian Frontier settlement living.

Under the sponsorship of the Harrison County Bicentennial Committee and the West Virginia Humanities Foundation, the "Friends of the Fort" cordially invites the public to visit the fort with a free entry to the open house from 1 to 5 p.m. today. A variety of activites features blacksmithing, basketry, spinning and weaving, hearthside cooking, ballad singers, and story telling. The current regular staff will be spotlighted on this day which marks the close of the public season for 1984 with the exception of the Harvest Weekend - October, 13 and 14 and the annual Christmas Celebration on Dec. 8 and 9.

Refreshments will be served at the sign of the "Green Tree" tavern as well as the offerings of different periods of entertainment. Fort New Salem may be reached by exiting US Rt. 50 at the Junction 23 exit at Salem.

Anmoore - Origionally Ann Moore's Run

By LLOYD LEGGETT

Originally known by several different names, Anmoore was settled in 1894 when Silas Ash brought 214 acres of land three miles east of Clarksburg. During the next decade, Ash continued buying land adjoining his holdings.

In 1903, Ash sold 218 acres to Edward R. Davis and Lynn S. Hornor, who divided the farm into building lots and established the unincorporated village named "Steelton" and then "Grasselli" after the Grasselli Chemical Company had been established there in 1903. The plant was closed in 1927 and all operations were moved to Spelter.

In 1904 the National Carbon Company moved its new electrode factory to Anmoore to be near an abundant supply of cheap natural gas. The original plant included a pot calciner, equipment for crushing and mixing coal particles, a horizontal extrusion press, and pit-type baking furnaces. Taxes collected from the Carbon Plant helped subsidize the town.

The carbon industry attracted settlers so that when Grasselli incorporated as Anmoore (for Ann Moore's Run) — the name already used by the post office — on Nov. 13, 1950, the population already totaled 1,107.

Anmoore is governed by a five-person council elected every two years. The city government installed street lights in 1951, and the citizens organized a volunteer fire department in April 1951. Using the Clarksburg water system as a source of supply, the city installed a water distribution system with the $150,000 cost financed by revenue bonds on Aug. 15, 1954. Interstate 79 bypasses the town thus adding to its accessibility.

From 1970 to 1973, the streets of Anmoore were blacktopped and upgraded. Mercury vapor street lights, eventually totaling 105, were installed. A $150,000 revenue bond issue was paid in full September 1983. A 300,000 gallon water storage tank was installed at the highest point in the city. A sewage system, also acquired through federal funding, serves over 400 homes. Cable service is also provided the citizens of Anmoore with the residents of Stanton Road recently receiving service. The name of Stanton Road was changed recently to North Oak Street.

In 1984, the city employs three full-time police officers and one part-time officer. The city of Anmoore boasts a two-police cruiser force, a well-manned and maintained fire department, two fire engines and three emergency vehicles, staffed by a paramedic and several emergency medical technicians on duty 24 hours a day. In March 1984, the city received a $36,000 grant, which is being used to add additional storage space for city vehicles. It is also being used to help renovate the auditorium in the upstairs of the City Building and for the dredging of the run, which occasionally overflows. In July and August of 1983, improvements were made to the City Hall Building. Siding was installed along with insulation, spouting and venting of the heating system.

The future of Anmoore looks brighter and healthier as the malls and businesses move closer to the city.

From the Beginning Harrison County Bordered On Greatness

BY HARRY J. BERMAN

Our story concerns the historical origins of Harrison County some 200 years ago this year, it's first 72,849 days with the exception of Monday, April 5, 1920. From its onset, Harrison County bordered on Greatness. Greatness County bordered Harrison County on the north and east consisting of New York, New Jersey, Delaware and Greenland. What lay south of Harrison County was Insignificant. Insignificant County consisted of Kentucky, Tennessee and all the territory south of the Amazon River. As we all know, everything west of Harrison County was Harrison County, including Kansas, Hawaii and Guam, but not North View, which at that time belonged to Doddridge County, and Columbus, Ohio which was in Genoa County, Italy.

This was all the known world except for Washington, B.C. (This was called B.C. because it was Before Columbia). As we all know Washington was named after George Washington, who was the father of the country because he slept everywhere. George had a brother, Harry Washington, who took over George's surveying business when George flipped his wig and joined a bunch of long-haired patriots and marched against the government. Harry started surveying everything west of Washington — which of course, was not called Washington yet and was known as Occupant Unincorporated.

However, I am sorry to say, Harry had a drinking problem. He couldn't find water. The farther west he went, the drier he got. There were no rivers, no streams, only Interstate 70 leading to Hagerstown.

Harry called on his son "Son," he said, "we need water desperately. We need it for our horses. We need it for ourselves. Keep going west until you find water." They had to use horses because of the oil shortage.

So Harry's son went west in search of water. On his way west he met the famous Arctic Explorer Captain Perry, who was somewhat off his beaten track to either pole to say the least.

"Captain Perry," said Harry's son, "Do you have any water?"

"No, I don't son," he replied "How about a beer?"

Harry's son looked at him dolefully and said, "No sir, I'd rather have some water," and he crawled on.

"Wait son," said Captain Perry. "Let me give you some advice, you'll die without drinking something. Take a few sips of my beer, take big deep breaths and gets lots of air until you find water."

Harry's son followed Perry's advice and trudged on over I-70 to Hancock, Rt. 40 to Cumberland, Rt. 48 to Morgantown, and I-79 to Clarskburg where he discovered the beautiful Elk Creek, which incidentally was then filled with water.

After taking a few drinks of this long sought water, Harry's son cried forth, "I declare all this land I have traveled and all to the west as far as Guam — except for North View which belongs to Doddridge County, and Columbus, Ohio which belongs go Genoa County, Italy — I and I shall name it for myself, Harry's son!"

And that is the origin of Harry's son County.

Harry's son, however, became rich from one ingenious idea.

"This water in Elk Creek," said Harry's son, "is truly more valuable than all the wine in France. I shall name these waters of the Elk Creek in honor of the men who saved my life with a sip of beer and two words 'suck air.' For my friend Captain Perry, I shall name these waters 'Perry Air' and I shall put them in tiny little bottles and sell them for a buck apiece."

Well, that's how Harry's son County got its name. Later thousands of French and Belgians came here to blow the little glass bottles in which to put Perry Air. And farmers came from all over to raise crops and cattle. Today Harry's son — now spelled Harrison — County is made up of all the descendants of the glass blowers and bull throwers — and there is no doubt which of these categories you're going to put me in.

The Humanities Foundation of West Virginia

POST OFFICE BOX 204
INSTITUTE, WV 25112
(304) 768-8869

August 12, 1985

Mr. James M. Pool
Harrison County Bicentennial Committee
404 West Pike Street
Clarksburg, WV 26301

Dear Jim:

The exhibit produced during your project, "Clarksburg-Harrison County Bicentennial," has been selected by the National Endowment for the Humanities (NEH) as one of four projects funded by the Humanities Foundation of West Virginia which may be featured in future NEH publications about state humanities programs.

The NEH Public Affairs office has asked for xerox copies of graphics or photos from your exhibit. The xerox copies will be maintained in a file for use in a future publication. When selected for use in a publication, NEH will contact you to arrange to borrow the original.

Would you select a few of the best photos or graphics from your exhibit and forward the xerox copies to me?

Thank you for your help. Congratulations also on being selected from among several hundred grants, to be featured in a national publication.

If you have any questions, please call me.

Sincerely,

Susan E. Kelley
Associate Director

SEK:sk